THE ROUTLEDGE DANCE
STUDIES READER
SECOND EDITION

The second edition of *The Routledge Dance Studies Reader* offers fresh critical perspectives on classic and modern dance forms, including ballroom, tango, hip hop, site-specific performance and disability in dance.

Alexandra Carter and Janet O'Shea deliver a substantially revised and updated collection of key texts, featuring an enlightening new introduction, which tracks differing approaches to dance studies. Important articles from the first edition are accompanied by twenty two new works by leading critical voices. The articles are presented in five thematic sections, each with a new editorial introduction and further reading. Sections cover:

- making dance
- performing dance
- ways of looking
- locating dance in history and society
- debating the discipline

The Routledge Dance Studies Reader provides access to over thirty essential texts on dance and expert guidance on their critical context. It is a vital resource for anyone interested in understanding dance from a global and contemporary perspective.

Alexandra Carter is Professor in Dance Studies at Middlesex University, she edited *The Routledge Dance Studies Reader* (1998) and is the author of *Rethinking Dance History* (2004).

Janet O'Shea is Associate Professor in Dance, in the department of World Arts and Cultures at the University of California, Los Angeles. She is the author of *At Home in the World: Bharata Natyam on the Global Stage* (2007).

THE ROUTLEDGE DANCE STUDIES READER

Second edition

Edited by

Alexandra Carter and Janet O'Shea

Routledge
Taylor & Francis Group

LONDON AND NEW YORK

First published 1998
by Routledge
2 Park Square, Abingdon, Oxon OX14 4RN

Second edition published 2010
by Routledge
2 Park Square, Milton Park, Abingdon, Oxon OX14 4RN

Simultaneously published in the USA and Canada
by Routledge
270 Madison Avenue, New York, NY 10016

Routledge is an imprint of the Taylor & Francis Group, an informa business

Typeset in Goudy by Taylor & Francis Books
Printed and bound in Great Britain by
CPI Antony Rowe, Chippenham, Wiltshire

British Library Cataloguing in Publication Data
A catalogue record for this book is available from the British Library

Library of Congress Cataloging in Publication Data
A catalog record for this title has been requested

ISBN 10: 0-415-48598-3 (hbk)
ISBN 10: 0-415-48599-1 (pbk)
ISBN 10: 0-203-86098-5 (ebk)

ISBN 13: 978-0-415-48598-2 (hbk)
ISBN 13: 978-0-415-48599-9 (pbk)
ISBN 13: 978-0-203-86098-4 (ebk)

CONTENTS

CONTRIBUTORS

Ann Cooper Albright is a performer, choreographer and feminist scholar, and Professor of Dance and Theatre at Oberlin College. She is the author of *Traces of Light: Absence and Presence in the Work of Loie Fuller* (2007); *Choreographing Difference: The Body and Identity in Contemporary Dance* (1997) and co-editor of *Moving History/Dancing Cultures* (2001) and *Taken By Surprise: Improvisation in Dance and Mind* (2003).

Adam Benjamin is a Rayne Fellow and lecturer in Theatre and Performance at Plymouth University. He is author of *Making an Entrance* (2001). An award winning choreographer with an interest in cross-arts collaboration, International Arts Council fellow, inveterate improviser, he is one of the pioneers of integrated dance.

Melissa Blanco Borelli is a Lecturer in Dance Studies at the University of Surrey. She currently works on *mulata* corporeality and comparative social dance histories in Cuba and New Orleans and has created a multi-media performance piece entitled *Mulata Madness*. Her work appears in *Women and Performance* and *Dance Chronicle*.

Carol Brown is a choreographer and Senior Lecturer in Dance at Auckland University, New Zealand. Her work is performed internationally through touring, commissions and cross-artform collaborations. In generating performance dialogues with the fields of architecture, music, visual arts and science, and in close collaboration with dancers, she develops installations, performance landscapes and site-specific events.

Theresa Jill Buckland is Professor of Performing Arts at De Montfort University and Vice Chair of the International Council for Traditional Music Study Group on Ethnochoreology. Edited collections include *Dance in the Field: Theory, Methods and Issues in Dance Ethnography* (1999) and *Dancing from Past to Present: Nation, Culture, Identities* (2006).

Ramsay Burt is Professor of Dance History at de Montfort University. His publications include *The Male Dancer* (1995, revised 2007), *Alien Bodies*

(1997), *Judson Dance Theater* (2006) and, with Valerie Briginshaw, *Writing Dancing Together* (2009). In 1999 he was Visiting Professor at the Department of Performance Studies, New York University. With Professor Susan Foster, he is founder editor of *Discourses in Dance*.

Alexandra Carter is Professor of Dance Studies at Middlesex University, London. She edited the *Dance Studies Reader* (1st edn, 1998) and *Rethinking Dance History* (2004) and is the author of *Dance and Dancers in the Victorian and Edwardian Music Hall Ballet* (2005). Further research interests embrace theories of historiography and early-twentieth-century British theatre dance.

Pallabi Chakravorty teaches in the Department of Music and Dance at Swarthmore College, USA. Founder and artistic director of Courtyard Dancers, she is an anthropologist, dance maker, and cultural worker. Her book *Bells of Change: Kathak Dance, Women, and Modernity in India* is the first critical study of Kathak in the context of postcolonialism and globalization.

Chandralekha was a leading contemporary dance artist who was known for her commitment to activism and social change. Her choreography combined Bharata Natyam, yoga and the martial art form, Kalarippayattu. She established a centre in Chennai and toured internationally, influencing a range of artists across dance genres.

Emilyn Claid is Professor of Choreography at Dartington College of Arts. Her book, *Yes? No! Maybe… : Seductive Ambiguity in Dance* (2006), interweaves her experiences as performer, choreographer and director with theoretical perspectives. She is currently training in Gestalt psychotherapy, extending her practice of relational processes for collaboratively devised performance.

Merce Cunningham danced with Martha Graham's company from 1939 to 1945, during which time he created many important roles, before establishing his own company in 1953. In creative partnership with John Cage, Cunningham was renowned for his radical questioning of what constitutes dances' processes, subject matter, structures and vocabulary. Known especially for his work with chance processes, video and, more recently, computer programs, his influence on succeeding generations of dance makers is undeniable.

Elizabeth Dempster is a Senior Lecturer in Performance Studies at Victoria University, Melbourne. She is the founding and continuing co-editor of the journal *Writings on Dance*.

Sherril Dodds is a Senior Lecturer and Director of Graduate Studies in Dance at the University of Surrey. Her teaching and research interests focus on cultural analysis of popular and screen dance practice and her publications include *Dance on Screen* (2001) and a forthcoming monograph *The Value of Popular Dance*.

Richard Dyer teaches Film Studies at King's College, London. His books include *Stars* (1979), *White* (1997) and *Pastiche* (2007). He is currently working on a study of the film composer Nino Rota.

Annabel Farjeon joined Sadler's Wells Ballet School at the age of twelve in 1931. She danced with the Company between 1933 and 1941 during which time she started her first novel. For over twenty-five years she was ballet critic for the *New Statesman* and the *Evening Standard* and has published a biography, novels and children's stories.

Susan Leigh Foster, choreographer and scholar, is the author of *Reading Dancing: Bodies and Subjects in Contemporary American Dance* (1986) and *Choreography and Narrative: Ballet's Staging of Story and Desire* (1996) and editor of *Choreographing History* (1995) and *Corporealities* (1996). She is Professor of World Arts and Cultures at University of California, Riverside.

Jens Richard Giersdorf's research focuses on the politics of dance and other movement practices in a global context. He has published articles in *Dance Research Journal*, *Theatre Journal*, *GLQ: Gay & Lesbian Quarterly*, *Forum Modernes Theater*, *Jahrbuch für Tanzforschung*, and *Maska*. He is Assistant Professor of Dance at Marymount Manhattan College.

Martha Graham studied and performed with Denishawn from 1916 to 1923 before establishing herself first as a solo performer, then with her own company. Although she continued to choreograph after retiring as a performer in 1969, it is her early repertoire of expressionist psycho-dramas which is now seen as the most significant in terms of their choreographic innovation and historical influence. Graham's technique, now evolved, has formed the basis for the training of dancers in succeeding generations the world over.

Shobana Jeyasingh has produced numerous works for stage and television, as well as site-specific commissions. She holds honorary degrees from de Montfort University and University of Surrey. She is a Research Associate at ResCen (Middlesex University) and received a NESTA Dream Time Fellowship in 2005. She was named Asian Woman of Achievement 2008 for her contribution to art and culture.

Stephanie Jordan is Research Professor in Dance at Roehampton University, where she directs the Centre for Dance Research and the doctoral programme. She has authored three books: *Striding Out: Aspects of Contemporary and New Dance in Britain* (1992), *Moving Music: Dialogues* *with Music in Twentieth-Century Ballet* (2000) and *Stravinsky Dances: Re-Visions across a Century* (2007).

Deborah Jowitt has written about dance for *The Village Voice* since 1967. She has published two collections: *Dance Beat* (1977) and *The Dance in Mind* (1985) and is the author of *Time and the Dancing Image* (1988) and *Jerome Robbins: His Life, His Theater, His Dance* (2004). She teaches at New York University's Tisch School of the Arts.

Anthea Kraut is Associate Professor in the Department of Dance at the University of California, Riverside, where she teaches courses in critical dance studies. She is the author of *Choreographing the Folk: The Dance Stagings of Zora Neale Hurston* (2008).

Janet Lansdale, Emeritus Professor, University of Surrey, developed academic programmes in dance over a quarter of a century, focusing latterly on the doctoral programme. Her publications include six books, with most recently an in-depth analysis of interpretive strategies in *The Struggle with the Angel* (2007), and an edited text *Decentring the Dancing Text* (2008).

Yatin Lin is Assistant Professor at the Graduate Institute of Dance Theory, Taipei National University of the Arts. Her PhD dissertation (2004) for the University of California, Riverside was on Cloud Gate Dance Theatre. She researches on contemporary dance from Taiwan and has contributed to *Dialogues in Dance Discourse*, among other publications.

Juliet McMains is a performer, choreographer, scholar and teacher of social dance practices and their competitive theatrical expression. Her book *Glamour Addiction: Inside the American Ballroom Dance Industry* received the CORD 2008 Outstanding Publication Award. She is an Assistant Professor in the Dance Programme at the University of Washington.

Vida Midgelow is a Reader in Performance Studies and Dance at the University of Northampton, specialising in European dance practices, choreographic methodologies and the radical reworkings of the classics. She is also an accomplished choreographer and director of the Choreographic Lab.

John Mueller is the author of the prize-winning *Astaire Dancing* (1985). He directs Ohio State University's Dance Film Archive, has been a dance critic and columnist, has produced scripts for two musicals deriving from Astaire films, provides the DVD commentary track on the Astaire–Rogers film, *Swing Time*, has been a Guggenheim Fellow, and is also a Professor of Political Science.

Cynthia Novack was a writer, teacher and dancer who specialised in improvisational methods of creation and performance. She became

Associate Professor of Dance and Women's Studies at Wesleyan University. Amongst other publications, she was the author of the influential *Sharing the Dance: Contact Improvisation and American Culture* (1990). She was a key figure in dance anthropology and in critical studies of dance.

Janet O'Shea is Associate Professor of World Arts and Cultures at the University of California, Los Angeles. She is the author of *At Home in the World: Bharata Natyam on the Global Stage* (2007), a text that investigates the twentieth-century history of Bharata Natyam, considering transformations in choreography, presentation, and pedagogy as they intersect with large-scale social, political, and economic concerns. Her current research examines politics of representation within international dance festivals.

Betty Redfern, after teaching in various schools and colleges, went on to study philosophy and became a freelance lecturer and writer. She obtained her doctorate in the field of aesthetics at Manchester University. Her published work includes *Dance, Art and Aesthetics* (1983) and *Questions in Aesthetic Education* (1986).

Philipa Rothfield is a Senior Lecturer in Philosophy at La Trobe University, Melbourne, Australia. She writes on philosophy of the body largely in relation to dance. She is engaged in an ongoing but intermittent performance project with Russell Dumas (director Dance Exchange, Australia) and reviews dance for *RealTime*, an Australian arts magazine.

Marta E. Savigliano is the author of *Tango and the Political Economy of Passion* (1995), and *Angora Matta: Fatal Acts of North–South Translation* (2003). She is Professor of Critical Dance Studies at University of California, Riverside, Director of Body, Performance, and Dance International Center, and co-founder of GLOSAS (Global South Advanced Studies) located in Buenos Aires.

Anna B. Scott is an Assistant Professor at University of California, Riverside, in the Department of Dance where she works with and performs cultural interfaces with digital modalities and intersectional studies of blackness in the African Diaspora.

Marcia B. Siegel is the author of *The Shapes of Change: Images of American Dance* (1985); *Days on Earth: The Dance of Doris Humphrey* (1993); *Howling Near Heaven: Twyla Tharp and The Reinvention of Modern Dance* (2006), *Mirror and Scrims: The Life and Afterlife of Ballet* (2010) and four collections of reviews. She is an internationally known teacher, lecturer and dance critic.

Helen Thomas is Research Director at London College of Fashion, University of the Arts London. Her research interests centre on the sociology of dance and culture. Her books include *The Body, Dance and Cultural Theory* (2003), *Dance, Modernity and Culture* (1995) and, co-edited with Jamilah Ahmed, *Cultural Bodies* (2004).

Editorial notes

Parts

The book is organized into five Parts in order to cluster common themes. This strategy allows ease of use for the reader and reveals interesting juxta-positions and diverse perspectives on similar debates. However, we are aware that some of these groupings are arbitrary, for example many chapters contribute towards 'debating the discipline' and/or offer 'ways of looking' at dance. We are aware, therefore, that Part headings in this cur-rent *Reader* are fluid and that the chapters therein might also be placed in other Parts. Readers are encouraged to look across chapters/Parts to discern complementary topics and threads of debate.

Further reading

The texts which are suggested as further reading after each Part introduc-tion are those which, in the main, were published after the first edition of the *Reader* (1998). They are examples of key texts, not already referred to in the individual chapters.

ACKNOWLEDGEMENTS

Thanks to Susan Foster, Jens Richard Giersdorf, Tim Shireman, the faculty and graduate students of the department of World Arts and Cultures at UCLA, and the dance department at Wesleyan University for feedback on versions of the introduction. Thanks to Rosemary Candelario for extensive legwork, bibliographic compilation and general editorial support sometimes at short notice. Colleagues at Middlesex University have provided vital time in work programmes. We also gratefully acknowledge the initiative of Catherine Foley of Routledge who steered the initial process, Ben Piggott who has supported us along the way and Chris Shaw, the copy editor, who is himself involved in playing for and teaching traditional English, French and Breton dance. Lastly, we extend our thanks to all those contributors, old and new, for allowing their work to be included in this edition of the Reader.

Permission given by the following authors and copyright holders is gratefully acknowledged:

Melissa Blanco Borelli, 'Hips, Hip-notism, Hip(g)nosis: the *mulata* performances of Ninón Sevilla', abridged from *Women and Performance*, 18:3 (2008) Taylor & Francis Ltd., http://www.informaworld.com. Reprinted by permission of the publisher © Taylor & Francis.

Ramsay Burt, 'Nijinsky: modernism and heterodox representations of masculinity', abridged from *The Male Dancer: Bodies, Spectacle, Sexuality* (London: Routledge 1995). Reproduced by permission of Taylor & Francis Books UK © 1995 Ramsay Burt.

Chakravorty, Pallabi, 'From interculturalism to historicism: reflections on classical Indian dance', *Dance Research Journal*, 32:2, Winter 2000/01

Chandralekha, 'Reflections on new directions in Indian dance', from *New Directions in Indian Dance*, ed. S. Kothari (Mumbai: Marg Publications 2003) © Estate of Chandralekha.

Merce Cunningham, 'Torse', abridged from *The Dancer and the Dance: Merce Cunningham in conversation with Jacqueline Lesschaeve* (London: Marion Boyars 1985) © 1985 Marion Boyars.

Elizabeth Dempster, 'Women writing the body: let's watch a little how she dances', abridged from *Grafts: Feminist Cultural Criticism*, ed. Susan Sheridan (London: Verso 1988) © 1988 Elizabeth Dempster.

Richard Dyer, analysis of 'Dancing in the dark', abridged from 'I seem to find the happiness I seek', in *Dance, Gender and Culture*, ed. Helen Thomas (Basingstoke: Macmillan Press 1993). Reproduced with permission of Palgrave Macmillan © 1993 Macmillan Press.

Annabel Farjeon, 'Choreographers: dancing for de Valois and Ashton', from *Dance Chronicle* 17:2 (New York: Marcel Dekker Inc. 1994) © Estate of Annabel Farjeon.

Susan Foster, 'Choreographing history', abridged from *Choreographing History* (Bloomington: Indiana University Press 1995). Reprinted with permission of Indiana University Press © 1995 Indiana University Press.

Jens Richard Giersdorf, 'Dance Studies in the International Academy: Genealogy of a Disciplinary Formation', abridged from *Dance Research Journal* 41:1 pp. 23–44 (2009) © Jens Richard Giersdorf, reworked and reprinted by permission of *Dance Research Journal*.

Martha Graham, 'I am a dancer', abridged from *Blood Memory* (New York: Doubleday 1991). Used by permission of Doubleday, a division of Random House Inc. © 1991 Martha Graham Estate.

Shobana Jeyasingh, 'Getting off the Orient Express', reprinted from *Dance Theatre Journal* 8:2 pp. 34–7 (1990) © Shobana Jeyasingh.

Stephanie Jordan and Helen Thomas, 'Dance and gender: formalism and semiotics reconsidered', abridged from *Dance Research* XII:2 (1994) © 1994 Stephanie Jordan and Helen Thomas.

Deborah Jowitt, 'In pursuit of the sylph: ballet in the Romantic period', abridged from *Time and the Dancing Image* (New York: William Morrow 1981). By permission of HarperCollins Publishers/William Morrow & Co. Inc. © 1988 Deborah Jowitt.

Anthea Kraut, 'Recovering Hurston, reconsidering the choreographer', abridged from Ch. 2 in *Choreographing the Folk: The Dance Stagings of Zora Neale Hurston* (Minnesota: University of Minnesota Press 2008) © University of Minnesota Press.

Yatin Lin, 'Choreographing a flexible Taiwan: Cloud Gate Dance Theatre and Taiwan's changing identity', first published as 'Chorégraphier Taïwan dans sa flexibilité: Le Cloud Gate Dance Theatre et l'identité changeante de Taïwan', in *Danses et identités: de Bombay à Tokyo*, (Pantin: Centre National de la Danse, May 2009) © Centre National de la Danse.

Vida Midgelow, 'Reworking the ballet: stillness and queerness in *Swan Lake, 4 Acts*', abridged from Ch. 4 in *Reworking the Ballet: Counter-narratives and Alternative Bodies* (London: Routledge, 2007) © Routledge. Reproduced by permission of Taylor and Francis Books UK.

John Mueller, analysis of 'Dancing in the dark', abridged from *Astaire Dancing: The Musical Films* (London: Hamish Hamilton 1986). Reprinted by permission of Alfred A. Knopf Inc. and Penguin Books Ltd. © John Mueller.

Cynthia Novack, 'Looking at movement as culture: contact improvisation to disco', reprinted from *TDR/The Drama Review*, 32:4, Winter 1988 pp. 102–19 © New York University and the Massachusetts Institute of Technology.

Betty Redfern, 'What is art?', abridged from *Dance, Art and Aesthetics* (London: Dance Books Ltd 1983) ©1983 Betty Redfern.

Philipa Rothfield, 'Differentiating phenomenology and dance' reprinted from *Topoi*, 24: 1 pp. 43–53 © Topoi with kind permission from Springer Science and Business Media.

Marta Savigliano, 'Gambling femininity: tango wallflowers and femmes fatale', abridged from pp. 166–90, *Angora Matta*, 2003 © 2003 Marta Savigliano and reprinted by permission of Wesleyan University Press.

Anna B. Scott, 'What's it worth to ya?', Abridged and reworked from *Discourses in Dance* 2: 1 pp. 5–21 (2003) © *Discourses in Dance*.

Marcia Siegel, 'Bridging the critical distance', abridged and amended from *Looking Out: Perspectives on Dance and Criticism in a Multicultural World*, ed. David Gere, co-ed. by Lewis Segal, Patrice Clark Koelsch and Elizabeth Zimmer (New York: Schirmer Books 1995) © 1995 Marcia Siegel.

1

ROOTS/ROUTES OF DANCE STUDIES

Janet O'Shea

The first edition of the *Routledge Dance Studies Reader* (1998) came out at a time that, in retrospect, appears pivotal for dance studies. The period from the late 1980s to the early 2000s was one of intense activity in dance scholarship, characterized by fundamental shifts in the field. Dance writers no longer concerned themselves only with the dance work and the artist's biography but also with how dances engage with their social, historical, political and economic contexts. Publications of the mid- to late 1990s speak of the emergence of 'new dance scholarship' framing its major preoccupations, including the overt acknowledgement of the need to translate the moving body to the written word, the consideration of dance as 'text', the relationship of the practice of dance to its theorization, and the interconnections between the dancing body and individual and group identities (Morris 1996, Desmond 1997a).[1]

These concerns positioned dance studies as an interdisciplinary field as they indicated both the approaches it borrowed from other fields and the ways in which it could inform other disciplines. At the same time, scholars legitimized the field by claiming its distinctiveness, especially from theatre, music and physical education with which it had been conventionally associated. While new dance scholarship is no longer new, its tenets continue to inflect research and writing on dance today. Moreover, this subfield has produced its own legacy. It is now possible to discern at least two generations subsequent to that which launched new dance studies.

I am interested in the development of this influential subfield because I am, in this sense, a second-generation new dance studies scholar; I received my PhD from the University of California, Riverside, and studied with several of the authors I cite below. In addition, I worked for six years at the University of Surrey, where educational methods fed into some of the pivotal work that established dance studies as a separate field. Generations in academia produce themselves quickly so I have participated in the training of a new group of scholars, through mentoring graduate students at the University of Surrey, Middlesex University and now at the University of California, Los Angeles. Many of my graduate-school colleagues are engaged in this kind of mentoring work and, as such, we are assisting in the creation of a third generation of new dance studies scholars. As such, new dance scholarship has extended from an innovative challenge to a discourse that establishes the parameters and investments of the field.

Given this development of influence, I think it is necessary to examine the key investments of this field, historicizing them and aligning them with the socio-political concerns of the time of their emergence (1980s and 1990s) as well as with issues in choreographic production. Moreover, I want to place new dance studies in a broader context, linking its interests to those of the writing that preceded it. My purpose is to consider these intellectual antecedents, placing them alongside innovative 'first generation' new dance studies texts as well as putting them into dialogue with subsequent work that draws on new dance studies. I also want to raise the question of what futures dance studies might pursue, given this history. Therefore, I historicize the concerns of this subfield with an eye toward considering what opportunities this opens up for dance studies.

I suggest that four strands of intellectual activity, each of which predate the emergence of dance studies as a separate arena, laid the ground for the present-day field: anthropology, folklore and ethnography; the writings of expert viewers and dance analysis; philosophy, especially aesthetics and phenomenology; historical studies including biography and dance reconstruction. These categories are not exhaustive or watertight; there is some overlap between them. All of these approaches transformed over time to address issues of identity and their articulation in dance, a shift from an authoritative position to a multiplicity of voices, and changing relationships between performance, choreography and writing.

Many, although by no means all, of the texts I address here come out of the US and the UK. Others emerge out of former British or US colonies. In dance studies, as in other fields, English operates as the *lingua franca*. While recent conferences have attempted to challenge the exclusionary effects of this English-language dominance, the exchange still moves primarily in one direction – English-language texts into translation more than non-English texts translated into English. Dance studies is, however, developing in exciting ways in languages and places that are beyond my scope here.

A volume like this, created at this historical moment, grapples with a set of concerns around globalization and representation. There is a temptation to fall into a collection mode, seeking out individual examples so that a single text written on dance studies within Africa would speak for a whole continent. I have resisted this kind of tokenization, focusing on approaches to dance studies that I can represent with a degree of familiarity and relying on writings from regions I have experience with (primarily South Asia, North America, the UK and, more briefly, the Philippines), while acknowledging the need for greater exchange and awareness across national approaches to the subject matter of dance.

My intent is to sketch out a history that comprises debates around the nature of the field, its politics, its investments and its strategic manoeuvres. I track changes in the discipline over time but do not propose these changes as constitutive of a narrative of progress. Furthermore, although I problematize a number of the approaches taken here, they are not ranked hierarchically. Approaches accrue strategic force at different historical moments and in different social and political contexts. As such, each venture functions as an engagement with the specific intellectual and social concerns of its time.

Anthropology, ethnography and dance disciplinarity

Some of the earliest academic dance writings came out of anthropology and folklore studies. There are several reasons why the social sciences, and anthropology in particular, were useful to dance studies. The ascribed ephemerality of dance only becomes a problem when viewing dance in relation to art forms that produce material objects, such as paintings, sculptures or novels. When viewed from a social sciences standpoint, dance is no more ephemeral than other aspects of lived experience, whether those are economic, ritual or linguistic.[2] In addition, anthropology, with its emphasis on the historical 'others' of the west – some of whose cultures were conflated with dance in popular representation (Shea Murphy 1995) – allowed its writers leeway to explore marginalized aspects of society. Anthropology subsequently widened its attention from structuralist and functionalist studies that emphasized kinship, hierarchy, etc., to symbolic anthropology and semiotic anthropology, which included ritual (Victor Turner) and the body (Claude Levi-Strauss), thus integrating bodily practices into the study of culture.

The anthropological interest in dance, however, created a problematic legacy for dance studies. Curt Sachs (1937), for instance, proposed a comprehensive model for understanding dances from all over the world, ordered according to an evolutionary ranking. This collection approach, while now recognized as linked to imperialist taxonomies and ethnocentric values, nonetheless influenced subsequent projects.[3]

In other cases, this collection mode was tied less to overarching knowledge than to imperatives toward preservation. For instance, Cecil Sharp's collection of folk dances in nineteenth-century England operated with the understanding that collection would lead to preservation, a postulate that the emergence of the British folk dance revival seemed to support. This collection approach aligned with the concerns of its historical context, rooted in nostalgia and post-industrial anxieties about the loss of 'authentic' community experiences and of opportunities for healthful recreation.

A preservation model carried forward into early US anthropology. Authors such as Gertrude Kurath (1931 onwards) and Franziska Boas (1944 onwards) participated in early-twentieth-century American anthropology's collection and recording of the practices of marginal populations. Anthropology, despite its claims to scientific knowledge, operated as part of a fascination with cultural difference and with fetishistic display that characterized European and North American artistic, literary and scholarly production from the eighteenth century until well into the twentieth century. Similarly, dancers and choreographers of the early to mid-twentieth century, such as Ruth St. Denis and La Meri, collected the dances of 'others', interpreted them, and displayed them for the viewers of the West.

Francesca Reyes Aquino took a similar approach in her extensive cataloguing of Philippine folk dance forms, a process that fed back into curricular development at the University of the Philippines and the professional stagings of folk dance by companies like Bayanihan. Scholars have since problematized Aquino and Bayanihan's use of ethnographic collection to stand in for a dominant national identity (Gaerlan 1999). On the one hand, Reyes Aquino, as a middle-class woman based in Manila practised a level of exoticism in her claim that the 'real' Philippine culture lay in outlying regions among the rural workers and tribal populations.[4] On the other hand, methods of ethnographic collection offered cultural 'authenticity' as a focal point for anti-colonial resistance.

In mid-twentieth-century US, anthropology served a progressive end in the work of choreographers like Zora Neale Hurston, Katherine Dunham and Pearl Primus. Following the impulses of the Harlem Renaissance, such choreographers looked for antecedents of African American traditions. Some, like Dunham, were formally educated in anthropology but chose to channel their efforts and present their 'findings' in performance, rather than in text. Others, such as Hurston, explored the roots of African American cultural practices in both literary and choreographic form (Kraut 2008).

The 1970s saw the emergence of theories for analysing dance and movement practices cross-culturally with, for example, the work of Adrienne Kaeppler in the US and John Blacking in the UK. Anthropologists like Kaeppler brought a structuralist approach to the study of dance, drawing out units of movement as an indication of dance's overall patterning and locating dance within larger events, but giving less attention to meaning and representation (Foster 1986: 233).[5]

The investigation of structure laid the ground for subsequent modes of engagement with dance, such as those that disassociated dance from subjective impression by identifying components that could be extracted and read. However, a structuralist approach also assumed an overarching vantage point that awards the author a totalizing and objective view. Joann Keali'inohomoku (1969/70), by contrast, used anthropology in order to critique Western dance history's misrepresentation of the rest of the world. This manoeuvre anticipated the identitarian critique that formed the basis of much dance writing of the late 1980s and 1990s, signalling a turn toward reflexivity and the investigation of the politics of representation in dance studies.

The legacy of anthropology in dance has since bifurcated. On the one hand, dance writers such as Andree Grau, Theresa Buckland and Deirdre Sklar work within the field of anthropology, retaining a focus on the cultural creation of meaning through dance while also considering intentional cultural production and applying historical approaches to the study of dance. Cynthia Novack (1990) and Sally Ness (1992) deployed cultural description within an anthropological context, while attending to its limits, locating the practices they studied historically – a significant challenge when articulated within a discipline that had defined itself as ahistorical – and situating them in relation to political as well as cultural concerns. Other dance anthropologists, such as Brenda Farnell and Adrienne Kaeppler, have moved away from the term 'dance', maintaining that the separation of dance from other practices is a Western construct. For these authors, the category of 'human movement' has proved more helpful.

On the other hand, dance scholars have also deployed an 'ethnographic turn' (Coles 2000) in the humanities, detaching fieldwork and its related practice of cultural description from anthropology (Clifford 1988: 24, Buckland, Chapter 30). The refiguring of fieldwork and ethnographic description characterized dance writings of the 1990s, both within dance anthropology and outside it so that dance scholarship integrated direct experience with historical analyses of dance forms (Savigliano 1995, Browning 1995). Later dance studies authors, such as Francesca Castaldi (2006) and Juliet McMains (2006) intertwined personal experience with the ethnographic in a more traditional sense – understanding and describing the experience of others – while continuing to place ethnographic studies of dance in dialogue with history. In my own research, I moved from an early training in anthropology to an interest in intentional cultural production rather than in culture as implicit consensus or as a way of life (O'Shea 2006). In these studies, an attention to the scholar's positionality and their process of participation guides, frames and delimits the project, as authors attend to categories of identity – such as gender, race, nation, class and sexuality – and work interdisciplinarily across history, ethnography, cultural studies and choreographic analysis.

Newer dance studies approaches, then, attended to culture, not solely as an inherited social context for particular practices, but also as part of conscious, politically defined attempts at creating identity. As such, it aligned ethnographic practice not only with anthropology but also with postcolonial and critical race studies' critique of the production of knowledge. Dance studies, with its focus on representation, offers a means of joining the study of the overt production of difference to the study of 'culture' in challenging ways.

From expert viewership to dance analysis

Some of the earliest source materials on dance rely on a close relationship between the watching of dance and writing about it. Skilled viewership and dance writing have historically supported one another. Cross-disciplinary exchange is less at the crux of choreographic analysis but emerged as a later preoccupation, once the devices for providing close analyses of dance had been established.

Many of the early texts on dance were written by dance instructors, dramaturges and critics. Dance criticism – the analysis and evaluation of dance works – focused on not only assessing the work of choreographers but also highlighting the aesthetics of a dance form and validating a form of practice. For instance, the consolidation of modern dance owed much to the efforts of critics such as John Martin (Franko 1996) and English-language dance criticism furthered the bharata natyam revival (Singer 1958). Dance criticism also integrated dance studies into the academy as critics produced writing that addressed the social and cultural significance of dance, taught on university faculty and offered training in dance criticism (Copeland and Cohen 1983).

While dance critics take viewing and description as their base, from which they offer evaluation and interpretation, other dance writers attended to the question of how dance is viewed and described in the first place. For these authors, an interest in identifying fundamental units of a practice and in exploring how these units form a whole facilitated the analysis of dance material. One of the most pivotal shifts for dance studies was the expansion of semiotics into the analysis and interpretation of choreography. Recourse to structuralist thought allowed dance to establish itself as an autonomous field, demonstrating that dance possessed a legibility that rendered it available to analysis.

Janet Lansdale (writing as Adshead 1988), for example, proposed such a method for the observation, description, interpretation and evaluation of a dance work. In her early work, Lansdale did not take up a textual metaphor directly but her attention to the breaking down of a dance into its components parallels structuralist studies of language.[6] Her explicit discussion of the process of dance analysis indicates the extent to which an informed viewer can 'read' a dance, interpreting its meanings by understanding its fundamental units.

As in the case of ethnography, post-structuralist texts complicated the analysis of dance by highlighting the constructed nature of knowledge and its intertwinings with the structures of power, challenging the idea of objectivity and encouraging a shift away from scientific models in the humanities. Susan Foster (1986), for instance, drew upon both structuralist and post-structuralist positions. Contesting the ephemerality, naturalness and ineffability of dance, Foster also argued for its legitimacy as an area of academic inquiry. Her text, by mobilizing literary and rhetorical theory in the interest of the analysis of dances, located the interpretation of meaning in the work itself through a consideration of its codes and conventions, while also engaging the cultural and historical construction of those codes, a move that brought dance into a dialogue with the more recognized disciplines of English and philosophy.

The historical appearance of dance analysis texts aligned with the concerns of the choreography of the period that preceded it, intersecting with the formalism of work like Cunningham's as well as the task-like approach of postmodern dancers associated with Judson Dance Theater (Foster 1986: 242). These publications of the mid-1980s also emerged at a time between the communitarian politics of the 1970s and the difference-based identity politics of the mid-1980s to 1990s. The attention to the act of reading rather than the act of creation acknowledges the difficulty of speaking for 'others' and suggests that reading and writing are both shot through with investments that are tied to the position of the reader or author. As such, these texts foreshadow the politicized approaches that followed.

As in the case of anthropology, the legacy of textual analysis in dance studies is bifurcated. For some authors, such as Stephanie Jordan, formal scrutiny and the combination of formalism with semiotics remain primary (Jordan and Thomas, this volume). For others, attention to form and to the close study of dances provides the background against which further interpretation can be carried out. A significant shift for dance studies was the interpretation of dances in political terms, especially, those associated with the politics of identity, such as gender, race, class and sexuality. Gender interpretations influenced the early phase of 'new dance studies' scholarship, either tied to the close reading of a particular dance work (Daly 1987), to the politics invested in a specific dance form (Meduri 1988, Foster 1996b), or to the choreography of masculinity and femininity in particular cultural and historical circumstances (Adair 1992, Burt 1995, Franko 1995, Banes 1998).

Studies of identity extended to the production of race in dance (Dixon-Gottschild 1996, DeFrantz 2002, 2004a, 2004b, Chatterjea 2004, Manning 2004) and the reading of imperialist narratives in choreography (Desmond 1991). Political readings of dance also included economic and class-based interpretations of performance (Martin 1996, Graff 1997, Franko 2002), sexuality and performance (Desmond 2001) and the choreographing of nationalism (Manning 1993, Savigliano 1995). Choreographic analysis served a dual purpose for dance studies by clearly establishing a field of investigation as well as by attending to specific works in the interest of interdisciplinary inquiries, especially those focused on the politics of identity.

This turn to social, cultural and political meaning intersects with strategies deployed by artists working in areas that cross dance and performance art. Choreographer/performers like Bill T. Jones, Jawole Willa Jo Zollar, Blondell Cummings, Lloyd Newson, Pina Bausch, Emilyn Claid, Liz Aggiss,

Anne Teresa de Keersmaeker, Wim Vandekeybus, Chandralekha and Ishmael-Houston Jones created work in the late 1970s, 1980s and 1990s that brought issues of race, gender and sexuality to the forefront of performance, frequently using autobiography to attend to issues of exclusion and identification in contemporary dance. Such choreographers also rejected the formalism and minimalism of their predecessors. Choreography, like choreographic analysis, turned away from a sole attention to form and towards exploring how form and identity collide, intertwine and contradict one another.

Discussions of the politics of identity have developed, fragmented and become nuanced in the writings of second generation new dance studies authors. For instance, scholars attending to race have moved outside a black/white polarity. Yutian Wong has attended to the politics of identification in Asian-American modern dance and performance art, exploring intersections between dance studies and Asian American studies (Wong 2002), most recently through a rethinking of the choreographic legacy of modern dance pioneer Michio Ito (Wong 2009). Melissa Blanco Borelli (Chapter 12) investigates race through the ambivalent figure of the *mulata*, or mixed race woman, in transnational cinematic dialogues between the differently constituted, multi-ethnic societies of Cuba and Mexico.

Nationalism – as an arena in which identities are overtly produced in the interest of political ends – frequently intersects with cultural production and, hence, readings of dance as part of a nationalist project have been productive for the second-generation of new dance scholarship. Newer scholars have drawn upon early work that frames up dance in ideological terms, while also complicating analyses on nationalist terms, frequently through attention to the transnational circulation of dance forms. For instance, Pallabi Chakravorty (Chapter 26) aligns the nationalist reinvention of Indian classical dance forms with transnational interest in the 'exotic' and an embrace of interculturalism on the part of the West. I have extended this interest in the global nature of the nationalist refiguration of a particular Indian classical dance form, bharata natyam, by attending to the multiple, contradictory nationalist discourses at play in choreography, their relationship to the transnational trajectories that dancers and their work followed, and their intersection with the creation of new local affiliations in dance (O'Shea 2007). Diyah Larasati (2006) has studied the choreographic implications of politics at its most serious and most devastating: the production of national identities in contexts of war, political repression and genocide.

Dance studies, in the process of studying the intentional production of identity in choreographic form, has drawn upon postcolonial theory, feminist theory, queer theory and critical race theory. While this interdisciplinary exchange has been useful for dance studies, it has the potential to run both ways. Many of these disciplines emerge out of English literature departments and, as such, attend to identity as primarily located in text, either written or visual, and performance as articulated in speech. Its bodies are frequently static. Dance studies puts gendered, sexualized and racialized bodies into motion, a tactic that enables further discussions about bodily inscription and agency.

Dance philosophy: aesthetics and phenomenology

Philosophical inquiries in dance studies have examined what constitutes dance, what comprises understanding in dance, and what the relationship is of dance to feeling. Aesthetic philosophy, in particular, laid the groundwork for understanding dance from a philosophical perspective. However, the major Western philosophers tended to neglect dance (DeFrantz 2005: 93, Foster *et al.* 2005: 3). Of the classic Western philosophers, only Nietzsche gave sustained attention to dance. Indian aesthetic theory, by contrast, offered dance a position of regard. Texts such as the *Natyasastra* and the *Abhinaya Darpana* considered both abstract and expressive dance as vehicles for the artistic experience. However, these texts tended to explore dance within the context of multi-disciplinary spoken drama, as opposed to those practices based primarily around movement.

Dance writers have negotiated these areas of possibility and neglect in order to explore dance in philosophical terms. Aesthetics, with its consideration of artistic experience and phenomenology, with its attention to selfhood as constituted through bodily experience, offers obvious support to dance. Aesthetics provides a means of articulating the importance of dance to human thought and understanding. Authors such as Graham McFee (1992) have drawn out key ideas in aesthetics as they relate to dance, linking them to, for instance, Wittgenstein's discussion of the nature of understanding.

McFee's study of dance as art and as action and his attempt to locate dance in discussions of understanding emerges out of traditional Western theoretical concepts, just as his examples develop out of Western concert dance, ballet and modern dance. However, the study of aesthetics is not limited to European and North America artistic categories and practices. Art history has been of particular use in the study of African and African diaspora forms. For instance, Robert Farris Thompson (1966, 1983) identified major components of African art forms that constituted the aesthetic experience. Dance writers have adapted and reworked these categories in their exploration of African American forms deploying such aesthetic traits to explore unacknowledged Africanist influences in mainstream North American experimental dance (Gottschild 1996) and the extension of Africanist aesthetics in hip hop (DeFrantz 2004b). Dance writers also developed aesthetic theories that shifted their debates away from what constitutes beauty in a universal sense and towards what operates as beautiful within a specific cultural and historical context. Rooting his discussion in an exploration of beauty in African American concert dance, DeFrantz (2005), for instance, draws upon ethnophilosophy and feminist aesthetics in order to suggest that a consideration of beauty has political consequences.

A similar focus to that concerned with aesthetic features and understanding is that of the emotional effect of dance. Suzanne Langer (1953), for example, takes as central to her theory of art and feeling the notions of the symbol and the illusion, arguing that all art must have its own 'primary illusion'. She argues that the primary illusion of dance is that of virtual power. She distinguishes virtual power from self-expression through her emphasis on symbolism. As such, Langer's argument opens up the possibility of a semiotic analysis of dance, something later writers embraced explicitly.[7]

Phenomenology, as a system of thought that redresses the Cartesian mind–body split by emphasizing immediate, bodily experience, provides dance studies with an approach towards considering the significance of dance. Authors such as Maxine Sheets-Johnstone (1966) explored the intersection between phenomenology and dance, positing that an attention to lived experience enables a discussion of the 'essence of dance'. Sheets-Johnstone (1984: 131) suggests that this exploration of experience is pre-theoretical, arguing that phenomenological description enables 'a grasping of the essential nature of experience'.

While phenomenology focuses on the specificity of experience, as lived through the body, it has also tended to assume that 'experience' and 'body' can be taken as givens for intellectual inquiry. Such assumptions have prompted dance scholars to critique phenomenology while exploring some of its tenets. Authors have challenged the notion that there is an essential nature to experience and have questioned the assumption that any experience can be pre-theoretical, mobilizing phenomenology towards questions of what it means to have a particular body with a specific set of experiences and a distinct relationship to the world. For instance, Vivian Sobchack (2005) explores the phenomenology of disability. Tracking her experience with movement following the amputation of her leg, Sobchack (2005: 55) retains phenomenology's attention to 'the lived and living body as the common ground that enables all of our thoughts, movements, and modes of expression' while insisting that 'their myriad forms and satisfactions' are differentiated. Philipa Rothfield (Chapter 28) extends this claim, arguing for a culturally specific body in order to suggest that, although there is no universal, invariant bodily self, bodily experience nonetheless constitutes self-hood, albeit in a culturally and historically specific way.

Philosophy has held a particular appeal for choreographers. So, for instance, Isadora Duncan found validation in the writings of Nietzsche, Padma Subramaniam has validated her choreographic inquiries through reference to Sanskrit aesthetic theory, and Chandralekha referenced the roots of her postmodern but nonetheless expressive choreography in Upanishadic traditions. Some choreographers have also explored philosophy explicitly in written form, such as Carol Brown's examination of the artistic, conceptual and political implications of different conceptions of space (Chapter 6), Kenneth King's (2005) investigation of Nietzsche and Merleau-Ponty, Floyd Favel's (2005) consideration of Cree worldview as an explanatory frame for understanding dance and movement, and Leena Rouhiainen's (2003) use of phenomenology to frame the life experience of freelance dance artists in Finland.

The rethinking of dance philosophy suggests that dance can ground philosophical assertions, especially those concerned with bodily experience and artistic effect, in the specifics of a practice. Dance can offer philosophy interdisciplinary devices to unite dance, phenomenology and post-structuralist investigations of power.

History: from family trees to new histories

Dance histories – reflections on the past of particular dance forms, artists, practices or repertoire – appeared in print long before the establishment of dance studies as an academic discipline. History, like dance analysis, offered dance studies a tangible object for interpretation and thus served as a means to validate an otherwise ephemeral art. While dance analysis focused on producing an object that could be deciphered, history produced an object by identifying its past.

The dance field has conventionally produced writings that focused on biographies of particular artists or traced fields of influence. Especially in studies of modern dance and ballet, these works privileged the creation of 'family trees' that established through-lines of influence as they supported present-day practice (Guest 1972, McDonagh 1976). Such modernist histories represented a search for origins and an attention to causality that formed part of broader traditional history methods (Tomko 2004: 80).

Running alongside the creation of family trees and biographies was the recreation of dances from the past using source materials, including dance notation, verbal description and visual imagery. Frequently, the reconstruction of dances from sources helped to consolidate a tradition, as for instance, in the case of modern dance restagings where dancers and choreographers recreate 'classic' items of repertoire that are no longer in circulation. In some cases, performance of movement based on visual and textual sources intersected with the tenets of a living tradition to constitute a 'reformed' dance practice, as in the odissi revival, or to create new items of repertoire that are treated as within the bounds of tradition, as occurs in the bharata natyam field. These reconstructions function as sources of creative inquiry, as items of repertoire that are put back into circulation, and as the basis or product of scholarly investigation.

Dance studies gained visibility as a discipline at a time when scholars were critiquing traditional history. For instance, Hayden White (1980) argued that causality was a narrativizing device rather than a historical 'fact' and Michel Foucault emphasized genealogy and archaeology, particularly stratas of simultaneity, as central metaphors for understanding the past. Foucault maintained that time be understood as sets of epistemes and that the relationship between each episteme – that is, causality – mattered less than its constitutive workings of power. Such assertions prompted dance studies to move away from linear accounts and biographical studies into inquiries about representation (Tomko 2004).[8] New dance histories (Manning 1993, 2004, Foster 1996a, 2002, Daly 1995, Graff 1997, Burt 1998, Foulkes 2002, Carter 2005) organize themselves not by patterns of influence or even chronologically but topically, placing intersecting concerns in dialogue with each other so that issues, rather than time periods, structure the work.

Dance scholars who attend to past practice frequently draw not only from historiography but also from ethnography, post-colonial studies, feminist and women's studies, sexuality studies, critical race studies and literary analysis. While new dance scholarship, in its earlier incarnations, placed biography at a distance, recent work includes biography that is issue-based, rather than descriptive or chronological (Daly 1995, Cooper Albright 2007). Similarly, scholar/choreographers such as Emilyn Claid and Liz Aggiss integrate autobiography with critical history rather than providing mere descriptive accounts.

Dance reconstruction, like traditional historiography, has undergone critique and evaluation (Franko 1989, Thomas 2004) and has emerged with numerous possibilities for theoretical and creative reassessment. While some dance reconstructors continue to perform historical dances for their own sake, others use choreographic strategies to signal the distinction between the 'original' and the reconstructed work being presented.[9] Moreover, Lesley Main (2005) has argued for a rethinking of reconstruction along the lines followed in theatre, so that a distinction between 'choreo-grapher' and 'reconstructor' is replaced by a directorial role that allows for creative engagement with an existing 'text'. Performance studies scholar and contact improvization dancer Ann Cooper Albright (2007) suggests that a critical deployment of dance reconstruction can express itself in both written and choreographic form, arguing that dance history is understood differently when experienced through movement rather than only through archival sources.

Dance studies scholars have also actively embraced the fictionalizing manoeuvres of history, shifting attention from White's critique towards a consideration of the creative potential offered by this narrativizing impulse.

Performance studies scholar Priya Srinivasan (2007), in her re-evaluation of Ruth St. Denis's *Radha*, aligns a traditional historical angle with one that engages its creative potential.[10] Srinivasan, on the one hand, corrects the historical record and counters the self-mythologizing of St. Denis's account of finding the inspiration for *Radha* in an Egyptian-themed cigarette ad by pointing out that St. Denis saw Indian dancers at Coney Island two years before she created *Radha*. On the other hand, Srinivasan departs from conventional history by imagining possible interactions between St. Denis and the Nautch dancers and fictionalizing their respective reflections on the encounter. Authors who write in this vein see this 'work of the imagination' as crucial to the writing of history (Carter 2004, 2005).

This attention to issue-based history and the consideration of dance history through the creative devices of choreography and fiction align dance studies with strategies in new history. These interests also suggest that dance studies can offer methods back to history such as a consideration of the post-structuralist critique as a prompt not only to examine the production of history but also to consider the opportunities offered by this production. Through a metaphor of the historian's body as dancing with the bodies of the past (Foster, Chapter 27) and through strategies that can imagine a dialogue with their voices, dance studies provides a history that engages dynamically with its subject matter.

Conclusion

Each of these sub-disciplines in dance studies moves from the documentation of a phenomenon, to problematizing the production of knowledge, to mobilizing this fragmentation of possible positions vis-à-vis the subject matter in the interest of specific, topical approaches to inquiry. This exemplifies a more general move in the humanities, from a 'neutral' approach to knowledge gathering towards an acknowledgement of the relationship between positionality, power and knowledge production. For dance studies, this shift is at the base of the establishment of the field as a separate discipline. These strategies also align with broader societal changes, on the one hand, and with transformations in choreography, on the other.

Large-scale social and political changes, especially the destruction of imperial regimes, prompted the power/knowledge critique of post-structuralism and the destabilization of ethnographic authority.[11] The civil rights and American-Indian movements in 1960s' US and the international feminist and gay rights movements of the 1970s encouraged a questioning of the authority of writers to represent the rest of the world. 'New dance studies' attention to difference as constitutive of representation in dance, and to multiple forms of identity and exclusion, incorporated this critique and followed the subsequent shift away from the communitarian politics of the 1970s to identity politics of the 1980s and 1990s, in which identity is defined less by participation in a group than by multiple forms of difference.

Susan Manning (2004) frames the importance for dance studies of 'binary models' of identity, along the lines of gender, race, sexuality and class. Manning signals the usefulness of such models for destabilizing hegemonic viewing positions. However, she also points to their limitations, suggesting that these binaries also threaten to essentialize responses to the experience of dance (ibid.: xix).

Manning's critique suggests the possibility of nuancing the study of identity within dance writings. There are other categories of belonging and exclusion that the categories of race, gender, sexuality and class do not encompass. The politics of location does not fit neatly into binaries, even those of East–West or North–South, as global networks of power extend and economies refigure themselves in relation to the former colonial hierarchies. Legal restrictions on belonging, such as those imposed by citizenship and immigration restrictions, also urge a reworking of identity. Similarly, economic concerns extend beyond the category of class to a consideration of economic power differentials and their role in the movement of populations, dance forms and dance works. Seemingly neutral categories of experience, such as space and technology, have also acquired a political resonance.

Recent scholarship indicates that this redefining of politics and power in dance studies is already underway. For example, a panel at the 2007 CORD conference, in which Jens Giersdorf, Anthea Kraut and Yutian Wong spoke about the legal implications of dance, including citizenship and copyright, suggests such an extension of interests in power and representation beyond those that can easily be read in the dance text. Presentations, such as that by Jennifer Buscher (2009), exhibit a concern with understanding relationships between choreography, technology, economics and power. Anurima Bannerjee's (2007) conference presentation on Chandralekha's choreography as a practice that activates a particular definition of space augments discussions on the social implications of space and allows dance studies to understand the politics of choreography not only through moving bodies but also through their positioning in their environment.

These approaches do not exhaust the possibilities for rethinking issues of power, positionality and representation. Instead, they offer avenues for debate as dance studies moves forward into its new articulations. For example, one of the more recently visible fields of enquiry is that of dance and pedagogy in which the politics of 'power' in the studio and classroom, and how and by whom dance knowledge is created and controlled in an educational context, are key debates.[12]

Recent work suggests a diversification or even a fragmentation of interest that necessarily accompanies the development of the field. Our attention remains – as it should – on the dancing body and the dance work.

However, current and future discussions can move away from only those meanings that can be read in the dance 'text' to those which are articulated in engagement with it. Such an extension of interest would allow the field to build upon its areas of strength in its attention to power and representation, while further differentiating these considerations in response to the conditions of a changing world.

Notes

1 References are indicative of particular methodological moves; they are not comprehensive. I have borrowed the key phrase of the title – Roots/routes – from Emilyn Claid (2006).
2 Alexandra Carter (2004) argues that lived experience is, itself, ephemeral, highlighting the difference between the documentation of an event and the event itself. Marta Savigliano (Chapter 23) also makes the case for the ephemerality of more legitimized aspects of social life than dance, such as economics and government.
3 One example is Alan Lomax's choreutics project. See Suzanne Youngerman (1974) for a critique of Sachs and his legacy.
4 Sally Ness (1997) applies a parallel critique to Philippine 'neo-ethnic' ballet.
5 Kaeppler's later work, however, grapples with the politics of representation of dance events.
6 In more recent writings, Lansdale (2007, 2008) has embraced semiotics and textual metaphors directly.
7 Colleen Dunagan (2005: 29) uses her read of Langer to suggest the incorporation of aesthetics into post-structuralism and ideological critique.
8 Similarly, a post-structuralist scepticism towards 'facts' enabled dance studies to explore a range of materials as 'sources' (Hammergren 2004).
9 Examples include the work of Ingo Diehl, Lesley Main and Jody Sperling.
10 Savigliano (1996, 2003) also experiments with fiction, ethnography, and history.
11 James Clifford (1988: 23) attributes the challenge to ethnographic authority to 'the breakup and redistribution of colonial power in the decades after 1950 and to the echoes of that process in the radical cultural theories of the 1960s and 1970s'.
12 See CORD/CEPA (2009).

Part I

MAKING DANCE

Choreography, as a concept tied to individual authorship, is a modern, Western-derived invention.[1] However, even when the original contribution of a singular, individual creator is not privileged, writings for, by and about dancing masters, dramaturges and arrangers of dance material have held key importance for the study and interpretation of dance. As such, writing about the process of making dance underlies many contemporary and historical approaches to the study and theorisation of dance. Moreover, as modern, experimental and innovative dance works acquire a currency in a range of sites of practice, dance makers have, if anything, greater cause to reflect in writing on their own strategies for creating work as they interrogate not just the end result but the process of choreography. In this section, then, we have brought together the writings of dancers, choreographers, and scholars[2] who write about strategies employed in the creation of dance work, including, but not limited to those working within the Western modern dance tradition.

Annabel Farjeon, for instance, describes the choreographic approaches of ballet choreographers Ninette de Valois and Frederick Ashton from the perspective of a company member of the Sadler's Wells Ballet in the 1930s. Inevitably, the personalities of these choreographers were reflected in two very different modes of dance making which still have relevance today. De Valois came to the studio fully prepared. Her dancers were 'puppets', there to execute her 'private imaginings', and they knew little about the meanings or even the subject matter of the work in progress. Some laxity of interpretation was accorded to the principals, but the *corps* was allowed little deviation from de Valois's intent. Ashton, on the contrary, often appeared at rehearsal having thoroughly researched his theme but apparently with little choreographic material. He drew upon the dancers 'as though we were shapes with whom he was playing or experimenting'.

Merce Cunningham, a continent and a genre away, also engaged in choreographic play, but with a far more premeditated approach. Although discussing a specific work (*Torse*, 1975), Cunningham's general choreographic principles which govern most of his *oeuvre* can be extrapolated.

These include the democratisation of both the stage space and the kine-sphere of the body: the layering of movement phrases and tempi and the resultant, constantly changing flux of movement through time and in space. Although Cunningham is renowned for his use of chance procedures, this interview reveals the amount of forethought and preparation before the rehearsal stage, especially in the creation of dance phrases and the general structuring of the work. This exposition of the creation, selection and rejection of movement illustrates how Cunningham was able to work with chance, yet retain a distinct choreographic style. His procedures may appear to be 'play', but the playground is delineated and the rules are strict.

Anthea Kraut explores choreographic strategies while also problematising the category of 'choreographer'. Kraut's aims are two-fold: to revivify the work of African American artist Zora Neale Hurston and, in a closely linked argument, to ask to whom the appellation of choreographer might be ascribed and, significantly, what are the repercussions for those who might not qualify? As Hurston worked primarily with the pre-existing folk form of the Bahamian Fire Dance cycle, which she redesigned for the thea-tre in *The Great Day* (1932), in what ways might she qualify for this title? Kraut notes that the term has come to denote a separation between author/creator and executor/performer. As such, the act of improvisation sits uneasily within its remit, with an important repercussion that Hurston's Fire Dance 'played an important role in supporting the emerging bifurca-tion between black folk dance as improvisation and white modern dance as choreography'. Despite the problems of ascribing the term 'choreographer' to Hurston, not least those of viewing her as originator and thus denying the contribution of her forebears in the communal creation of the dance(s), Kraut argues for its appropriateness. Although acknowledging its discursive construction, she argues that the term has a materiality which attracts public recognition. It also implies a history of labour, of premeditation. By revealing this labour, Kraut argues that it is possible to ascribe the term 'choreographer' to the specificity of Hurston's activity in this particular staging. As such, it facilitates 'artistic credit – especially for those who have been historically denied the privilege of authorship – without losing sight of the complex, collaborative networks in which all choreographers are situated'.

Vida Midgelow's contribution similarly refigures discussions of origin-ality, this time focusing on reworking as a choreographic strategy. Mid-gelow investigates German choreographer Raimund Hoghe's *Swan Lake, 4 Acts* by looking at it as a staging of queerness, disability and non-norma-tive masculinity through Hogue's use of stillness, slowness and repetition. Midgelow argues that *Swan Lake, 4 Acts* both echoes and refigures the ori-ginal ballet, thereby challenging spectators through its play between pre-sence and absence and through its sense of provocatively unfulfilled expectation. Midgelow goes on to suggest that there is a politics to Hoghe's choreographic strategies. Slowness and repetition unsettle audience expectations of spectacle while his foregrounding of both his disability, that is, his difference from, and his body's anatomical likeness to that of his non-disabled dancers, trouble conventional narratives of disability and masculinity. Hoghe, Midgelow suggests, allows us to revisit history with a critical edge.

Dance maker/dancer/scholar Carol Brown considers the refiguring not of time but of space as she investigates the relationship between dance and its environment. She uses inter-related theories on corporeality and architecture to inform both her practice and her reflections upon it. Such an approach constructs the space of the dance not just as a neutral void but also as 'performative', as 'the interior spaces of the body' become entwined with 'the external spaces of performance'. Brown argues that the conditions of contemporary society have brought a shift in both experiential and conceptual attitudes to space from those that deem it a passive container of the body, an empty 'volume', to ones where space becomes fragmented in a continuum of interior–exterior interaction. This conception offers opportunities for the dance maker to deal with space '*for* dance that acknowledges *how* we are *here* in the contemporary moment'. Traditional performance spaces can alienate kinaesthetic experience and response; now, choreographers are questioning the dysfunctional nature of the received spaces of theatre. Brown concludes her exposition by offering examples from her collaborative work with designer–architect Dorita Hannah in which the materialities and qualities of the tomb, the labyrinth and the tower become spatial guides for creation and performance. Her descriptions are eloquent testimony to what can be achieved when choreographic and architectural imaginations meet and where 'choreography emerges through an unfolding between somatic awareness and scenic architecture'.

In contrast to a consideration of the choreographer's role in relation to abstract concepts such as space and time, postmodern Indian choreographer Chandralekha puts forward an argument about the dance maker's responsibility in and to society. Motivated by the dislocation she experienced between the poetic, classical dance work she began her dance career with and the realities of life around her, Chandralekha explores the changing relationship between dance and culture and considers the intersections between the engagement between the dancer and the dance and dance and society. She situates these relationships in a postcolonial context, arguing that 'for the East to be "contemporary" would mean to understand and express the East in its own terms' but this is not to dismiss lightly the tensions and possibilities, which arise from exploring – and exploiting – Western influences. She identifies how the function of dance has changed over the centuries, from that of a participatory, communal act of physical expression which embodied the material conditions of the people who danced, to one which became distanced from these conditions: where performer and spectator separated, and dance became spectacle. In such circumstances, asks Chandralekha, what role can dance play in recuperating and revivifying the human, most particularly in societies which have become increasingly alien to humanity? If, she asks, 'our life is alienated, can our dances and arts help to transcend that alienation?' Here, she suggests that choreographers have an obligation not just to aesthetic quality but also to environmental preservation and to economic and political justice.

Like Hoghe, Chandralekha looks to history with a critical edge, seeking change not for the sake of it, for there is much in Indian classical forms (as, arguably, in those of all cultures) which speak to today, not least 'the principles of wholeness and relatedness'.[3] There are inevitable tensions, however, in basing contemporary work on a traditional or classical movement vocabulary. Not least of these is the task of escaping the weight of the past which can stultify but, conversely, of resisting the pressures to 'update' in order to accommodate commercial imperatives. In summary, the task for the artist is how to 'initiate and consolidate the conjunctions between our traditional forms and our contemporary concerns'. Although Chandralekha uses the specificity of bharata natyam as central to her case, her argument that 'it is the task of the artist to modernise tradition through the creative process' is pertinent for all those who work with the longitude of dance's history and the latitude of present times.

Anna Scott likewise explores the possibilities raised by the choreographic investigation of history, in this case exploring adaptation as a strategy in Rennie Harris's *Rome & Jewels*. Together with his dancers, Harris has formed PureMovement, an ensemble that, as Scott suggests, operates more as a collective than a traditional, hierarchical dance company. PureMovement's *Rome & Jewels*, a collaborative multimedia event, aligns hip hop dance and music, film and video art, and classic British theatrical traditions. Scott embarks on her analysis of this piece by signalling the importance of dance to Shakespeare's original text, tracing the articulations of the ball/fight scene so that *Rome & Jewels* operates not only as an adaptation but also evokes the multiple adaptations of Romeo and Juliet that its audience is likely to be familiar with: Jerome Robbins's *West Side Story* and Baz Luhrmann's *Shakespeare's Romeo and Juliet*. This layering of adaptation conjures issues of masculinity, sexuality, race and the 'social construction of space'. Scott's piece, although a close analysis of one choreographic work, raises larger issues about the implications of adaptation, when she suggests that it 'explodes a system of sameness'.

The strategies discussed here – pre-planned design, play, improvisation, restaging, reworking an original dance work or a conventional dance language, the adaptation of works from other genres – are several among many approaches to the work of making dances. These entries are not intended to exhaust the possible approaches but rather they are meant to suggest that choreography takes many forms. These choreographic tactics, in turn, evoke multiple resonances ranging from the politics of specific identities to those of the global environment, from the politics and poetics of space to the role of the individual dancer.

Further reading

Aggiss, L. and Cowie, B. (2006) *Anarchic Dance*, London: Routledge.

Butterworth, J. and Wildschat, L. (2009) *Contemporary Choreography; A Critical Reader*, London: Routledge.

Gitelman, C. and Martin, R. (eds) (2007) *The Returns of Alwin Nikolais: Bodies, Boundaries and the Dance Canon*, Middletown, CT: Wesleyan UP.

Hay, D. (2000) *My Body, the Buddhist*, Middletown, CT: Wesleyan UP.

Limon, J. (2001) *Jose Limon: An Unfinished Memoir*, Middletown, CT: Wesleyan UP.

Ohno, K. and Ohno, Y. (2004) (trans. John Barrett) *Kazuo Ohno's World from Without and Within*, Middletown, CT: Wesleyan UP.

Notes

1 We use the term 'modern' here in both its temporal sense, to refer to the post-Enlightenment period, and its aesthetic sense, to refer to the modernist movement. As Susan Foster (2009: 145) indicates, 'choreography' initially referred to the notation of dances as the term was first deployed by Raoul Auger Feuillet in 1700 when he published his collection of notated dances. It was only in the early modernist period of the 1920s and 1930s that 'choreography' came to refer to the creation of a dance work (ibid.: 149). In both cases, however, the concept of choreography served to secure ownership over dance material (Foster 2009, Kraut 2009).

   In discussing the Western origins of the term, we do not mean to imply that the practice of making work is specific to the modern West as, even in traditions that do not celebrate an autonomous creator, dance works are constantly being created, recrafted, reworked and reinterpreted. Moreover, the Western notion of individual authorship, although spread as part of the discourses of colonialism, was taken up by those in colonial and postcolonial settings and refigured to acquire local meanings.

2 We have also included, and are especially interested in, the work of those who bridge those categories.

3 See also Shobana Jeyasingh on this topic (Chapter 17).

2

CHOREOGRAPHERS

Dancing for de Valois and Ashton

Annabel Farjeon

When I was a dancer with Sadler's Wells Ballet Company through the 1930s I was first a student in the school and then, two years later aged 14, given the roles of a Snowflake and a Biscuit in the original London production of *Casse Noisette*. From that time began more *corps de ballet* work, learning such classics as *Giselle*, *Le Lac des Cygnes* and *Les Sylphides* from the regular repertoire. For this we students were paid five shillings a performance until, suddenly, there was a salary of £3 10s a week and one was in the company. By 17 I had a flat of my own in Canonbury Square, Islington, and was independent.

Ninette de Valois and Frederick Ashton were the two main choreographers who worked on me – and at me – when I was a dancer. In their manner of composition, in their manner of getting what they wanted out of artists, they had very different methods. De Valois was cold and reserved, outwardly sure of herself, so that one was never exposed to her personal feelings or a sense of participation in the creation of a ballet. Ashton was hot and subject to violent emotional whims which would sometimes hinder, sometimes forward, his work, but with which nobody in the company could resist sympathy, so exposed and tender were his sensibilities.

Of course, we members of the *corps de ballet* were of minor importance as far as the choreographer was concerned, save as a group, being expected to do what we were told without fuss. But this subservient state gave all the more opportunity for observation with a curious and critical eye. It is the same with servants, who are generally far more astute and accurate in assessing their masters than is any equal friend or relative, since servants' judgments are not nearly so swayed by personal prejudice or sentiment. Thus I watched de Valois and Ashton carefully, judging each mood, each decision, each joke and each *pas de chat*.

Although the prospect of a new ballet such as *Checkmate* or *The Wise Virgins* was obviously of great importance to the company, both financially and artistically, it always seemed to me odd that nobody, or practically nobody, in the *corps de ballet* knew what this creation was to be about: neither the story or who had composed the music or who would design the decor. We were never told. The title with a cast list would be pinned to the notice board by the stage door – that was all. In the case of Ashton, this lack of information stemmed from a kind of unconcern; his feelings were so intense that he thought the theme must almost immediately become apparent without the bother of an explanation. In the case of de Valois it was partly her secretive nature, partly her policy of separating director from work force. She needed solitary power, for her own satisfaction and for the management of the company. From our point of view both methods had at least one advantage: they lent excitement to every new discovery, to every new rumour.

At the first rehearsal de Valois would remain cool, concentrated and often humorous. She was already primed with ideas and knew what she wanted: it had been written down in a notebook. Save for a pianist or merely using the score, she had marked out the details of the whole ballet in private. She was inclined to use dancers as puppets to be manipulated and there was little elasticity to the system. Now and then she would alter some step, rearrange a pattern or bring a character more to the fore, but it was seldom necessary. Her private imaginings had been pretty accurate.

De Valois never ranted and raged at rehearsals of her own work as she did when dealing with that of other choreographers. Then she would abuse dancers for lack of vitality, lack of technique, of being 'perfectly hopeless'. Once, in the fullness of exasperation, she cried to the young girl dancing Clara in *Casse Noisette*, 'Haven't you any temperament? You stupid little Anglo-Saxon!' For her own ballets impatience was merely at some slowness of understanding or forgetfulness of a move, which is common enough in newly fledged dancers, who are expected to memorize the choreography of twenty or more ballets at an early stage in their career.

De Valois stumped into the Wells Room for the first rehearsal of *Checkmate* with her feet, as usual, well turned out and a determined look on her face. It was a surprise to learn that she knew nothing about the game of chess or the moves of the pieces, since the story concerned a battle on a chessboard. The fact that the designer dressed us in red and black as opposing forces made me suspect that he did not know the game either.

Hilda Gaunt sat at the battered upright piano, a cigarette drooping from her mouth as she gossiped in a husky, smokey voice. Often she was the only filter through which information about a new ballet could be sifted. Now it seemed that the music was by Arthur Bliss and the decor by E. McKnight Kauffer. De Valois sat down in the middle of the long bench with her back to the window that looked on to Rosebery Avenue. 'Come along! I want the eight Red Pawns,' she said in a voice as sharp as the snip of scissors.

Now, I was understudy for the six Black Pawns. It was lucky that one of them, Margot Fonteyn, was almost immediately elevated so that I took her place. But first, as understudy, there was time to watch, admire and criticize.

The Red Pawns were ranged down one side of the room, the smallest girl in front, graded up to the tallest at the back. 'Fourth position, right foot in front, left hand on your hip, right arm straight forward, hand turned down from the wrist. Now – like soldiers drilling! Music!' De Valois would stand up to demonstrate, then hurry back to her book, open on the bench where the hieroglyphics could be studied. Sitting on the end of the bench, I wanted to get my hands on that book to see how her notation looked, but I never dared peep. When one of the Pawns yet again got out of line and then lost her way I gave an involuntary gasp of exasperation. De Valois turned in surprise, then gave a quick nod and lift at the corners of her mouth as a sign of recognition, so that I felt we were momentarily allied in the same cause.

The plot of the ballet evolved jerkily, for scenes were not rehearsed in their final order. Every detail of footwork, each turn of the head and arms had to be fixed to de Valois's satisfaction before she would move on. With soloists in whom she put her trust it was different; they were allowed to interpret movement almost in their own way – almost. But as the Red King, Robert Helpmann took the character entirely into his own hands. He became a dithering senile old man, pushed in every direction by his Queen and his Knights. Unable to make up his mind, with arms shaking, he tottered from square to square as though blown by a violent storm, to be ultimately hoisted prostrate on the staves of the Black Pawns and carried to his checkmate. I enjoyed every minute of being a Black Pawn.

To dance in de Valois's finest ballets, such as *Job*, *The Gods Go a-Begging* or *The Rake's Progress*, was another delight. Technically the steps were not difficult, but to get the style correct – that balance between restraint and display, that sense of period and character – was a problem that these ballets always posed. In *Job* it was a mixture of Blake and the Bible, in *The Gods Go a-Begging*, Watteau and neoclassicism, in *The Rake*, unadulterated Hogarth. During the brothel scene, when we chorused with the street singers 'Oh deary me, I do want to pee, and I don't really care who sees me!' (words not intended to carry, composed by Constant Lambert), I stuck my tongue out at the audience one night. A moment later I grew nervous that de Valois might pounce as I came into the wings and tick me off with one off her magnificent tirades for deviating from her choreography.

Frederick Ashton arranged his ballets in quite another fashion. He loved the feel of dancers, both physically and mentally, and he greeted them with warmth. His long face and sad eyes would light up with joy as readily as a child's when we danced well. But there were days when he would turn up to rehearsal seemingly without an idea in his head, and in my experience he never wrote anything down. Sitting on the bench before the window, his cheeks and neck would turn peony pink with anxiety. There was stillness and silence in the room.

At last he would go to the piano and, leaning over the music to hide his embarrassment, say, 'Play this bit, Hilda.' Hilda Gaunt would lay her cigarette on the fingerboard and play. After a moment he would pick on a favourite dancer. 'Do something! Go on, darling, do something!' Then he, too, would start swooping about the room, drag a couple standing at the side by the hands. 'Try it like this. Try lifting her – no, one leg like this! No – yes! Lovely! Now reverse the whole thing.' It was as though we were shapes with whom he was playing or experimenting, as a little boy might.

On other occasions he knew just what he wanted, but movements were always open to improvement. 'Look at the way Wenda flopped her head then. I want you all to flop your heads like that; it looks charming. Flop your heads!' So we all flopped our heads as Wenda had done.

In *Le Baiser de la Fée*, a ballet first produced for Ida Rubinstein with music by Stravinsky and choreography by Nijinska, then in 1935 by Ashton, I remember at the age of 16 the misery of not being strong enough on pointe, and how kindly forbearing Ashton was to me. There was a terrible quick-change in the wings from the first peasant scene into a new costume plus pointe shoes, which added to my agony. Pearl Argyle, as the wicked fairy, looked divine and danced with a numb elegance that left me longing for a spark of imperfection. The prologue of the mother and baby floundering back and forth in a snowstorm struck me as sentimental and incongruous. It would be interesting to know how Nijinska coped with this scenario.

Ashton taught us the peasant dance during one long afternoon but then, next day, arrived in a frenzy of dissatisfaction and scrapped the whole thing. He had thought up a new plan in the night. This, of course, was a dismal waste of rehearsal time, time that was hard enough to come by, what with the opera rehearsals, our regular repertoire, and classes for both company and students. All day every room in the theatre was filled with dancers leaping and singers shrieking, while the auditorium resounded with the players of music and the tap of a conductor's baton on his desk as he stopped the orchestra mid bar, saying, 'Now, go back to C, I want those five notes much softer.'

During an early staging of *The Wise Virgins*, which we rehearsed on tour in Brighton at the start of the war in 1940, Ashton produced a book of photographs of baroque churches in southern Germany, with their curli-cued plasterwork and the asymmetric poses of saints and madonnas who look at the same time so beautiful and so unnatural. He explained how our limbs should express the formality and elegance of Bach's music, how they should match the pinnacles around which cherubs spun, the altars of fluffed clouds, and angels disporting themselves with such absurd affectation.

'You see,' he said, smiling at Fanny's charming pose as she aped a saint, 'Fanny understands. She sees herself like this in the afterlife, floating about heaven with beautiful thoughts, laid out on a mauve cloud.'

Fanny's face expressed distress. She was one of the few serious Christians in the company. Quickly Ashton showed his contrition by turning attention away from the sensitive one, to cry, 'Pamela, you shall massage my dowager's hump after the rehearsal!'

In this ballet, where I played the Bride's Mother, he would say, 'Come on now, what about your ancestors, Annabel? Let the Jewish momma in you take over – your daughter is getting married so howl, howl from head to toe! Go on – HOWL!' That a mother might howl at the marriage of her daughter had not occurred to me before, but immediately I saw drama in this sorrow and it affected every gesture I made.

Often, after searching for clues among his dancers, Ashton would suddenly begin a flow of movement that seemed to take hold of choreographer and dancer alike, until both became instruments on which his imagination would improvise for hours with a facility and professionalism that entirely belied all that early agony and dither.

Ashton was no moralist, but there was one socially conscious ballet he produced at the beginning of 1940. The war with Germany had begun, although so far there had been no direct attack on Britain. Ashton, the romantic, chose as his subject the battle between the forces Good and Evil, set to Liszt's *D'après une lecture de Dante*, arranged for piano and orchestra by Lambert, and called the ballet *Dante Sonata*. With awareness of Nazi concentration camps, with photographs of Jews being abused in German streets, revulsion surged up in him, always a man full of sympathy for the underdog. Unlike de Valois, he was not a natural autocrat. Again we were shown a picture book, this time of engravings by Flaxman of Dante's Inferno, where bodies happily spiralled up to heaven or tumbled in agony down to hell.

As so often, Constant Lambert, our conductor, collaborated with the planning and suggested the music. In a broadcast he later explained, 'The general layout, by which I mean not the dancing as such but the association of various characters with various themes and the general dramatic sequence, was then established by Ashton and myself. I played the piano at almost all the rehearsals while the choreography was being created, so that when it came to finally orchestrating the ballet, I had the whole stage picture in mind.'

We danced *Dante Sonata* barefoot on the stage, the choreography designed in a free, almost Martha Graham style, though as I remember with a wider scope of movement. It was a release from the restrictions of classical ballet and pointe shoes, for so-called 'modern dance' is far easier to execute.

Fonteyn and Somes were the leaders of the Children of Light, while Brae and Helpmann led the Children of Darkness. Of course Fanny was one of the Good, while I was one of the Evil group. Ashton cast his dancers with care. We fought and parted without a victor and in the final tableau there was no triumph. On opposite sides of the stage, mounted above their followers, Helpmann and Somes hung as though crucified. Some critics found this ending trite, while others felt it to be a step toward a much needed social consciousness within the Sadler's Wells Ballet Company.

Certainly, this ballet, fraught with emotion, was appreciated by us, we who interpreted the tortured ecstasy that runs through Liszt's music. And the sorrow and anger we expressed seemed to identify us more closely with the terrible drama surging across Europe. We the dancers thought that *Dante Sonata* would be a creation to last through generations, as it was handed down by example and word of mouth. Some years later, with a different cast, a larger stage and changed attitudes, the ballet failed and has not survived. There was probably too much passion in it and not enough artistic decorum. But I still remember Ashton's choreography as marvellously balanced, full of power and romance, and above all – beautiful.

Frederick Ashton aimed at beauty. Ninette de Valois aimed at truth. That was the difference between them.

3

TORSE

There are no fixed points in space

Merce Cunningham with Jacqueline Lesschaeve

JACQUELINE LESSCHAEVE: *Merce Cunningham, the choreography for classical or modern dancers follows often predictable sequences: mainly soloists doing variations in relation to (or against) a background of a group of dancers. You deliberately broke with that procedure of repeating familiar sequences, and you involved yourself in exploring the range of possible movements. Starting with one of your recent dances, could we take note in some detail of what differentiates it from the older, more traditional forms?*

MERCE CUNNINGHAM: Imagine going to the other extreme of what you described. Say you have eight people each of whom is doing different sequences, all of whom are being soloists. That is immediately far more complex. Think of how they divide the *corps* in classical ballet: you have eight girls on each side of the stage, eight girls moving symmetrically which you can perceive at a glance. If you have these two groups of eight girls doing totally different phrases, that's not very complicated but it's already more unexpected. Now go further still, take each eight. Have four do one thing, four something else. You immediately see that you can go to the extreme: you can take all sixteen and have each dancer doing clearly different movements. That would be done not just to be complex but to open up unexplored possibilities. Further, in classical ballet as I learned it, and even in my early experience of the modern dance, the space was observed in terms of a proscenium stage, it was frontal. What if, as in my pieces, you decide to make any point on the stage equally interesting? I used to be told that you see the centre of the space as the most important: that was the centre of interest. But in many modern paintings this was not the case and the sense of space was different. So I decided to open up the space to consider it equal, and any place, occupied or not, just as important as any other. In such a context you don't have to refer to a precise point in space. And when I happened to read that sentence of Albert Einstein's: 'There are no fixed points in space', I thought, indeed, if there are no fixed points, then every point is equally interesting and equally changing.

I began to work in that direction, for it opens up an enormous range of possibilities. As you're not referring one sequence to another you can constantly shift everything, the movement can be continuous, and numerous transformations can be imagined. You still can have people dancing the same phrase together, but they can also dance different phrases at the same time, different phrases divided in different ways, in two, three, five, eight or whatever. The space could be constantly fluid, instead of being a fixed space in which movements relate. We've grown up with ideas about a fixed space in the theatre to which spectator and dancer refer. But if you abandon that idea you discover another way of looking. You can see a person not just from the front but from any side with equal interest.

Taking nothing else but space, you see how many possibilities have been revealed. Suppose you now take the dimension of time. Our eight dancers can be doing different movements, they may even do them to the same rhythm which is all right, there's nothing wrong with any of it! [*laughter*] – but there is also the possibility that they can be doing different movements in different rhythms, then that is where the real complexity comes in, adding this kind of material one on top of and with another. One may not like it, but it seems to me anyway that once one begins to think this way, the possibilities become enormous. One of the points that distinguishes my work from traditional choreographies, classical and modern, is certainly this enlargement of possibilities.

JL: *Your dancers often enter into unison groups and break up from them. These movements give a sense of exploding or changing in time and space, but it's disconcerting to those used to more linear changes.*

MC: But just think of a group of six people walking along on the sidewalk together. At any moment they can all walk off in different directions, at different rhythms.

JL: *It's especially visible when you see children, grouping and separating, walking off, going off, in very different dynamic modes. The same holds for flights of birds, at once fluid and abruptly changing.*

MC: One of my recent works, *Torse*, is very clearly made in that way. The groups of dancers are constantly changing. I finished it in 1975. The whole piece was done using chance operations so as to have the possibility of any formation of the dancers appearing. Say, for example, that you had two groups, not with the same number of dancers, one downstage and one upstage, somewhat diagonal, and say they were simply to exchange places, though they're doing two different phrases. Now obviously they could pass through each other, but say the movement wouldn't allow for it. Let's suppose that this group's tempo is slower, and that I want both groups to end at the same time (that could happen, yes ...). I could for instance have the first group start, stop for a while, start the second one that would pass through the first one. Because of the different rhythms, they could end together, as the first one would start more rapidly to go to a stop and then go on, while the other group would go more slowly but regularly.

The other fact in that dance that I like very much, actually, is that if you saw the whole dance – it is fifty-five minutes long when the three parts are danced one after another – you would see that each one of the ten dancers appears at some point as a soloist. You have to watch, really use your eyes, but if you see it a few times, you see that each one comes out separately at one point, some way, back or front, as a soloist. And though the general feeling throughout is that the dance remains a dance of ensembles, it is very individualized as well, each dancer at one point or another has a chance to appear outside the group. It's subtle enough; it doesn't happen in an obvious way or place, but I'm sure it's felt. Or it may come about that there are no groups on stage, just two solo dancers. That was decided as well through chance means, which included this constant appearance of soloists. And as I worked it out from step to step, I didn't decide any of it ahead of time. As chance made a solo possible, long or short, I would see which dancer could do it, and in what way.

JL: *I especially admired one of the sequences where, leaving them all very distinct, you set a whole group of dancers in a small part of the stage, leaving the rest empty, which by comparison seems much bigger; after which you shift them all on the other side in a continuous flow, which gives the feeling of much more space than if the dancers had been spread about all over.*

MC: If you don't divide a space classically, the space remains more ambiguous and seems larger.

JL: *I think* Torse, *because of the many questions it brings up, would be a good basis for studying the composition process.*

MC: I'm going to give it in a workshop. I will not be able to show it the way my dancers do it, but I will show students the basic process. What's interesting in it is that all the elements were dealt with simultaneously, and even though to some people *Torse* looks like classical work, it isn't really. The movements do have a certain emphasis on line but the line is not at all a classical ballet line.

JL: *The coherence of a certain type of movement through* Torse *gives the impression that the way it seems to float in space is achieved by means that are very precise and used throughout, and that gives the flowing sensation that is so beautiful.*

MC: I figured out the phrasing and the continuity ahead of time, before the dancers came to rehearsal. Not, of course, the way they would dance the phrases, but the phrases themselves. It took a long time. I worked on it by myself with the help of video. There are sixty-four phrases, because that's the number of hexagrams in the *I Ching*. The phrases are formed like the numbers themselves. For example, one has one part in it, two has two, three has three, up to sixty-four. But I didn't make it as though one were one rhythmic beat, and so forth, metrically. Let us take the second phrase, it will be clearer. The counts are related to *weight changes*. That is, if you stand on your foot, that's one; if you bend your knee, that's a weight change, so that's two. Now that could be done slowly or quickly. At sixty-four, you have sixty-four weight changes. Or say, in phrase ten, for example, you have to produce ten weight changes, which means you're on one foot or both or whatever – but you might stand on one foot for a long time and circle the arms, which is not a weight change but changes completely the structure of time for this phrase. I figured them all out ahead of the rehearsal period with the dancers or I never would have been able to finish the piece in the rehearsal time available. And I allowed for repetition within a phrase, for instance: thirty-six is nine times four, or six times six.

That was for the sixty-four movement phrases. But then you take the space and you have a similar process. I numbered the space with sixty-four squares, eight by eight. Then I used the *I Ching* as it comes out: the hexagrams come out double most of the time, one over the other, for example thirteen over fifteen, that means phrase thirteen along with phrase fifteen. Then I would toss to see how many people did each phrase among the men, the women or both. Gradually all the combinations would come out and I would see them more and more clearly and try them out. Most of the paperwork had to be done ahead. But the crucial moment is when you try it out physically.

Sometimes you would have all the dancers doing the same phrase. That was decided by chance, the number forty-nine, for instance, comes up a couple of times alone, and in that case they danced in unison. Let's look at all this more closely: for instance, this is hexagram thirteen over hexagram twelve, and say that the following one is by chance the five or seven. I had prepared what would be phrase five, and working on it with the dancers I would see how it could move through the space, starting from where they stood before. I did the same with the space they occupied, numbered as you remember from one to sixty-four: someone was standing in space thirteen and someone in space twelve. I would choose how many dancers would come in those two spaces, and to go to forty-nine in terms of space – forty-nine is a specific place – they all go in that direction, but they can do it by such or such a detour according to the phrase they have to dance. This last point is important, as the dancers may as well go straight there as go while forming circles or whatever figure is suggested by the dance phrase to get them there. The dance phrase itself was generated, as you remember, by its own number. So I made a space chart and a movement chart, both in sixty-four distinct units, and I had to deal with them both, this chart and the movement chart. Then there would come up the possibility of exits or entrances or the possibility of a duet and that's done by tossing coins, according to which some dancers leave the stage or not. I would toss a coin to see what to do. That's how those trios and duets appear in the piece. What it amounted to was a *continual change.*

JL: *There are only about ten dancers, but one gets the impression of a flock of them. This constant shifting makes them seem to be everywhere.*

MC: I know. A lady saw *Torse* once and said, 'But you must have sixty dancers!' For a lot of people, especially people accustomed to classical ballet, it's very difficult to watch. They're disturbed because they realize it's clear but they can't see it, can't deal with it at first sight.

JL: *It's at once precise and strict, and in constantly shifting motion. I understand better now why someone I know well, who is a mathematician, liked* Torse *so much. He literally saw* numbers at work. *To give this continual sensation of flux, you must have been quite selective in the choice of the movements themselves.*

MC: I did leave certain movements out, you're quite right. I was thinking about the torso, as the title indicates, and I retained mainly the range of body movements corresponding to five positions of the back and the backbone, positions with which I mostly work: upright, curve, arch, twist and tilt. Those five basic positions are very clear and the leg and arm positions in relation to those are clear, too. When you assemble all this to form the phrases, the possibilities are numerous though they stay within a certain vocabulary. It's wide but strict. I remember, though, when the dancers danced *Torse* for the first time, they found it very difficult to do. Now they're used to it, some of them even do it extremely well, the ones who've danced it often like Chris Komar, Robert Kovich, Ellen Cornfield and Meg Harper.

JL: *To what extent do the dancers know the complexity of the structure they're working on?*

MC: I think they're aware of it, because even if you're only dancing a part, after a while, you begin, if you're at all conscious, to develop a sense about what the others are doing, and you realize they're doing something else. You have to begin to know where the other dancer is, without looking. It has to do with time, the relationship with the timing. If you paid attention to the timing, then, even if you weren't facing them, you knew they were there. And that made a relationship. It depends also on how you think something can be created, too. If you always think that relationships are only one way, then that's the way you do it. But if you think relationships can be many ways, then that comes into your possible perception. It's like a cat. It doesn't have to turn around and look at something, it knows it's there. In human beings, it comes by experience, and certainly my pieces develop this faculty.

JL: *A word about the music for* Torse.

MC: The music is by Maryanne Amacher. I don't know how to describe it, you almost don't hear it. Sometimes there are no sounds at all. Every once in a while I hear a railroad train. It's quite like subliminal sounds. It's very quiet. Sort of still.

JL: *What indications did you give for the music?*

MC: None. I asked John [Cage] who he thought might make some music for *Torse*, and he suggested Maryanne.

JL: *Did he know of the piece you expected to do?*

MC: I'm trying to remember ... I think he must have known somewhat, because I was working on it so much before I did the piece, making all those charts.

JL: *I'd like us to jump ahead to your work with video, by talking about the splendid film (double screen) of Torse that you made with Charles Atlas, and for which you were one of the cameramen!*

MC: Yes, it's a colour film of the whole piece, fifty-five minutes long as well. We chose the double screen because of the nature of the choreography. It wouldn't have been possible with one screen. We did the shooting in a large theatre in Seattle where the dance company was in residence, that allowed for very good camera work. And in that case, too, we prepared all the takes in advance. The shooting itself only took three days. The idea is that on the two screens you see everything that happens on the stage. When half the company appears on one of the screens, the other half appears on the other – that's the simplest case. We didn't do much that way because the dance itself opens and closes so much. The other extreme case is where all the dancing can be happening on one screen for a few seconds, while the other screen is empty. At first, I felt strange as a film cameraman ... and I was afraid of having wasted film and time, but it turned out the camera wasn't working! One of the three cameras was stationary and took the whole stage, and the other two, moveable, were placed slightly lower. The stationary camera was handled by a technician, the mobile ones by Charles Atlas and myself. We followed the groups of dancers and took what close-ups were possible. After that Charles Atlas edited the film. In its final version it is projected on two screens using two synchronized projectors.

4

RECOVERING HURSTON, RECONSIDERING THE CHOREOGRAPHER

Anthea Kraut

> But this I do know, that people became very much alive to West Indian dancing and work songs. I have ... felt the influence of that concert running through what has been done since. My name is never mentioned, of course, because that is not the way theater people do things, but that concert and the rave notices I got from the critics shoved the viewpoint over towards the natural Negro.
>
> (Hurston 1996: 284–5)

In her 1942 autobiography, *Dust Tracks on a Road* (pub. 1996), Zora Neale Hurston takes stock of her presentation of black diasporic folk songs and dances a decade earlier. She notes both the impact of her concert and the public's failure to remember her association with it. In a departure from what Hurston chalks up to the ways of 'theater people', this essay seeks to restore credit to Hurston for her staging of black folk dance by adding 'choreographer' to the list of accomplishments – novelist, folklorist, anthropologist and playwright – that more frequently accompany her name. At the same time, I explore some of the implications of employing naming as a strategy of remembrance. While use of the term 'choreographer' helps remedy the long-standing neglect of Hurston's dance contributions, this retroactive designation also poses certain dilemmas. Consequently, I hope to show that the act of remembering Hurston's performances is one that requires a careful rethinking of our disciplinary definitions of artists and artistry.

The concert to which Hurston refers in her autobiography premiered on 10 January 1932, at the John Golden Theatre in New York. Titled *The Great Day* and billed as 'A Program of Original Negro Folklore', Hurston's revue was based on the anthropological research she conducted in the southern United States and the Bahamas during the late 1920s. The narrative of the concert traced a single day in the life of a railroad work camp in Florida, from the waking of the camp at dawn to a rousing Bahamian Fire Dance at midnight (Programme 1932). Over the next few years, Hurston produced her folk concert in slightly different versions and under various titles – *From*

Sun to Sun, All De Live Long Day, Singing Steel – in cities and towns across the country. Although she continually reworked the revue, the enactment of the Caribbean dance finale remained a fixture that was by all accounts the high point of the production. In addition to these full-length concerts, Hurston presented portions of her revue at several venues around New York, twice at the National Folk Festival (in St Louis in 1934 and in Washington DC in 1938), and under the auspices of the Florida Federal Writers' Project in Orlando. Along the way, her Bahamian dance material captured the interest of choral director Hall Johnson, Russian-born jazz dance promoter Mura Dehn, theatre director Irene Lewisohn, modern dance artists Ruth St. Denis, Doris Humphrey and Helen Tamiris, and ballroom dance icon Irene Castle. Despite this attention, Hurston's contributions to the field of dance remain all but forgotten.

The project of recovering the history of Hurston's stagings of black diasporic dance is therefore one of 'revisibilization': unearthing what Brenda Dixon Gottschild (1996) has described as the 'invisibilized' black influences on American culture. Certainly Hurston is no stranger to the revisibilization process. From the 1970s to the 1990s, this African American artist – and her 1937 novel *Their Eyes Were Watching God* in particular – catapulted from near-complete obscurity to canonization within the academy. While Hurston's current renown makes the neglect of her dance practice all the more striking, the rise of her literary star also proves instructive as we set out to recuperate her dance productions. As a number of black feminist critics have pointed out, the reclaiming of Hurston as foremother to a black woman's literary tradition has elevated her to the position of pure origin, a move that not only naturalizes and decontextualizes Hurston's own artistic production but also privileges her representation of a reputedly 'authentic' black folk heritage over and above other African American experiences and histories.[1]

In rectifying the erasure of Hurston from the dance historical record, then, questions about the politics of recovery are paramount. To be sure, the history of Hurston's dance stagings was never really 'lost'. Information about her successive enactments of the Fire Dance survives in the 'disparate residual traces' (Foster 1995: 4) that each staging of the dance left behind, from programmes, press releases and newspaper reviews; to photographs, film footage and sound recordings; to written correspondence, published and unpublished research, and autobiographical accounts. The task of recovery requires assembling these archival fragments, speculating about the archive's absences, and formulating conclusions about what it all means. Writing the history of Hurston's dance undertakings thus involves both a literal re-membering of the scattered pieces of evidence and a more figurative re-membering of Hurston herself, for knowledge of her dance enterprise surely shifts our overall understanding of her. Yet how best to remember Hurston as a dance artist? Especially pressing is the issue of naming: bluntly put, to what extent can and should Hurston be considered a choreographer?

At first blush, the term may appear inappropriate. Clearly, Hurston did not function as a choreographer in the conventional sense of composing new dances. The Bahamian Fire Dance that served as her concert's finale was a pre-existent, communally created and sustained folk form. The archive provides no evidence that Hurston ever referred to herself as a choreographer, nor did she ever use the related term 'choreography' to describe her dance endeavours. It is worth bearing in mind, however, that in the 1920s and 1930s, terminology such as 'arranged', 'staged' and 'directed' was much more commonly used to recognize dance artists working on the theatrical stage. And indeed, the programme for a 1939 exclusive presentation of the Fire Dance listed Hurston as 'Dance Director' (Programme 1939). Whereas she employed both a musical arranger and a chorus director to help train her singers for the New York debut of her concert, Hurston alone took on the responsibility of transforming the Fire Dance folk cycle from its Caribbean vernacular incarnation to its American theatrical manifestation. The question thus remains: does Hurston merit the label 'choreographer' for her staging of black folk dance?

As I've worked on this project over the last several years, other scholars first learning of Hurston's involvement with dance have responded with both surprise and delight. Yet my contention that Hurston 'choreographed' – as opposed to 'staged' or 'orchestrated' – the black folk dances that appeared in her revues has occasionally met with scepticism. This reluctance to grant that the nature of Hurston's dance work constituted a kind of choreography, I believe, indicates that there is much at stake in how and to whom we give the designation 'choreographer'. Evidently, dance scholars have invested a great deal in the term – but what kind of investment and for what reasons? Recognizing the controversy that attributions can engender, I aim to give careful consideration to the advantages and pitfalls of applying the label 'choreographer' to Hurston.

In recuperating the history of Hurston's stage presentations of black folk dance, I want to ask not only how we might re-member Hurston differently, but how we might differently conceptualize the categories that define dance studies. In particular, I hope to place pressure on the term 'choreographer' by asking questions about the kinds of work the term has historically performed. Who has been entitled to wear the mantle choreographer, and who has been excluded from the category? What are the consequences of drawing lines between those who can and cannot claim the appellation? While an in-depth investigation of the history of the term 'choreographer' is beyond the scope of this essay, a brief consideration of how the term has traditionally been used helps lay the ground for scrutinizing its relevance for Hurston.

What is a choreographer?

In its most common usage, 'choreography' refers to the art of making dances, and the term 'choreographer' designates the artist responsible for a dance's creation and arrangement. What exactly this means, however, is a matter of significant historical contingency. With its etymological roots in the Greek *'choreia'* for dance and the French *'graphie'* for writing, the word 'choreography' referred, in the seventeenth and eighteenth centuries, to the written notation of dances. The nineteenth and twentieth centuries saw a shift in the meaning of the term as the emphasis came to centre on the 'actual invention and sequencing of movements' (Foster 1996c: 295, n.57). But because the choreographic tradition was a European ballet-based one, it took some time for white American modern dance artists to appropriate the appellation 'choreographer' for themselves (Huxley 1999). Though modern dance in the United States began as a solo form, it legitimized itself in the 1920s and 1930s in part by adopting the elite art model of the separation between the author and the aesthetic object. Under this model, 'the individual choreographer was conceived of as the creative source of the work executed by the dancers, as the person who shaped and set the work of art until it was ready to be presented before an audience' (Novack 1990: 23).

Though today the label is considerably less restricted, claimed by those working in concert dance, Broadway and MTV alike, it is clear that 'choreographer' has historically been a term of privilege, functioning both to authorize and to exclude. Accompanying the separation the term marks between the artist/creator and the dancers/performers has been a division between choreography and improvisation, with the former perceived as premeditated and intentional and the latter seen as impromptu and haphazard. While recent scholarship has helped complicate the accepted dichotomy between choreography and improvisation (Foster 2002; Albright and Gere 2003), this binary has not been without its utility for certain parties.[2] In the early twentieth century, the constructed opposition between the choreographed and the improvised served to elevate white creative artistry, which implicitly – and often explicitly – defined itself against the putatively 'natural' expressive behaviour of black performers. In fact, as I argue elsewhere, Hurston's Bahamian Fire Dance played an important role in supporting the emerging bifurcation between black folk dance as improvisation and white modern dance as choreography (Kraut 2008).

For a number of reasons, then, the attribution 'choreographer' was not available to Hurston at the time she staged the Bahamian Fire Dance. Prime among these was the perception that the dancing that appeared in her revue was unrehearsed, spontaneous expression – in other words, the opposite of choreographed. The critic Arthur Ruhl's testimonial that *The Great Day* embodied the ideal of 'natural and unpremeditated art' epitomizes this view (Ruhl 1932: 11). However much Hurston actively cultivated the impression of naturalness, this discourse played right into entrenched racist stereotypes about instinctive black performativity, stereotypes that left little if any room for the recognition of methodical black artistry. As a black woman working with 'low art' black vernacular forms at a time when dance was struggling to establish itself as a respectable field, Hurston faced a convergence of racial and artistic hierarchies that made it unthinkable for her to identify herself as a choreographer. If my employment of the term to describe Hurston is therefore anachronistic, it is my hope that this usage will help further trouble the binaries between choreography and improvisation, the individual and the communal, and the modern and the folk.

Still, it would no doubt be possible to problematize these dichotomies and interrogate Hurston's dance stagings without relying on the word 'choreographer'. As it happens, there are some rather sound reasons *not* to apply the term to Hurston. By no stretch of the imagination did Hurston create the Bahamian Fire Dance. Transported to the Caribbean by African slaves, the dance commingled with European practices before finding its way to Florida, where Hurston stumbled upon it during a research expedition in the late 1920s. Though I do not subscribe to the belief that such collective folk forms are 'authorless', it could certainly be argued that the Western idea of the individual choreographer is an inadequate way of characterizing the kind of collaborative artistic production that is responsible for generating and sustaining idioms like the Fire Dance.

Even in taking the position, as I do, that there are judicious reasons for treating Hurston as a choreographer despite her failure to fit conventional understandings of the category, it is important to be alert to the perils involved in limning Hurston's contributions in this way. Much as it has in literary studies, appointing Hurston the 'originary' source for subsequent stagings of Afro-Caribbean folk dance would once again threaten to reify her by obscuring the entire matrix of influences and historical forces that shaped her own artistic practice. In particular, describing Hurston as a choreographer risks glossing over of the contributions of the innumerable folk artists who created and sustained the Fire Dance for years before and after she incorporated it into her concert. Yet calling Hurston a choreographer need not necessarily elide or undermine the contributions of these Bahamian artists. Their authorship of the Fire Dance in its vernacular form is undeniable, even if their individual identities cannot be known. There is room, I would argue, for both Hurston and her Bahamian sources to be understood as choreographers.

Despite the various hazards, then, I believe that there are compelling grounds for treating Hurston as a choreographer and that the values of doing so ultimately outweigh the risks. To better understand these grounds, it is helpful to return to the label choreographer and probe beneath its casual associations. Rather than hammer out a new definition of the term, I want to focus on its 'author-function' – what Michel Foucault (1977b) has

articulated as the operation and effects of the figure of the author in discourse. While the meanings and effects of the designation 'choreographer'
unquestionably fluctuate in accordance with the contexts in which it is
invoked, I want to flag two levels at which the term performs a fundamental
kind of ideological work that are essential to recognizing its significance for
Hurston.

First and most obviously, calling someone a 'choreographer' assigns
credit to that individual for a given dance production; the term thereby
serves as an assertion of authorship. Notwithstanding post-structuralist
proclamations about the death of the author, 'Our investment in [the]
institution [of authorship]', as scholars such as Peggy Kamuf have con-
tended, 'is massive. All sorts of values are exchanged within its construction' (Kamuf 1988: x). Indeed, authorship continues to hold a good deal of
economic, legal, and political – as well as aesthetic and cultural – capital.
Granting that authorship is a figure of discourse, then, should by no means
eclipse its material effects. Following the insights of both Foucault and
those who have contested the death of the author, it behoves us to recognize that assertions of authorship – like those the term 'choreographer'
enacts – are discursively constructed and entail real repercussions.

Secondly, and perhaps more tacitly, the designation 'choreographer'
acknowledges a history of labour: the use of the word simultaneously
assumes and establishes that an executed dance has been worked out in
advance. It is here that the distinctions between choreography and improvisation tend to get inscribed. While the term choreography marks dance as
predetermined, improvisation is used to describe dance that is composed
on the spot. Yet as scholarship on African American expressive forms like
jazz and tap has demonstrated, improvisation depends equally on a history
of labour.[3] A more accurate account of where the two modes of production
diverge, I believe, would centre on their different objectives, including the
different ratios in each between what Susan Foster has characterized as the
'known' – that 'set of behavioral conventions', 'structural guidelines' and
individual predilections that condition and delimit an improvising body's
choices – and the 'unknown' – 'that which was previously unimaginable'
(Foster 2003: 3–4).

Both implications of the term 'choreographer' were of consequence to
Hurston. The fact that she sought copyright for a number of her plays
stands as a reminder of her serious interest in authorship. So too does the
entreaty she made to her friend, the writer Annie Nathan Meyer, to attend
an upcoming production of one of her plays: 'Do come and like a good
Zora rooter Yell "Author, author"!!' (Hurston 1925). Hurston's concern for
recognition of her dance work is evidenced in her 1942 autobiography, in
passages like the one that opened this essay. Declaring her satisfaction in
knowing that her folk revues 'established a trend' and that 'people became
very much alive to West Indian dancing' in their wake, she insists – perhaps

a bit too emphatically – that she is 'not upset by the fact that others have made something out of the things I pointed out,' even while her own name is 'never mentioned' (Hurston 1996: 284–5, 173).

If in spite of themselves, these remarks convey a sense of Hurston's regret about being denied public acknowledgment for the authorship of her dance productions, her investment in the other dimension of the term 'choreographer' – its invocation of a history of labour – was more equivocal. With artlessness and simplicity at the cornerstone of her marketing efforts, affirming too much labour threatened to undermine the perceived naturalness and therefore diminish the value of her folk concerts. When Hurston referred to the estimation of a critic who 'said that he did not believe that the concert was rehearsed, it looked so natural,' she did so not deploringly but as proof of her project's success (ibid.: 172).

To a great extent, it is Hurston's reliance on the rhetoric of spontaneity – at a time when black performance was judged primarily if not wholly on the basis of its perceived authenticity – that propels me to assign the label 'choreographer' to her retroactively. Granting Hurston a status she was not afforded in her own time is a deliberate tactic, designed to bring to light aspects of her stage practice that have gone under-appreciated or altogether ignored. To that end, the remainder of this essay examines the nature of Hurston's choreographic labour – the various kinds of preparation she carried out to mount the Bahamian Fire Dance on the theatrical stage – while keeping one eye to the larger questions about what the work of the choreographer entails and who merits this designation.

Hurston's choreographic labour

Learning the fire dance

Hurston's first encounter with Caribbean folk dance and music, as mentioned earlier, occurred in the late 1920s during an anthropological expedition to southern Florida. The dancing of a group of Bahamian migrant workers there struck Hurston as 'so stirring and magnificent, that I had to admit to myself that we had nothing in America to equal it' (ibid.: 281). The Fire Dance that she found so captivating was actually a cycle of three dances. In the first two, the Jumping Dance and Ring Play, a circle of players took turns in the centre, stepping, leaping and posing to the rhythms of an accompanying drum. In the subsequent Crow Dance, a soloist performed an imitation of a buzzard 'flying and seeking food' (Programme 1939). In October 1929, Hurston travelled to Nassau to find out more about Bahamian music and dance. There she not only took three reels of film of the dancing, she also 'took pains', as she later reported in her autobiography, to learn the Fire Dance movements herself (Hurston 1996: 281).

Before she could even think about staging the Fire Dance in her own concert, then, Hurston first had to master all the facets of its choreography. This included learning to 'read the drum': discovering how to hear and anticipate the dynamic subtleties of the drumming so that she could coordinate all of her movements to fit its varying rhythms and tones (Hurston 1999: 154). The process of learning to perform the Fire Dance was no doubt similar to that she followed to assimilate the folk songs she encountered during her research expeditions. As she once explained to an interviewer,

> I just get in the crowd with the people and if they sing it and I listen as best I can and then I start to joining in with a phrase or two and then finally I get so I can sing a verse and then I keep on till I learn all the verses and then I sing them back to the people until they tell me that I can sing them just like them and then I take part and I try it out on different people who already know the song until they are quite satisfied that I know it and then I carry it in my memory.
>
> (Hurston 1939)

Acquired through comparable methods of immersion, trial and error, and embodiment, the Fire Dance also became lodged in Hurston's muscle memory, where she could 'carry it' around with her. Knowledge of the general framework of the Fire Dance thus remained with Hurston when she grew ready to transform it for the proscenium stage.

Transmitting the fire dance

Back in New York in the fall of 1931, as she fine-tuned the script for the production that would become The Great Day, Hurston took the initial step of assembling a 'troup [sic] of sixteen Bahamans who could dance' (ibid.: 281). Information about precisely who these dancers were, how Hurston recruited them, and what their dance backgrounds were is extremely sketchy. Among the known members of the troupe were Leonard Sturrup, also known as Motor Boat, Carolyne Rich, Alfred Strochan, John Dawson, Joseph Neely (or Nealy), William Polhamus, Reginald Alday, Lias Strawn and Bruce (Mabel) Howard.[4]

As Hurston began conducting rehearsals in her apartment on West 66th Street and wherever she could find space, she discovered that her research footage could be put to a perhaps unanticipated use. In a letter dated 15 October to her white patron, Charlotte Osgood Mason, she made the following plea:

> Godmother, may I show Mr. Colledge the fire-dance films from the Bahamas? ... He wants to see first a sample of all the materials and while I am training the group it takes so long for the preliminary

showing and that holds back definite arrangements. Then too, seeing the films would refresh *my* memory on details. Please, may I?

(Hurston 1931)

Preparing to audition her concert material for a producer at the Steinway Theatre, Hurston gingerly requests permission to borrow back her own film footage. Her explanation of how she plans to use the films – as a concrete representation of what she intends to present on stage and as a visual reminder to herself of the folk dances – vividly demonstrates the interconnections between her anthropological and theatrical work. In transferring the Bahamian folk dance cycle to the stage, Hurston followed what VéVé Clark (1994) termed a 'research-to-performance' method, translating her anthropological findings into a live presentation in the public theatre. Yet, crucially, Hurston's allusion to the 'training' of her performers suggests how mediated this translation process was. While some of her cast members may have been familiar with the Fire Dance, clearly not all of them were. The Fire Dance that eventually appeared in *The Great Day* thus followed a circuitous path from Bahamian bodies to Hurston's body to film, back to Hurston's body, and finally to the sixteen bodies of her ensemble. Attention to this sequence of interpolations seriously complicates claims of spontaneity with respect to the staged Fire Dance and attests to the work that underpinned the appearance of authenticity. At the same time, these interpolations, involving the body to body transmission of movement material, must be recognized as vital components of Hurston's choreography.

Staging authenticity

Though most of the details of Hurston's choreographic process and rehearsal methods are lost to history, some choreographic decisions were obligatory. As scholars of staged folk dance routinely point out, the process of transforming participatory dance forms for presentation on the proscenium stage involves any number of artistic choices. These encompass the selection of movement material, decisions about how much improvisation to allow on stage, and considerations of 'time, space, and spectacle', all of which are constrained by Western theatrical conventions (Ramsey 1997: 363). Hurston faced this same set of issues in preparing the Fire Dance for her revue. After settling on which portions of the dance to stage and in what order, compressing and plotting their duration within her own concert must have been one of her foremost decisions. While it is impossible to determine how much improvisational freedom Hurston allowed her dancers and drummers, certain concessions to the proscenium stage were conspicuous, from forgoing the presence of a live fire, to arranging her dancers in a semi-circle rather than a closed ring, which would have obstructed the audience's view of the soloists. She may well have also coached her dancers on the precise spacing, degree of virtuosity and movement scale for each section of the Fire Dance cycle.

At the same time, it is clear that much of Hurston's choreography involved masking the various capitulations she made to the Western theatrical stage. Determined to present black expressive practices in a way that bore a closer resemblance to the folk from whom she had collected her material than to the black artists and entertainers who populated the New York stage, Hurston purposely sought out cast members who did not fit the Broadway mould. This included darker-skinned performers with less experience in the professional theatre. In the same letter of 15 October in which she requested use of her film footage, Hurston described to Charlotte Mason the 'black' and 'dark brown' singers she had assembled, concluding, 'No mulattoes at all.' Hurston also touted the 'gawky' and 'naïve' singer she had enlisted for *The Great Day* (1931). The fact that, according to Hurston, her concert was the first public performance for some of her Fire Dancers suggests she took a similar tack in recruiting dance performers (Hurston 1996: 284). Such casting decisions made it possible for her to contend that *The Great Day*'s dances had 'not been influenced by Harlem or Broadway' (Anon. 1932).

Concomitantly, Hurston adopted performance conventions that diverged from the polished norms of the mainstream theatre. The best evidence of this can be found in the recommendations for improvement offered by Rollins College president Hamilton Holt in response to a 1933 production of *From Sun to Sun* in Florida. 'They need to keep their eyes much more to the audience,' he wrote of Hurston's performers, 'and they need to do their swinging more in unison. Some did it from the right side and some from the left side' (Holt 1933). The asymmetry and lack of self-consciousness that Holt objected to as amateur were, for Hurston, a closer approximation of the black folk aesthetic she embraced and endeavoured to bring to the stage.

Hurston did not reject mainstream theatrical principles outright, however, and on several occasions she referred expressly to the need to 'polish' her troupe before presenting them (Hurston 1933). One such reference came in her autobiography, in an account of a disturbance among her Bahamian dance troupe in 1932:

> one of the men, who was incidentally the poorest dancer of all, preached that I was an American exploiting them and they ought to go ahead under his guidance. Stew-Beef, Lias Strawn and Motor-Boat pointed out to him that they had never dreamed of dancing in public until I had picked them up. I had rehearsed them for months, fed them and routined them into something.
>
> (Hurston 1996: 284)

When she deemed it necessary, Hurston thus found ways to affirm her choreographic labour, even when it may have contradicted her repeated claims of naturalness. Subtly, but surely here, she shores up her originality and authority by ventriloquizing the defence of her lead dancers. Not only do they verify that it was her idea in the first place to stage the Caribbean material, they also emphasize the work she undertook to discipline, finesse and 'routine' her dancers into 'something' worthy of the public theatre.

Hurston's choreographic rendering of the folk, then, was by no means a straightforward or unmediated operation. Rather, the cultivation of a performance aesthetic located somewhere between professionalism and amateurism demanded that Hurston make a series of careful calibrations in everything from casting to training to staging. Although her work in this capacity certainly didn't qualify her for choreographer status at the time, conceding the term to her today helps redress a historical blind spot by granting her credit for the labour that underwrote her danced representations.

Admittedly, calling Hurston a choreographer is still not a fully precise way of describing her relationship with the staged Bahamian Fire Dance. In placing so much emphasis on Hurston the individual, assigning her the term 'choreographer' may, despite my intentions, detract from the contributions of her assembled troupe of performers and the countless creators and practitioners who forged the dance out of the African and European cultural traditions that blended and collided in the Caribbean. Yet I am by no means trying to assert that Hurston choreographed the Fire Dance per se. Instead, I maintain she should be recognized as the choreographer of the version of the Fire Dance that appeared in her revues. Rather than abandoning the term, it should be possible to preserve its ability to allocate artistic credit – especially for those who have historically been denied the privileges of authorship – without losing sight of the complex, collaborative networks in which all choreographers are situated.

In the end, treating Hurston as a choreographer is a move that should force us to confront her calculated, labour-intensive orchestration of moving bodies in time and space *and* the structures and relations of power that have long inhered in the designation. It is also a move that may ultimately raise as many questions as it answers. Yet the generation of new questions – both about the term 'choreographer' and about Hurston as an artist – seems a fitting outcome to a recovery project such as this. While the task of revisibilizing Hurston's contributions to American dance requires uncloaking and identifying that which has been forgotten or obscured, historical subjects like Hurston and historical events like her dance stagings are never fully recoverable, as much as they were never fully lost. Neither can Hurston, with her discipline-defying endeavours and her notorious evasiveness, be made to fit into any neat or totalizing classification systems.[5] If we are to avoid reifying black woman artists like Hurston as iconic figures, the work of remembrance can never be done.

Notes

1 See especially duCille (1993), Carby (1994), and Dubey (1995).
2 The term 'devising', which appears to have become current within the British dance scene in the latter part of the twentieth century to denote the process by which dancers create performances using collectively developed structures, also blurs the distinction between choreography and improvisation. See Claid (2006).
3 See, for example, Stearns and Stearns (1968), Berliner (1994), Malone (1996) and Valis Hill (2000).
4 The names I list here are derived from various archival sources, including a comparison of multiple programmes for performances of the Fire Dance throughout the 1930s.
5 See Hemenway (1977) and Boyd (2003).

5

REWORKING THE BALLET

Stillness and queerness in *Swan Lake, 4 Acts*

Vida Midgelow

The choreographers of reworkings have contradicted, criticised, dislocated, fragmented, updated, celebrated, refocused and otherwise reimagined the ballet on stage. Operating as unruly forms of critical discourse reworkings refer intertextually to pre-existing dances, thereby evoking a bidirectional gaze that has the potential to shift our perceptions of both the past and the present. In doing so, reworkings have enabled identities to be (re)constructed, as choreographers have read against the grain of accepted representations and dismantled received meanings to challenge perceived norms.

I focus here on *Swan Lake, 4 Acts* (2005) by Raimund Hoghe. This is an austere and poignant reworking of *Swan Lake* and, through close reading, I consider the ways in which Hoghe's reworking queries and queers the ballet. This is a dance for Hoghe and four other performers – Ornella Balestra (the only female dancer and an accomplished ballerina), Bynjar Bandlien, Nabil Yahia-Aissa and Lorenzo de Brabandere. Structured in four main parts the work is marked by the placement of objects and rearrangements of space – a miniature theatre, a row of chairs, rows of small paper swans, a large square of ice-cubes, a ripping up of the stage flooring revealing a white layer under the black dance mat and a final layering of white sand. Contact between the performers is minimal and actions are equally small, precise and discreet – an arm ripple, a head tilt, a glance to the side, a walk across the stage. Following neither choreographic nor narrative conventions, this is a dance formed around image making and understated relationships.

Marked by internal contradictions and historical disruptions, *Swan Lake, 4 Acts* presents images of the body, gender and sexuality that have the potential to radically reconfigure the status quo. Via his pared-down approach and de-emphasising of conventional choreographic forms, Hoghe brings attention to the materiality of his own body – a non-normative body, marked by deformity due to his spinal curvature and resultant hump of his upper back. In doing so Hoghe reconfigures what we mean by dance and what kind of bodies can dance. Further, masculinities and sexual identities are constructed anew, for, in contrast to the disembodied ideals of ethereality and illusion embedded in conventional *Swan Lakes*, Hoghe locates the materiality of the body, with its history and experiences, identity and flesh fully intact. Using his own queer and disabled male body he brings to the fore the specificity of bodies, and the hierarchical value placed upon differing bodies, by locating the idiosyncratic and non-normative at the centre.

Raimund Hoghe

Hoghe, born in Wuppertal and now living in Düsseldorf (Germany), is a respected and well-established journalist/dance writer and a dance-maker. Throughout the 1980s he was dramaturge for Pina Bausch and her Wuppertal Tanztheater, which became the subject of two of his books. Throwing his own body into the fight (to paraphrase the title of his 2000–2001 performance lecture), he has for the last ten years created conceptually, politically and choreographically challenging works that have been performed throughout Europe. He produced his first solo for himself, *Meinwärts*, in 1994, which, together with *Chambre séparée* (1997) and *Another Dream* (2000), constituted a trilogy of pieces for the twentieth century. Describing *Another Dream*, one critic notes that Hoghe 'invites us into his world of on-stage play, ritual and enjoyment of music and memory' and that he takes these performance principles, 'whittling them down to their barest form' (Phillips 2005: 25). As is typical of Hoghe, he uses the stage as a canvas to be filled with (fragile) memories, allowing space for us to read ourselves – with all our own frailties intact – into his work. Using intimate material that draws on historical events, his own life and the unique characteristics of his body, Hoghe explores themes of love, loneliness, xenophobia and racism. Formed with an economy of means, his works are meticulously crafted, involving ritualistic, minimal movement with almost ceremonial rigour, as they resonate with emotion. Gerald Siegmund writes:

> Raimund Hoghe's Tanztheater manages to be explicitly political without neglecting form. The ritual severity of Japanese theatre combines with American performance art, German expressionism and his own interest in human feelings and socio-political states to create his minimalist pieces ... He formulates his memories so that the historic events are called to mind through subjective and purely private moments. His body, which due to his hump does not correspond with society's norm, holds a place for us all and our personal memories. He opens up spaces between things, words and songs for personal reminiscences and affective moments. They are moments for reflection but also for laughter.
>
> (Siegmund 2006)

Using highly recognisable music from the classics to the popular, Hoghe draws on the archive of collective memories, for, as he states: 'People know them and have memories associated with them: for example, they remember the life of the singer, or the moment when they first heard a special song for the first time' (cited in Johnson 2005: 339). Several of his dances have also referenced ballet – for example, *Tanzgeschichten* (2003) opens with music from *The Nutcracker*, the second part of *Another Dream* (2000) uses Stravinsky's *Le Sacre du Printemps* following a series of popular songs, and *Sarah, Vincent et moi* (2004) contains images from *Swan Lake*, as do *Dialogue with Charlotte* (1998) and *Tanzgeschichten*. These references have been extended in his dances that use music from *L'Après-Midi d'un Faune*, *Le Sacre du Printemps* and *Swan Lake*.

Hoghe's reworking of *Sacre* is a duet with his collaborator Lorenzo de Brabandere, a young untrained performer. Together their contrasting bodies pulsate with a tender, touching intimacy. Yet, while complex and desirous strings resonate between them throughout, the relationship never becomes remotely sexually explicit or homoerotic. Their connection is unselfconscious, undramatised, as they mirror each other's simple movements and balance against each other, establishing a remarkable equivalence, despite their differing physicalities. De Brabandere and his connection with Hoghe are also central to *Swan Lake, 4 Acts*. Here too their relationship has an aura of intensity, while remaining similarly ambiguous throughout the duration of the performance.

In the gaps and absences

Hoghe operates within the gaps of the ballet, bringing to the fore those things which are absent in order to create a work which speaks from a position not so much of 'What can I do with *Swan Lake*?' but, rather, 'What does *Swan Lake* mean to me?' and 'How can this material, this cultural artefact, be useful to me?'

Swan Lake, 4 Acts references the ballet directly in its title and music, and also through the use of reminiscent images and gestures. Throughout, Tchaikovsky's score is played in a seemingly random order and is at times distorted. While it provides an important reference in terms of coming to understand the dance, it is in the main ignored by the performers who move without reference to the tempo and rhythms of the music – working instead at their own internal, or task-derived, pace. In addition to the music, the ballet *Swan Lake* is present through the use of paper cut-out swans and ice cubes that melt to form miniature lakes. These objects frame the space and encapsulate Hoghe's compressed approach. In addition, Hoghe's repeated arm actions (that reach forward and extend behind him as his torso bends forward in a swan-like beat of the wings), together with the movements of the other performers (such as an arm flutter at the side of the body and small beats of the feet) and the costume and danced references of former ballerina Ornella Balestra (who at various points wears a knee-length black tutu and pointe shoes), connect us to the ballet – as does the simple but carefully executed exchange of one black and one white T-shirt, which sparingly connote Odette and Odile, the white and black swans. Out of context, unadorned and bearing little elaboration, these references to the ballet, however obscurely made, form the mainstay of the work. Yet they are presented as if recalling distant memories, as if searching to retrace forgotten actions, and are so small that they appear lost.

Here then *Swan Lake* is appropriated *and* erased, as layers of meaning and signification are written, and written over, like a palimpsest. Playing between absence and presence, the ballet is always in the process of simultaneous manifestation and dematerialisation. While structures of presence (that which is visible) and absence (that which is invisible) tend to value presence over absence, here the two are conflated. For, while making visible references to *Swan Lake*, it is the invisible ghost text that resonates most strongly. For example, the work (purposefully) omits the famously virtuosic *thirty-two fouettés rond de jambe en tournant*, yet our cultural knowledge of this choreography affects our reading of the dance. We note the absence. The choice not to include this celebrated act leads to an awareness of what replaces it or, rather, what does not replace it.

The paring away of such overt virtuosity and the locating of the only extended and recognisable movement from the ballet tradition in the supine position (the dancers lay on their backs and perform movements akin to *port de bras*, *développés* and *petit battements*) is an important deviation. Using a shared cultural knowledge of convention, Hoghe stages a dance that is full of unfilled expectations and expressions of horizontality – creating a resonance of loss and sadness – not because these things are themselves 'losses', but rather because we experience the presence of absence. Hoghe points us to this absence causing us to note and question our perhaps nostalgic desires for the past, for coherence, for completion, for the vertical.

Thereby, full of reference and denial, Hoghe establishes ambiguous relationships with *Swan Lake*, for here the ballet exists in a series of deconstructed images and in our hazy memories. The play between absence and presence, visibility and invisibility engenders an empathic force for a past that is missed but never to be recuperated fully. For this past is never taken whole (for that is not possible or desirable); rather it is cut up, examined, turned over and questioned, speaking across time without evoking a nostalgic or mythic sense of past. Instead, past and present productively collide. For this reworking transforms the past while repeating it in a continuous playground of recollection and reaction. Revealing a complex relationship with history, Hoghe embodies the desire to revisit history, not to recuperate it, but to live alongside it or perhaps in the face of it. Through this process we come to understand the past, not to repeat it, but to understand it from a new perspective.

Stillness

Formed as dance of stillness and repetition, Hoghe casts aside established ontologies of dance. Eschewing familiar virtuosity and expectations of the body, Hoghe, through his non-action, rather than action, breaks expectations of 'dance', for dance has almost always been related to action.

Challenging conventional aesthetic values, the flow and virtuosity of ballet is replaced with an economy of motion, for actions and image are reduced, fragmented and stretched out over duration. For extended periods Hoghe and his performers kneel or lie, waiting upon the floor. At other times they stand facing each other, or facing the audience, their bodies motionless and expressionless. Further, objects, having been steadily and carefully arranged, are left for us to contemplate. These acts of stillness are significant, for as André Lepecki has convincingly argued, 'the insertion of stillness in dance, the deployment of different ways of slowing down movement and time, are particularly powerful propositions for modes of rethinking action and mobility through the performance of still-acts, rather than continuous movement' (Lepecki 2006: 15).

Lepecki writes that the 'still-act' can usefully reconfigure the 'unquestioned alignment of dance with movement' (ibid.: 16). This is important, he suggests, for 'dance ontologically imbricates itself with, is isomorphic to, movement' (ibid.: 2). This break of dance from movement, from mobility, enables a rethinking of the body and might blur divisions between 'the sensorial and the social, the somatic and the mnemonic, the linguistic and the corporeal, the mobile and immobile' (ibid.: 15).

Hoghe's use of expanded duration and stillness, perhaps due to our expectation of dance to involve movement rather than performers standing still, is uncomfortable, even torturous at times. This sensation is heightened by the contrast with Tchaikovsky's score that continues to run onwards whilst little 'happens' on the stage. Yet this feeling of increasing discomfort becomes precisely the point of Hoghe's approach. Our expectations, it seems, are purposefully unfulfilled. For, if we can surpass our frustration, Hoghe suspends our usual experience of time – in particular, theatrical and metered time. Requiring us to slow down, the work provokes us to enter into a more contemplative level of engagement through which it is possible, in self-reflexive manner, to note that which is unfulfilled, yet craved for, and consider the value systems at work within those very desires.

> Thus [Lepecki writes] 'the still-act ... requires a performance of suspension, a corporeally based interruption of modes of composing flow. The still *acts* because it interrogates economies of time,

because it reveals the possibility of one's agency within controlling regimes of capital, subjectivity, labor and mobility.'

(ibid.: 15)

Lepecki relates these ideas to those of Gaston Bachelard to suggest through stillness, through shifts in temporality, we might come to experience a 'slower ontology' (Bachelard 1994: 215). This connection is useful for understanding the impact of duration in *Swan Lake, 4 Acts* as, for Bachelard, notions of stillness and silence are not passive. Rather, in creating a space of silence in and around a text a sense of contemplation emerges, enabling a critical listening or viewing. Bachelard's notion of 'slower ontology' then echo Hoghe's focus upon the hidden and the miniaturised – for it is through the small gestures and objects that the inside/outside voices are merged, beyond sensory divisions and sensual speculations and sensuous delimitations.

When Hoghe places ice cubes in a square around the edge of the stage, positioning these items with meticulous care, he simply takes the time it takes to fulfil the task. As we wait, these ice cubes are left to slowly melt into small puddles. With time to gaze upon the objects, it is the waiting, the lack of action, which enables us to enjoy the poignant simplicity of the image and to ponder. Allowing the images to reverberate long enough for the range of intertexts and tangential thoughts to emerge and intertwine, also allows us to lose ourselves for a moment in our own subjective experiences.

Thereby the images Hoghe creates resonate precisely because of the slowness of unfolding and the attention to the micro, taking on the force of political action by delaying and withholding gratification. For in contemporary society, which tends to focus on movement, action and consumption, our capacity to concentrate on stillness, to be in the moment and to experience duration are qualities that embody radical potential. Shifting experiences of the temporal and relocating our attention to the small, the quiet and the unspoken, Hoghe challenges his viewers to reconsider their expectations and values. The power of this challenge to established ontologies of dance is that Hoghe's use of stillness is not a negation of dance; rather his approach is affirmative, for, as Una Bauer (2006: 145) writes, when he moves, Raimund Hoghe is not trying to say: ' "Look at me, I am not dancing," but precisely the opposite: "Look at me, *I am dancing.*" '. In doing so, Hoghe expands concepts of what it is to dance and what we mean by dancing.

Dis/ability

Hoghe uses his diminutive stature, spine curvature and resultant hump to unmoor expectations, and the particulars of his body do not go unnoticed.

Critic Katja Werner (2003) describes him thus, 'Raimund Hoghe, small, hunchbacked, the perfect impersonation of loneliness', and Sanjoy Roy (2007) writes, 'Hoghe is a tiny, middle aged, hunchback', while Ramsay Burt (2005) notes his 'twisted spine and disabilities'. For these reviewers, and I would think most of the audience, Hoghe's body creates a disjuncture, a jolt to established expectations.

Taking this disjunction as a point of departure, I am going to consider for a moment the implications of Hoghe's homosexual, 'disabled' body, when it is placed alongside the *Swan Lake* of collective memory, and thereby at an intersection with all those idealised bodies that conventional versions of the ballet contain. For it is pertinent to consider, as Ann Cooper Albright (1997: 57) asks, 'what happens when disabled people move into the role of dancer, the very same role that has been historically reserved for the glorification of an ideal body?'

Albright asks this question in an insightful discussion about dance and disability which she begins with a description of the Romantic ballerina Marie Taglioni by Théophile Gautier. Emphasising her lightness, delicacy and transcendence, Gautier provides 'a tantalizingly elusive vision of the spectator's desire' (ibid.: 56). Albright goes on to note that this is, of course, all about creating illusion and that it obscures the dancer's sweat and pain. She uses this starting point as a foil through which to question the ways in which dance has equated 'physical ability with aesthetic quality' and suggests that, through the 'disabled' body it might be possible to re-envision 'just what kinds of movements can constitute a dance, and by extension, what kind of body can constitute a dancer' (ibid.: 57).

Hoghe provides a site for just such a re-envisioning. As a dancer with a physical deformity, he purposefully and meaningfully challenges concepts of the body, specifically dancers' bodies, and, in this process, forces the viewer to reassess aesthetic values. For, as Johnson writes, Hoghe's body 'interrupts the canonical exclusion of the non-normative body from the traditions of dance and theatre, to claim these spaces anew for atypical bodies' (Johnson 2005: 37). Establishing complex questions about normality and beauty, his humped back, and resultant somewhat stiff, awkward phy-sicality, create a poignant contrast to images embedded in ballet, thus destabilising and refiguring such images along with conventional ideals of the body.

Avoiding the studied illusion of ethereal transcendence in conventional *Swan Lakes*, Hoghe makes no attempt to disguise or surpass his hump; rather, we are made acutely aware of it. Kneeling centre stage, his body bent forward, he extends his arms forward over his head, and then reaches them around behind his back. His arms and hands twitch – like a half-remem-bered mimic of Odette or a swan that can no longer fly. This 'swan motif' occurs repeatedly and, each time he kneels down or raises his arms, his hump and his stiff awkwardness clear. As the stigma of his body is reiterated throughout – lest we should forget – Hoghe uses the framing of theatre and the expectations of spectacle (which are never fulfilled) as a context for us to experience his disabled body, and this experience is palpable.

His repeated performance of the swan, which never complies with expectations, unsettles notions of completion, for each repetition builds upon the previous manifestations of the same gesture, to the extent that the 'message' is magnified to such a point that we really start to note the detail – and the detail creates complications and complexities. Through this repetition Hoghe destabilises conventional ways of seeing and expressing dance, as his body emerges as the constant subject. And this body is a site of abnormality, a site of dissonance.

If this was not enough, he steadily exposes his body through the duration of the work: he first removes his jacket, then his t-shirt, until at the end he lies on the floor fully naked. These actions are in no way gratuitous; he removes his clothing cautiously, gradually revealing to us his deformed, (seemingly) vulnerable, back. And, as Johnson writes: 'Hoghe refuses to apologise for putting his body on stage, for the discomfort you might feel, for showing you up for not being accustomed to the encounter' (Johnson 2005: 37).

Albright (1997: 58) suggests that we are forced to watch with a 'double vision' when viewing 'disabled' bodies dancing, for the negotiation between theatrical representation and the actuality of physical experiences is made acute. We become aware that 'while dance performance is grounded in the physical capacities of a dancer it is not limited by them' (ibid.: 58). Hoghe, through his non-action (for, as discussed above, he tends to stand rather than 'move') and his (disconcerting) body places a gap between expectations and that which confronts us, refusing to 'fit in' to the discourse of normative bodies. By doing so he goes against aesthetics that are often located in ideals of beauty and/or athleticism, for dance, specifically ballet, has tended to reiterate the 'classical' body and action.

Performed by Hoghe's non-normative body, the 'swan motif' evokes images of a swan that are uncomfortable, isolated and vulnerable. The specifics of his body in performance creates a resonance with Odette's desire for retransformation back into her human state, and even more strongly with her experience of imprisonment in her swan body. Hoghe's physical difficulties in kneeling and extending his arms backwards bring this to us anew, so that which is usually hidden by the beauty of the swan is here exposed as excruciating and frustrating. His insertion of his own body into the history of *Swan Lake* in this way thereby brings about a reconsideration of Odette's experience.

This reference to the Odette figure is heightened further by the contrast established between Hoghe and Balestra. As Hoghe lies curled up on the floor, behind him Balestra performs the coded choreography of Odette. Her body, marked by years of ballet training and performance, is the embodiment of the ballet swan. Her rippling arms and shimmering feet are in stark contrast to Hoghe's uncomfortable postures and stillness. Yet the poignancy of the contrast marks both performers, for we are reminded of the vulnerability of Odette and Hoghe, and we note the beauty of them both.

Hoghe highlights such differences then, not to maintain them but rather to point to the similarities between bodies – between his body and those of others about him – his co-performers and us, as members of the audience. As he and de Brabandere stand face to face they mirror each other's actions and support one another's weight. The contrast between them couldn't be more pronounced. Hoghe, short, slight in build, middle aged and humped; de Brabandere, average height and build, young, able-bodied. Yet the differences between them are blurred. Their touch is sensitive and tender, for neither body attempts to occupy the space of the perfect body. By performing each action without artifice, Hoghe emphasises the individuality of everyone's body – theirs and ours.

In these ways Hoghe brings about a rethinking, challenging us to reconsider representations of the body and bodily ideals. For, as Hoghe suggests, being confronted with a body that does not conform to conventional ideas of beauty requires us to question our own experiences of the body (Hoghe cited in Johnson 2005: 37). The possibility of his radical reconfiguration lies, then, in our connection with his disabled body as it resonates within our own bodies. Working to elide the all too easy binary between able and disabled bodies, Hoghe challenges the narratives of (dis)ability. This is an important task for, as Shildrick and Price (1996: 96) note: 'So long as "disabled" is seen as just another fixed identity category, an identity that we might carry with us into all situations, then the boundaries which separate us, one from the other, are left undisturbed.'

Through extended periods of stillness and the specifics of his own body, Hoghe provokes a reconsideration of what it is to act or to take action and, fundamentally, what it is to dance. For his is a dance in which the relationships between kinetic/non-kinetic, absence/presence, abled/disabled, passive/active are blurred. Through *Swan Lake, 4 Acts* the experience of temporality is profound, enabling the audience to 'time-travel' – into personal reveries and histories – as the resonances of images and shifts in the body are brought to the fore. Yet, lest we should forget the individual uniqueness of every body, Hoghe quietly observes the importance of flesh and the proximity of our bodies to theirs (the performers) and our gaze on his stigmatised body.

Beyond queer

Hoghe stages his homosexuality quietly through his enactment of a male–male relationship with de Brabandere. But Hoghe's choreography is not overt, and certainly not homoerotic. Since he refuses artifice or effeminate coding his homosexuality is rendered almost, but not quite, invisible, for, while the intimacy between de Brabandere and Hoghe is no way demonstrative, it is nevertheless clear. As they mirror each other's movements, slowly raising and lowering their arms, rest their hands upon one another's shoulders, and use ice cubes to trace over each others bodies, their relationship is enacted through a series of slow and studied caresses. Their performance, while avoiding camp or homoerotic coding, and remaining uninflected and unselfconscious, is still (or perhaps because of this ambiguity) readable as queer. For the ghost of the ballet and the ballerina – her feminising presence and *Swan Lake*'s emphasis upon romance – in combination with their staged intimacy, drive towards Hoghe and de Brabandere's pairing, as they dance a dance of unconventional erotic relations, both real and imagined, that evoke a queer queerness. For, as de Brabandere lowers his weight onto Hoghe's back and they rest back to back, and later as he covers Hoghe's body with a fine white powder, the presence of their relationship disrupts the conventional understanding of 'queerness'. For queerness, in line with poststructuralist legacies, has construed the body as an inscribed surface, tending towards exteriorised models of corporeality. Yet here we are required to consider the way in which identities and sexualities might be fundamentally located in an (auto)corpography, in which the materiality of the body, and the sexed experiences of the body, are brought to the fore in a refusal of such exteriority and of any overt 'queer' coding.

Further, the specificity of Hoghe's bodily disability gives rise to important questions as to the ways in which his disability interacts with his male, homosexual body, and in turn extends, or at least presses upon, queer theory. For, in a parallel manner to the ways in which earlier feminisms were challenged by questions of how gender intersects with other social characteristics, disability too complicates our understanding of gender, race and sexuality. Disability studies have just begun to raise these debates, asking for instance: 'How does disability affect the gendering process?' and 'How does it affect the experience of gender?' (Gerschick 2000: 1263). As bodies are central to the recognition of gender, for gender is enacted through the body, Gerschick usefully highlights the ways in which 'the bodies of people with disabilities make them vulnerable to being denied recognition as women and men' (ibid.: 1264).

In line with Gerschick's observations, Hoghe's homosexuality, disability and profession combine to emasculate him. In other words, Hoghe is a man rendered not-male, for here masculinity collides with disability to contradict masculine privilege. Further his disability is combined with his homosexuality and located within the stigma of the feminised stage space. Yet disability and homosexuality emerge as dual figures that haunt the recesses of the 'normal', and it is these deviant bodies that combine to remake the world, to nurture profound alternatives and articulate the future. Hoghe's bodily deviance unmoors the territories of broken and whole, beautiful and grotesque, homosexual and heterosexual, existing in-between to challenge the aesthetic values inherent in normative definitions of the body and of dance. He reappropriates his not-male status to contribute to the creation of alternative gender and sexual identities, and his queer queerness reveals that gender and sexuality are provisional and that bodies do not always (or indeed generally) comply to match easily defined categories.

By inserting his own queer body into history, Hoghe reveals *Swan Lake* as provisional and open to contestation. The ballet's potential queerness (for there is clearly a perverse queerness in the tale of a man's sexual desire for a bird), which normally remains hidden, is brought to the surface, and the heterosexual contract embedded in the ballet is challenged and destabilised. This asserts that the ballet's representation of sexuality per se, and specifically unitary heterosexuality, is a fiction.

6

MAKING SPACE, SPEAKING SPACES

Carol Brown

Opening in

Can architecture inhabit us as much as we see ourselves inhabiting it?
(Grosz 1995: 135)

As a choreographer, I am interested in making connections between bodies and environments, in making space speak through a dynamic exchange between dance and architecture, and in shifting audience expectations about how and where one might come to experience a dance. This writing explores spatial practices in dance through an understanding of architecture as an inhabiting force within choreography.

Relationships between space, corporeality and architecture are core to the taking place of dance as performance and become entwined within practices of making. Through working at the interface of choreography and architecture in collaborations with performance designers and architects, spatial praxes become generative forms for new choreographies. In writing out of and into this experience of making dance-architectures, I draw upon critical practices in architecture and theories of corporeality to (re)inscribe the spatiality of my practice and open it to questions concerning relationships between the insides of the body and its constitutive outsides.

Matrixial spaces

Choreography situates the moving body in time and space. As Phelan describes it, 'while it is true that bodies usually manage to move in time and space, dancing *consciously* performs the body's discovery of its temporal and spatial dimensions' (Phelan 1996: 92). Traditionally, the architectural container of the choreography catalyses frames and constrains the possibilities for these dance discoveries. However, we can think of the 'taking place' of choreography as an emergent matrix of relationships shaped by states of flux between the body and the built, performers and audience, corporeality and virtuality, ephemerality and the seemingly permanent. In this context, the threshold between inside and outside, interior and exterior is a complex enfolding as we embody, incorporate and extrude spaces, assimilating given places through somatic awareness and generating a sense of place through tangibly manipulating space as a material of the dance.

Through dancing, space is experienced as a continuum between inside and outside, outside and inside. The dancer traces an embodied awareness of interior and exterior spaces and audiences can follow this movement like a Möbius strip: in rotating the undersides of corporeal surfaces; in (dis) embodying narratives of place; in measuring space through sequencing bodily articulations; in mapping body parts to points in space; in extruding lines; in shifting scale; in changing orientations; in hollowing volumes; in scribing geometries; in drawing spaces; and in spiralling dimensions. The dancer (dis)articulates space, producing a set of relationships between body, space and architecture, which can be described as matrixial.

A matrixial field can be understood as a transgressive threshold of co-emergence for the dancing subject and the unfolding spaces within choreography as encounter. Such a view of the spatial praxis of contemporary dance subverts historical legacies that situate the dancing body as the central organising force within a void-like space, as space itself is understood as an agent within the work. Space is performative. No longer conceived as a three-dimensional continuum, space becomes a discontinuous, plurality of spaces containing multiple dimensions.

Space has a history

If the early twentieth century led to the birth of modern dance by radical women intent on bringing 'the inside out', the early twenty-first century reconfigures the relationship between inside and outside by entwining the interior spaces of the body with the external place of performance. This disjuncture between early modern dance and contemporary choreographic conceptions of space is revealing of how understandings of the body are radically affected by the history of spaces and the impact of technology in shifting our sense of scale, interiority, dimension and proximity.

Twentieth-century modern dance, particularly in its Central European incarnations, broke with nineteenth-century models of pictorial representation in its rediscovery of space or *raum* as a material of choreography. Writing of Mary Wigman, John Martin (1939: 231) explained how: 'Space assumed definite entity, almost as a tangible presence in every manifestation of movement'. The idea of space in the modern era was conceived as a dynamic field of forces acting on and through the body. As Martin describes it, the dancer 'is continuously engaging the forces within him with those forces which press upon him from without, sometimes yielding to them, sometimes opposing them, but ever aware of them, and finding his own identity in this dynamic process' (ibid.: 231). The work of Laban is central to this development. In *Choreutics*, he describes space as a pre-condition of movement and movement as a 'visible aspect of space' (Laban 1966: 4). In understanding how movement composes three-dimensional space through trace-forms, Laban articulated a vision of dance as a 'living architecture' and his work has continued to influence the ways in which choreographers and dance educators articulate and imagine space (ibid.: 5). Mapping diagonals through the centre of gravity of the upright body in an imaginary cube, Laban composed a three-dimensional form orientated to length, breadth and depth.

Other Central European choreographers such as Mary Wigman and Gertrud Bodenwieser combined Laban's insights into the dynamic properties of space with an awareness of the unconscious drives of Freudian psychoanalysis to develop a genre of *ekstatic* dance. Dances which, in their contents and form explored *being-outside-of-oneself* and which embodied states of rapture, delirium and an intensity of projection, represented the unconscious depths of the dancing body and projected this depth into an outside where it transcended the space–time of the present.

The concept of *Raumempfindung* or 'felt' volume in space underscored both developments in the spatial thought of dance and ran parallel with contemporary developments in architecture. Architect Bernard Tschumi describes how 'space' was rarely discussed at the beginning of the twentieth century but by 1915 the influence of German aesthetics saw the proliferation of ideas about *Raum* and *Raumempfindung*. By 1923, 'the idea of felt space had merged with the idea of composition to become a three-dimensional continuum, capable of metrical subdivision that could be related to academic rules. From then on, architectural space was consistently seen as a uniformly extended material to be modelled in various ways' (Tschumi 1995: 14). Contemporary methods of practice in dance continue to work compositionally with this understanding of a pliable, abstract volume of space through the use of algorithms, mathematical sequencing and geometrical patterns founded on Euclidean geometries.

And, yet, we have experienced a profound shift in our perceptions of space. A post-Euclidean understanding of space de-stabilises structures of belonging that previously anchored bodies to place. In the post-humanist landscape, space is fractured.

We live in an age where skyscrapers and their occupants are turned to dust, where civilians can be destroyed by remote control and where the body itself has become utilised as a bomb in London, in Casablanca, in Baghdad and elsewhere. Alongside this explosive phenomena we live in a time that Jean Baudrillard terms 'implosive': a collapse of space–time reality into complex matrices of data that evade physical limits (Kellner 1994). The kinds of world we embody through dancing are to some extent an effect of the ways in which we understand the spaces and times in which we live. The collapse of space–time in the digital age, the surveillance and security systems of a time of terror, the relativity of an Einsteinian universe together with the virtuality of cyberspace have brought about a paradigm shift in our understanding and perception of space to the degree that the limits of the kinesphere are radically reconfigured. The somatic language of the dancer has shifted away from perceiving and representing the body in only three dimensions, which relate to Euclid's mathematisation and axiomatisation of a space considered as homogeneous, universal and regular.

In refusing to conceptualise space as a three-dimensional container, a passive receptacle or void, whose form is given by its content, we come to know space as 'a moment of becoming, of opening up and proliferation, a passage from one space to another, a space of change, which changes with time' (Grosz 2001: 119). The dancer is perceived in this context as a conduit between spaces, meeting, incarnating and exhuming spaces.

In moving beyond dualist understandings of the spatialised subjectivity of the dancer, relationships between inside and outside, figure and ground are reconceived, opening the spatial praxis of dance to new forms, alignments and varieties of space. Untethering the body from its moorings to an anthrocentric point of view and from the Euclidean geometries of twentieth-century modernists, spatial practices in dance are increasingly exploring this continuum through enfolding inside and outside. Following the critical practice of my collaborator, performance designer and architect Dorita Hannah, the contemporary body is both 'contaminated' and a 'contaminant', erupting and displacing borders between soma and city, the organic body and the built environment, corporeality and virtuality, container and contents, inside and outside (Hannah 2007: 135). Through this crossing we might consider choreographic processes which explore the outside of the body from the point of view of the inside, and the inside of the body from the point of view of the outside. Under the influence of architectural theory and practice, this critique of the binary between interior and exterior spaces, opens choreography to the possibilities of imagining, conceiving and incorporating spaces *for* dance that acknowledge *how* we are *here* in the contemporary moment.

Listening to the space we are in

With eyes closed, I might invite you to pay attention to the spaces between joints, to deepen your awareness of those cavities through which we hinge movement, levering physical articulations of jointed bone through multiple dimensions of space and finding a place to settle momentarily, unexpectedly. A movement trace is drawn and space is secreted. The separation between bones creates an in-between space, a space defined by boundaries, a potential space into which memory/image/sensation can take their bearings and a connection can be made between outside and inside. To hinge other spaces into your dancing imagine that these spaces between bones are listening to the space and air that surrounds you. Negotiating the interior spaces of the body with the coordinates, qualities and characteristics of the exterior space, pay attention to the sounds of the building. What information do these sounds contain about the volume of space, its materiality and dimensions? Play the spaces between bones, orchestrating these with the sounds of the building you are in, tuning your movements to create a somatic architecture.

To listen is not only to hear but also to concentrate, to pay attention and to make aware. Choreographers and dancers frequently invoke 'listening to the body', one's own or another's, as a form of embodied awareness which opens perception to the body's liveliness and the minutiae of its articulations. But 'listening' can also generate information about the space we are in. According to sound artist Brandon LaBelle, legacies of thinking about space tend towards 'a fixation on the logic of opticality leaving behind the atmospheric, the haptic, the sonorous, and the sensorial' (LaBelle 2008: 159). Sound is acoustically absorbed and resonates through space, it is both 'out there' and 'in here'. People and sounds interpenetrate. An 'outside' sound is both a force and a medium forming the basis for a way of knowing which is immediate, non-representational and tactile. In privileging listening over seeing we invoke hearing as a tool for perceiving. Our ears, positioned either side of our heads, displace the power of frontal gaze and orientation with the breath and breadth of the space we are in. In *listening to* rather than *looking at* space, a conversation between body and building is opened. We can think of this conversation as a process of building connections. In building connections between the materiality of my body and the qualities, textures and sounds of the environment I inhabit, I also build myself. Not in the traditional sense of building as a mastery over materials and nature, but in the sense of a cultivation of a relation between two entities. Loosening the volumes of internal space brings a porosity of exchange with exterior spaces through which a sense of depth and a thickening of perception and awareness to our inhabiting of place can be conceived. This process allows my body to be both receiver and inscriber, becoming a conduit between one space and another, unpredictable and furtive.

Choreographing place

If the process of dance-making frequently incorporates real, virtual and/or imagined exterior spaces into the compositional building of choreographic material through sensate experience, the taking place of dance as performance is largely determined by boundaries shaped by historical conceptions of theatre. Key to the 'taking place' of dance performance is a being present within the space and time of a shared experience. This shared temporality is what distinguishes the spaces of live performance from that of other arts and media. To make space speak through this shared condition, however, many artists acknowledge the increasing irrelevance of traditional venues such as the proscenium arch theatre, the concert hall and the play-house as well as its modernist incarnations, the black box theatre and the white cube gallery.

Performers Leslie Hill and Helen Paris (Hill and Paris 2006) describe how the voids of modernist spaces of performance deny a sense of danger or risk-taking through adherence to health and safety legislation creating theatres designed *not* to 'set the world on fire'. Dorita Hannah writes of the increasing irrelevance of traditional spaces such as the playhouse, in the age of *liquescence*, 'where nothing is stable, where fiction constantly folds into reality, and where sedentary structures can no longer house the mediatized spectacle of daily life' (Hannah 2007: 135). Arnold Aronson goes so far as to claim that 'performative borders have shifted in ways so profound as to call into question the very notion of theatre and performance as it has been understood for over 2,500 years' (Aronson 2008: 23).

Practices of dance bring a further set of priorities in relation to the 'taking place' of performance. Historically, modern and contemporary dancers have struggled to find homes for their practices through suitable studio environments and performance spaces appropriate to the kinaes-thetic and embodied. Most dance artists house their practices within studio environments which are paradigmatic spaces for dance containing a flat, horizontal, bare and ideally sprung floor. Conversely, the theatre, concert hall and proscenium of the classical stage with its emphasis upon figure–ground relationships and the separation of audience and performer have provided the traditional contexts for dance as performance. Unlike the studio environment, such spaces can be viewed as spaces more suited to the visual and aural senses in performance than the kinaesthetic and proprio-ceptive of contemporary dance, given the distancing effects of the per-spectival. Alternative spaces such as the black box theatre and the white cube gallery environment have also provided significant homes for con-temporary dance production, but these spaces bring with them modernist connotations centred around the dialectics of absence and presence and the bare, empty volume of space which is presumed to be universal and homogeneous. In this way, bodies inscribed by one cultural milieu, dance, find themselves 'spacing' their practices within the architectural forms of others.

Horizons inside and outside

We know then that the 'presentness' of the horizontality of space is a product of a multitude of histories whose resonances are still there, if we would but see them, and which sometimes catch us with full force unawares.

(Massey 2005: 118)

Unlike classical ballet dancers, contemporary dancers have a strong relationship with the horizontal plane, as they explore the floor and the ground through touch, yielding weight and resistance. Methods of practice frequently begin with lying on the studio floor in a feedback relationship to ground, body and environment. Different modes of relating to the horizontal continue throughout dance practice as we explore moving between the floor and the surrounding space, breath and air, and integrating horizontal, sagittal and vertical dimensions in our dancing through the support of the ground. The horizontal is connected to landscape, reciprocity and being-in-relation to another; from a somatic perspective it is highly integrative as I gain a sense of my whole body and its expansiveness as it reaches across space. Rolling, crawling, falling and stumbling put us in touch with the horizontal dimension and a mammalian, developmental corporeality through non-dominant bodily schemata such as radial geometry. Movement patterns such as radial geometry practised over time have a profound influence on the perceived morphology of the dancer and the architecture of her movement. Lying on the floor, freed from the constraints of gravity, the dancer visualises six limbs radiating out from her navel, following an in–out pattern of breath she condenses and expands, initiating vectors of movement from navel to limbs and from limbs to navel. With this pulsating movement pattern, developed through the work of Irmgard Bartenieff, connections are made between core and distal movement, centre and periphery, body and environment. In mapping morphological structure in this way, the dancer can access a multiplicity of spaces, resisting the limits of a classical cruciform figure with its upright torso supported by two legs. And yet, drawing as they do upon the history of perspectival vision and the classical figure, most of the spaces in which we perform privilege this upright and vertical figure, installing sight lines for a front end audience which compromise the visilibity of any floorwork and the radial geometries of a multidimensional figuring of space. Coupled with this, the economics of dance production frequently require the maximising of audience numbers within given spaces, further removing the possibility for a closer, more proximate relation to the dancer which might allow for the kinaesthetic sensation of the dance to be better communicated to audiences.

The built environment of the theatre provides the context and coordinates for contemporary forms of dance as representation, and yet the embodied practices of dance might be better suited to a closer, less stable relationship between audience and performer. According to Lepecki (2006), when we 'topple' the vertical plane by performing choreography in the horizontal dimension, we inscribe a different history for dance, one that bears a relation to visual practices of space marking, drawing and the grapheme.

To align contemporary dancing bodies with the coordinates of contemporary spaces requires a rethinking of inherited conventions about the practice and making of space and the relationship between studio and stage environments. If, following Grosz (2001: 33), 'the limits of possible spaces are the limits of possible modes of corporeality', choreography as an embodied art form is particularly vulnerable to the givens of traditional theatrical venues. Choreographer Siobhan Davies (2002) describes the moment we step into a theatre, as a falling into a long history of received conventions and habits of viewing. Alternatively, she states, we might ask what happens when we *discover* a dance where we don't expect to find it? As the infrastructure and resources for contemporary dance in the United Kingdom have developed over the past twenty-five years, many choreographers, including Davies, have made the transition from studio practice to public presentation by shifting the production of their work out of traditional venues and into diverse spaces exploring different models of presentation that place the dancers and audience in new relationships to one another.

The tomb, the tower and the labyrinth

Space is real, for it seems to affect my senses long before my reason.

(Tschumi 1995: 20)

Space makes possible different kinds of relationships between dancers and audience but in turn is transformed according to the dancers' relations with it. Our relations with our own bodies provide the basic spatial concepts for orientation in choreography: our sense of size, direction, location, dimension and volume are felt through the joints, fascia and organs of the body. As a choreographer I work with this embodied information to direct the sequencing of spaces and the dancer's exploration and habitation of these.

In my choreographic work the transmutation between interior and exterior spaces is made possible through collaborations that build connections between architectural forms and corporeal states. Together with performance designer and architect, Dorita Hannah, the works *Aarero Stone* (2006), *Her Topia* (2005) and *Touch Tower* (2003) were created through transdisciplinary conversations in which the coordinates of an architectural imagination (hers) met a choreographic imagination (mine). In working collaboratively to create performative spaces between dance and architecture we explore the possibilities of a third space at the constitutive edges of each other's disciplines, a space of interaction, without hierarchy, where design is not a backdrop to action but is a kinaesthetic component of space and where choreography emerges through an enfolding between somatic awareness and sceno-architecture.

Tomb

Te Papa Soundings Theatre, Wellington, New Zealand, 4 March 2006. A mist fills the stage and auditorium as the audience enter. The lights dim, and a large black gauze 'veil' drops from the proscenium. The misty atmosphere dissolves and a 'landscape' of 'inky shapes and dark reflections' emerges from the darkness (Trubridge 2007). A steely grey wall faces the audience. It contains a single dark cavity beneath which a pool of still water lies and is reflected in a mirror suspended above. A tomb of black acrylic butts into the pool containing white rocks, another cantilevers into the auditorium space offering a promontory. Within the onstage sarcophagus rubble-like rocks evoke the 'curves and lumps of the body' (Trubridge 2007).

Balancing, through the sustained tension of a vibratory stillness, on the minimum amount of outer surface necessary of my right shoulder, arm, hip bone and thigh, I orientate my body to face the audience as the lights go up. Held in this stress position of contained energy I become a gravity defying form suspended and entombed within the tight black lacquered box embedded into the grey wall. For the audience, the visual image is shaped and thickened by the glow of stage lights as these touch and contour my near-naked skin, moulded in stillness. The architecture of the tomb finds its incarnation in the text of a haunting soundscape. Coming into the light, a gravelly voice recounts Sibyl of Cumae's story.[1] Sibyl, who has been preserved in a cave for seven hundred years and who has shrunk with the centuries until her body threatens to disappear, leaves only the sound of her voice echoing through the rock. Through this intimate yet epic staging, one world leaks into another as I offer my body as host to a series of stone stories: the stone body of Niobe; the petrified standing stone dancers of Belstone, Dartmoor; the sandstone back of the Maori woman who offers her spine to her son to sharpen his adze, Hine-tua-hoanga.[2] A dense matrix of associated images culled from these stone stories forms the foundation and backbone of the choreography allowing me to build the dance from the corporeal ground imagined as geological strata. From this opening, I negotiate a series of encounters with the performance landscape, creating a chorus within the singularity of the solo. From these fossilised gestures a monument of mourning emerges.[3]

If theatre is where we meet the dead, I make a dance in the shape of a monumental ruin (Cixous 1995). I inhabit the entombed state of a primitive architecture, making a memorial by embedding movement memories in a slowly unfurling state of vibratory stillness, mutating between deep folds, juddering extensions and probing extremities and imagining a metamorphosing from flesh to stone to dust to phantom. Memory and monument coalesce through a performance space that emerges at the boundary between the present and the past. The theatre in which this work is premiered, Soundings Theatre, is part of a museum, Te Papa Tongarewa, the

National Museum of New Zealand, a place for the collections of the dead, but enduring.[4]

In this work, the entombed spaces of the design become a performance landscape shaped by a corporeal history born in myth. In embodying transcultural myths of metamorphoses, from flesh to stone, the corporeal logic of the dance becomes sedimented in the permanence of the theatre, but a theatre that is exposed and laid bare through a history of trauma. The Moscow Theatre siege (Nord-Ost October 2002) with its mediated spectacle of female suicide terrorists, 'black widows', lying slumped over theatre seats, had provoked us to ask, 'how do we occupy the stage in the time of terror and when the body has been turned into an incendiary device?'

Aarero Stone is imagined as a performative landscape that choreographically negotiates between the proscenium, the dark void of the stage and the auditorium. In juxtaposing the landscape and the building we sought to create a tension between container and contents. Mirrors, mist, sounds, cantilevered forms, light and the movement of air incorporate the audience, blurring the boundary between land and stage. If the design inscribed a topographical dimension for the work as a 'landscape', the choreography became cartographic, as it negotiated this landscape by embedding movement memories in its strata, marking space through the piling up of steps and gestures, like the white stones piled up on the 'tomb'.

In *Aarero Stone* the theatre is imagined as a living memorial, a site of memory and loss. The liveness of the landscape and the embodied narratives of the choreography question this stasis by rupturing its frame, mirroring its contents and performing rituals of recovery.

Labyrinth

Athens, Greece, 7 October 2005. A dance studio, a paradigmatic site for dancing, its features are a flat sprung wooden floor, a wall of mirrors, a bare volume of space, an entrance and an exit. A space that does not look out on the world, it exudes a sense of interiority and privacy. Through a performative journey that began as the sun set over the concrete ruin of a neighbouring aqueduct outside, the audience has been led inside to sit on one side of this dance studio turned performance site. Five dancers holding mirrors above their torsos are lying on the ground in front of us, at once amplifying the habit of this space as a dance studio, through the ubiquitous presence of mirrors, and augmenting their presence through a low-tech virtuality. We, the audience, see ourselves in the reflection of the wall mirror in the background and we see their faces and bodies through the shifting planes and reflections of these held mirrors. As they move, fixing the mirrors to highlight and focus zones of attention on the minutiae of their bodies, our vision is splintered between their raw and reflected appearances. We are implicated in this action as they also catch glimpses of their audience – a virtual other – mixing these images with their own, they capture and splice one body with another, vivisecting a corporeal remix and resisting a directly apprehending gaze.

A red stitch which the audience has followed to find this space, marks the floor and leads the eye up to a single mannequin, our phantom Ariadne, whose 'body' is weighted with stones attached to red ribbons. Ariadne is known as the first architect, as she provided the thread for Theseus to unwind his way through the labyrinth. In *Her Topia*, Dorita and I extend the idea of the labyrinth to the sequencing of spaces within the work as a whole by using a red stitch as a 'performance seam' to suture one space to another, enabling the audience to negotiate their pathway through the site-specific work. Like prehistoric labyrinths that defined paths for ritual dances leading to ecstatic states, the event culminates in a spectacle of spotlit dancing by women placed on rooftops dotted across the Athenian night sky.

The studio described above is part of the Isadora and Raymond Duncan Dance Research Centre in Vyronas, Athens. *Her Topia* (October 2005), a commission for the centre, was a dance-architecture event performed by fourteen dancers and engaging a team of multimedia artists directed by Dorita and myself. The centre was conceived in 1903 by the Duncan family as a utopic space, a temple for dancing inspired by the mythology and history of the ancients. However, with little awareness of the political, social and economic realities of Greece at the time, the Duncan family abandoned the project in the 1920s. Rebuilt by the Greek government in 1980, the rough stone structure modelled on the Temple of Agamemnon represents the first known attempt to build a space specifically for modern dance and is today a working centre for contemporary choreographic research.

Hannah and I explored the building, its adjoining site (an abandoned aqueduct) and the surrounding neighbourhood, and devised images that linked historical women with mythical women and the contemporary site with its history and archaeology. The figures of Ariadne, Arachne and Niobe as well as Duncan's own life story provided content for the creation of performance vignettes that were sited in individual rooms and surrounding parts of the building. These were stitched together as a 'fluctuating temporal continuum' weaving the audience through interior and exterior spaces in which bodies were 'fragmented, multiplied and dematerialised in an orchestration of sound, light, video, mirrors and movement' (Hannah 2008: 199).

The labyrinth is specifically evoked in the room of Ariadne but the concept of a labyrinthine space underpins the work as a whole. According to Bernard Tschumi, labyrinths engage the sensual experience of space because they allow us to feel a portion or fragment of space, never its whole dimensionality or objectlikeness. In the Ariadne room of *Her Topia*, the dancer stimulates a sense of labyrinthine space by dissecting her movements, leading the audience on a journey where the destination is not given, suggesting that they are part of a larger spatial conception whilst depriving them of a coherent vision of the space as a whole. As a time-based art form, dancing carries this paradox of temporality, that in live performance it can only be in one place at a time, even if that place is multifaceted and transdimensional.

The Duncans imagined their dance house as a utopic place for the integration of dancing and living. The dancing they conceived was both of its time and of another time as it sought to recover classical Greek forms. In working with this site, Dorita and I sought to cite this legacy through a performative architecture which was 'heterotopic', incorporating fragments of the Duncan's utopian vision and floating these within the studio by turning distorted mirrors on reality, provoking maps for possible other worlds (Foucault 1997). The room of Ariadne is where the architecture of the labyrinth finds its home, as it is where she provides the thread to negotiate the labyrinth, in other words the narrative to make sense of the journey.

The movement of the audience in relationship to the movement of the performers thickens the sense of space, giving it dimension and meaning as each audience member composes their own narrative of the journey. Compared with the static image of the theatre as a monument in *Aarero Stone*, this modelling of performance space shifts understanding from form to experience as one finds one's own way through the labyrinth.

Tower

Vystaviste, Prague, 14 June 2003. A group of women in identical red uniform dresses and black Louise Brooks wigs greet visitors at the bottom of a seven-metre-tall tower: the anatomical tower. Leading the visitors up a set of narrow stairs, encased in an opaque white skin, they hear breathing, heartbeat, the rustle of clothes, the brush of skin against skin and the shimmering pulse of movement. They are inside the sonorities of a body amplified to an architectural scale. Their own breath and footfall mix with the recorded sounds of this body to create a resonant architecture. At the top of the tower, the audience comes to stand on a narrow platform and peer down a vertical slot to see a performer seven metres below, lying, standing, speaking on a stainless steel table tilted to a 45-degree angle. On this table/slab/bed, I move in and out of the narrow frame whilst narrating stories in fragments: *How can we encounter each other without annihilating our differences? How can I touch you if you are not here?* Here, the relationship between performer and visitor is defined by the vertical rather than more customary figure–ground relationship, and by a mediator, as one of the guides stands close to the visitor, close enough to invite touch. Dizzying the hierarchy of perspectival vision, the audience experiences vertigo in the shaky balance of the scaffold platform and, in looking down, peering over a ledge to experience a wounded cut, a slice of lived corporeality. The seven-metre gap between the voyeuristic gaze of the spectator above and performer below is held in tension with the proximate touch of the performer's voice that fills the void. Distance, proximity and fragmentation are further amplified as the visitor is led back down the steps and into a tall black silo where, invited to lie horizontally at the base of the tower, their gaze is directed upwards to a live video feed of the performer in close-up.

The *Touch Tower* formed one section of a much larger performance event, *Heart of the Senses*, for the Prague Quadrennial of Theatre Architecture and Scenography in 2003. The installation was one of five scaffolding towers each representing a different sense and organised around a long table bound within an undulating timber landscape. As a part of this larger event, choreography and design sought to intertwine the physiological structure of the body, with its history as a material object and cultural artefact. Stitching itself into the landscape, the tower formed a vertiginous panoptic, an anatomical theatre focusing on the body, laid out on a slab, suspended within a viewing slot, and forensically captured by live video. In acknowledging the influence of technology on the senses, it created a mediated sensorium referencing the long-distance touch of contemporary medical science and communication technologies as well as the prosthetic extension of the body through technology. The tower folded the audience into the work, inviting them to inhabit a range of postures and physical orientations whilst encountering the live and mediated actions. Spatially and sensorially, these were intended to induce a reorientation of perception, a turning of the insides out and a shifting of their relationship from being outside the work as spectators or visitors to becoming participants and themselves subjects within the work.

Opening towards

Dancing, which stimulates the senses, gives signals about the concept of space the choreography embodies. In this way the materiality of the body coincides with the materiality of the space. In *Aarero Stone*, *Her Topia* and *Touch Tower* three different species of space – the tomb, the labyrinth and the tower – become leaky containers for inviting particular dancer–audience relationships and sensate-perceptions. As architectural forms that are met by corporeal states, their space–time coordinates build deep maps for choreography, creating an architectural organism.

As a dematerialised architecture, space becomes defined by patterns rather than shapes and is full of openings. These openings resist the dialectics of inside and outside through being perceptible thresholds that do not tell us whether they are opening outside or inside. In this way, we might say that, *I become the space where I am.*

Choreographic research is often about working with external referents as triggers and catalysing agents. Material from outside one's own experience finds it way inside through the making of unexpected connections. This process allows material to be transformed from within, as the physical body of the dancer becomes the meeting place between spaces and between worlds.

Through practices of embodying space, even remote spaces become entwined with the dancer's corporeal self. Experiencing space on the 'inside' transforms it from objective into subjective, as the experience of a fragment of a larger context allows us to 'see' it from the inside. In choreographing, the resonance of a specific location, a fragment of a larger context, or the set of architectural coordinates that relate to a site or building become known and familiar and can be incorporated through *the eyes of the skin*. In this way, the feel of the space is captured in the graphy of choreography.

Choreography is situated in corporeal, social, institutional and conceptual spaces. In its discovery and embodying of spaces, choreography makes places as temporary cartographies of energy and force rather than fixed forms. In its practice it embodies a multiplicity of understandings of space as physical, psychic, metaphoric and virtual. Corporeality, as the material condition of the work, involves a turning inside out and an outside in of the body. So that, following Deleuze in his discussion of Foucault we might say:

> The outside is not a fixed limit but moving matter animated by peristaltic movements, folds and foldings that altogether make up an inside: they are not something other than the outside, but precisely the inside *of* an outside.
>
> (Deleuze 1988: 96–97)

We are living in a time which has extended the parameters of performer-audience exchanges and the spaces of performance, challenging conventions of spatial practices within dance and opening new sites and situations for choreography. As choreographers increasingly mix dance with other art forms, new genres of performance practice emerge, such as dance installation, screen dance, dance-performance, site-responsive dance, place-sensitive dance, dance-architecture and interactive dance. In departing from the history of concert or theatre dance, these new varieties of dance performance take dance out of its traditional homes – the black box theatre, the concert stage and the proscenium – and into the street, gallery, live art space, landscape and digital infrastructure.

Architecture, as a way of looking at and manipulating space, invites understanding of these changes to ways of making and perceiving dance. Through dance, movement unfolds and actualises space, opening space to time and making space particular, distinct. In this way, space is an effect of matter and movement and we make space between us (Massey: 2005). Given this, we can say that location is always defined by action, refusing the conceptualization of space as a neutral medium, a container and a passive receptacle whose form is given by its content. Alternatively, we see space in a more heterotopic way, as an opening to a proliferation of other spaces, or as a labyrinthine passage from one space to another, a space of mutability that changes over time. This re-enervation of space requires us to think and enact space as heterogeneous and mutable.

In attempting to move beyond a hierarchy of the senses enforced through perspectival vision, choreographers explore the tactile, vibratory, aural, kinaesthetic and proprioceptive senses in performance and explore design processes which allow these senses not just to be communicated but also experienced by audiences through a mediated sensorium. In this way, the morphological resonance between the dancing body and the environment of performance is amplified through a reorientation of sensory and perceptual information. In choreographing through the sensory and perceptual feedback received from the environment one is in, be that virtual and/or physical, we produce specific concepts of spatiality beyond the visual. In listening to space in this way, choreography speaks space through a somatic language that exposes and makes vulnerable the outside of the body from the inside, and the inside of the body from the outside.

Notes

1 In Ovid's *Metamorphosis* 14, Sibyl of Cumae is a prophetess who, offered a wish in exchange for her virginity, takes a handful of sand and asks to live for as many years as the grains of sand she holds. However, in failing to ask for eternal youth, her body shrinks over time until only her voice is heard resonating through the rocks of her cave (Ovid: 2004).

2 Marina Warner (2002) in her short story, 'Stone Girl' writes of the standing stone ring of Nine Maidens on Dartmoor. Condemned to petrification for dancing on the sabbath they come to life under the moonlight and dance again.

3 Comprising two solo performances, *Aarero Stone* was an interdisciplinary collaboration with New Zealand Maori performance artist Charles Koroneho and designer Dorita Hannah. The solos examined themes of lamentation, myth and ancestral voices through two different perspectives, that of an indigenous Maori (Koroneho) and a Western European (Brown). Though sequentially structured as distinct works the solos shared the performance landscape designed by Dorita inviting audiences to perceive each work through the traces of the other, troubling its aura with pre-European and postcolonial narratives of mourning.

4 Rather than cultural artefacts becoming inert museum objects, the Maori consider them to be cultural treasures, *taonga*, which carry deep spiritual truths for the living. In writing of the Maori ancestral story of Hine-tua-Hoanga, Margaret Orbell (1995) describes how her son, Rata, faced with the task of avenging his father, needed a *waka* and therefore a sharp adze, so his mother, offered her advice. In one version her instructions were to sharpen his adze on her back. She was known as 'Woman with a Sandstone Back'.

7

REFLECTIONS ON NEW
DIRECTIONS IN INDIAN DANCE

Chandralekha

One of the crucial experiences that shaped my response and attitude to dance was during my very first public dance recital (*arangetram*) in 1952. It was a charity programme in aid of the Rayalseema Drought Relief Fund. I was dancing 'Mathura Nagarilo' depicting the river Yamuna, the water-play of *sakhis*, the sensuality, the luxuriance and abundance of water. Suddenly, I froze, with the realisation that I was portraying all this profusion of water in the context of a drought. I remembered photographs in the newspapers of cracked earth, of long, winding queues of people waiting for water with little tins in hand. Here, Guru Ellappa was singing 'Mathura Nagarilo'. Art and life seemed to be in conflict. The paradox was stunning. For that split second I was divided, fragmented into two people.

Through the years this experience has lived with me and I have not been able to resolve the contradiction which, of course, is a social one. On the one hand, a great love for all that is rich and nourishing in our culture and, on the other, the need to contribute positive energies towards changing the harsh realities of life. For me, to be able to respond to the realities of life is as crucial as to remain alive and tuned to sensuality and cultural wealth. I have struggled to harmonise, to integrate these diverging directions in order to remain sensitive and whole.

Being inheritors of colonial structures and institutions of education, language, liberal values and perhaps even notions of aesthetics, we cannot overlook the mediation of the West in shaping our approach to our traditional arts. Problems of revivalism, nostalgia, purity, exclusiveness, conservation, preservation need to be examined. There is a tendency to swing between the polarities of rejecting the West to seek the security of our little islands, or of accepting the West at the cost of a wealth of traditions, without any attempt to try and listen to what they have to tell us.

Such conflict stems from a lack of consciousness and an inability to comprehend the central and basic issues which, ultimately, are connected with integrated and humanised existence on our planet. The East in order to be 'contemporary' would need to understand and express the East in its own terms; to explore to the full the linkages generated by valid interdisciplinary principles common to all arts and central to the creative concept of *rasa*; to extend the frontiers of the loaded cultural language of our soil.

I see dance as a visual, tactile and sensual language, structured with a specific vocabulary and idiom, with space–time, with organic bind, principles and, most importantly, related to the dynamics of energy and flow with a capacity to recharge human beings. The internal relation between the dance and the dancer and the external relation between dance and society are questions that cannot be taken lightly.

First of all, dance is an expression of physicality. In the course of human evolution, for a long time physicality was a communal possession to be collectively expressed. The remnants of tribal societies show the basic unity of material life and physical expression. So we start from the fundamental premise that dance does not originate from the heavens, that it has a material base, that it is rooted in the soil, the region, the community, in usages, work rhythms, habits and behaviour, food patterns, and social relations, and in racial characteristics like nose, skin, eyes, hair – a whole lot of accumulations that go by the name of culture and intimately related to body attitudes and physiognomy, and to work and tools. Even in its most stylized form, dance retains a certain universality of idiom and is an extension of and a supplement to spoken language.

The history of dance, then, cannot be separated from the history of the various stages of society. The variations in form are like variations in soil, climate, trees, vegetation. Over a long period of time, however, dance along with other arts and social functions became integrated into the evolving hierarchical structures of society effecting a transformation in its role – from communal participation to communal consumption.

The codification of dance in a society that admitted a hierarchical structure introduced a process of rigidification in the roles of the performer and the spectator, propelling classical dance and dancers towards limiting, though exotic, specialisation and to a fossilisation of the form. Increasingly, the dances became a class preserve expressing an ideological content.

However, through all the distortions of the medieval period, the body retained a certain primacy and sensuality and played a vital role in maintaining human dignity in spite of much privation. It is when we come to contemporary times and an industrial/urban society that a sudden and harsh break occurs. The vital link, between body and nature, body and work, body and ritual, snaps. Dance becomes, almost totally, a spectacle.

A reversal, too, takes place. While traditional thought conceptualises the human body as a unique centre, a centre of the universe, expanding outwards into the cosmos, industrial society converts the human body into the prime target of attack: as citizen, attacked by the political system; as consumer, attacked by the economic system; as individual, bombarded by the media, denied contact with nature, incapable of self-renewal, suffocated by poisons in air and water, isolated and deprived of directions for change.

The question then arises: What role can dance play in such a society? Can it recuperate energies? Can it initiate a living flow between individual and community? Can it integrate human perspectives? Can it infuse people with joy for life, radical optimism, hope, courage and vision to negate all that is ugly, unjust and hurtful? If our life is alienated, can our dances and arts help to transcend that alienation?

I have experienced dance as a sensual language of beauty and of essential freedom; a language of coordination as against alienation; a movement towards the human essence, the sap, the vitality, the *rasa*. It is this aspect of classical dance and its unflagging potential to regenerate the human spirit that constitutes for me its *contemporaneity* and the reason why we need to work with the form. Any human mode with a capacity to touch, to ener- gise, to transform is potent. Otherwise art is primarily to be lived. It is nothing but the quality of all that is made.

Besides several negative features in the prevailing dance situation like spectacular mindlessness, archaic social values, faked religiosity, idealisation leading to mortification of the form, numbing sentimentality, literalism, verbalism, dependence on *sahitya*, on word, mystification and dollification, perpetuation of anti-women values, cynicism within the solo dance situation and its senseless competitiveness, there are also more serious questions: Why have classical Indian dances become so insular and unre- sponsive to the dramatic social, historical, scientific, human changes that have occurred in the world around us over the past forty years? What blocks and complexes prevent classical dancers from initiating basic chan- ges? What makes them resistant to contemporary progressive social values? Why is it that even purely formal exercises and experiments have eluded these forms? Why have not attempts been encouraged to explore the power and strength of these forms, as, for example, their links with martial arts?

At the same time, the criteria, the parameters, the references, the direc- tions for what constitutes 'new' and 'contemporary' in the realm of classical dance is a sensitive area and there can be no easy formulae and solutions. I believe one can make only one small step at a time with feeling and sin- cerity. The principles of wholeness and relatedness that form the core of traditional thought are the most relevant for us today. Through these we get some idea of the directions for a fresh search, questions of perceptual and creative levels, exchange and transmission, movement and control, art and experience, tradition and modernity, inner and outer, space and time, individual and collective, integrity and rupture, quantity and quality.

With my root and training in a classical dance form, Bharata Natyam, with its ancient lineage and formal purity, I had to contend with several contra- dictions inherent in working within 'traditional' form in a contemporary context.

I have increasingly been disturbed by current Western critical opinion which so effortlessly glamorises and valorises Eastern 'traditions' in an uncritical manner, entirely from an 'orientalist' and patronising perspective. For us, in our Eastern contexts, both our 'traditionality' and our 'modernity' are complex and problematic areas which are not abstract theoretical categories but real everyday concerns – both of life and of performing arts.

If our so-called 'traditions' are largely superficial post-colonial 'inventions' which subsume the genuine experience and accumulation of the past, with its treasure-house of complex and holistic concepts of body/energy/ aesthetics, then our so-called 'modernity' has turned out to be a movement that privileged the 'bourgeois' self, enabling an elite aesthetic to distort and de-eroticise the real and the liberating energies of the body. Those of us engaged in a battle for 'recovery' in several artistic and intellectual fields, therefore, find ourselves simultaneously battling on two fronts, often tending to get isolated and marginalised by national and international markets, by official state policy and dominant cultural constructs.

If I battle on regardless, it is entirely because of the pleasure I derive, on the one hand, from knocking the narrow-mindedness and vested interests, at both the national and the international level and, on the other, from a real vision of the full blooming of a form that, I am convinced, can make a difference to the way we look at ourselves.

In our contexts, I believe dance is a 'project' that would enable a recovery of the body, of our spine, which for me, is a metaphor for freedom. Dance, for me, is not spectacle, or entertainment, or virtuosity.

It is not about seduction or titillation or loaded effects or exotic representations. For me, it is all about evoking human energy and dignity in an increasingly brutalising environment. Working with – and making a departure from – the exclusive classicism of Bharata Natyam, therefore, the questions before me have been: how to explore, expand, universalise the form; how to comprehend its inherent energy content; how to see it in relation to other allied physical disciplines in India – such as yoga, ancient martial arts and allied life activity with its investment in physical labour; how to interpret the purity of the Bharata Natyam line; its principles of balance and flexion; its body geometry of squares, circles, triangles, coils, curves; how to visualise this body-geometry in terms of space-geometry – the inner/outer correspondence; how to slash across the dead weight of the 'past' suffocating dance in the name of 'tradition'; how to pare dance of its feudal and religious acculturations, sticking like unhealthy patinas to the form, as also from the increasing pressure on it of the demands of the commercial market.

There are more questions: how to understand dance as a language in its own right, self-sufficient and with a vocabulary of its own – so as to free it from the tedious god/goddess narratives and staged religiosity, to give it a secular space of its own; how to demystify its content, which reinforces nostalgia and revivalism, promotes esoteric self-indulgence, and idealises a deep woman content; how to recover and celebrate its abstract content of space and time; how to initiate and consolidate the conjunctions between our traditional forms and our contemporary concerns.

Any work with dance, therefore, in my context, involves engaging with the body and its primitive accumulations, its social complexes, its cultural stratifications. The 'content' of the body is vast and complex. There are no limited or fragmented concepts of the body in indigenous cultures. Here, the body is seen as a unity – with respect to itself as well as the society and the cosmos. Neither specific parts of the body nor physical systems are seen in isolation. For example, the traditional martial art form Kalaripayattu, with its swift leaps and spinal stretches, is integral with a scientific understanding of secretive points in the body – such as *marmas* and *chakras*. An ability to hurt presumes an ability to heal.

In this cosmology, the arts and sciences, too, are interdependent and richly cross-referenced. Dance, music, architecture, sculpture, yoga, medicine, martial arts, linguistics, grammar are not isolated and mutually exclusive. This is the larger meaning of 'tradition' – to be integral, to be whole. Once this is understood, it is not 'tradition' we will need to break as much as the conditions that create isolation, exclusivity, specialisation, competition. It is binary categories which promote narrow beliefs and linearity, against the joys of a world view and curvature, that we need to break.

So, with all its contradictions, conflicts, tensions, splits, and ruptures, tradition, for me, is not a museum piece or fossil form, hermetically sealed forever, which precludes ideation, commentary, questioning, critique. I see tradition as open and fluid in terms of our times, in interactive relation with the past, accepting as well as foregrounding the tensions and disjunctions. This is the only way to locate tradition here and now – as a prerequisite for renewal of our energies at the level of our everyday life.

The issue, for me, is not 'tradition' versus 'modernity'. I do not see them as two different things. The task of the artist is to modernise the tradition through the creative process.

Not transplanting, borrowing, imitating or becoming a 'shadow culture' of some other culture. It has to be an inward journey into one's own self; a journey constantly relating, refining the reality of the in-between area; to enable tradition to flow free in our contemporary life.

8

WHAT'S IT WORTH TO YA? ADAPTATION AND ANACHRONISM

Rennie Harris's PureMovement and Shakespeare

Anna B. Scott

End shelving

At the level of production, the dance idiom of Rennie Harris and his company reflects the periphery of the late capitalist, post-urban world in which he grew up – fits and starts, shape shifting and time displacement, parody and mimicry as codes of exchange and consumption, lots of consumption, but of goods that have no actual materiality to them, no physicality as of yet. Funky, indeed. Unlike the *corps de ballet* that is organized like a standard capitalist factory – *corps*/workers, *prima*/shop manager (costume, props and music all reside within the span of the shop manager), artistic director/mid-level management, and finally board of directors/capitalist – PureMovement is more akin to a collective, each dancer prized for his or her particular interpretation of the rhythm and the set-moves, not the ability to replicate a corpus of movements: that's boring. However, in order to pull off *Rome & Jewels*, Harris had to force the issue of mastery, bringing into alignment the particularities of each dancer to match the vision. Be not mistaken. It is by no means his vision alone, and he is very clear about that. In classic hip hop style, the production is an ensemble effort. Instead of a conversation between the DJ, rapper and breakers and audiences in the cipher, *Rome & Jewels* owes its existence to a series of choreographies on film, a choreographer, six playwrights, a DJ, an MC, several dancers, a videographer, and the unfortunate settings/scenes of the murders of Tupac Shakur and Biggie Smalls, sworn microphone enemies. Though it toys with mass-produced items and idioms, even delving into Fordist choreographic strategies, *Rome & Jewels*, because of the alleged conflict between what's in sight/site, a bunch of black men doing 'urban dance', and what's in mind, an old white man writing a masterpiece of theatre, forces the question about reproduction: why y'all so hung up on cloning?[1]

Drip droppin
over the line
we find that there ain't enough
time
to relinquish this grip
that's got our soles
a piece of time wound round itself
it's never too late
or too early
to start counting
your blessings
but any fool knows
that infinity
is simply unfathomable
so why bother with abstractions
like numbers and meters
drop your chin
now lift it with your ears
can't you feel the millions
that march on across the seas
wound round itself
time
ain't money
and it sho don't start over every time
a somebody call
a somebody respond
it hovers
between memory and premonition
stacking up on our backs
shaking down our spinal columns
accumulation
of beats per minute per
forever
the interminable loop
that keeps heads rockin

Units, moving units

Bodies everywhere. Strewn about like the popopopop of bullets. Death and living coalesce, coagulate on the stage as the lights can't finish coming all the way up, or like the curtain that couldn't even close – too much seepage. What did I do to be so black and blue? A lanky figure backs into the scene, miraculously stepping over the carcasses. He knows death intimately. He lives it, is it. Dark, tall, swooping, buzzard lopin' bassackwards across familiar terrain to the sound of helicopters that we can't afford to see. This is not Miss Saigon. It will not play on more than one stage at a time. Our Death is draped in fly cream-coloured Adidas gear. A real killa.

Back in the black, another figure, more tentative than the first, gingerly makes his way into what is looking more and more like a Rodin sculpture, ass first. Unborn, always already dead, he is the *abiku* that we keep wishing will not die so soon after its birth; the one we keep trying to tie down here in the market place of our desires with the weight of human flesh. He is fleeting, not of this world nor made for it. He is love. He is black. Pimped out and mad that he can't seem to get his groove on in any consistent way on either side of this life and death thang. He is about to reach the centre of the stage. He pauses, the lights shift from wings to the fly overhead. Reds, harsh, like Sleeping Beauty's apple, draw his gaze upwards, smack dab in the middle of the whole stinking thing. Life begins again. The Dead walk once more.

Poppin', lockin', punkin' and uprockin', the Always Already Dead make their way back into the story, trying to catch us up with the speed and brevity of their lives. A two-hour traffic that will blow your mind. This is *Rome & Jewels*, Romeo & Juliet Illadelphia style, courtesy of Rennie Harris's PureMovement.

Repetition as accumulation, party lines

In *Rome & Jewels*, the party challenge scene speeds up the rate of our return to the beginning of the play. Rather than a ball that he is crashing, Rome and his crew are invited to attend a neighbourhood jam, as are Tibault and his posse. Dance's central force to the possibility of the story struck me almost dumb as I watched film after film. Each version of *Romeo and Juliet* took the party as the frame within which to do the most updating of Shakespeare's text. The party is even moved within the flow of the narrative in some instances. In Shakespeare's play, the masquerade ball occurs in Act 1, Scene 5 and it is the elder Capulet that gets the party started right.

CAPULET

Welcome, gentlemen! ladies that have their toes
Unplagued with corns will have a bout with you.
Ah ha, my mistresses! which of you all
Will now deny to dance? she that makes dainty,
She, I'll swear, hath corns; am I come near ye now?
Welcome, gentlemen! I have seen the day
That I have worn a visor and could tell

A whispering tale in a fair lady's ear,
Such as would please: 'tis gone, 'tis gone, 'tis gone:
You are welcome, gentlemen! come, musicians, play.
A hall, a hall! give room! and foot it, girls.
Music plays, and they dance[2]

In *Rome & Jewels*, the party itself is the central focus; we end–start there, work our way back to it, watching it flashback into the action of the play through out the evening. In *West Side Story* as in the film *Shakespeare's Romeo & Juliet*, the party scene happens approximately in the first act, and Maria and Tony/Romeo and Juliet see each other for the first time across the crowded room. But all is not Shakespearean. Dance, in all instances, serves to broaden the gulf that separates the warring factions – the Caps vs the Monster Qs; the Jets vs the Sharks; the Capulets vs the Montagues – but at the same time the dance mitigates the impending doom, providing an opportunity for communal, non-destructive interaction that ultimately capitalistic desire cannot allow to manifest.

Classically (if you can say that about break dance), the crowd encircles the performers, shoving in closer and closer while the dancer does his thang. In hip hop worlds this is known as the 'cipher'. I use the term 'de/cipher' along those lines, in an attempt to show that everyone is performing and there is a third space between the call and response, 'the unmaking of play'. In *Rome & Jewels* Rennie has opened the circle to accommodate the 'audience', but the performers refuse to relinquish the sacredness of round spaces, trying valiantly to tug the audience into closing the circle, to join in the making of the piece itself. On the tape from Jacob's Pillow, the Vermont crowd just didn't get it, and politely sat waiting to be mesmerized by the swoops, kicks and stunts. In Long Beach at the Carpenter Centre, where I saw it in 2000, the culturally mixed audience was schizophrenic. Youth of Colour were on their feet, shouting back at the stage, letting the performers know that they had to step up. They in turn complied, getting the MC and DJ in on the act, giving us 'mad love'.

In contrast, season ticket holders sat stunned at the players' ability to stay focused amidst the participatory gaggle of young humans. My colleague and I, being college professors and all, even though we broke out our flygirl wear for the event, constantly turned to each other in amazement as Evil Tracy pulled us further and further back in the stacks, with the dancers responding with old school tricks that most kids don't even know how to do nowadays. And then, of course, there was the Shakespearean text placed next to an embodiment of Prince's 'International Lover'. We were speechless by the time we realized that we had already seen the party scene, practically throughout the entire performance.

Rennie's dance challenge scene, true to the streets (think Michael Jackson's *Beat It* video or Mardi Gras Captains dancing off for right-of-way in the narrow streets of the *quartier*), is also true to most West African stage dance forms: the dancers break into two groups, cross each other in the middle of the floor, usually in a line pattern, complete a riff together, then break again, crossing each other one more time, forming 'camps' on either side of the stage, sending out their best dancers to bust the chops of the competition, usually through improvisation.

Finally released from the handcuffs of unison, the boys set out to school us not on their characters, but on themselves throwin' it down at the jam. Though the solos are rehearsed to make sure there is dramatic tension between the camps, each playa rolls his pimp his own way, slippin' in improv moments, seeking liberation of identity in the security of the half-cipher. The audience cheers and we call out the dancer's name, known' full well that they couldn't give a damn about no Shakespeare at that moment, they just tryin' to lay it down. Folks don't know what to do with the only woman on stage, 'cause she ain't Juliet, it ain't exactly clear that she is there as a 'she' and she a white girl. Though she got some moves, any solo she does ends the same way; makes you kinda wonder if she gets it. We wriggle at the fella's head spinnin', hand walkin', yoga back bends that stop mid-roll, shoulder bouncin' around the stage, old school lockin', and capoeira spins and half moons. We are delirious with their expertise, sweatin' up a storm way back in the Carpenter Centre, getting hoarse from giving it up to the now superstars rockin' it out on the stage.

This moment, merely signalled by Shakespeare, without even so much as a time limit (though I suppose that if you went through all the folios, you could roughly figure out how long the dance sequence should be and who should figure prominently), provides space for both nostalgia and trepidation. Directionless, those adapting the text must discover the prerequisite juju in order to turn their trail of breadcrumbs into the yellow brick road. Breasts and penises, skirts and slacks, heels and flats, fine jewellery and cravats, the bodies in motion at the ball step into a world of suspended time, or proto-carnival, happily delivering us a communal moment that the Bard understood as practically impossible when strident calls of kinship meant death to the unrelated, and not of the *petit mort* type either.

On the dance floor, difference, both cultural and gendered, sparkles as a lighted buoy demarcating the switching lanes on an otherwise placid night sea, slicing the monotony of darkness and waves with angular illuminations, recreating phantasms from the shadows. A cold hard shaft cutting into the play space of the stage, Juliet is not exactly a luminous angel in *Rome & Jewels*. An imagined love interest in the shape of her lover's tool, Jewels, literally, the female love interest, in all its perfection, has no form; is perhaps only longing, lengthening an insatiable masculine desire for the refuge of rounded out spaces, the (w)hole; and, in this case, the cipher. The displaced desire to get straight to the point, to the issuance almost at hand, drives this scene in each of the versions. Here, the players are caught like puppets dangling in a series of *pas de deux* motivated by the expectations of decorous behaviour, even though the master puppeteer seems to have crossed all the lines, forcing entwined bodies to unwrap themselves merely to collide once more with the fact of their sexualized fates. Tantalus had it easy.

Back in the simulacrum, Jerome Robbins took the grand ball scene to highlight ethnic identity through dance in the classic *West Side Story*. Though his idea of Puerto Rican male identity is questionable – they are all marked as Spanish toreadors through costume and movement – his emphasis on the hip serves to undergird the fundamental differences that the Jets and the Sharks have with each other: the rhythm of their day to day and the social reality that they must share a dance floor in a choreography that they don't recall auditioning for. The European Jets soar, leap and twirl, moving like a row of pistons, generating white heat and rage. The Sharks, by contrast, are quick on their feet and twisted in the torso, beguiling in the offset of their line so that one does not notice the extreme amount of footwork they are doing as their hips absorb the frenetic contact with the flooring. Robbins' choice of mambo is awkward yet fitting: it was a 'Latin' dance craze at the time of the film, 1950, like the one we are going through now with salsa. Mambo, however, is Cuban, that other craze that was just starting to happen when *West Side Story* went from the stage into a film.

Jaded, alone in my sunny den, I have been shocked by my pleasure at this sinister collection of photographs, so alluring in their ability to make me believe. Natalie Wood is too angelic, too impossible; I'm loving the grit and dirt of an over-painted Rita Moreno. The white boys are left adequately pasty, trying to really make the darkened Greeks, Jews and Mexicans look Puerto Rican. Jerome Robbins is a badass muthefucka is all I can think. I have to give it up: no detail is left unsignifying: the costumes, the lights, the makeup, the songs, oh my god the songs. And the performances. Those kids got schooled. They believed that it was gonna be legendary. I could tell. By the time I realized I was grinning ear to ear, waltzing in my seat to 'I Feel Pretty', one of those quirky scene splices began and, suddenly, it was all hips and then some. The party redone, again. Robbins had a point to make. He wanted to be absolutely clear: didn't nobody own that party. None of the participants could call the shots. The Man, the State, that's the what inside the choreospatial reality.

Jammed into a circle celebration, the delinquents revolt against the decorum of a bygone era, cock-sure that it coulda never ever existed given the tightness of their soles and aspirations. Having their 'get together' dance on terms that are at once reasonable and wholly unsustainable, the 'kids' must break the circle with crisscrossed lines, lest their need for each other be revealed, just so they don't realize that their need for alterity is really just one more joke of the system. We are shown the distance of telecommunications, not the promise of teles nor communitas as they relay, reincorporate their bodies into the proper slots, like adapter plugs on an old switchboard: 'Hold please, while I disconnect you.' A duel, the line drawn, the battlefield cut from gym class sweat and sheer gumption, the challenge is issued, we all gon' go back to the kitchen, or out on the corner, 'cause we didn't know nothing about no ball rooms and open fields of maypole green: 'MAMBO'! And the African ghosts dance and dance, weapons on the bodies of both sides of the Games. I smirk.

Baz Lurhman's party scene in *William Shakespeare's Romeo & Juliet* follows very closely that of Shakespeare except the Capulet soliloquy is given already in the midst of the frivolity, oh yeah, and somebody invited the ghost of Sylvester to perform. Here, the hidden cod piece is all the more important as Lurhman makes a point to underscore the erotic tensions between Romeo and Mercutio, between straight parties and gay club culture. Prancing down the stairs, reminding us of Madonna reminding us of Bette Davis's 'Best Friend', Mercutio floats like a butterfly and stings like a bee across a Miami techno-house mix that sounds an awful lot like the Mambo from the Rogers and Hammerstein score of *West Side Story*. White wings fluttering against his black skin, competing with the red sashes against alabaster stairs and purple sequined sugar plum 'fairies', girlfriend handles the stairs in his four-inch stacks like an old pro, cutting off spectatorial distance with a corny grin and vicious stare that acknowledges our secret pleasure at looking for his cock amidst the whirl of hips, extreme close-ups and sudden tableaux of ballroom decadence. And those lips. Tucked and hidden, his penis just a piece in his pants, his hips suggest labial eruptions somewhere below the waist, but we are continually drawn to the camp trace of his moustache, stomping around his seductive other set of lips, glimmering under a gloss that only a queen like himself could pull off.

He is every woman. The Deva Tantrika so potent that she cannot partner, only copulate. The camera obeys and worships, almost slipping into a top/bottom relationship that is perversely out of place with his sanctity. As the edits force us to actuate the Goddess/Trickster, the dizziness of the camera motion itself transforms us into willing horses for the machinations of the Divine. We are possessed. He is possessive, and pierced through.

The boys, the bard, the bizness

Masculinity is both a choreography and a dance partner in all of these works; its representation – b-boys and hip hoppers, toreadors and tumblers, Sylvester and everybody else – is its interrogation. Cool pose or radical defiance, the manoeuvring of the male form in *Rome & Jewels* begs the question: is it fundamentally a dick thang and we females will never understand? Stranded in dead-in identities, gender starts to look like the new nationalism as homies struggle to keep their focus on the light, on Jewels. Absent yet placed into evidence, the cipher of Juliet perhaps generates the muscle isolations that we as audience misread as competence, as mastery of the physical self – even while the male self is revealing itself as an unfinished, undone textual entity.

Rome, as if to underscore the brutality of love to the masculine, rather, the macho, gives a soliloquy that is almost pornographic. Humping the light, in effect, doing the worm on the stage, undulating in place, then getting doggy by taking vinyasa A into imagined crevices while reciting the lines of Prince's 'International Lover' (here taking the place of Lurhman's use of 'When Doves Cry' in *William Shakespeare's Romeo & Juliet*), hip hop homeboy revels in, reveals, a self-analysis that would do Freud proud. Dancing with his own dick, Rome ponders the neediness of his subjectivities (and they are multiple, a dose of lithium would do this character some good) for a trip back home, detached from his man-child self so as to have more freedom to express itself. Masculinity in *West Side Story* is pulsed through heteronormative relationships, even where the potential for homoerotics is stronger, more plausible, than Dick and Jane riding a bike. Interestingly, the Jets are rarely seen without female counterparts. In fact, when Ginger and her girls aren't around, the boys make very bad decisions indeed, like the rumble scene under the overpass. In a similar vein, a female waiting at home or even trying to insert herself in the plans on the Sharks' side prevents all-out race war, mitigated first by the swinging, yet searing 'America' roof top scene, then again by Maria's unyielding love. Whereas her soft feminine counterpart, Little John, requires the utmost care and handling (he is precious and merely needs schooling in the ways of a man), the female body in the land of the Jets, however, as the spunky side kick Anybodys (tellingly named), is a male point of ridicule. Played like a bat out of hell by Susan Oakes, Anybodys is a deformation of the 'clear' ordering of things, a poisonous knot of instigation and self-hatred that ultimately ruins the possibility of true love. And she didn't even have a black pointy hat or poisonous snake.[3]

Corporeally, such undetermined bodies, mobile sites of contestations invigorate the story with an indeterminacy that belies the pathological quality of fixed identities, standardized choreographies. That lone white girl on the stage in *Rome & Jewels* spins us back to the baby dike who wants to run with the big boys, who wants to be spatially defined and defining, undeniably present in the day to day of the neighbourhood. Merc dies in Rome's arms like the way we must imagine the invisible Jewels must die: a retracing and mapping of desire, of repetitive steps that force the question of the veracity of true love altogether. Is love just a simulacrum dependent on extenuating political economies? Socio-cultural trajectories of ill-defined space?

S.W.A.T.

There is a progression, of sorts. We are relieved, some of us, to recognize the bump and grind of the cadence of the actors' delivery. We was scared that we was gonna need Cliff Notes[TM] to keep up. We shoulda known better from the six writers listed in the programme: Sabela Grimes, Rennie Harris, Ozzie Jones, Rodney Mason, William Shakespeare, Raphael Williams. Then it happens. We realize that most of it is iambic pentameter. Most of what they're saying is Shakespeare's text, and, more frightening yet, when they ain't exactly saying what he wrote, they are moving it through their bodies. It gets worse. Each character has his own kinaesthetic delivery. Let me break that down. Rome (Rodney Mason) pimps across the stage with a roll coming from deep in the hips. Ben V. (Sabela Grimes) is an upright menace whose torso rattles back and forth like a trap door that's been sprung. Merc (Clyde Evans, Jnr) has a bip-bop roll to his pimp, moving from squats to solid stances in the blink of the eye. Tibault (Ron Wood) is almost priestly, tutting around the stage in yogic poses, but right on the edge, mayhem flashing from his eyes as he collapses into ferocious pacing every time he talks. The narrating MC (Ozzie Jones), the spectre of Death and All-Knowing Rhymes, has a coldness that is reptilian; a puppet master that swoops like a buzzard, glides like a 'gator. They keep it steady, so you can study up on the science they droppin'.

Somewhere in one of the soliloquies we recognize that the talkin' mouth ain't always sayin' the same thing as the talkin' body. Our minds stutter, but the catch and release of the poppin' is lucid, almost fluid as it re-enacts the magic of the camera – 32 pictures = one frame, 32 hits transports us into another body other than the one we are seeing. ...

The Monster Qs and the Caps stalk each other, struggling for territory in a war that ain't no body gonna remember when they all dead any way, which they already are to begin with. The gunshots ring out again. They are killed again. Then the B-boys get up while the Lockers spin-off stage and proceed to 'beat love down'. ... Mercutio's speech sounds too much like 'beat that ho down. Smack that bitch's ass and split'. ... time changes as this thing goes on. But the rules of the game do not: kill or be killed, love and be killed, stand up and be killed, dance and be killed, question and be killed. Be killed; die already, damn.

Synergistic organizations

Rennie Harris refuses to make equivalencies of language and gesture, format and structure. In so doing, he manipulates one of the highest standards of white normative aesthetic and linguistic production, Shakespeare, providing evidence that conflicts which may arise in the conjugation of (usually) anachronistic form with contemporary content are largely a product of market, of audience. The art of adaptation by definition explodes a system of sameness, for at its centre is the idea that disparate vantage points can coexist in one production without resolving. Specifically, I am interested in the place of dance in this adaptation since it appears to take on the inscrutability of Shakespearean texts by rendering it even more indexically challenging through a transposition of those textual moments into kinetic investigations. But only non-black folks face an oblique interpretation. Black people (more specifically young people of all races, ages 10–38, who identify with black culture) in the audience have a charged and immediate experience and understanding of the 'text' at that moment since the movement is indexically liberating for them; they have notes that match the outline.[4]

We could talk then about the Social Life of Steps: of walking around, through, in, towards, away, against, down, between, against, across. In the challenge of hip hop dance or urban dance or break dance (all of these mean almost the same thing depending on who is appropriating who, but people fight over the fractions of difference), resides a voracious capacity for mimicry, but it is a retracing, a stepping into a world that requires a familiarity with the terrain of the everyday life of those particular steps: de/cipherin'. *Philadelphia Inquirer* critic Elizabeth Zimmer (2000) raved about how 'Joycean' the text was in its referents, but completely missed a similar, more incisive quality within the movements, the footprints.

B-boying is a mastering of the Psychology of Footprints in one's own neighbourhood. There are particular steps to learn, but the doxa of your block, your crew, dictates the quality of the stepping. A dancer's stance and delivery tells it like it is. Bluesy, soulful, rockin' the bells, whatever, your footprints must represent, without revealing too much. Stepping out into the leftover movement now marked on the floor by the imprint of a dirty sole, the dancer is in effect mapping or retracing the positionality of all dancers who have ever rolled with the crew. Homage or deconstruction, it's a history that defies reification as period. Instead, we are confronted with a Geography of Meandering, following the twists and turns in styles and motions, learning perhaps more about the material reality of the performer than the internal dialogue he is having with himself. We gaze across the stage, recognizing from the blocking and positioning of bodies that now we are running with them over the tops of buildings or along fences. This is a particular place, a specific location that triggers memory bounded by geographies of flight and yearning to which we are not privy, unless we are from Philadelphia and have raced away in the dead of night from the cops in a particular section of town. It is about the preciousness of turf, the ability to have a territorial claim for the siting of your memories.

That struggle for a spatial definition of self, family, group, neighbourhood is the ultimate manifestation of human existence within late capitalist society: The Choreography of Un-Alikes. Forced into conflicts that better protect the flow of capital, people and their stepping vie for increasingly smaller space within urban zones, the space required to create place, signify home. We are thrust again into the Psychology of Footprints as some steps are deemed unreliable, unnecessary, illegal, exotic, unofficial, out of line, too plentiful. Stereotypes blossom from the dust of our treading, drawing our attention away from the machination of capital itself, convincing us that it is some other pedestrian's fault that we lack control over the design of our daily comings and goings.

Walls, turfs, territories, neighbourhood names that are different than what realtors use, the Social Construction of Space, the repetition of the components of passing by, our desire to keep it real by repetition of the same ole same ole, not to be in a rut but in a groove, is the impetus of a Configuration of Cultural Spatial Consciousness. So spaced out, the body in motion emerges tagged and ready for identification, inclusion or exclusion. We create our Alikes by the thuds of our heels striking pavement, dirt, flooring, from the way we allow our spine to reflect that contact, our extremities to organize around the rhythm of our epistemology. Racialized, gendered, classed and broken into specific religious clusters, the walking body is now a strolling socialization whose gait we read like a book, react to like a gazelle on the plains smelling danger.

Returning to poppin', lockin' and breakin', they more aptly appear as analytical processes that kinaesthetically seek to unfetter the socialized stroller by placing the familiarity of its movements into contexts, spaces other than the ones of its daily enactments. As 'internal pantomime', poppin' signifies spaces of difference, but collapses them by retracing, redistricting across various footprints. This simultaneity ridicules and celebrates the pedestrian, providing avenues for other perambulations, like Shakespeare, for example. Intense muscle isolation to rhythm, almost manic in its attack and performance, poppin', and to a lesser extent, lockin' (which is more fluid) requires a Zen-like self-awareness: knowing the self relinquishes the grip of selfhood, of positionality, opening up the possibility of becoming anyone, anything, in any place, at any time. Layer across this a Black and Blue sensibility within a consumerist society and any and all things are up for grabs, for play into the cipher, onto the stage.

Notes

1 Esteemed social theorist and policy maker Philomena Essed is currently developing a theory, in collaboration with Theo Goldburg, to better articulate the reason why, after all of the policy and lawmaking that attempts to redress racial and gender difference in the workplace (primarily), most workplaces remain rather homogeneous, even when difference is present. That is, that a body that is visibly differentiated through dress, skin colour, gender from the normative and networked group must always bring itself into 'compliance' with the network's cultural imaginary and ethics. However, such copying or mimetic shift is unsubstantial and must actually more closely resemble a process of cloning, since gendered and coloured bodies cannot necessarily remove their genetic markings which make them stand apart from white male networked normativity, these different bodies, though desired legally, must ultimately be removed lest their presence throw into high relief the ways in which cloned behaviour is expected

from other whites who are not part of the network (Center for Ideas and Society, June 2002).

2 http://etext.lib.virginia.edu/shakespeare/works/

3 For the complete cast list to the original 1961 film, see http://www.westsidestory.com/site/level2/archives/productions/movie.html

4 One of the phenomenon of urban dance and hip hop culture is geographic elasticity and resulting racial indeterminacy. hip hop, though clearly a practice of the African Diaspora, has always been a production of transnational crews and therefore absolves competing racial categorizations of its practitioners. See DeFrantz (2004b).

Part II

PERFORMING DANCE

Like the words of dance makers, the writing of dancers and of those who reflect on the experience of dancing has been pivotal to the development of dance studies. Until recently, the accounts of dancers were primarily auto-biographical. However, the modernist reflection on philosophy and the postmodernist interrogation of form and content prompted an inquiry into the building blocks not only of dances but also the process of performing them. In addition, dancers, writers and those who bridge both categories have turned to phenomenology and auto-ethnography to examine and theorise their experience of dancing. Dance writers have attended to the intertwining of their own bodies with the research process[1] and have attended to the strategies mobilised by individual dancers.

It is fortunate for our heritage that one of the most important figures in the development of modern dance, Martha Graham, has been eloquent in the expression of her beliefs. In her personal manifesto for the dancer (and, by implication, the choreographer), she allies the experience of life with the experience of dance. Learning, in both, is acquired through practice and achieves a philosophical significance; as such, the dancer becomes 'an athlete of God'. The training of the dancer requires a holistic approach to body/mind and the cultivation of the whole being. Graham pleads for openness to the past, the 'blood memory' of the body, and to the present. The dancer must be 'reborn to the instant', permitting feeling and vulnerability. Graham's writing, not only in its content but also in its metaphysical style, reflects the aesthetic beliefs which are embodied in her choreography. Working within the aesthetic framework of abstract expressionism, Graham attempts to deal with the 'inner landscape' of humankind and the role of the subconscious and of memory. For Graham, the dancer/choreographer was a unique, special individual, an Artist. For the next generation of postmodernists, 'Art' became 'art' and a more pragmatic sensibility pervaded writing about performance. Graham's writing, therefore, not only presents in its content her own strongly held principles but also, in its very style, holds traces of the specific cultural and aesthetic beliefs of her time.

The notion of 'traces', formed by 'a footprint, mark or impression of a person or event' is central to Albright's research on the early modern dancer Loie Fuller. Despite her fame in her own time, and her influence on the work of other artists, Fuller has been a difficult figure to place within the modern dance paradigm. Often, her instrumental role in relation to new ideas about lighting and technology defined her contribution to the exclusion of her achievements as a dancer. Albright, however, chooses not only to investigate Fuller's dancing but also to do so through her own dancing body, in order to produce an 'integration of conceptual and somatic knowledge'. In a recreation of a Fuller work, and in further referential pieces, she attends to her own bodily responses: to the premeditation needed for the negotiation of swathes of material; the strength needed to manipulate these; the impact of light on the body in movement; the sensory experience of the movement itself. As such, traces are made between the conventional texts that mark our understanding of historical subjects and between dancing bodies across time – Fuller's and Albright's own. Although such a strategy exposes the impossibility of closing the gaps between the present and an absent past, it opens up the possibilities which arise from improvising in this space in order to create an historical presence.

Adam Benjamin investigates less the process of performance than the significance of the performer's identity in relationship to the changing possibilities for and limitations within the dance field. Benjamin, with Celeste Dandeker, co-founded the British-based integrated dance company Candoco. He notes the developments which have occurred since his first foray in to the field of dance and disability: the willingness of professional choreographers to meet the challenges of making work in this context; increased opportunities for performers with disabilities and the necessary adaptation of performance spaces. As such, 'the divide between professional dance and disability became more porous' and impacted on policy and public attitudes. Nevertheless, Benjamin argues, mainstream companies and even worthy cultural events still marginalise or exclude dancers with visible disabilities.

Drawing parallels with the organic movement, Benjamin claims the potential for inclusivity in dance to promote both the uniqueness of individuals and their social interconnectedness. But, he warns, the higher profile of inclusive work perhaps comes at a cost of these performers being 'included' in a dominant model of high-level skill, achieved through near-conventional technical training, in order to achieve 'parity of abilities'. Perhaps 'parity', however, is not appropriate, for this is being achieved at the cost of difference not only in performing skills but also in the creation of new vocabularies. It is, hopes Benjamin, not a striving towards the same but the uniting of 'different elements in unexpected ways to create new and utterly surprising outcomes' that should be the ultimate target.

Like Albright, Melissa Blanco Borelli reconstructs a historical subject through the extraction of choreographic traces. She investigates performance as a strategy mobilised by the figure of the dancing *mulata*, here a mixed race Afro-Cuban woman, in Mexican films from the golden age of cinema. Blanco Borelli considers the complex gender, race and national politics of the *mulata* figure, usually played by a white Cuban woman, imported into Mexico in order to star in films where she plays a *rumbera*, a performer of the Cuban dance genre *rumba*. In investigating the political implications of this dancing figure, Blanco Borelli works against the tragic *mulata* figure as she appears in literature and, indeed, in film narratives. Tracing the articulation and rotation of the *rumbera*'s hips, Blanco Borelli posits a *corpo-mulata* who, contrary to the literary *mulata*, achieves an agency through her dancing. Mobilising her concept of hip(g)nosis, Blanco Borelli suggests that the moving body asserts its resolutely non-tragic status and allows the possibility for the dancer to choreograph her own identity. Here, dance performance becomes a way of reading against the grain of conventional narratives.

'As I sense myself still, I become more alert', asserts Emilyn Claid in the introduction to her chapter on the place and possibilities of stillness in dance making, performing and spectatorship. Like Benjamin, Claid considers the significance of difference, here not only rooted in identity categories but also in a range of particularities of experience. Using theoretical underpinnings drawn from Gestalt psychotherapy and her own experiential knowledge from both a long history as a choreographer and her current work in the studio, Claid centres on the notion that 'stillness makes room for discovery'. It draws attention to the physiology of the body, its internal adjustments and potentialities and its strategies for preparation for movement and for recovery afterwards. Stillness carries knowledge of personal histories, present in the body and the perceptions of informed spectators. The ways in which we perceive others in the studio forms the basis of Claid's practice-led research, in which her dancers engage in a 'slowing down to notice how we see or do not see each other, becoming aware of our individual styles and ways of making contact'. In these moments, a space is made for 'dialogic relations' between performer and performer and performer and choreographer, a space which opens up the potential for improvisation and creation.

These contrasting definitions of performance – the place where the dancer displays a training that aligns the body and the spirit, as a site where history can be reconsidered, and as a locus for the performance of identity and the meeting of difference – signal the importance of attending to the experience of dancing. Investigating and theorising the performance of dance as well as its crafting opens up multiple perspectives for considering the social, cultural, political and historical implications of dance. Contrary to those who would argue for the ephemerality and ineffability of dance, these authors, among others, insist that performance allows not only description but also reflection, examination and theorisation. In looking closely at the performance of dance, these authors signal a fruitful arena for debate, where the significance of dance lies as much in its moments of enactment as in its creation and design.

Further reading

Albright, A.C. and Gere, D. (eds) (2003) *Taken By Surprise: A Dance Improvisation Reader*, Middletown, CT: Wesleyan University Press.

Bales, M. and Nettl-Fio, R. (2008) *The Body Eclectic: Evolving Practice in Dance Training*, Champaign: University of Illinois Press.

Benjamin, A. (2001) *Making an Entrance*, London: Routledge.

Eichenbaum, R. (2008) *The Dancer Within: Intimate Conversations with Great Dancers*, Middletown, CT: Wesleyan University Press.

Gottschild, B.D. (2005) *The Black Dancing Body: A Geography from Coon to Cool*, Basingstoke: Palgrave Macmillan.

Note

1 Examples of such an inquiry into the writer's bodily involvement in the production of the text include Susan Foster (1995) and Ann Cooper Albright (2007, and Chapter 10 this volume).

9

I AM A DANCER

Martha Graham

I am a dancer

I believe that we learn by practice. Whether it means to learn to dance by practising dancing or to learn to live by practising living, the principles are the same. In each it is the performance of a dedicated precise set of acts, physical or intellectual, from which comes shape of achievement, a sense of one's being, a satisfaction of spirit. One becomes in some areas an athlete of God.

To practise means to perform, in the face of all obstacles, some act of vision, of faith, of desire. Practice is a means of inviting the perfection desired.

I think the reason dance has held such an ageless magic for the world is that it has been the symbol of the performance of living. Even as I write, time has begun to make today yesterday – the past. The most brilliant scientific discoveries will in time change and perhaps grow obsolete as new scientific manifestations emerge. But art is eternal, for it reveals the inner landscape, which is the soul of man.

Many times I hear the phrase 'the dance of life'. It is an expression that touches me deeply, for the instrument through which the dance speaks is also the instrument through which life is lived – the human body. It is the instrument by which all the primaries of life are made manifest. It holds in its memory all matters of life and death and love. Dancing appears glamorous, easy, delightful. But the path to the paradise of the achievement is not easier than any other. There is fatigue so great that the body cries, even in its sleep. There are times of complete frustration, there are daily small deaths. Then I need all the comfort that practice has stored in my memory, a tenacity of faith.

It takes about ten years to make a mature dancer. The training is twofold. First comes the study and practice of the craft which is the school where you are working in order to strengthen the muscular structure of the body. The body is shaped, disciplined, honoured and, in time, trusted. The movement becomes clean, precise, eloquent, truthful. Movement never lies.

It is a barometer telling the state of the soul's weather to all who can read it. This might be called the law of the dancer's life – the law which governs its outer aspects.

Then comes the cultivation of the being from which whatever you have to say comes. It doesn't just come out of nowhere, it comes out of a great curiosity. The main thing, of course, always, is the fact that there is only one of you in the world, just one, and if that is not fulfilled then something has been lost. Ambition is not enough; necessity is everything. It is through this that the legends of the soul's journey are retold with all their tragedy and their bitterness and sweetness of living. It is at this point that the sweep of life catches up with the mere personality of the performer, and, while the individual becomes greater, the personal becomes less personal. And there is grace. I mean the grace resulting from faith – faith in life, in love, in people, in the act of dancing. All this is necessary to any performance in life which is magnetic, powerful, rich in meaning. In a dancer, there is a reverence for such forgotten things as the miracle of the small beautiful bones and their delicate strength. In a thinker, there is a reverence for the beauty of the alert and directed and lucid mind. In all of us who perform there is an awareness of the smile which is part of the equipment, or gift, of the acrobat. We have all walked the high wire of circumstance at times. We recognize the gravity pull of the earth as he does. The smile is there because he is practising living at that instant of danger. He does not choose to fall. At times I fear walking that tightrope. I fear the venture into the unknown. But that is part of the act of creating and the act of performing. That is what a dancer does.

People have asked me why I chose to be a dancer. I did not choose: I was chosen to be a dancer, and, with that, you live all your life. When any young student asks me, 'Do you think I should be a dancer?' I always say, 'If you have to ask, then the answer is no.' Only if there is one way to make life vivid for yourself and for others should you embark upon such a career. You will know the wonders of the human body because there is nothing more wonderful. The next time you look into the mirror, just look at the way the ears rest next to the head; look at the way the hairline grows; think of all the little bones in your wrist. It is a miracle. And the dance is a celebration of that miracle.

I feel that the essence of dance is the expression of mankind – the landscape of the human soul. I hope that every dance I do reveals something of myself or some wonderful thing a human being can be. It is the unknown – whether it is the myths or the legends or the rituals that give us our memories. It is the eternal pulse of life, the utter desire. I know that when we have rehearsals, and we have them every day, there are some dancers, particularly men, who cannot be still. One of the men in my company is not built to be still. He has to be moving. I think at times he does not know what he is doing, but that is another matter. He's got the essence of a man's inner life that prods him to dance. He has that desire. Every dance is a kind of fever chart, a graph of the heart. Desire is a lovely thing, and that is where the dance comes from, from desire.

Each day of rehearsal for a new ballet I arrive at a little before two in the afternoon, and sit alone in my studio to have a moment of stillness before the dancers enter. I tease myself and say I am cultivating my Buddha nature; but it is really just such a comforting place for me to be – secure, clear and with a purpose. It is that order of these elements together that led one writer to call dance 'glorified human behaviour'. I sit with my back to our large mirrors so that I am completely within myself.

Outside my studio door, in my garden, is a tree that has always been a symbol of facing life, and in many ways it is a dancer. It began as a sapling when I first moved here and, although a wire gate was in its way, it persisted and grew to the light, and now thirty years later it is a tree with a very thick trunk, with the wire embedded within. Like a dancer it went to the light and carried the scars of its journey inside. You traverse, you work, you make it right. You embody within yourself that curiosity, use that avidity for life no matter whether it is for good or for evil. The body is a sacred garment. It's your first and your last garment; it is what you enter life in and what you depart life with, and it should be treated with honour, and with joy and with fear as well. But always, though, with blessing.

They say that the two primary arts were dance and architecture. The word ' theatre' was a verb before it was a noun – an act, then a place. That means you must make the gesture, the effort, the real effort to communicate with another being. And you also must have a tree to shelter under in case of storm or sun. There is always that tree, that creative force, and there is always a house, a theatre. The spine is your body's tree of life. And through it a dancer communicates: his body says what words cannot, and if he is pure and open, he can make of his body a tragic instrument.

I am absorbed in the magic of movement and light. Movement never lies. It is the magic of what I call the outer space of the imagination. There is a great deal of outer space, distant from our daily lives, where I feel our imagination wanders sometimes. It will find a planet or it will not find a planet, and that is what a dancer does.

And then there is inspiration. Where does it come from? Mostly from the excitement of living. I get it from the diversity of a tree or the ripple of the sea, a bit of poetry, the sighting of a dolphin breaking the still water and moving toward me – anything that quickens you to the instant. And whether one would call that inspiration or necessity, I really do not know. At times I receive that inspiration from people; I enjoy people very much and for the most part feel it is returned. I simply happen to love people. I do not love them all individually, but I love the idea of life pulsing through people – blood and movement.

For all of us, but particularly for a dancer with his intensification of life and his body, there is a blood memory that can speak to us. Each of us from our mother and father has received their blood and through their parents and their parents' parents and backward into time. We carry thousands of years of that blood and its memory. How else to explain those instinctive gestures and thoughts that come to us, with little preparation or expectation. They come perhaps from some deep memory of a time when the world was chaotic, when, as the Bible says, the world was nothing. And then, as if some door opened slightly, there was light. It revealed certain wonderful things. It revealed terrifying things. But it was light.

William Goyen, in *The House of Breath* (1950), wrote that 'we are the carriers of lives and legends – who knows the unseen frescoes on the private walls of the skull'. Very often making a dance springs from a desire to find those hidden frescoes.

In Burma, on our second Asian tour in the 1970s, I had been asked to present flowers at the tomb of the Burmese Unknown Soldier. This I did in the presence of our [the American] ambassador and the Burmese minister of culture. When I had finished, there was a tremendous stir, great sounds of conversation. The Burmese wanted to know who had coached me to present the flowers in precisely the correct manner, steps and gestures that would be appropriate to a Burmese woman of my age and station. No one had. Just as no one had taught Ruth St. Denis to touch back generations in east Indian dance to find the true path and spirit for her solos which even the Indians at that time had lost.

But for this you must keep your vessel clean – your mind, your body; it is what the Zen masters tell their students who get too full of themselves, too wrapped up in theory and too many thoughts. They ask them, 'That is all very good; but have you cleaned your dish?' For the Buddhist student lived by begging food, and how could he receive it if his bowl was not clean? He is being asked if he is ready for his next meal. A clear instruction to get back to basics. It is so easy to become cluttered.

I think that is what my father must have meant when he wrote to me when I was away from home. 'Martha,' he said, 'you must keep an open soul.' It is that openness and awareness and innocence of sorts that I try to cultivate in my dancers. Although, as the Latin verb to educate, *educere*, indicates, it is not a question of putting something in but rather of drawing it out, if it is there to begin with.

Dancers today can do anything; the technique is phenomenal. The passion and the meaning to their movement can be another thing.

At times I will tease my dancers and tell them that they are not too bright today, that all of their jumping has addled their brains. And yet they move with grace and a kind of inevitability, some more powerfully than others. This moment of rehearsal is the instant that I care about. This is the very now of my life.

The only thing we have is the now. You begin from the now, what you know, and move into the old, ancient ones that you did not know but which you find as you go along. I think you only find the past from yourself, from what you're experiencing now, what enters your life at the present moment. We don't know about the past, except as we discover it. And we discover it from the now. Looking at the past is like lolling in a rocking chair. It is so relaxing and you can rock back and forth on the porch, and never go forward. It is not for me. People sometimes ask me about retirement and I say, 'Retire? Retire into what?' I don't believe in retirement because that is the time you die.

There are always ancestral footsteps behind me, pushing me, when I am creating a new dance and gestures are flowing through me. Whether good or bad, they are ancestral. You get to the point where your body is something else and it takes on a world of cultures from the past, an idea that is very hard to express in words. I never verbalize about the dance as I create it. It is a purely physical risk that you desire to take, and that you have to take. The ballet I am doing now is a risk. That is all I can say because it isn't fulfilled yet. I let no one watch, except for the dancers I am working with. When they leave I am alone with the ancestral footsteps.

Somewhere very long ago I remember hearing that in El Greco's studio, after he died, they found an empty canvas on which he had written only three words: 'Nothing pleases me.' This I can understand.

What I miss some days in a dance class is not perfection, because some of them will never achieve that moment of technical expertise. I don't demand, at the beginning, any vestige of perfection. What I long for is the eagerness to meet life, the curiosity, the wonder that you feel when you can really move – to work towards a perfect first or a perfect fifth position. There comes an excitement, an avidity, a forgetfulness of everyone about you. You are so completely absorbed in this instrument that is vibrant to life. The great French poet St John Perse said to me, 'You have so little time to be born to the instant.' This I miss in class very much. I miss the animal strength, the beauty of the heel as it is used to carry one forward into life. This, I think more than anything, is the secret of my loneliness.

I do not feel myself unique by any means, but I do know that I agree with Edgard Varèse – and I'm going to use a word that I never use regarding myself or anybody else. And that word is genius. Varèse, a wonderful French composer, who wrote some music for me, opened up new areas of musical strength in the way he used percussion that I had never experienced before. He said, 'Martha, all of us are born with genius, but most people only keep it for a few seconds.'

By genius he meant that curiosity that leads to the search for the secret of life. That is what tires me when I teach and I come away alone. Sometimes you will see a person on the stage who has this oneness with themself – it is so glorious it has the power to stop you. It is a common gift to all of us but most people only keep it a few moments.

I can never forget the evening I was staying late at the school, and the phone rang. I was the only one there and I picked it up to hear a mother ask about classes for her child. 'She is a genius. Intuitive. Unique. It must be nurtured now.' 'Really,' I answered. 'And how old is she?' Her mother replied, 'Two years old.' I told her that we only accepted children at nine (today much earlier, thanks to vitamins and computers and home training). 'Nine!' she cried. 'But by nine she will have lost all of her genius.' I said, 'Madame, if she must lose it, it is best she lose it young.'

I never thought of myself as being what they call a genius. I don't know what genius is. I think a far better expression is a retriever, a lovely strong golden retriever that brings things back from the past, or retrieves things from our common blood memory. I think that by every act you do – whether in religion, politics or sex – you reveal yourself. This, to me, is one of the wonderful things in life. It is what I've always wanted to do – to show the laughing, the fun, the appetite, all of it through dance.

In order to work, in order to be excited, in order to simply be, you have to be reborn to the instant. You have to permit yourself to feel, you have to permit yourself to be vulnerable. You may not like what you see, that is not important. You don't always have to judge. But you must be attacked by it, excited by it, and your body must be alive. And you must know how to animate that body; for each it is individual.

When a dancer is at the peak of their power they have two lovely, fragile and perishable things. One is the spontaneity that is arrived at over years of training. The other is simplicity, but not the usual kind. It is the state of complete simplicity costing no less than absolutely everything, of which T.S. Eliot speaks.

How many leaps did Nijinsky take before he made the one that startled the world? He took thousands and thousands and it is that legend that gives us the courage, the energy and the arrogance to go back into the studio knowing that, while there is so little time to be born to the instant, we will work again among the many that we may once more be born as one. That is a dancer's world.

My dancer's world has seen so many theatres, so many instants. But always I have resisted looking backward until now, when I begin to sense that there was always for my life a line through it – necessity. The Greek myths speak of the spindle of life resting on the knee of necessity, the principal Fate in the Platonic world. The second Fate weaves, and the third cuts. Necessity to create? No. But in some way to transcend, to conquer fear, to find a way to go on.

How does it all begin? I suppose it never begins. It just continues.

10

TRACING THE PAST
Writing history through the body

Ann Cooper Albright

*Let's begin with traces. Traces of the past. Traces of a dance. Traces of light …
and colour and fabric. Traces of a body, animating all these sources of movement.
Traces of a life, spent spinning across nations, across centuries, across identities.
How do we trace the past? Reconfigure what is lost? Are traces always even visible?*

*Perhaps we should lose the noun, which renders us nostalgic, maybe even mel-
ancholic at the extreme. Replace our ambition to find out what happened with a
curiosity about how it came to be that it was happening. Replace traces with tracing – the past with the passion. Tracing the contours of fabric which spiral
upward and outward, we spill over beyond any one historical or aesthetic discourse.
This act of tracing can help us become aware not only of what's visible, but also
what is, has been, will always be, less clearly visible. Beyond the image into the
motion.*

With a nod to the meanings embedded in historical study, Walter
Benjamin wrote: 'To dwell means to leave traces' (Benjamin 1999: 9).
Indeed, traces are the material artefacts that constitute the stuff of historical inquiry, the bits and pieces of a life that scholars follow, gather up
and survey. The word itself suggests the imprint of a figure who has
passed: the footprint, mark or impression of a person or event. These
kinds of traces are omnipresent in the case of Loie Fuller. Some traces
are more visible than others, some more easily located. But all traces –
once noticed – draw us into another reality. *Someone passed this way
before.*

Loie Fuller is one of the most interesting and paradoxical figures in early
modern dance. Born in 1862 in Chicago, Fuller began performing in her
teens, first as a temperance speaker and later as a member of the Buffalo Bill
troupe, touring America on the vaudeville circuit. Her various dramatic
roles included cross-dressed ones, such as the lead in the fast-paced melodrama *Little Jack Sheppard*, but it is as a 'Serpentine' or skirt dancer that she
became well-known. In the 1890s, Fuller created an extraordinary sensation
in Paris with her manipulations of hundreds of yards of silk, swirling high
above her and lit dramatically from below. She embodied the *fin-de-siècle*
images of woman as flower, woman as bird, woman as fire, woman as

nature. One of the most famous dancers of her time, Fuller starred as the main act at the Folies Bergère, inspiring a host of contemporary fashions and imitators. Fuller's serpentine motif is also visible in much of the decorative imagery of Art Nouveau, and she was the subject of works by such renowned artists as Rodin, Toulouse-Lautrec and Mallarmé, among others. Yet, despite the importance of her artistic legacy, Fuller's theatrical work fits uneasily within the dominant narratives of early modern dance. Most historians don't see Fuller in light of the development of expressive movement, but rather relegate her to discussions concerning dance and lighting, or dance and technology.

I had been thinking about writing a book on Loie Fuller for some time, but it took me a while to come to terms with how I wanted to respond to the less visible traces of her work (Albright 2007). My project began with a question: why do so many critics and historians dismiss the bodily experience of her dancing in their discussions of Loie Fuller's theatrical work? The question grew into a dance. The dance, in turn, taught me how to write history from inside the vibrations of its ongoing motion. This essay carries the story of an intellectual approach to the past that not only recognizes the corporeal effects of the historian's vantage point, but also mobilizes her body within the process of research and writing. It is the story of a dance shared across a century of time and two continents, a dance that takes place at the meeting point of physical empathy and historical difference.

I am engaged in writing on Loie Fuller. I use this term 'engaged' very consciously, for I want to highlight both the sense of binding oneself to another person and its etymological meaning as 'interlocking', a literal as well as a figurative meshing with someone or something. I have chosen to work on this project in a way that integrates conceptual and somatic knowledges, connecting to my physical as well as my intellectual and analytic facilities. Dancing amidst clouds of fabric in elaborate lighting effects, I try to understand something of Fuller's experience from the inside out. I also dance with words, moving with my writing to see how ideas resonate in my body. Then too, as I weave my way through archival materials and historical accounts of cultural milieus, I practice staying attentive to what I have learned through that dancing experience. This research process challenges traditional separations between academic scholarship and artistic creation, between criticism and autobiography – in short between dancing and writing. More than just another layer of historical excavation, my dancing creates a strand of physical thinking which weaves back and forth between the presence of historical artefacts (posters, reviews, photos, memoirs and paintings) and the absence of Fuller's physical motion.

This essay is an attempt to articulate the theoretical implications of my embodied approach to this study – an attempt to understand the very conditions of its possibilities. In what follows, I identify two strategies – two practices, if you will – that guide my scholarship on Loie Fuller. While one is primarily intellectual and the other is based in physical study, both practices refuse the conventional separation of scholarship and the studio, folding themselves into a mix of dancing and writing that houses a certain physical receptiveness at its core. These strands of embodied study create a textured fabric in which aspects of Fuller's work are made visible through my body as well as my writing.

> In all writing, a body is traced, is the tracing and the trace – is the letter, yet never the letter, a literality or rather a lettericity that is no longer legible. A body is what cannot be read in a writing. (Or one has to understand reading as something other than deci-pherment.) Rather, as touching, as being touched. Writing, reading: matters of tact.
>
> (Nancy 1994: 24)

Despite its linguistic unwieldiness (an effect, no doubt, of the difficulties of translation), this quotation from Jean-Luc Nancy's 'Corpus' signals what is for me a profound difference from more traditional approaches to histor-ical work. Moving from traces to tracing incorporates the tactile, and thereby refuses the traditional separation of object from subject. Reaching across time and space to touch Fuller's dancing means that I allow myself, in turn, to be touched, for it is impossible to touch anything in a way that does not also implicate one's own body. (Ask any kid who has just been burnt.) Touching, then, becomes the space of our interaction, a mutual engagement. As I touch Loie Fuller through my historical research, both textual and physical, I am touched in return.

This metaphysical conundrum (How is one touched by history?) has, in my case, a very physical complement. Much of my dance experience over the past two decades has been generated by Contact Improvisation. In Contact, the actual point of contact (defined, most usually, in terms of physical touching, although it can be rhythmic, visual or kinaesthetic) cre-ates an improvisational space in which assumptions as to what the dance will be like (future tense) are eschewed in favour of a curiosity about what is happening now (present tense). The meeting point of Contact creates an interconnectedness of weight, momentum and energy that channels a common physical destiny. The partnering in Contact is not simply an addition of one movement to another, but rather a realization that both movements will change in the midst of the improvisational duet. In addi-tion to learning how to meet others in a dance, Contact dancers train in extreme spatial disorientation. Releasing the uprightness of the body and learning how to be comfortable upside down, rolling and spiralling in and out of the floor, falling without fear – these are all aspects of a training that redirects visual orientation into a kinaesthetic grounding.

In a variety of ways, I think of the physical aspects of my research on Fuller in terms of a Contact duet. My body is influenced by her dancing as I imagine how she must have used her spine, her head, her chest. Suddenly, historical descriptions of Fuller laid up in bed with excruciating pain and ice packs on her upper back make sense to me. Spinning with my arms raised high and my head thrown back, I realize that Fuller must have slipped a disc in her cervical spine. These kinds of biographical details become intelligible as I literally incorporate some aspects of the physical tolls her nightly performances must have incurred. Even on an intellectual or metaphysical level, I think of our interaction as a contact duet, a somatic meeting set up by the traces of history. I believe that envisioning this relation in terms of an improvisational duet usefully redefines the traditional separation of a historical subject (treated as the 'object' of study) and the omniscient writer of history. When, for instance, I review the enormous variety of images of 'La Loie' – the posters, photographs, paintings, prints and programme covers – I try not only to analyse the visual representation of her work, but also to imagine the kind of dancing that inspired such visions. That is to say that I allow myself to be touched (these 'matters of tact') by what remains only partially visible.

Loie Fuller's work embodies a central paradox of dance as a representation of both abstract movement and a physical body. Her dancing epitomizes the intriguing insubstantiality of movement caught in the process of tracing itself. Surrounded by a funnel of swirling fabric spiralling upwards into the space around her and bathed in coloured lights of her own invention, Fuller's body seems to evaporate in the midst of her spectacle. Nonetheless, Fuller's body is undeniably present, and discussions of her sartorial style and physical girth break through these romantic representations of her ethereality and femininity in interesting ways. Splayed across history and geography, Fuller's dancing takes place at the crossroads of diverse languages, two centuries and many cultural changes.

Intellectually, the material is fascinating. But there is something even more compelling for me in this subject. It's a gut thing. I find that many scholars cover over the kinaesthetic and material experience of her body in favour of the image, rather than reading that image as an extension of her dancing. Descriptions of her work get so entangled with artistic images or poetic renderings that historians easily forget the physical labour involved. Then too, there are all those apologies and side notes about how Loie Fuller didn't have a dancer's body, or any dance training really, as if the movement images were solely dependent on the lighting, as if it were all technologically rendered. (One typical example: 'The influence of Loie Fuller upon the theatre will always be felt, particularly in the lighting of the scene and in the disposition of draperies. *But she was never a great dancer. She was an apparition*' [emphasis added] Flitch 1913: 88). There is an odd urgency in my responses to these commentaries, my whole body revolts with the kinaesthetic knowledge that something else was going on. *My body tells me this.*

Ten years ago, I made a dance called *Traces of Light*. It was the first time I incorporated light as a source of movement and stillness within choreography. The first time I experienced what it was like to dance in, with, through and next to light. The following year, I traced another dance which used light as a partner for movement. I recreated Loie Fuller's *Le Lys* dance (1895), or, at least, something approximating it. It was part of an evening-length choreography and although we meticulously reconstructed Fuller's patented design for costume and curved wands, I didn't think about this dance as a historical reconstruction, but rather as more of an interesting effect plundered from the abundant resources of early modern dance. Because of budget constraints, we used parachute material, not silk. Purple not white.

I remember the first time I danced in her costume. It felt odd to be cloaked in yards of fabric, me, so used to dancing in pants and a top, with nothing in my way, every movement and each direction easily accessible. Within her costume, I have to prepare each step in order not to trip on the extra fabric. Twisting to one side, and then to the other, I gather my strength and then launch the spiral, catching the air underneath the fabric and opening my arms and reaching towards the sky. Two minutes later, I collapse, exhausted and dizzy. I am awed by the upper body strength and aerobic stamina Fuller must have had to keep the fabric aloft and swirling for upwards to 45 minutes a night. How odd that some historians insist that she wasn't a dancer. Was it that she didn't look like a dancer? That she didn't act the way they thought a dancer should? Clearly she had a trained body and specific movement techniques in her body. In order to make a mere 12-minute solo with much less fabric than she used, I had to train my upper body intensively for several months. *In motion, my body talks back to historical representation and teaches me to look again, to read beyond the visual evidence and into its source.* Ironically, then, where others savoured the image of her disappearance (into the dark, into the folds of cloth, into the ideal symbol), I have come to appreciate the dynamic of her vital presence, those moments of becoming, and becoming again.

In the ensuing decade, I would return to the costume and her dancing each time I taught early twentieth-century dance history. Taking history from the classroom to the studio, my students would try on Fuller's costume. But nothing happens until you begin to move and spin. Some students would get caught up in Fuller's whirl, the mystique of her dancing. Their enthusiasm inspired me. Eventually, I became aware of a need to write on Fuller. Part physical, part intellectual, this desire was fuelled by the intriguing complexities of a cultural moment in which a short, stocky lesbian from Chicago arrives in Paris to inspire a famous poet's evocation of the dancer as at once feminized and yet also decorporealized into a vision of pure movement.

I began to conceive of this twisted relationship between dance and image, as a möbius strip, one in which the interconnectedness of figure and body would never entirely line up, but always exist just across the fold.

What is so fascinating for me about dance as a historical phenomenon is the many different kinds of layers and information we need to excavate in order to understand that kinetic and artistic experience. What constitutes the dance as staged in Western theatres? Is it the movement? ... the dancers embodying the movement? ... the narrative plot or libretto? ... the entire theatrical apparatus including sets, costumes, music, choreographer, technicians, and company managers? ... the social and cultural context in which it was created? ... all of the above? In other words, what do we need in order to know the dancer and the dance?

In the introduction to their collection of essays, *Acting on the Past*, Mark Franko and Annette Richards describe this process of culling many different kinds of historical sources when they write:

> Absent performative events have conceptual, imaginary, and evidential, as well as actively reproductive bases. They are especially characterized by movement between present and past, one in which archive and act, fragment and body, text and sounding, subject and practice, work in provocative interaction'
>
> (Franko and Richards 2000: 1)

I see my work as taking place in the midst of this 'provocative interaction' – right at the imaginative intersection of the past and the present. I visualize this (double) crossing spatially, marked in the centre of a vast, cavernous space – much like the old wooden dance studio where I teach and work. At one end is the stage of the Folies Bergère. My view is from backstage, with all the workings of its magical effects revealed. Programmes, posters and images of Loie Fuller, as well as pages from her autobiography and countless other articles about her, dot the floor, creating a historical landscape and defining various pathways through the space. Improvising my way through these artefacts, I come to the opposite end where I also envision a backstage. This time, however, it is backstage of the theatre where I work. There is a new Plexiglas floor in the middle, underneath which we will project lights in multiple colours, reinventing Fuller's lighting designs within a contemporary context. It is the motion between these two backstage spaces (one in the past, one in the present) as well as the dancing pathways I construct from source to source that inform my research methodology.

As a major attraction in Paris at the end of the nineteenth century, Fuller left her mark on the imaginations of many poets and artists of her time. My scholar's cubicle in the library is filled with images of Fuller's dancing: posters, sculptures, photographs, articles about her. How do I respond to these traces? Looking at the reproductions, reading texts, I am fascinated – and moved. What would happen if I took these images, these ideas, into the studio? *I grab my notebook and sprint out of the library.* Inspired to move as well as to write, I take the plunge back into the physical, using my body both as a point of departure and as a moving vehicle, a method of transportation into history.

In an early essay entitled 'Rereading as a woman: the body in practice', feminist scholar Nancy Miller discusses the ways in which readings of literary texts are very much affected by the cultural experience of the reader. She writes: 'To reread as a woman is at least to imagine the lady's place; to imagine while reading the place of a woman's body; to read reminded that her identity is also re-membered in stories of the body' (Miller 1995: 47). My studies in feminist theory, inspired by the work of scholars such as Nancy Miller, have taught me to be aware of how I produce a double reading – as a scholar, as a woman. These days, I am challenging myself to push the implications of Miller's essay even further, that is to say, to read (and, by extension, to write) as a dancer, allowing my body to be present even in the midst of a scholarly project.

Because I have decided to posit my dancing body as a research tool or guide (perhaps assistant is a more apt expression, for my body certainly has a mind of its own and it doesn't always follow my instructions), I feel compelled to grapple with the relationship of my body to history. In the dance field, there often seems to be a split between researchers who focus primarily on reconstructing a dance from the past on bodies from the present, and those scholars who use dance as the hook into a broader cultural study of modes of production, representation and reception of artistic endeavours. Now, of course, we all might quickly assert that we do both, but it is rare that I read an essay in which I feel that the writer's bodily knowledge was a crucial part of the scholarly process. Indeed, although *theoretically* we might be interested and excited by the possibilities of a dialogue between the dancing body of the researcher and that of the subject they are researching, we are rarely willing to confront that methodologically murky territory for ourselves. With this work on Loie Fuller, I am asking what it would mean to research a historical body; a dancing body; a desiring body precisely through the intertext of an 'other' body – my own. How can I use my embodied knowledge to move beyond the traces of artistic and literary representations of Fuller's dancing into the physicality at their core?

Over the past several years, I have developed a series of solo performances inspired by my work on Loie Fuller. These dances take place at the intersection of historical research and choreographic expression. Although they delineate a movement vocabulary that references Fuller's work, these choreographies are not reconstructions of her works. Spinning, spirals circling out of the upper body, and large expansive gestures of the arms with an upward gaze of the face, these motifs constitute much of the dancing. My first solo, 'Searching for Loie', was a structured improvisation which used my earliest writings on Fuller as a sound score. Playing with the juxtaposition of poetic and expository prose, the read text created an open field (semi-serious, semi-playful) in which to explore my physical response to Fuller's historical legacy. Later, the dance morphed into a performative lecture entitled 'Acts of passion: tracing history through the body'. In this more recent incarnation, I interrupt an academic discussion with dancing that pairs my movement with slide images of Fuller's dancing. Moving back and forth across the stage, my body interrupts the projections, flashing my shadow onto the screen. In these moments, Fuller's image is joined by my image, creating a complex duet involving interpretation, interconnection and reflection. Bringing myself into the dancing in this manner forces me to reflect on my own intellectual position and physical experience, as I ask myself, 'So what does this embodied experience tell me about history?' My answers to this question encompass both specific details as to her movement, staging and lighting techniques, as well as a more general sense of her performance energy and the role light played within Fuller's own personal cosmology.

Loie Fuller thought of her theatre spaces as laboratories in which to combine lights and movement in increasingly sophisticated ways. Fortunately, I have a wonderful collaborator and lighting designer in my colleague Jen Groseth, who also became quite interested in Loie Fuller's work and legacy. We were able, over the course of one year, to spend a significant amount of time experimenting with lighting in the theatre. Our university situation gave us the luxury of time to create the lights and movement both simultaneously and interactively. Although we were not attempting to reconstruct her dances per se, we did use Fuller's original design patents and depictions of her staging (with live lighting technicians above, below and to the sides of her specially raised platform) to inform our updated use of her lighting inventions. For instance, we created a floor out of Plexiglas, with intelligent lights revolving above and below its surface. The result was a twelve minute performance entitled 'Dancing with Light'.

Collaborating with a lighting designer for days on end brought me closer, I believe, to the reality of Fuller's working environment. Not only did I begin to understand the physical labour involved, I understood why she is always pictured wearing shoes (the stage floors of variety theatres being notoriously dirty and riddled with nails and bits of this and that). I also realized that the reason she never mentions using haze to intensify the rays of light (an effect every critic comments on) was because the theatres were already so dusty and smoky, one didn't need any additional stuff in the air. It seems so simple and obvious, but the physical experience of making a dance in the middle of a busy theatre jerked me out of the modern dance paradigm of solo artist working alone in the studio, waiting for inspiration, and brought me headlong into the gritty realities of popular theatre. While it is true that at the beginning of her career, Loie Fuller was mostly known as a soloist, she never performed anything without the committed assistance of a whole crew of technicians. Both an artist and a craftsperson in the theatre, she transcended a deep and still omnipresent division between artists and technicians, directors and staging hands, dancers and electricians.

One of the most important aspects of 'Dancing with Light,' for me, was a new appreciation of the experience of moving in strongly defined lights. In contrast to lighting which has the sole purpose of illuminating the dancers, the lighting we created was an equal partner in the dance. Sometimes the light obscured me, sometimes it revealed my dancing, and sometimes I was simply a screen onto which a variety of moving lights were projected. At various times, I felt sheltered and enclosed, inspired, at times even dis-oriented (especially when dancing on clear glass with lights shining from underneath). The palpable presence of these lights reminded me of otherworldly spirits.

Returning to my study, I began to understand more concretely the spiri-tual role that light played for Loie Fuller. I believe that Fuller experienced a certain kind of euphoria when dancing that was intensified by her dramatic approach to lighting. Her dances generally followed a classic creation nar-rative. They began in a total blackout (which was highly unusual for that time), with the first strands of music calling forth a dim illumination of the small motions of her hands and fabric. The lights, movements and music would generally crescendo into a final frenzy of colour and motion which faded abruptly back into a primordial darkness. The idea that light had spiritual overtones for Fuller is confirmed by her own writing – both her published autobiography and unpublished letters and fragments of a book she was writing later in her life. While I don't always know what to make of this visionary aspect of Fuller's work and life, I do know that I would never have understood its significance without having danced in a light so defined I could pierce it with my body.

In her essay 'The concept of intertextuality and its application in dance research', Janet Adshead-Lansdale identifies the imaginative possibilities of an approach to dance research that resonates with my own. She writes:

> These methodological shifts of position are sometimes in harmony and often not, but they can be tolerated and made to function by seeing that it is in the spaces created between a multiplicity of texts and traces [that] there is the opportunity, indeed, more strongly, the demand, that each reader should engage in this process of constructing meaning by unravelling what seems to be implied by

the work, or the method, or the discipline, while simultaneously creating their own threads from their own experience

(Adshead-Lansdale 1999b: 111)

This layering of texts forms a web of signifying practices that merge and emerge depending upon the historical or methodological lens one chooses to use. Yet these intertexts can also produce a misleading sense that we have captured the thing itself – the *presence* of a dancing body.

I want to introduce the concept of intertextuality, not in order to add simply another historical layer or methodological option, but rather to point out the space between these texts. While this space may figure as an *absence*, it is not necessarily a loss. Rather, I see it as a distance (both historical and cultural) across which desire always pulls interpretation. At once opportunity and demand (which I sometimes experience as an internal command, an urgency that compels action or speaks to a particular direction of thought), this intertextuality marks the space of improvisation possible within historical work. It recognizes the gap between myself and the subject of my inquiry – that historical distance – while simultaneously foregrounding the desire to close that gap, to build bridges and cross over from one period to another. Not every subject would necessarily elicit such mobile strategies. But given the elusive quality of Fuller's work and reception in combination with the unpredictable edge of my physical commitment to exploring her dances, this methodological fluidity seems right at the moment.

Writing a scholarly book on Loie Fuller while making a series of dances incorporating aspects of her oeuvre opens up an intertextual space which can become the site of a negotiation between past and present bodies, between history and desire. More than a post-structuralist ploy (one in which movement is simply a slippery strategy of evasive criticism), however, this approach presses beyond the seams of traditional historical inquiry. Researching with my own body brings me face to face (body to body) with my own physical predilections, intellectual interests, artistic agendas and writing desires. Using my kinaesthetic imagination to embody images of Fuller has fuelled much of my scholarly work and helps me to understand aspects of her dancing (its own vibrant expressivity) that are often overlooked. This process has also given me one of the most satisfying experiences of reading, dancing and writing that I have had to date in my academic career.

Tracing the past – the past in light of the present. Present tense, the tension produced by the conjunction of movement and time – the subjunctive mode – the connection of her and me. She. Aware of my desire to read history through choreography, to write with my body, I trace another's dancing with my own.

11

CABBAGES AND KINGS

Disability, dance and some timely considerations

Adam Benjamin

Across the world, there seems to be remorseless pressure to operate on an ever larger, impersonal scale.

(Prince Charles 2008: 21)

When I first began teaching with Celeste Dandeker in 1990, 'Disabled time' was a phrase we used to explain why it took so long to get half a dozen people in wheelchairs, a couple of blind and other assorted dancers into a workshop, or out of a workshop for a coffee (and back), or to look round a theatre with no ramps, or for that matter, to make a costume change. We inhabited a world that went at a slower pace; no less valid, no less attuned, but a world in which the obstacles to contributing, let alone competing, in the mainstream of British dance seemed daunting. Celeste and I founded CandoCo Dance Company in 1991, and our subtext in many ways was to get up to speed with contemporary dance. We fought against marginalization, against the practice of placing companies associated with disability at the end of the programme, rather than alongside others performing in the same festival, against the notion that our work should be any less compelling, less demanding, less artistic than any other dance company. It would have been impossible at that time to imagine that the list of choreographers to have worked with disabled performers would come to include those such as Javier de Frutos, Emilyn Claid, Fin Walker, Nigel Charnock, Stephen Petronio Siobhan Davies, Filip Van Huffel and Hofesh Shechter (to name but a few). It is unlikely, before 1980, that any of these choreographers would have considered making this kind of work.

The question of whether disabled people could earn a living through dance (a question repeatedly posed during the early 1990s) has been effectively answered through the long-term presence and success of CandoCo and companies such as StopGap, Axis, Blue Eyed Soul, Remix, DIN A 13, Joint Forces, Dancing Wheels and l'Oiseau Mouche. The careers of Celeste Dandeker, David Toole, Chris Pavia, Laura Jones, Bill Channon, Marc Brew, Chisato Minamimura, Clare Cunningham and Caroline Bowditch represent a generation of disabled dance artists who have made an impact on dance in the UK. This marks a radical departure from the 1980s when disabled dancers had virtually no profile in Europe, and when Emery Blackwell and Bruce Curtis were only just beginning to be noticed in the USA. At the time of writing there is evidence of a 'next phase' in which disabled artists, previously confined to these professional inclusive companies, have begun to migrate to projects and performances with other professional companies and dancers: David Toole and James Cunningham to DV8, Caroline Bowditch to The FATHoM Project and then with Dan Daws, Cornelia Kip Lee and Michael King to Scottish Dance Theatre, Welly O'Brien to work with Victoria Fox, and so on. The divide between professional dance and disability becomes ever more porous. This is significant in a number of ways: it reflects an acceptance of the professionalism and skills of disabled performers; a newfound mobility of disabled people within the arts and a departure from early disability dance projects of the 1970s, which were often located within or attached to institutions 'for the disabled'. Lastly, it reflects a gradual shift in society at large; each time a disabled person engages in a new project within the mainstream there must be an examination of the accessibility of the physical environment in which that project takes place, and a change in attitudes amongst artists and organizations with whom they work. Arguably dance has never had such an immediate dialogue with public attitudes, architecture and social policy as when it embraced disability.

The advent of the disabled dancer represented a two-pronged assault, first on the construct of dance and the type of performer audiences might expect to see, and second on the construction of dance theatres themselves: the elevation and accessibility of the stage, access to auditoriums, access to changing rooms. Ramps were built, corridors widened, doors removed. As dance practitioners we were forced to reconsider our physical workplace and our aesthetic and ethical values. The result was a theatre more permeable, more flexible, more connected to humanity; more a place of exchange and learning. Today inclusive companies (the word 'inclusive' has replaced 'integrated') and disabled artists permeate the British dance scene, but perhaps we still struggle to recognize the journey, its significance or the lessons learned along the way.

A time to dance

In CandoCo we have had a policy of creating our own work, as well as inviting in choreographers we admired to work with the dancers, ensuring a rich melting pot of ideas and a fertile exchange of experiences. Works like Emilyn Claid's *Back to Front with Side Shows* (1993) and Guilherme Botelho's *Trades and Trusts* (1996) not only exposed audiences to a new experience of disabled people as dancers but also, just as importantly, to an experience of disabled dancers as people, replete with the same aspirations, urges and neuroses as the rest of us. By 1997 Judith Mackrell, in the *Guardian*, was able to write: 'CandoCo reinvented the boundaries of dance by proving that virtuosity wasn't confined to the able bodied'. Three years later saw the publication of the *Oxford Dictionary of Dance* which was described in its preface as:

> A new reference book for the twenty-first century, its scope designed to reflect an art-form that has never been more diverse. The boundaries of dance are constantly being redrawn.
>
> (Mackrell and Craine 2004: v)

Mackrell was joint editor of the dictionary. Arriving on the bookshelves almost a decade after the birth of CandoCo, and nearly twenty years after that of Amici in the UK, Dancing Wheels and Joint Forces in the USA and l'Oiseau Mouche in France, no mention was made in the dictionary of integrated or inclusive dance, or of disability and dance at all. Perhaps the boundaries Mackrell referred to had still to be given cartographic significance. Perhaps it was the caution of editors reluctant to write anything into dance history before it had proven itself. Perhaps, at some deeper level, it was a continuation of the idea that disability and dance constituted a diversion from 'the real thing'. Whatever the reason, it was clear that academic and literary acceptance of dance and disability was slow to emerge and had yet to be given their proper weighting; it could, of course, be argued that dance itself still lacks that recognition. The urge to research and read about dance represents a continued unearthing of the art form, in which disability and the ideas associated with it play an unlikely, but to my mind, central role.

An idea whose time had come

CandoCo was an adventure into the unknown, at the time both ground breaking and naively ambitious. We dreamed not only of changing attitudes toward disability through dance, but also of changing dance and dance education itself. In 1995 I wrote:

> Although it is possible for non-disabled students to study how to teach, help, and care for people with disabilities through the medium of dance, there have, as of yet, been no opportunities for disabled and non-disabled students to study and train together. It is little wonder therefore that teachers graduating from such courses continue (albeit unintentionally) to reinforce attitudes of inequality, or that people with disabilities should, after their first dance session and the inevitable encounter with bean bags, parachute and

squeezy foam balls, beat a dignified yet hasty retreat for the nearest door and become Olympic athletes.

(Benjamin 1995)

With the dearth of real opportunities in the 1980s, and the continuing perception that dance therapy was the only option for disabled people interested in moving their bodies, competitive sport and the Paralympic movement seemed to offer the only 'grown up' alternative. In the 1990s a new engagement between high-profile, mainstream choreographers and integrated companies was established, bridging what had been, until then, two virtually separate worlds. The sheer volume of CandoCo's output in the remainder of the decade and the range of choreographers with whom they worked, ensured that there was an ever-growing repertoire against which each new work could be compared. The result was a more rigorous criticism; the gloves were off (or perhaps, more aptly, the cotton wool had been removed) and integrated dance finally achieved an equality of critical appraisal that matched that of any work on the professional stage. As the work attracted the press and gained a wider audience, so the numbers of disabled people watching, attending workshops and eventually performing increased dramatically. Just as disabled athletes had transformed perceptions of what being disabled meant for physical accomplishment, so disabled dancers began to address perceptions of beauty and, as Mackrell noted, virtuosity. It became evident that physical difference was no obstacle to artistry in dance. Far from reducing or restricting the art form, disability brought an unexpected burst of creativity and a reappraisal of what a contemporary, body-centred art form had to offer.

One of the first inclusive performances at The Place was by the aptly named Common Ground, a dance company of deaf and hearing performers (London, 1986). The idea of a common ground for dance was to resonate throughout the coming decades as more venue managers/programmers awoke to their attitudinal assumptions and the architectural shortcomings of their buildings, an issue made in pointed fashion by the *Stare Cases Project* (1999). This was a promenade piece I directed with Danny Scheinmann which saw Tom Saint-Louis bedecked in tutu improbably descending the stair railings of London's Royal Festival Hall in his wheelchair.

Although figures are not readily available, there is overwhelming empirical evidence that theatres such as the Queen Elizabeth Hall and The Place (now the Robin Howard Theatre) have seen an upsurge not just in the numbers of disabled people performing, but also in the numbers of disabled people coming to watch dance of all descriptions, both dance which includes and dance which 'omits' or 'excludes' disabled performers. 'Omit' and 'exclude': I use these two words to highlight a difference and to explore some important definitions relating to dance and disability. There are plenty of dance and physical theatre companies that could quite easily employ disabled performers. The ethos and working methodology of these companies would not have to undergo any great changes; that they have not yet done so could be considered, for the time being at least, an omission. In contrast, there are other companies whose criteria and physical requirements (to fulfil particular activities) continue to exclude disabled performers. Here, for example, we might place most ballet companies and a good many contemporary dance companies, whose repertoire seems to rule out the introduction of bodies that do not fit the conventional, 'classical' mould. Nevertheless, it is not beyond the bounds of imagination to suppose that, at some point in the next decade or two, we might see a high-profile ballet company addressing this issue on its main stage. Certainly there are choreographers working with ballet companies today who could tackle such a challenge. In the meantime we are more likely to see the kind of multi-cast, multi-art productions by choreographers such as Lloyd Newson, Alain Platel, Maguy Marin and Bill T. Jones utilizing a range of performers who might include ballet dancers, disabled performers and others. When Newson employed a cast of disabled and non-disabled performers in DV8's production *Can We Afford This/The Cost of Living* (2000), wonderful use was made of David Toole, while a number of other less visibly disabled performers in the piece appeared to be noticeably under-used. Why were they cast for the show but marginalized in the performance? Work that includes disabled performers holds with it an imperative; it must offer a new reading of everyday stereotypes if it wishes to disturb preconceptions and overturn prejudice, if it wishes to 'deviate' from the norm. Although there is resistance to using the word 'integration' (because of its association with medical models of rehabilitation), its etymology refers to 'being in touch' and of not only playing an integral part in a larger picture, but of changing that picture. Thus as an aim, or methodology, it still has much to offer. Inclusion, in itself, is not always enough.

While the classical ballets are to be enjoyed in their own right, they also hold, embedded in their technique and modus operandi, reminders of a particular and socially conservative ideology. Ballet originates in the courtly dance of the royal families dating back to Louis XIV of France, a stylization of movement intended to distinguish those who owned the land from those who laboured upon it. It was the first step, or series of steps, that were to take the agri (field) out of 'culture' and begin dance's gradual disassociation from the 'common ground' to be placed instead at the service of kings and nations; its seasonal and social tenets increasingly replaced by political ones. The use of ballet to demonstrate mastery of (and over) the human form demanded ever more agile and eventually, ever more trained dancers, while mastery over the elements of space and light required ever more controlled environments. Within an increasingly technical theatre the choreographer came to mimic the regent as a singular directorial power exerting control over infinitely pliable, uniform and *replaceable* dancers/individuals.

In 2008 the world was treated to one of the most extraordinary commissions of recent times. The miraculous choreography of the opening ceremony of the Beijing Olympics was an opportunity for China to pronounce its own cultural message to the world: endless ingenuity, outstanding artistry and enormous, overwhelming political will. It was a performance that was breathtaking in scale and execution and, if it was possible to read between the lines of immaculately synchronized performers, troubling in its message of uniformity and social control.

Of the thousands of Chinese performers in those awe-inspiring performances (directed by Zhang Yimou, with choreography by Shen Wei) none were visibly disabled (though some were deaf). When a report from the BBC (Michael Bristow BBC News 12 August 2008) revealed that the beautiful little girl singing 'Ode to the Motherland' was miming to the voice of another child considered 'insufficiently beautiful' to represent her country, more than a few eyebrows were raised in the UK; not that the West is inured from its own attraction to image over substance, something we have gladly embraced since The Monkees were produced and marketed to adoring teenagers in the 1960s. More worryingly, from a Western perspective, was that there was no mention of the award winning ballerina Lin Yau who was due to perform the only solo in the ceremony, but who was paralysed in a fall 12 days before the performance, when a piece of apparatus malfunctioned. It was an utter failure on the part of the Chinese, who managed so many aspects of that extraordinary Olympic theatre with such aplomb, to have misread the likely international response. Had the news been acknowledged and shared, rather than hushed up, there might have been far greater rapport and empathy between nations, and an opening to real dialogue about such artistic endeavour and risk not to mention the acceptance and role of disabled people in society.

Accidents can fracture lives, they can fracture everyday perceptions of the world, but they can open us to new experiences and ideas about how the world is construed both physically and temporally. The evolution of dance in the UK and its embracing of difference reflects this ability to uphold new and possibly fragile realities that we might ordinarily pass over. Aargh!! Isn't that what we were struggling to avoid, the association of disability with frailty? Well, yes and no.

In the 1980s dance and disability inhabited a similar territory to the organic movement: something rather strange, carried out by an eccentric few and with no great relevance to the rest of society or bearing on the world at large. Today the organic movement lies at the centre of the debate on sustainable food resources. Although it has grown rapidly, it continues to advocate the notions of interconnectedness and scale that are central to its beliefs and practice. Of all the unexpected and idiosyncratic turns that dance has made in the past thirty years, the embracing of physical difference is arguably the most significant. To pursue the 'organic' analogy a little further, the wedding of dance and disability resonates with a view of the world that recognizes the importance of (bio)diversity over uniformity, and insists on the interconnectedness of things, even when these connections may not be immediately evident. The value it places on the individual and on differing notions of time and action is written (literally and metaphorically) into its DNA, for the work is inevitably made with individuals who are unique and irreplaceable. Work made with Christian Panouillot will not fit Welly O'Brien; work made for O'Brien will not transfer to a dancer like Kaz Langley. There is a value here placed on those who do not fit into categories. The contribution of the individual is significant, and this binds dancers and audiences into a very particular relationship with each other. This is as close as dance has come to an ecological statement of intent. As the organic movement provides an alternative to a world increasingly reliant on manufactured beauty, cosmetic surgery and genetic manipulation, so integrated dance offers an alternative movement that accepts human beings as they are, as different, difficult, diverse and obstinately, intimately connected to place. It is this principle that underpins the theatre of WILDWORKS, that engages local people, local landscapes, even local food, within its performances; or the film *Bruit Blanc* (1998), choreographed by Mathilde Monnier and autistic dancer Marie-France Canaguier which captures the place and time of a dance in its 'once only' uniqueness.

When CandoCo took part in the 2008 Olympic ceremony it was a very public acknowledgment, national and international, of how highly disabled people in dance, and in society, are valued. The performance, which included dancers from the Royal Ballet, hip-hop dancers from ZooNation, a bus and David Beckham, said a great deal about British diversity, while managing to say nothing at all about British art. To have made some kind of artistic/cultural statement in the face of the staggering scale of China's presentation was always going to be a challenge, but one that could only have been realistically addressed with adequate artistic resources and adequate time were it to have avoided falling into the oldest of clichés. The experiences of recent decades of integrated dance in the UK make British dance audiences as discerning of the choreographic frame, and the individual performances of inclusive dance, as we would be of the performance of any other professional work. We are capable of detecting an underused or 'token' performer, and, perhaps more important, we are able to comment on it in a way that wasn't possible in the 1970s, when the mere presence of a disabled person on stage was so much of an innovation as to mute critical thought. While the dancing at the handover ceremony from the present to the future Olympic host nation represented the multiplicity of British society, few British dance artists could have revelled in the performance itself. None of the dancers seemed able to make the kind of statement that could reflect the riches of the previous thirty years of dance in the UK, though, to be fair to the artists involved, there can be few greater choreographic handicaps than having to dance with a bus.

That disabled people are on the professional stage and are no longer a side show is part of a natural and welcome progression that can be traced back to and beyond the democratization of the dance space (Cunningham), the exploration of pedestrian or found movement (Rainer), the acceptance of gravity, and of the dances for ordinary bodies in ordinary spaces (Paxton/ Nelson). This paring down of dance to simple and 'honest' movement principles (notably by the Judson Church Group) was in part a response to the large-scale deceptions of the Nixon era in American politics of the 1960s. These unadorned dances acknowledged gravity, reinstated the role of the ground and sought to embody open and democratic principles within the work, a position that was taken up and evolved by the X6 Dance Collective in the UK.

Had disabled people not succeeded in entering the world of dance then, in a sense, the promise of this earlier work would not have been fulfilled. The ideas being passed on and explored by all of these artists centred round the liberation of the dancing body from either choreographic or technical constraint; the principles that underpinned this work were those of freedom of movement which, as it turned out, were the same principles that were being fought for by disabled people through their demands for access and equal opportunities in the wider world. In a sense the former group were fighting their way out of the theatre while the latter were fighting their way in.

Parallel bars

As disabled performers reach new heights of physical accomplishment, and as the choreographic demands and responses to those demands rise, a new category of disabled dancer has emerged. These dancers, for the most part, are capable of learning and interpreting the traditional dance lexicon, albeit on wheels or crutches. That early discovery, and the new language that emerged is now taken for granted. What we see today is a constant sharpening and refining of that language. The complexities, however, in Petronio's *Human Suite* are known complexities, the language recognizably Petronio's, albeit modified to meet the exigencies of different bodies and chairs. This in no way detracts from the accomplishment of either choreographer or dancers, but a close look at the type of disabled dancer in these works reveals an ever more conservative and categorized body. While CandoCo champions the idea of difference, it also reflects a preference for a very able, 'dancerly' body, be it in a wheelchair, on crutches or on two legs. CandoCo has shaped itself as a contemporary dance company at the top end of the very competitive dance industry, and finds itself using similar (though less formalized) categorizations to those used in sports to establish a parity of abilities across the company and ensure that performers can meet the rigorous demands of its touring schedules. It has effectively placed its disabled dance artist alongside the modern day Paralympian in physical accomplishment and hierarchy. Disabled time has effectively been done away with, as has the body that obstinately demands a slower pace.

CandoCo's intricately woven *Journey* (Fin Walker 2005) or *Human Suite* (Stephen Petronio 2004) are as complex and demanding as anything we might see on the professional stage; disabled and non-disabled performers pushed to their limits by outstanding choreographers. Emerging from these performances impressed by the professionalism and artistry, I search my senses for some missing element, like some illusive taste, disappointingly absent from a favourite dish. Perhaps it's that an interpretation of dance that once reached out into the world, that caused barriers to be knocked down, ramps to be built and new doorways to be created, now, through its own success, locates itself behind a less visible but equally problematic barrier to accessibility, one shared by a great many companies performing in theatres around the world: the fourth wall.

Thinking outside the (black) box

2004 saw the publication of the second edition of *The Oxford Dictionary of Dance*. Although new headings of 'sport' and 'shoes' were added, 'disability' remained conspicuous in its absence. In 1990 this might have been something we would have been rather proud of, believing at the time that there was no need to mention 'disability' to describe what we were doing, and that a disabled person being part of a dance company should not merit any particular mention. At that time I wrote that we only needed to use the word 'integrated' to describe what we did because we lived in a society that was in so many ways 'dis' integrated (Benjamin 1993: 46). The picture has altered beyond recognition: disabled artists are now embedded within the UK dance scene. That it was not always thus, indeed that it was not so even twenty years ago, needs to be marked. It is a revolution in the portrayal of dance, and an evolution in the art of dancing as radical as the rejection of the pointe shoe by Isadora Duncan. This chapter is itself evidence of a new reading and a new readership as disabled students find their way into higher education to study, and the subject of inclusive dance becomes the focus of an increasing number of graduate and postgraduate essays/theses written by non-disabled students. Disabled performers have rightly striven for equality of opportunity and equality of provision in the performing arts, and I have been an ardent supporter, yet I wonder whether the arena that we have entered, like the Birds Nest in Beijing, holds all that we, or at least I, thought it might.

Wait a minute

Perhaps then, when we seek to secure the spirit of integrated practice we should not make the mistake of thinking that a conservative, or conservatoire, model of training will provide all that the early work promised. The training requirements of the new professional level disabled dancers need to be met, but I would argue that it needs to be a far less regimented, perhaps more chaotic environment where experimentation is valued as much as excellence, that the creation of new dance languages (movements that speak to us in new ways) will evolve, and where we might expect to see artists emerging who will continue to question and challenge rather than dance to whoever calls the tune. In the early days of CandoCo's education work, I came across a young community dance artist working for East London Dance. I remember him dancing with a community group of disabled youngsters, every one of his gangly, oddly coordinated movements serving the dancers around him, making wonderful sense of the chaotic assortment of bodies. By 2007 the young man, Wayne McGregor, had become Resident Choreographer at the Royal Opera House making radical new work for the Royal Ballet while maintaining an active involvement in East London community dance. This has no direct connection with disability but everything to do with integration: bringing together differing elements in unexpected ways to create new and utterly surprising outcomes. McGregor's non-classical, eclectic background draws out a new language from the Royal Ballet, and creates an opening for dialogue with the contemporary world. As the late Chris de Marigny personally observed on his first encounter with CandoCo, the most interesting developments seem to arise from the margins of the dance world. McGregor's career indicates that the margins are a different kind of boundary, less absolute, less easily defined and therefore more porous to new ideas. If Mackrell was correct and CandoCo reinvented a boundary it is perhaps worth considering whether it is the artist's role to reinvent boundaries or to dissolve them. Of course CandoCo set new standards for performance and has continued to raise the bar in terms of expectations and accomplishment, but it may be that the dissolution of boundaries rather than the creation of new ones lies closer to the heart of anything we might term integrated dance.

> 'The time has come,' the Walrus said,
> 'To talk of many things:
> Of shoes – and ships – and sealing-wax
> Of cabbages – and kings
> And why the sea is boiling hot
> And whether pigs have wings.'

> (Lewis Carroll 1984: 26)

We are only just beginning to recognize the intricately woven fabric of the world, the need to value its many different ecologies, and the kinds of footprint we might leave as signs of our dance upon it. Since the early

1900s dance has reshaped itself to meet new challenges. Modern Dance, Post-Modern Dance, Contemporary Dance, New Dance: the names tumble over each other, each succumbing to the inevitable progression of the very element they seek to outpace: time. Ever since we ceded the measure of our lives to choreographer kings and forgot the metre of a day and the phrasing of the seasons, the element of time has come to govern and define our uniquely human race.

If there is a challenge for dancer artists today perhaps it is to help reinstate that connection severed in the lordly attempt to dominate the world rather than partner it; a connection, not solely between people (something which we continue to champion through the Community Dance Movement), but between people and the places in which we live and work; between the body and the body politic, between culture and agriculture, between cabbages and kings. This entails a return to ecological concerns, to activity not only in but also beyond the theatre, to regard for a human scale and tempo rather than grandiose design and the relentless, Olympian urge to get ahead. It is only place (the longevity and patience of the ground) that can hope to bear witness to human activity and measure its importance and its long-term impact. It was with the ground that our dancing began, a seemingly unproductive activity (and certainly not an industry), a treading of ground away from the treadmill, its purpose rarely agreed on, but didn't we stumble upon it right at the off and then race on by? In this fast-paced, furious world, might dance not help us, if not to stop, then at least to slow down, or should that be 'disable' time?

12

HIPS, HIP-NOTISM, HIP(G)NOSIS

The *mulata* performances of Ninón Sevilla

Melissa Blanco Borelli

Subtle lighting envelopes tables and chairs ... cigarette smoke dances in the air. Glasses sound against one another. Glasses, filled with tequila or rum, and held by men's gnarled hands. Alcohol to assuage a wounded masculinity that hides beneath heavily invested performances of *machismo*. Suddenly, the sound of maracas, drums, pounding, pulsing ... a bright spotlight shines upon a curvaceous figure ... a woman. Not just any woman, but a *rumbera*, a woman dancing *rumba* ... or mambo, or cha-cha-cha – Cuban rhythms. Her hips, decorated with sequins, feathers or fringe, move to the incessant rhythm of the drums, hips swaying, pulsing, rotating and gyrating. Audience's eyes transfixed. Hip-notism.

What I have briefly described alludes to scenes found in many of the films from Mexican cinema's golden age, particularly the *cabaretera* or cabaret genre. During this time (1935–59), many Cuban *vedettes* were literally imported into Mexico in order to perform Afro-Cuban dances in elaborate musical numbers. Mexican film popularized the archetype of the *rumbera*, a sultry, seductive woman who enticed her audience with transgressive body movements, specifically her ever-revolving hips dancing *rumba*. The *rumba*, a highly eroticized and heterosexual dance, evokes a precoital mating game when danced with a partner. In contrast, these *rumberas* danced alone, moving their hips and enticing anyone and everyone to partner with them. The *rumba*, as a dance 'historically derived from associations with Cuba's black underclass, their lifestyles, attitudes and cultures', was somewhat sanitized by the *rumba*-dancing *mulata* characters made popular in Cuban theatrical stage productions of the late nineteenth/early twentieth centuries (Moore 1997: 169). The dance, still coded as dark and underclass, gained certain respectability performed by a lighter-skinned body, accentuating the erotic qualities of the *mulata* body, particularly her hips. The *rumba* was further eroticized when predominantly white Cuban bodies, such as Ninón Sevilla, exported and displayed it in Mexican film, extending its association not just with Cuban *mulatas*, but a feminized *cubanidad* based on ample, agile and entrancing hips.

It is from these bewitching hips that the idea of hip-notism, and the ensuing theory of hip(g)nosis arises. I set forth the theory of hip(g)nosis and the embodied reality of *corpo-mulata* in order to contest the idea of the *mulata* as a merely tragic figure of colonialism. These theories demonstrate how a body racialized as *mulata* choreographs identity through gestures, bodily articulations and socio-historically inscribed movement repertoires associated with this particular corporeality. By developing this sign/theory/ movement and the sentience 'corpo-mulata', my intention is to show the complexities that bodies add to history, as well as their impact on cultural production and notions of territoriality, nationalism and citizenship. Finally, by providing examples of these theories through a close reading of Ninón Sevilla's performances of the title character in *Mulata*, I provide a way to rethink the *mulata* as something other than 'tragic'.

Mulata depicts various stereotypes of the *mulata* figure: fatherless, poor, virtuosic dancer, sexualized yet infantilized, and tragic. Many other characters in the film are reminiscent of Cuban *teatro bufo*: a *gallego* man who lusts after the *mulata*, the *gallego*'s wife/counterpart who dislikes the *mulata*, a *mulato* suitor and a white suitor. Despite the limited and stereotypical qualities assigned to the *mulata* in the film, Ninón's Caridad (this particular name tying her to *la Virgen de la Caridad del Cobre*, the mixed-race patron saint of Cuba that is syncretized with the Santería goddess Ochún) offers a nuanced rendition of the tragic trope. Although Ninón's Caridad does die at the end, her death signifies a return to her matrilineal heritage, and the culmination of her life's journey to be in a 'place' where her colour and black inheritance do not matter. This *mulata* must leave the material world as it has no place for her. Her path to this 'transcendence' includes several hip-shaking moments where she asserts her material reality as a *corpo-mulata* using hip(g)nosis.

Although the film *Mulata* remains marred by the trope of the tragic, displaced, desired yet unloved *mulata*, it demonstrates how a *corpo-mulata* might utilize her interpellated status as a means for survival. The *mulata*'s demise caused by the excesses associated with the cabaret and her *mulata*-ness neatly package the widely circulated and known *mulata* trope throughout Spanish-speaking America (safely assuming that audiences in countries in Latin America other than Mexico and Cuba saw the film). Despite the notoriety and circulation of the trope, I am suggesting an almost counter-intuitive means of watching the film, the choreography, and Ninón's body through the theories of hip(g)nosis and the materialization of the *corpo-mulata*. As theories based on corporeal knowledge and rhetoric, they enable a body – in this case Caridad's fictional one, and Ninón's 'real' one – to contest the tragic narrative implicit in *mulata*-ness.

A fascination with the *mulata*'s shaking hip appears in literary scholar José Piedra's essay 'Hip Poetics'. In it, Piedra turns to the Cuban dance form of the *rumba* as a way to both read the body of and find a voice for the *rumbera*, the 'woman-of(f)-colour' dancing *rumba*. He notes that the 'Rumba provides a partial form of liberation and also a form of revenge that shakes and undresses the motives of those who watch to pay for the shaking and the undressing' (Piedra 1997: 107). He further elaborates:

> a *rumbera* is not simply a person who exists through her hips and her duties to men but also through her own mind and rights. The *rumba* hips, exaggerated, voyeuristic, exhibitionist, deified, and prostituted as they might appear to be, might also be a signifier of both acceptance of our bodies and defiance of foreign impositions, and even further: a substitute for the silenced or muffled voice, and not just for women or through women.
>
> (ibid.: 108)

Influenced by Piedra's postulations, I diverge from his examples of the hip as a source of liberation for women in that I don't read the hip as a static text. His analysis comes from textual examples of *rumbera* hips as canonized in Caribbean literature and poetry. In contrast, the hips that I refer to belong to corpo-realities constantly moving them. I am interested in the visceral, the corporeal, the flesh moving, sweating, watching and being watched. Following the example of Saidiya Hartman (1997: 51), I have chosen to begin 'counterinvesting in the body as a site of possibility'. If *mulata* is incarcerated by its own cultural constructions, why not liberate it by the *corpo-mulata*'s own pleasurable performance of those cultural constructions?

The shaking, rotating, revolving hips usually associated with primitive sensuality and vacuous carnality become a repertoire of movement associated with not just a Cuban body, but particularly a Cuban *mulata* body – *la mulata de rumbo*, a *costumbrista* adage used to connote the *mulata* of the party, the unstable *mulata*, the *mulata* that always searches for a party (Lane 2005: 21). It is this archetype of the *mulata* that Ninón Sevilla's 'brownface' performances both engage and contest.[1] The pleasure her *mulata* character finds in her body's liberation from, yet enactment of, *mulata*-ness crystallizes how historically marginalized corporealities utilize their bodies as sites of defiance, empowerment and sensual affront. In this vein, how could a living body ever be tragic?

Both a history and a lived experience, the *mulata* exists primarily as a narrative trope. The body is read, or interpellated, as if it is separate from its inhabitant. This distance between the person who *is* a *mulata* and the trope that binds the *mulata* creates a series of tragic mis-encounters with the social, as the person who lives the reality is engaged as a living character in an extended melodrama, not as a material witness to social processes and machinations of power. The real tragedy here is not the body as evidence of miscegenation, but the violence of language. For these reasons, I have constructed the sentience, '*corpo-mulata*'.

The term *corpo-mulata* serves as a means to address the method through which different corpo-realities use, manipulate, (de)activate, subdue and mobilize the various signifiers of '*mulata*' within this market-space of colonized histories. *Corpo-mulata* exists as a confluence of different factors: colourisms stemming from colonial hierarchies based on skin colour, gendered realities, monetized sexual exchanges, and distinct processes of domination depending on which type of patriarchal system acted as the hegemonic power. Additionally, a *corpo-mulata* foregrounds the discourses and debates about purity, beauty and truth. The hybridized, miscegenated, mulaticized body – otherwise known as the *corpo-mulata* – disrupts these idealized conditions constructed by Western cultural imagery. As a type of narration, the *mulata* disappears. She becomes tragic, a victim of historical and literary representations based on hegemonic discursive practices. Yet, as a materiality, as a *corpo-mulata*, she is always present and visible, staking out space, territory and meaning. More importantly, she is powerful through this materiality as represented through her hips and their transnational indexicality. As a result, the *corpo-mulata* is not a labourless body, but one that actively labours by problematizing how definitions of beauty and purity affect its interpellation and how the machinations of history amplify this interpellation.

Corpo-mulata exists as an incorporated marking. It is a widely distributed and recognizable 'embodiment' or character that pertains to specific market forces and systems of interpellation primarily between a Europeanness and an Africanness, sauntering into a 'New World-ness.' *Corpo-mulata* can be circulated like capital, expended, used and wielded. Unlike an uttered performative, like the 'I do' of J.L. Austin's 'How to do things with words,' the *corpo-mulata* as a body is not a linguistically driven state of being. When a corpo-real choreographs *corpo-mulata*, she uses the incorporated markings of the *corpo-mulata* performance and mobilizes them through bodily gesture.

Caught within the *mulata* trope, a *corpo-mulata* has situational agency, not projected agency. She cannot completely decide for herself how she wants to be seen because her body pertains to an economy of visibility within which it is assigned loaded signifiers: they supersede her. In the film *Mulata* for example, the *mulata* Caridad is stereotypically hailed as *mulata cochina* (dirty mulata), *mulata asquerosa* (filthy mulata), and at one point as having '*el diablo metido en la cintura* (the devil in her waist)' because she presumably 'tempts' men with the sway of her moving body. The *mulata* can also have aesthetic agency because of the different forms of value imposed on her skin, body, hair or other features, and then use this aesthetic agency to its advantage (or not). Yet without hip(g)nosis, the *corpo-mulata* has no potential to be anything more than an amalgam of signifiers speaking for her across her skin on her behalf in the service of white patriarchal capital formations. Signifiers will always speak due to their culturally defined circulation, yet they do not speak a body into being, only into knowing. Although her sign labours for her, a *corpo-mulata* exerting hip(g)nosis allows the body to dialogue and even overtake the battery of signs overworking the body even when it is still. Hip(g)nosis provides a method for a corporeal to actively organize how the *mulata* signifiers dance around its physiological facts. Thus, materializing as a *corpo-mulata*, she can contest the fixity of an essentialized *mulata*-ness, and mobilize it in order to dismantle the tragedy inherent in it.

The genesis of the term/theory hip(g)nosis stems from a play on the words hip, hypnotism and gnosis. By evoking the trance-like state of hypnotism, I consider the audience reaction to dancing *mulatas*, specifically remembering the *mulatas* I witnessed at the Tropicana cabaret in Cuba during one of my research trips. I place the 'g' in parentheses to highlight its usefulness in associating certain hip movements to choreographies of worship in Africanist/Lukumí praise dancing featured in the film *Mulata*, while at the same time allowing for hip movements or hipnosis to be a theory of corporeal knowledge not specifically linked to Africanist cosmology, for example when the *mulata* in the film dances the secular cha-cha-cha. Either way, the corporeal knowledge shared through the mobilization of the *corpo-mulata*'s hips asserts the powerful force of her body and its non-tragic state.

Power lies already in the hip, but only those conversant in this particular corporeal language have access and can understand its multilayered knowledge. That is to say, only those that can accept kinaesthetic knowledge as valuable and female-made cultural production as essential can 'hear' what these hips say. Mere reliance on the visual component of hip(g)nosis brings forth a hypnotism which counters what the corpo-real's hips mobilize and, more importantly, express – a lived, gendered and racialized history.

Just as anybody can witness and/or comprehend hip(g)nosis, anybody can have access to, and perhaps even wield, hip(g)nosis. But, hip(g)nosis does depend on specific histories and technologies of power. A movement is not simply a movement, but a sum of its parts – the ideologies and histories where the movement developed, gained notoriety, value and carved out space. Additionally, as a historicized bodily theory situated in specific racial and gendered states of being, hip(g)nosis problematizes the hips' own commoditization. What happens when differently privileged bodies learn, use and wield hips, and what does it mean for the flows of/between corporeal knowledges? Anybody's access to hip(g)nosis or performance of hipped enunciations demarcates the risks in de-historicizing and removing the labour intrinsic in hip(g)nosis.

I want to draw a relationship between this claim I am making and what Anna Beatrice Scott writes in 'Dance', the essay featured in *Culture Works: The Political Economy of Culture*. She states, 'If dance is particular to the body that performs it – and that body is a person particular to a certain family, locale, region, nation – then dancing takes on meaning as an identity marker and demarcates territory, both real and imagined. Crossing these boundaries engages discourses of power, and requires scrutiny of the concepts of authenticity, appropriation, misinterpretation, and misuse' (Scott 2001: 108). Hip movements can be practised and learned, for a body is pliable and capable of being docilized in order to mobilize musculatures in disparate ways. This exposes hip movements as consumable and commodified forms, not as natural qualities of a body. As a commodity, hip movements then can be branded, packaged and sold by anyone.

This branding of hipped activity results in an opportunity for the *corpomulata* to be an agent in her own self-making. These forms of technique and muscle memory substantiate Scott's claim that 'muscle memory is not only epic and explosive, but traverses and manipulates space and time in its various manifestations, creating potential ruptures in hegemonic perceptive devices by simultaneously stripping and manipulating sight/vision of its primacy' (Scott 2002: 6). Rather than merely looking at the curve of the hip, consider its movements as speech, its paths as drawings of a map, a space where similarly literate bodies might find moments of connection, cohesion, and relevance.

As a trans-territorial bodily theory, hip(g)nosis interpolates (in the mathematical sense) different nationalized bodies. Because of this, hip(g)nosis does not have to remain solely attached to the Cuban cultural context that I use to theorize it; it can traverse time and territory. As a result, hip(g)nosis appears on Mexican celluloid, wielded first by a Puerto Rican *mulata*, Mapy Cortes, who was the first *rumbera* and 'showed her aptitude' in *Cinco Minutos de Amor* (Five Minutes of Love), then later by many white Cuban women – for example, María Antonieta Pons, Rosita Carmina and Ninón Sevilla – and eventually by an American-born dancer of Swedish/Spanish and French-Tahitian ancestry, known as Tongolele. These were performances of racialized and nationalized hips, yet commercially elided by the signifier of the rhythmic and universalized 'Latina' product covered in ruffles. In other words, the hip-notism of the mulaticized product under the guise of 'Latina' enabled the dissemination of such a product specifically in the *cabaretera* films of Mexico's Golden Age.

La mulata Caridad

Ninón Sevilla was born in Cuba and is famous for her performances of *cubanía* in Mexican films of the 1940s and 1950s. She capitalized on Mexico's Golden Age of Cinema as a *rumbera-cabaretera* archetype, moving her hips beneath ostentatious outfits in films like *Aventurera*, *Perdida* and *Sensualidad* and playing a Cuban mulata in *Mulata* and *Yambaó*. She choreographed her own dance numbers and was instrumental in introducing

Santería/Afro-Cuban ritual dances into her choreography. Ninón serves as an example of someone who traffics in hip(g)nosis. In the film *Mulata*, she inhabits a materiality that doesn't belong to her, that of the *rumba*-dancing *mulata*, but because of territoriality – her (white) Cuban dancing body – she's able to use hip(g)nosis and become a *corpo-mulata* to gain both economic and cultural capital. So, although in the film *Mulata* she plays a 'tragic mulata', Ninón was quite the contrary. In this film, two versions of hip(g)nosis appear: the fictional Caridad's quasi-liberation through her dancing, and Ninón's own use of hip(g)nosis as a brand signifying Cuba in order to achieve fame in Mexico and Latin America in the *cabaretera* genre.

The narrator of this tale is Martín (played by Pedro Armendariz, a famous Mexican actor in the Golden Age), an errant sailor who arrives in Cuba. We are on his boat as he watches over Caridad (Ninón Sevilla), who lies feverish in bed, mumbling inaudibly to herself. His narration introduces Caridad with a loaded term, 'poor', setting her up as tragic from the beginning. He tells his tale of Caridad through flashback, his narration of Caridad's story situating her in a masculinist, linear history, a history antithetical to the motion of her hips. We only gain access to Caridad through Martín's memory. Caridad continually refers to her strong relationship to 'blackness', her inheritance of the legacy of Santería left by her mother, and the limited opportunities she has as a *mulata*. When she shares her history with Martín, he dismisses her 'inheritance of old stories' as worthless. For him (as a representative of patriarchy and 'proper' history) these circulated texts of *orichas* (deified forces of nature in Yoruba/Santería cosmology), her legacy of 'blackness', and her consistent contextualization of her racialized identity are of no value because they are not tangible, visible. His proof for the importance of things stems from occularcentrism. He says that it is better to focus on the tangible or material things that one can touch – 'touch things like you ... come, rest and forget about everything'. His insistence that she forget and acquiesce to his desires instantiates how her corporeally situated history not only comes secondary, but takes no precedence over the power contained within patriarchal desires. She is just an object for him and will only be situated in history as a thing in his ledger books.

Caridad's dancing ability in the film is constructed as 'natural' and instinctive. Even she claims she doesn't know where her natural affinity for dance comes from; somehow it is part of her bodily composition. Alluding to Caridad's inheritance of 'blackness', these danced iterations of her identity outside of the confines of the trope 'mulata' are where I witness Caridad's hip(g)nosis in the film. In these moments, unmarred by others' descriptions of who she is/what her body does, her hips forcibly speak about all of those things that Martín insists she forget.

Hip(g)nosis speaks a boisterous, rambunctious language especially for those who can follow it. Here, hip(g)nosis reveals its sleight of hand, or more accurately, sleight of hip. Although floating signifiers want to forcibly envelop the *corpo-mulata* and silence her, hip(g)nosis forces the focus to the body wielding it and choreographing *corpo-mulata*-ness. Bodies set these markers of identity into play. By choosing to perform whatever aspect of *corpo-mulata* necessary for agency and recognition, Caridad enacting hip(g)nosis has some agency in how she is perceived. Such hip(g)nosis occurs on the cabaret stage where she becomes a star.

El Cabaret Las Vegas

Martín takes Caridad to Havana where he brings her to a cabaret. While she sits and watches him surrounded by, and flirting with, other women, a *cha-cha-cha* begins to play. She approaches him wanting to dance. He asks her, 'Do you want to dance for me, mulata?' and then proceeds to lift her up onto the bar which doubles as an elevated stage. She starts to *cha-cha-cha*, not only for him but also for the entire cabaret. I read her dance as a corporeal affront to Martín having ignored her. Initially, it appears as if she dances to please him, but with each flip (dip, sway, pulse, pump) of her hips, she carves out a hip(ped) response to not just having been ignored by him and what he expects/wants from her, but by what he represents: *machista* notions of being. The cabaret audience adds to Caridad's affront, showing how her dancing body can attract more than one pair of eyes.

Only when she dances, improvising through a *cha-cha-cha*, pummelling her audience ever so gently with the enunciating curves of her hips and buttocks, does she seize pleasure ever briefly through her hip(g)nosis. Hip(g)nosis posits the idea of female sexuality through the body, specifically the hip, as a means for that very body to exhibit power, potentiality and prowess. It follows, then, that the hipped enunciations of *mulatas* marked as tropes shift from being erotic suggestions for the patriarchal gaze to becoming historicizing declarations about and for Othered women's labour and lives: she is a deployment, a *corpo-mulata*.

The beginning of her dance number has her filmed from the waist up, leaving the film audience to infer the hip sway occurring beneath. The neighbouring bystanders' gazes shift to her dancing body and, eventually, the camera pulls away and the film audience gets the opportunity to experience her enunciating hips and buttocks. The *cha-cha-cha* is a combination of duple and triple time: 1, 2, 1-2-3, 1, 2, 1-2-3, and so on. When danced, the feet alternate stepping to this rhythm while the arms, torso and more importantly the hip/butt complex can play with the rhythm by improvising how to move in the space to the rhythm. Because of the alternating foot action and slight weight transfer between them, the hips must sway to the corresponding side of the weighted foot/leg. Ultimately, the hips become the focal point demonstrating the dancing body's finesse. Caridads *cha-cha-cha* has her tapping her feet and pumping her pelvis back and forth, like a piston. Between swaying, pulsing and circulating motions, Caridad's hips mesmerize her audience. The bartender gazes wide-eyed up at her, and, even when she moves out of the frame, the camera lingers on his transfixed state showing the effectiveness of those moving hips to indeed hip-notise.

Guevara, the cabaret owner, arrives during her 'show'. Several point-of-view shots from his perspective situate Caridad as the spectacle of the cabaret. Martín goes over to speak with him and we find out he has unsettled debts. Guevara offers Martín money only if Martín can persuade 'la mulata' to work for him. For them, she exists as an exchangeable commodity going from one man to another; 'Convince the *mulata* to stay here and sign a contract with me and I'll help you find the money to get your boat back,' Guevara enticingly offers Martín. Quick to demonstrate which 'item' he prefers, Martín abandons Caridad to the life of the cabaret. After Martín leaves, Guevara conveys the news to her in his office. She has been 'sold' for a boat:

> 'Now what are you going to do, *mulata?*'
> She throws a shot glass, walks over to the door, and opens it to look out onto the cabaret. She turns, looks straight at Guevara and says:
> 'They've always sold us. They've kept us as slaves. But now, I, the *mulata* slave will avenge herself. Martín and you, my new owner, want me to burn in the hell of the cabaret. Hmph! But a lot of people will burn with me!'

Having been 'abandoned' and 'sold' to the cabaret, a quick edit cuts to Caridad's triumphant entrance onto the cabaret after she pronounces her revenge.

The mulata's revenge

Caridad enters stage left with arms diagonally stretched outwards from her body, presenting that very same body to an audience. As she enters facing front, she continues with elevated arms to move sideways/across the raised stage. Her hips below snap to the left and then to the right, like a rhythmic pendulum. She executes a small, syncopated jump – almost like a double jump – and then the hip that corresponds to the foot where her weight has shifted to punctuates the downbeat. These 'jumps' are abrupt, quick knee flexion bounces with alternating hip pumps from side to side.

When she arrives stage right, hips swinging from side to side and arms still above, she descends stairs that take her through tables filled with cabaret onlookers. While she walks down the steps, she shimmies her shoulders and brings her arms down to be level with her shoulders and suddenly pauses. She does basic *rumba* steps with corresponding hip swirls, takes the last two steps and when she arrives at ground level, which is the cabaret main floor, she straightens her legs, bends her torso forward and salutes an onlooker behind her with her bottom jutting out.

Her bottom hides behind a huge multilayered tulle bow and train that bobs according to her pelvic enunciations. She continues on the main cabaret floor, flutters her shoulders and traces a full circle around the floor to wind up in the centre facing forward. She has been shot wide angle up until now, allowing the audience outside of the film set to ingest her entire moves on the screen and to witness the reaction of the audience within the film.

What follows is a series of improvised *rumba* steps with legs bending and weight shifts enabling hip dips, sways, swirls and circles. After several counts of the *rumba* step facing her audience, she turns around and the big white tulle bow makes figure eights, illustrating the shapes her hips trace in space. Perhaps she thinks we may not have had enough of her big white bow, so she does a quick jump, leans forward with her back still to us, and on the balls of her feet she runs in place, tracing little circles with her hips/butt/bow. Circles become semicircles become ovals become half circles swinging side to side like a swing set, all at the discretion of the rhythm and this *corpo-mulata*-cum-*rumbera*'s improvisational technique. She kicks one leg towards the drummers and turns around to face her adoring public once again. Camera shots are generally wide ones, encapsulating her entire dancing body, permitting ample witnessing of how it not only moves through the cabaret space, but how other corpo-reals react to its moving and performing presence. All eyes rest on this dancing *corpo-mulata*. She is the main attraction, the cocktail special of the evening: the new infamous *Mulata* served at Cabaret Las Vegas.

By performing hip rotations, undulations and pelvic movements associated with her presupposed intemperate sexuality and brazen nature, through an acute awareness of the material value of those kinaesthetic iterations, the *corpo-mulata* appropriates the very body that has been used against her. This is hip(g)nosis at work. In so doing, she removes her body's status as fetish, as victim of violence and iconographic subjugation, while at the same time highlighting the socio-politically constructed nature of race. It is through this performativity based on epidermal realities that she asserts her historically denied subjectivity and makes claims for citizenship. Thus, her body serves as both cultural construct and site of redress, further complicating notions of race, gender and subjectivity. The *corpo-mulata* moves, entrenched in a consistent struggle between the state, consumerism and consumption, machismo in all of its different cultural forms, and her construction of self-hood attesting to the fact that 'power is everywhere; not because it embraces everything, but because it comes from everywhere' (Foucault 1977a: 93). If this is the case, then there lies power in the practice of *corpo-mulata* and in the theory/sign/movement of hip(g)nosis. It is not simply the power to dazzle, enliven, enthral, swindle or entice, but the power to contest the multiplicity of force relations acting upon that body. She can thus enact a contestatory resistance through the seemingly 'natural' revolution of her hips.

At the refrain of the 'bow dance', the camera moves in for a tighter shot. This time, she inhabits the frame from mid-thigh to the top of her head-dress, and we see the bow move closer. Interchanging between wide and medium close shot, she continues to hip-notise her public.

Another barrage of *rumba* steps follow as the buttocks lead the way back towards the drummers, all combined with fancy footwork: jump, cross right in front, across left, jump cross left in front, across right. During a drum solo she imitates the male version of the *rumba*, the *columbia*, in that she lifts her knees alternating them while her torso quickly rotates from left to right, the movement initiated by the waist, hips stable. With her back to the audience yet again, she jumps and lands on the floor, knees bent, back arching until she touches the floor with her back, neck craned to look at audience. Meanwhile her arms are outstretched, perpendicular to her torso and she shimmies her shoulders to another percussive drum solo, while lying half supine on the floor. When she gets up, her energy and pace slows down, she does several *rumba* steps facing the audience, stops as the music flourishes to an end, lifts her arms triumphantly and smiles. A *corpo-mulata*'s vengeance achieved through hip(g)nosis.

These examples of hip(g)nosis within the confining narrative of the *mulata* Caridad acknowledge hip(g)nosis's ability to assert the corpo-real's lived presence. What is more, hip(g)nosis forges a real or, quite specifically, a material response to the impositions of the interpellated *mulata*-sign. If body movements or, more precisely, if a corpo-real's wielding of her own body/body part can be considered an assertion of identity, a veritable choreography of the self, then it becomes crucial to consider bodies – racialized, gendered, sexualized and sensual – as sites of knowledge, history and power.

Note

1 I use the term 'brownface' to connote white Cuban Ninón Sevilla's performance of *mulata*.

13

STILL CURIOUS

Emilyn Claid

For hours I would stand quite still, my two hands folded between my breasts, covering the solar plexus ... I was seeking and I finally discovered the central spring of all movement, the crater of motor power, the unity from which all diversities of movement are born.

(Duncan 1927: 75)[1]

In the beginning, I wanted to speak of arms and legs, of jumping up and down, of bodies tumbling and spinning. Little by little ... the things I wanted to do seemed finally to be of no importance ... Now emptiness is all that remains: a space, no matter how small, in which whatever is happening can be allowed to happen. And no matter how small, each and every possibility remains.

(Auster 1998: 86)

Most of us live in fear of slowing down our thinking; because of the possibility that if we succeed we might find that in fact nothing is happening. I guarantee this is not the case. Something is always happening.

(Goulish 2000: 82)[2]

These three artists' impressions suggest we slow down to notice more in the world, so that stillness becomes a resource for discovery. As I sense my self still, I become more alert. The practice of stillness reaches inwards towards a somatic being and outwards into the world. Stillness is being here in this moment now as a perpetual point of tension within movement, not something that happens when movement stills. It is the breath out as it pulls towards life. A still body blows open the ambiguity of 'Once upon a time', zooming in on the empty 'O' with its fullness of the past and scenes about to be introduced. In Gestalt psychology stillness is the moment of demobilising, a necessary space between the beginning and end of each cycle of experience, that holds all possibility: 'And we find when we accept and enter this nothingness, the void, then the desert starts to bloom, the empty void becomes alive, is being filled. The sterile void becomes the fertile void' (Perls 1969: 57). Stillness is the moment of not knowing before knowing emerges. It is a quality of movement within all movement. Slowing down allows us to meet each other differently. Still here, still there, 'still' also suggests ongoing-ness, process and duration. The still point resides within the constancy and continuity of movement.

> In performance perhaps what we have here is a dramatic tension – a doing, which IN ITSELF is tensed by non-doing, by interval, tensed by what-is-not-done-and-yet-is, tensed by 'what-is-not-yet' and yet we know is potential in the vacuum.
>
> (Smith 2008)[3]

I am writing about stillness because the physical practice of cultivating stillness has initiated important political, philosophical and psychological shifts in choreography – for performers, spectators and makers. 'A dance that initiates a critique of representation by insisting on the still, on the slow' offers the opportunity to interrogate 'choreography's political ontology' (Lepecki 2006: 45). Lepecki proposes that the emergence of minimalism and the 'still-act' in dance (Seremetakis 1994) has uprooted the modernist project – that of a continuous and exhausting 'being-toward-movement' (Sloterdijk 2000: 36). The modernist ontology is displaced by the still-act with its:

> Insistence on politics, its fusion of the visual with the linguistic, its drive for a dissolution of genres, its critique of authorship, its dispersion of the art-work, its privileging of the event, its critique of institutions, and its aesthetic emphasis on minimalism.
>
> (Lepecki 2006: 135)

Suggesting how the embodied practice of stillness becomes political in performance between performers and spectators is the first intention of my text. But there is a further purpose and that is to explore how an embodied practice of stillness evokes the potential for a meeting of difference between self and other. For this I turn to my current studio-based research with MA students in Transitions Dance Company to pose a question: how do we meet?[4]

As a writer writing I am looking sideways to embrace two worlds. One is Gestalt psychotherapy, my current training and research. The other is my experiential field of performance and choreography, as a dance practitioner and academic. As I stretch into both directions I see how the relational practices of humanistic psychotherapies, such as Gestalt, have been closely interwoven within my choreographic processes since the 1970s. I am thinking particularly of the parallels between devising methodologies and the Gestalt focus on dialogic relations.[5] Humanistic therapies have dissolved the strict structures of classical psychoanalysis, just as devising processes dissolve the fixed hierarchies between choreographers and performers. At X6 our new dance experiments were affected by the incoming tide of relational practice.[6] I was not aware of Gestalt theories then. Now, the parallels in theory and practice are revealing. We were living in practice, yet the theory was there all along. The dialogic tools of presence, phenomenological enquiry and inclusion – tools familiar to Gestalt psychotherapy – also shape a devising process. The core of the dialogic meeting is an awareness of 'self as contact', an experience I approach through a bodily practice of stillness. So, as I return to work in the studio with Transitions, I am drawing with me, and interweaving, theoretical parallels and a therapeutic understanding of Gestalt psychology. Here I am documenting the hesitant beginnings of a pathway.

> I want to watch watching arrive. I want to watch arrivances.
>
> (Cixous and Calle-Gruber 1997: 4)

We enter the journey with the words of French feminist theorist Hélène Cixous. She speaks of her writing process, offering a parallel to the physical practice of stillness. Her words slow us down; we're gathering perception and information, capturing the curiosity and excitement of something potentially different happening. Giving attention to stillness makes room for discovery. Since the 1960s minimalist performances at Judson Church and the 1970s new dance experiments in the UK, dancers have embraced body–mind somatic practices such as Alexander Technique, Contact Improvisation, Body Mind Centring and Release technique. Each in its own way attends to stillness as an integral element for questioning the fundamentals of human movement. Mabel Ellsworth Todd emphasises the complex work required just to stand still.

> Since all parts of the human body are constantly moving, each separate unit is dropping of its own weight; the momentum is determined by the size of the unit, its density, type of support and distance from the ground. These forces, which operate exactly as they do upon weights outside the body, must be met by the body with resistance equal, or more than equal, to counter them in their manifold expressions and combinations.
>
> (Todd 1937: 55)

Standing still, we are focusing on a somatic body–mind attention to a myriad of sensations. Internally we experience a mapping of downward, upward and crossing imaginary lines, towards the earth and the centre of gravity and upwards through the top of the head into space. A still balance in the body is an attention to multiple, rapid, skeletal and muscular adjustments (Paxton 1986). Our bodies are caught in stillness, holding and held by forces, poised on a current, between gravity and weightlessness. Thinking in our bodies through stillness holds the possibility of shifting habitual movement pathways, working *with* our bodies rather than against, acknowledging the paradox whereby 'change occurs when one becomes what he is, not when he tries to become what he is not' (Beisser 1970: 77).

Remembering Paxton's *Small Dance* (1986), a particular experience stays with me. This is the sensation of approaching movement and movement approaching. In stillness we can imagine taking a step, or a step taking us, without actually doing the action. We can notice what happens in our bodies as we sense the preparation preceding the action. We extend the moments before and after movement.

A somatic practice looks inwards. But this is no longer the only focus. Rather, the practice also allows us to notice more fully what is happening outside. Just as the silence of 4'33" (Cage 1952) evokes the presence of sounds in the world, so the still dance exposes movement. Slowing down allows us to perceive, not only the beginning of action, but how we make contact in relation to others, how we make meaning of the world. Choreographer Michael Parmenter writes of the reach of intentionality, a philosophical principle that lies at the core of phenomenology. Embodied, intentionality becomes a physical movement of desire for being in the world, a grounding of self while reaching to the other (Parmenter 2008).[7] For Gestalt phenomenologists Chidiac and Denham-Vaughan, this is a practice of presence:

> It is this combination of fully 'being-while-doing' that the dialectical synthesis of 'will' and 'grace' becomes manifest. Here, will can be defined as directed action ... and grace as a quality of receptivity and surrender.
>
> (Chidiac and Denham-Vaughan 2007: 9)

I am watching Jonathan Burrows' graceful practice of embodying stillness, his approach to movement as a tension between still here and moving there. From Yvonne Rainer (*Trio A* 1966) to Jonathan Burrows and Jan Ritsema (*Weak Dance Strong Questions* 2001), watching and dancing stillness continues to be an unlearning and a political act. 'In a walking moved by awareness, we can take a small "preparatory step" towards the over-coming of our metaphysical tradition' (Levin 1985: 291).

To introduce *Weak Dance Strong Questions* Jonathan and Jan are meandering about the performance space wearing loose trousers, t-shirts and shoes. The stage is stripped, brightly lit with non-theatrical working lights; the seats are arranged intimately in a half circle. Jonathan tells us they will perform for fifty minutes. Then it will be over.

Jonathan walks backwards, slips and slides over his own feet, creating a limping affect as he walks. He begins a step, hesitates, changes direction before completion, and pauses mid-movement before reaching any identifiable line or position. Each arm gesture dissolves out of a never-defined recognizable image. The movement language is stripped of climactic phrasing and expressive depth, shifting away from a stylized presentation towards pedestrian movement. Speaking of their work together Jan says,

> It is about the availability of the body and mind, not driven by impulses to produce, but to reach a state of non-productiveness, of not-needing each other, of reaching a state of potentiality.
>
> (Ritsema 2004)

Jonathan's body holds a history of performing with the Royal Ballet where he absorbed the fast moving flourish of illusionist spectacle. Now he rejects that on his body. But its absence is present (Claid 2006). He/we carry those embodied memories even as he/we unfix them. Watching, I sense a paradox of past and present. Echoing Parmenter's reach of intentionality, I am caught by my desire to observe in the present *and* interpret what I see with what I know. We do not perceive something without also understanding it *as* something. I draw a parallel here with Staemmler's discussion of Gestalt methods of diagnosis, whereby we move between the constantly changing process of observation and description *and* a fixed interpretation based on past facts. Grounded in 'cultural coinage, our personal history, our material conditions' we do not separate our perception from our understanding of the world (Staemmler 2006: 20). Our interpretation or understanding of a situation 'begins with a prejudice, or, to put it a little milder, with a pre-understanding' (ibid.: 21). My pre-understanding of Jonathan's history, together with my own background of dance experience, becomes the basis of interpretation. The challenge is to simultaneously bracket my presumptions. I can do this if I slow down the constant mobility of my thinking body to observe, in the present moment, now. So the work of watching Jonathan is that of perceiving, knowing and unknowing as a crossing of past/present contradictions between my body and his body that I watch.

I am engaging with Jonathan's dance more for what I know is not there than what is there. Jonathan opposes convention so radically that he draws attention to the convention's absence. In this way, I connect with the memory of illusion of the spectacle, where the illusion recalls itself through its absence.[8] Jonathan's movements of stillness contest choreographic expectations. As I watch, I know, in my body now, what is not there within his movements. The work represents an era in dance performance when knowledge of convention, for performers and spectators, informs the absence of convention in the work (Claid 2006). Pre-understanding, perception and interpretation of Jonathan's dancing interweave, and watching becomes a conscious act of questioning what it is to make meaning and where meaning resides.

Moreover, watching itself is physical. Jonathan's quality of liminal non-spectacle – his attention to the present moment – triggers expectations in my body. As one gesture begins to happen, Jonathan's stillness contains the action. The gesture does not flow through to an external expression. I can feel, in my still watching body, an expectation of the line extending to completion. My body memory expects a particular flow, but that memory is abruptly broken. I experience this jolt physically and the smooth habitual familiarity of watching dancing is disrupted. A still space opens in my body for awareness of the approach to movement.

Watching Jonathan's slowness seduces me into a 'critique of representation' that refashions an assumed choreographic ontology.[9] *And* I am not forgetting that we are both engaged with a physical act of stillness. He is grounded in his body while moving. I sense his dance in my body initiating a disruption in my thinking. For me, the still dance is the process of the body thinking into movement. I want watching as not knowing but desiring to know. I want stillness as a process of curiosity between my body and yours, to notice you and what is not you, and perhaps what you do not notice about yourself.

> The other in all his or her forms gives me *I*. It is on the occasion of the other that *I* catch sight of *me* … It is the other who makes my portrait. Always.
>
> (Cixous and Calle-Gruber 1997: 13)

Cixous's poetic assertion serves as a bridge that joins the first and second parts of my text. I am moving to the studio to begin research with Transitions Dance Company. What interests me is how an attention to stillness might affect the creative liveliness of the contact we make. I come with a question to explore: how do we meet? We open up this question through a simple improvisational structure *still curious*. Two performers stand facing one another in stillness. Each performer looks at and looks away from her/his partner in a reciprocal exchange, sometimes making eye contact, sometimes not, to notice how *I* emerges through *not I*. 'I watch you watching me watch you watching me' (ibid.: 77). The point is to slow down the approach to eye contact, to notice what is happening in the body, with the potential for a different understanding of self and other.

Within the framework of Gestalt psychology the question – how do we meet? – is explored through the cycle of experience (Perls *et al.* 1951). Human behaviour exists as a constant formation and destruction of figures, emerging from a ground (also known as void, chaos or field) into contact, and collapsing back into the ground.

The cycle describes how we make contact in the world. Perls identifies the cycle as a continuum of stages towards, and away from, contact: sensation, awareness, mobilisation, action, contact, assimilation, satisfaction, withdrawal and return to the void from where sensation emerges. These stages are not consciously enacted; they are the self in process. Our interruptions, moderations, fixed repetitions and missed stages in the cycle define our individual experiences – our personalities. The self emerges as experience in the world and experience (change, growth) occurs at the 'surface-boundary in the field of the organism/environment' (ibid.: 258). Developing aware contact, at the boundary of self and other, is both the healing process and goal for Gestalt psychotherapy. But the boundary is not something *between* us.

> The contact-boundary, where experience occurs, does not *separate* the organism and its environment; rather it limits the organism, contains and protects it, and *at the same time* it touches the environment.
>
> (ibid.: 229)

At the moment of contact, organism and environment, self and other, are not distinguishable.[10] 'Subject and object here are arbitrary' (McLeod 1993: 27). Hence the notion of *self as contact*, a meta-theory in Gestalt psychology (Perls *et al.* 1951). 'Where there is no contact there is no self. Or more usually, where there is little contact there is little self, and where there is full contact there is full self' (McLeod 1993: 26). In the studio, we are slowing down to notice how we see or do not see each other, becoming aware of our individual styles and ways of making contact.

With the task of *still curious*, we are exploring how physical stillness can affect an approach to meeting with each other. I ask performers to describe what they learn about themselves. What do you notice? What do you need? Who has the power? Who initiates? Who invites? Who holds back? What are we afraid to see? What do we want to hide? How do we want to be seen? Who is the *I* that emerges in this particular exchange with this particular person? The performers' comments about themselves and each other become a rich source of shared knowledge for devising relational interaction.

The task takes a different tack. Standing at a distance from each other, two performers move towards each other to hug. Within the dance profession, hugging is a familiar mode of meeting. We hug to greet each other, to say goodbye, to congratulate, commiserate and support. The hug affirms a bonding between artists in a profession that accentuates communication through physical languages. But sometimes we move through the meeting of difference too fast to reach either a place of security and confluence or a place where one is subsumed by the other. Both these styles of contact can limit the potential risk, excitement and dynamic change of the moments of meeting. From a place of *still curious*, we hold the intention of the hug, but let go of the goal, to slow down this process of meeting. We explore the richness of the moments of contact before the hug and notice how contact changes at each stage. The slow approach is a key to bring us 'to the boundary but not marching through the boundary or controlling the other' (Yontef 1993: 34). For each one of us there is a personal spatial boundary, which, once crossed, can create sensations of excitement, fear, flight, fight or freeze. In living, we often pass this fragile line unaware. I ask each performer to notice that place/space, exploring the sensations that occur when a partner steps inside or outside.

Where is the fullness of contact? Is it in the hug, or is it in the moment before the hug? In eye contact? Or are there at least three different cycles of experience happening here, the initial eye contact, the hug and the drawing away? What role do you play in approaching the hug? What do you learn about yourself and the other in this moment of relationship? Whose arms go where and is this familiar? Which parts of your bodies touch? What do you feel – excited, nervous, angry, aggressive, sad? The discussion draws out information about how sensations of hugging are different for each person depending on whom they hug.

The process of *still curious* continues, as does the question: how do we meet? Still here and looking there, performers begin a dialogue, in words and then movement.

> The chief presupposition for the rise of genuine dialogue is that each should regard his partner as the very one he is. I become aware of him, aware that he is different, essentially different from myself, in the definite, unique way which is peculiar to him, and I accept whom I thus see, so that in full I can direct what I say to him as the person he is.
>
> (Buber 1965: 79)

Buber provides a fundamental text for Gestalt, offering a philosophical grounding for the practice of dialogic relations. Our experience of stillness facilitates the potential of dialogic encounters, encouraging a practice of 'separatedness, centeredness, and yet relatedness' as Gestalt psychotherapist Richard Hycner defines the dialogic relationship (Hycner and Jacobs 1995: 27). In the studio the performers begin with a verbal enquiry of difference. The phenomenological 'rule of epoché' (Spinelli 2007: 115), first proposed by Husserl (1931), requires a bracketing of expectations and assumptions to understand the different worlds of each other. So our questions are asked from a place of stillness, looking at, and responding to, each other. What is happening for you right now? How is it for you to see me here? What are you aware of in your body as you stand there looking?

We move *still curious* into gesture, embodying a quality of enquiry. In the duets that follow the performers are open to the unknown of each other. As Cixous aptly portrays:

> What interests me is what I do not know. It leaves me first of all silent. It strikes me with surprise, with a certain silence. But at the same time, it strikes my body, it hurts me.
>
> (Cixous and Calle-Gruber 1997: 71)

Still watching, I see creative differences as performers' personalities collide, while surprising, relational narratives emerge and dissolve. Slowing down to observe each other's movement dialogically, nurtures a response that takes the improvised journey somewhere unexpected. What is co-created emerges through a dialogue of separate relatedness. Here is a paradox. Curiosity of difference requires a separateness, yet we are also entering into each other's world, as a movement of bodily inclusion.

> Inclusion is the opposite of analytic objectification. It is the rhythmic back-and-forth ability of human beings to experience an event from the perspective of the other person while in the same moment maintaining one's own experience ... It is an immersion in the existential stance of the other without losing one's own existential position ... It is the basis of the possibility of all dialogue ... The paucity of inclusion has left human interaction emotionally and spiritually bankrupt.
>
> (Hycner and Jacobs 1995: 122–3)

Two performers, respectful and curious of each other's difference, include themselves in each other's world in a meeting of reciprocity. The becoming of one and the other offers an experience of I–thou (Buber 1937).[11] It is 'an experience of appreciating the "otherness", the uniqueness and the wholeness of another, while at the same time this is reciprocated by the other person' (Hycner and Jacobs 1995: 8).

I–thou is given a revered status in Gestalt. Aware contact between therapist and client *is* the healing process, so I–thou becomes a special moment. It is fleeting and unfixable, yet we know when it happens. For us in the studio we discover these moments in shared laughter, tears and fragments of precarious balance between performers. I mention I–thou here as a pleasure of dialogic relations. In teasing out the question 'How do we meet?', the potential of I–thou contact is not necessarily where we think it is, but somewhere else and perhaps somewhere else again along a process, the goal of which becomes another cycle beginning. We are enabling the will to take risk and the grace to submit; an ability to focus on how the meeting feels in the moment of now.

I am remembering how I have used the tool of *still curious* for many years as a devising methodology (Claid 2002).[12] I return to it here with the Gestalt maps of self as contact, enquiry and dialogic relations. The difference is my understanding of the inter-relational, the inter-subjectivity of experience, together with the paradox evoked by that understanding. Something about the contradictions of the paradox – the separateness and relatedness that the dialogic demands – necessitates a bodily sense of stillness in order to notice more of the other that I meet. *Still curious* explores a resource for devising, makes space for a pre-performance relational practice. *Still curious* offers a direct communication between performers and choreographer, a pathway that might inform a choreographic process, might affect performers' presence and influence meetings. Writing now, it is the process not the goal that intrigues me. I am not particularly interested in stillness as a performance product and I love fast-moving action. Stillness is a tool for aliveness. We are in the moment of each gesture, curious, while fully attentive to one another. 'Stillness is not what is achieved in display, but the pre-expression from which the best (most probable) action comes' (Smith 2008).

Words about stillness – performing, watching and devising – attempt to reveal how apparent nothingness has far reaching implications for relational performance practice. This is not new. I am revisiting something that dance practitioners have held dear to their hearts for a long time. I am reiterating a slowing down to stillness as a quality that holds potential for another way of relating. I would like to extend and expand the arc between a somatic ground and contact in the world to notice what is along the way. Perhaps I am saying that an experiential quality of stillness is held within the perpetually moving point of contact that joins and separates us. And perhaps I am suggesting that we might slow down our moment of meeting, to notice each other, to allow for the possibility of sensing something else – and I don't know what that is. I only know the immediacy of stillness at our meeting, a fused spark, and something is always happening.

> Or else, something does not happen. A body moves. Or else, it does not move. And if it moves, something begins to happen. And even if it does not move, something begins to happen.
>
> (Auster 1998: 81)

> Sink to the bottom of the now.
>
> (Cixous and Calle-Gruber 1997: 41)

With thanks to David Williams, Sarah Paul, Jill Lewis, Kay Lynn, Alys Longley, Michael Parmenter.

Notes

1 Cited in *Hand to Hand* (Parmenter 2008).
2 Matthew Goulish is co-founder of Goat Island Theatre Company. Cited in *a little by little suddenly* (Williams 2008).
3 Phil Smith, writer, dramaturg and site-specific performance maker. Email correspondence, 20 September 2008.
4 Transitions Dance Company is a postgraduate performance group at Laban, London.
5 Innovators of psychotherapeutic relational practice include Carl Rogers, Fritz and Laura Perls. Prof. K. Goldstein introduced Fritz Perls to Gestalt psychology

in 1926. Perls worked with Living Theatre, Max Rheinhardt and Anna Halprin amongst others in the 1960s. Laura Perls, his wife, was a dancer. Perls' work with Anna Halprin is documented in her book *Moving Towards Life* (Halprin 1995).

6 X6 Dance Space 1976–80 (Claid 2006).

7 Parmenter traces the roots of the term intention to 'the Latin *tendere* ... derived from the Sanskrit *tan* – "to stretch" or "to reach"' (Kirstein 1969, p.1). We find this *ten* in many English words, like 'intend', 'contend', 'pretend' and 'tent, a temporary structure maintained through stretching' (Parmenter 2008 p.13).

8 Cf. David George (1999: 19), 'Doubling' and Peggy Phelan (1993: 2), 'multiple and resistant readings'.

9 Cf. David George (1999: 33–4), 'performance ontology'.

10 The meeting of organism and environment is the sensory boundary that under-lies the relational boundary of self and other. An understanding of the inter-relationship of organism and environment is crucial to an understanding of ecology (Giannachi and Stewart 2005).

11 I–thou has roots in Jewish and Christian religions and is a slippery term to translate through Hebrew and German texts (Buber 1937). In Gestalt this term refers to the something else that is created when we give ourselves fully to the meeting from a place of separateness. Difficult to interpret, some call this the presence of God or spirituality.

12 *Back to Front with Side Shows* (Candoco Dance Company 1994), *Shiver Rococo* (1999), *Nobodies Baby* (2002) and *Remember to Forget* (2003) specifically used still-ness and looking as a tool for devising performance. The last three pieces were a trilogy of works for *Embodying Ambiguities* (AHRC research project 1999–2004 co-directed with Valerie Briginshaw).

Part III

WAYS OF LOOKING

Closely allied with the points of view of dancing masters and dramaturges has been the concern with analysing dance, identifying its elements and investigating a dance form or a dance work according to these components. Some of the large-scale textually oriented performance traditions have produced tracts that point to the building blocks of dance, for example the classical Indian dramaturgical texts, the *Natyasastra* and the *Abhinaya Darpana*, which examine dance in the context of a multidisciplinary drama that closely integrated dance with other art forms. In a later period, Raoul Feiullet developed his system of notation specifically for the recording of Baroque dances. Subsequently, the ways of looking privileged in dance writing shifted towards the creation of the role of the dance critic, as in the writings of Theophile Gautier.[1] The process of looking at dance remained tied to an interest in documentation, so that, for instance, Rudolf von Laban's system for identifying components of dance, Laban Movement Analysis, was closely allied with his Labanotation system.

Despite this longstanding attention to the systematic analysis of dance, it was only with the emergence of 'new dance studies' in the 1980s that authors investigated and problematised the process of looking at dance. Susan Foster (1986) aligned the 'reading' of dances with post-structuralist inquiries into the historical specificity of systems of meaning. Post-structuralism alerted scholars to their own positioning, following the Foulcauldian attention to the power/knowledge interface, which suggested that knowledge production is value-laden. Janet Adshead (now Lansdale) (1988) proposed a system for the analysis of dance works that aimed to be broadly applicable, while also encouraging the dance viewer to attend to the meaning and the contextual resonances of a dance work, distinguishing, for instance, between description and interpretation. These manoeuvres have encouraged dance scholars, such as those whose work appears here, to debate the process of investigating and analysing dance movement, to consider its terms, and to reflect on the implications of the choices made in the process of analysis.

Using Siobhan Davies' *Duets* (1982) and Ann Daly's analysis of the third theme from Balanchine's *The Four Temperaments* (1946), Stephanie Jordan and Helen Thomas exemplify the various perspectives offered by formalism, structuralism and semiotics. Taking gender as their theme, they illustrate ways in which these differing analytical strategies offer possibilities for multiple, sometimes contradictory readings. Furthermore, they argue that interplay between the 'poetic' and semiotic approaches can result in a richer appreciation of dance.

Janet Lansdale both builds upon and departs from her earlier work on dance analysis. Recognising the historical circumstances which produce analytical models, Lansdale argues that advocates of some systems (she cites Laban's specifically) have evaded their links with context, thus acquiring both a false universality and objectivity. The trajectory of Lansdale's own ideas have moved on to the more fluid notion of intertextuality as an analytical strategy. Identifying some of the authorial or 'narrating' voices – that is, who is telling the stories about the dance – Lansdale argues that the cultural positioning of these narrators results in different stories, 'none of which has a claim to be universal or all-embracing'. Authorial voices also speak the 'ancestral'; the histories and traditions which inevitably inform our understanding. Retaining her earlier model which identifies the components of the dance, Lansdale layers these with notions of 'trace, absence and flickering presence' which renders the process of analysis complex, multilayered and dynamic. As such, like dance itself, the perceptions of all those who encounter it and the theories which inform their ways of looking at it, are not context-free but are culturally embedded.

The notion of dance as culturally embedded is at the heart of Novack's influential chapter. Novack points to how historical and anthropological studies have neglected the body in movement as a key indicator of identity. Seen only as a referential guide to cognitive and social systems, the experience – and the significance – of movement has not been recognised. However, warns Novack, it is erroneous to examine movement as some kind of surface activity unconnected to material conditions, for structured movement systems like dance tell us not only about people and how their identities are constructed but also about the societies in which they act and which act upon them. Novack is alert to the patterns of movement which produce a recognisable cultural identity but argues that these, in their lack of specificity, are ambiguous and must be interpreted with care. To exemplify her argument, Novack traces the movement characteristics of contact improvisation and various forms of rock dancing, situating them within their historical and contemporaneous contexts. As the times changed, so too did the forms and functions of these movement systems/dances. Avoiding simplistic parallels, the argument is made that 'by looking at different dance forms ... as cultural realities whose kinesthetic and structural properties have meaning, possibilities emerge for articulating and clarifying our experiences of who we, and others, are'.

The notion of ambiguous cultural identities also informs Shobana Jeyasingh's argument. She opens her discussion by tracing the classical and colonial history of bharata natyam. Rehabilitated for a modern, twentieth-century India, it became, paradoxically, part of a mythical Orient constructed by the West. As the reality of this 'Orient' come closer to the UK through the process of immigration, bharata natyam was appropriated as an 'ethnic' dance, supposedly embodying a specific and long-standing cultural heritage. By viewing the dance as reflective of a particular religious/cultural background which needed to be interpreted within that frame, its movement language, performance skills and theatricality were lost to sight. Context, albeit misconstrued, dominated choreography. The classicism of the form, not in the sense of longevity but in attention to the dance and its qualities, was overlooked. Jeyasingh extrapolates these key features which comprise the classicism of the bharata natyam technique. Central is the display of 'technique for its own sake', or *nritta*, which is based on the idealised geometric form of the human body. All of the central features of the *nritta* are still conserved but Jeyasingh argues that this does not render the form redundant in changing times. 'It alone', she claims, 'has the tenacity to speak with confidence to the present without turning its back on the past.'

In an 'afterward' to her original writing in the first edition of the *Reader*, Marcia Siegel implies that dance, as she sees it in the USA today, has turned its back on the past. In her earlier contribution, she tackled issues which are crucial not just for the work of the critic but for any dance spectator. Notwithstanding the multicultural nature of many societies, we are still often faced with dance events which initially appear alien to us; in what ways, she asks, is it possible to approach the work of cultures with which we are unfamiliar? Furthermore, how is it possible to judge what is 'authentic', or is this quest for authenticity doomed logically to fail when culture itself is dynamic, ever-changing? Siegel argues that, however ideal an immersion into the context of a work may be, critics cannot be anthropologists. An acceptance of the many different functions of dance other than the theatrical can also engender a more open perspective and contribute to a celebration of dance in all its diversity. Writing two decades later, Siegel laments not the challenge of dealing with new genres or diverse practices, but the erosion of genre-based boundaries; a situation where 'style is becoming less a signifier than a new shade in a limitless movement palate'. As such, the specificity of dance's 'cultural and historical meanings' is lost. We are also losing, she claims, the expert knowledge, perceptions and writing skills of the professional critic. This might partly be remedied, she suggests, by the teaching and learning of these skills in university dance curricula. Although the notion of 'critical studies' in dance is now common in education, it is, perhaps, a timely reminder that these need to be presented with an attention to not only erudite and evocative writing but also to the immediacy of viewer response and to a potential (if imagined) readership.

Richard Dyer's and John Mueller's analyses of 'Dancing in the Dark' from *The Band Wagon* (1953) are included here as examples of the still rare consideration given to the choreography of dance in films. Dyer hints at the potential for readings informed by gender perspectives, which is the subject of the much longer chapter from which this brief extract is drawn. Mueller focuses on the narrative of the film, explicating the way in which a significant change in the relationship between the two protagonists (Astaire and Charisse) is charted not by words, but in dance.

The approaches taken here all signal a relationship between the close reading of dances and an interpretation of their broader significance. While the identification of the components of a dance may have once sufficed, now dance writers and viewers extend their analysis from the form itself into its engagement with its context. Inversely, these writings also remind us that the contextual study of dance does not give a full picture of its significance. These writings challenge us not only to look closely at dances but also to examine how we are looking and to note how this viewing process yields permutations of results that differ depending on the perspective taken.

Further reading

Hammergren, L. (1995) 'Different personas: a history of one's own', in Foster, S. (ed.), *Choreographing History*, Bloomington: Indiana UP.

Jordan, S. (2000) *Moving Music: Dialogues with Music in Twentieth Century Ballet*, London: Dance Books.

Ness, S. (2001) 'Dancing in the field: notes from memory', in Dils, A. and Albright, A.C. (eds), *Moving History/Dancing Cultures: A Dance History Reader*, Middletown, CT: Wesleyan University Press.

Shea Murphy, J. (2009) 'Mobilizing (in) the archive: Santee Smith's Kaha:wi', in Foster, S. (ed.), *Worlding Dance*, New York: Palgrave MacMillan.

Shimakawa, K. (2004) 'Loaded images: seeing and being in "Fan Variations" ' in Mitoma, J., Trimillos, R.D. and Jorjorian, A. (eds), *Narrative/Performance: Cross-Cultural Encounters at APPEX*. Los Angeles: Center for Intercultural Performance, <http://www.wac.ucla.edu/cip/appexbook/loadedimages.html>.

Stoneley, P. (2006) *A Queer History of the Ballet*, London: Routledge.

Note

1 It is worth noting, however, that Gautier was a libretticist as well as a dance critic. In this sense, like earlier dance writers, he bridged a now taken-for-granted gap between dance writing and dance creation.

14

DANCE AND GENDER

Formalism and semiotics reconsidered

Stephanie Jordan and Helen Thomas

The following paper was specifically intended as a collaboration between two writers whose work on dance incorporates different disciplinary frameworks: dance practice/history/criticism (Jordan), and sociology of dance/culture (Thomas), Thus, our interest in and our observations on dance are coloured by the theoretical and methodological positions we inhabit in our respective disciplines. We have sought to use these differences, as well as points of overlap, to our advantage. Through the process of writing and rewriting the other's writing, we have attempted to generate a more kaleidoscopic view of the topics and themes under discussion in this paper than we would have been able to do individually.

The two starting points for our paper might hardly seem compatible: Ann Daly's analysis of the third theme from Balanchine's *The Four Temperaments* (1946) in her article 'The Balanchine woman' (1987) and the work of the choreographer Siobhan Davies.[1] The latter is a leading British contemporary dance choreographer, one of the first generation of contemporary choreographers to emerge in Britain in the 1970s. But Daly's feminist analysis of *The Four Temperaments*, we found, suggested an interesting additional perspective for viewing Davies' work, and a consideration of that perspective reminded us of some fundamental issues inherent in reading art.

Daly reads the third theme of *The Four Temperaments* as an example of a man manipulating a powerless and vulnerable woman. It is a duet based on doublework, lifts and supports. Daly's view is that the goal of this joint venture is the display of the line of the woman's body, but that there are also violent, sadomasochistic undertones. The duet is an instance of ballet representing an ideology that denies women their own agency. Of course, it goes without saying that many other writers have seen very different things in this duet, and some have not seen any of what Daly saw.

Jordan (1987) described Davies' duet form as democratic, two people equally active, often presenting two distinct lines of dance in counterpoint, and with the woman motivating the man as much as vice versa. Davies' duet form seemed democratic in relation to most ballet and other established styles of contemporary dance. A closer examination revealed that most of the contact ideas introduced in Davies' duets use the man once again as the physically stronger and more powerful of the two. Even some moves which the woman could quite easily have achieved are given to the man. The woman lightly pushes the man's arm or foot or just touches him as a signal for him to move on. The man uses his strength to lift her or pull her up from the ground, but also acts as her support, which may not necessarily require much strength at all.

Is Davies' duet behaviour a mere token gesture towards the women's movement, giving the woman some agency, 'democratic', but really only superficially so? Perhaps we need to see what else her duets contain, information that emerged from the early viewings of Davies' work.

Our example is a series of related duets from *Rushes*, a piece that Davies made for Second Stride in 1982. These duets, performed by the grey couple in the piece, have been selected because they are in many ways typical of Davies' duet style of the mid and late 1980s. They can also be compared with *The Four Temperaments* duet, being likewise part of a non-narrative piece. Seen as a whole, *Rushes* progresses towards a violent rush of activity. The six dancers move slowly at the beginning, later dash from one spot to another, until at the end, in a state of tension, it is as if they have to leave the stage. A mob develops; solos and duets give way to quartets and sextets as the piece progresses. There is tension, even violence, but nothing as specific as character or story.

An important image that emerges in these duets is that of the body being pulled or pushed onwards, 'rushed', not stopping and being placed, but always going somewhere. Sometimes the dancers, each in turn, give the impetus or signal to move on to their partner and, as we have seen, the man more forcibly than the woman. But that is only one way in which this image arises; the dancers often carry it within their own bodies, as if they propel themselves or are propelled by an external imaginary force.

Another feature is the imaginary lines that seem to pull out from the dancers, as gestures, for instance, project beyond the body. Often there is counterpull, forces pulling in different directions to create spatial tension. This can occur within one body; in the second duet in the series, the woman arches and throws one arm way back, but her weight pulls her forward to become the force that wins. At other times there are pulls in opposing directions between the dancers who function independently: back to back (the moment occurs in both duets 2 and 3), the woman stretches one arm out to pull directly upwards, while the man pulls away horizontally. There are instances too when the spatial pull involves contact: in duet 1, the man pulls the woman back in an arch, while both take their hips forwards until they eventually fall and release the spatial tension into a run. This last example also emphasizes an important line within the structure of this duet, the diagonal line which is the territory of the duet. Physical manipulation of a partner to move him or her on or to hold the person back is therefore part of the general force field of the series of duets, and indeed of the piece as a whole, a powerful expression of tension, but nevertheless an ingredient in the general style of the work, one that complements and is complemented by other ingredients. It has implications well beyond those of the relationship between man and woman.

Lifts too take their place within the formal logic of the duets, expressing climax in more than one sense. There is the climax of level – there are no major jumps to compete as elevation. There is also a peak of dynamic excitement – lifts look especially energetic as lifts combined with turns, and the second lift in duets 2 and 3 raises the dynamic level one stage higher, each turning further than the last. These lifts can also be seen as climaxes of resolution, after counterpoint and spatial tensions between the couple. But they are temporary resolutions, as the dancers return immediately afterwards to expressing the tensions that are so characteristic of this piece.

So far, we have looked at the *Rushes* duets from a formalist perspective, which is what early viewings suggested. Many of the concerns behind such a perspective have a parallel in the analysis of music, but perhaps the most significant parallel lies in the linguistic analysis of literature which emerged from the Russian formalist school of literary criticism in the 1920s. The formalists were concerned with analysing how words were used and combined in a particular manner to generate a desired aesthetic effect, in much the same way as we have illustrated here. One of the problems with this kind of analysis, however, is that it is somewhat one-sided, and we would want to maintain that the words themselves or, in this case, the movements themselves, cannot be studied without any reference to meaning or in isolation from the whole work. When we say, then, that, despite the absence of a specific story or plot in *Rushes*, the work conveys tension and even violence, the concern becomes to ask how the work manages to achieve this. To that extent, we see ourselves as moving from a strict formalist perspective towards what might be more appropriately termed a structuralist analysis of *Rushes*.

It is important to note that structuralism does not embody a single theoretical framework, but, rather, it can be best described as a method of inquiry. As a mode of analysis, structuralism seeks to explain surface events, in this case a dance, in terms of the structures that lie below the surface level and that underscore it. Moreover, from this viewpoint, the art work is treated as a structure that functions as an emerging coherent whole, constantly in the process of structuration through its own determinate internal rules. The art work is not simply an aggregate of individual parts, but, rather, the parts conform to the same set of internal rules that determine the whole. The parts, then, have no existence outside the structure in which they are brought into being and through which they are ordered. But the structure is not static, because it is able to use transformational rules that provide for the possibility of new material being brought into existence to effect change and movement. So the concern becomes to look at the art work in terms of its specificity, dynamics, form, content and so forth in order to draw out the complex sets of interrelationships at work in it, which, combined together, help to create the aesthetic effect and give rise to the emerging integrated whole. Thus, individual movements in a dance have no meaning in and of themselves. Rather, meaning is determined by the relationship of the movement to all other aspects that are involved in the dance work. Consequently, although we are separating out certain sections of *Rushes,* to illustrate particular points, the concern is always to integrate these back into the emerging whole.

Our analysis, in general, privileges what Jakobson (1972) terms the 'poetic function' of language. Jakobson sets out six linguistic functions of communication which can be applied fruitfully to other modes of communication apart from verbal language: the referential, the emotive, the cognitive, the phatic, the metalinguistic and the poetic. The various functions run together and, in the same message, they can be seen to exist in various proportions. The dominant function is reliant upon the type of communicational expression. If, for example, the aim is to prevent confusion between the sign and the object or the message and the reality it refers to, then the referential or cognitive function will predominate. However, if the message ceases to be the instrument of communication and becomes the object of communication, as in works of art, then the poetic function will predominate. There are two major forms of semiotic expression, the referential (objective, cognitive) function, on the one hand, and, on the other, the emotive (subjective, expressive) function. These two functions are closely related and yet antithetical to each other. They combine what Jakobson (ibid.) calls 'the double function of language'. Each function involves different modes of perception, one with understanding, the other with feeling and, as a result, they embrace two different modes of meaning. The logical and the expressive signs have different and opposing characteristics and comprise two forms of signification that coincide with the polarity between the sciences and the arts. Where the referential function predominates, the concern will be with denotation or signing and conversely, where the poetic function is the determining function, then the focus will be on connotation or symbolizing.

Daly's semiotic analysis of *The Four Temperaments* is largely denotative in character. That is, she looks at the work to demonstrate how it reflects existing gender relations in the 'real world' outside the dance. The analysis points to, in a somewhat literal manner, a symmetry between the dancers' movements and the ways in which women are subordinated by the 'male gaze' or look, in a society seen to be organized on the basis of patriarchal relations. This type of semiotic analysis is largely extrinsic in orientation as opposed to ours which seeks to focus on the intrinsic, structural and connotative features of a dance work where the poetic function is treated as primary. Of course, this does not mean that the referential function is absent, but rather that it is subservient to the aesthetic dimension where the focus is on the symbol which is self-referring, as opposed to the sign which is concerned with denotation.

If we wished to read the first example we gave of the duet form in *Rushes* in a denotative manner, we might begin by considering the symmetrical and asymmetrical relations between the male and female dancers. As we suggested earlier, there is a symmetry between the man and woman in terms of physical activity, in the two distinct lines of counterpoint and in the reciprocity of movement motivation. However, when the contact element of the work is taken into account, these relations of symmetry are counterposed by other asymmetrical relations, with the male dancer taking on the traditional role of being physically stronger and more powerful than the female. In other words, 'democracy's body' in dance co-exists with its opposite, the traditional use of men and women's bodies within dance and without in the 'real world'. We could suggest that these relations of symmetry and asymmetry speak to and of the changes and continuities in contemporary gender relations in our culture. While there has been a movement towards women's liberation and equality of the sexes, at least in certain aspects of social life, these have been underpinned by the continuation of the status quo insofar as the traditional power bases in society remain male dominated.

This kind of analysis privileges the referential function of communication as opposed to the poetic function. Sometimes, or at least at some points during a piece, as we suggested before, one reading might conflict with or even cancel out another. Indeed, this is likely to happen in work such as that of Davies, where there is a good deal of analytical interest other than the gender relations. We consider that when other formal relationships come into play along with the man/woman relation, then analysis should be directed towards the interrelation of the parts to the whole work.

On reflection, perhaps it is significant that gender aspects of the piece seemed so quiet at early viewings (Jordan's). Conventional behaviour can so easily become invisible behaviour. Often, it is only when the rules of behaviour have been broken that we come to understand that, indeed, they constitute conventions of behaviour which are rule bound and subject to sanctions. As we pointed out earlier, it is important to get underneath the surface of appearances to reveal the hidden structural interrelations. However, it is interesting to speculate that, if Davies had shifted from the physical conventions between man and woman more than she did, the duet could well have developed into a statement about gender and obscured her formal issues (and the poetic function) in the process. If she had taken this idea to the extreme, the dance could have been reduced to a piece of agitprop with the concomitant loss of what Marcuse calls art's 'otherness'

(Marcuse 1977). By using the conventions of male/female behaviour in dance, Davies might be seen not to have put gender on the agenda.

So far, we have deliberately avoided talking about Davies' intentions as a choreographer, primarily because we have been focusing on the dance as an entity in itself, rather like a text, which is viewed as not being reducible to its creator and/or its viewers. Nevertheless, there is a tripartite relation at work here (author/text/reader(s), choreographer/dance/viewer(s)) that we feel requires consideration. So, it might be pertinent to introduce Davies' claim that she sees her dancers first and foremost as people, with dance personalities, not as men and women. Lifts, she describes as fulfilling 'a visual and dynamic need as much as anything else', like 'the rise and fall of a melody ... I don't want to restrict myself to not using that' (Davies 1989).

Davies then seems to have been touched by the consciousness of the women's movement – the relative democracy of her duet style demonstrates this – but only insofar as this does not reduce the richness of her formal content, which celebrates the poetic function of dance.

From what he said and accounts of his behaviour, Balanchine was certainly not touched by the women's movement, and it is crystal clear that women and men in his ballets are used as contrasting elements. In *The Four Temperaments*, this continues to be the case. However, we use the word 'elements' because it is possible to see the opposition of men and women as one part of the formal content of the piece. Other writers have read the ballet as a whole in formalist terms: as an essay about scale, the expansion and contraction of vision (Croce 1979), or as a piece about the construction of a ballet body (Copeland 1990). When we looked at the ballet as a whole (Daly does not do this – she generalizes from an examination of one section of the ballet, the one that can be most easily read in terms of man manipulating woman), we saw fragmentation and small-scale activity leading to a mass assertion of power in geometrical configurations, modernist architectural solidity after early waywardness, uncertainty and even occasional absurdity. Choleric, the last and the most powerful and self-sufficient of the four temperaments, is a woman! She becomes the leader of the mass into the final, highly formal, highly architectural, machine-imaged, aeroplanes-taking-off-from-a-runway apotheosis.

Given this analysis, which privileges the abstract, we see that lifts and supports can be read primarily in terms of increasing the effect of power. Two bodies combine to extend and dramatize the line of verticality, the pull between sky and earth, to create counter-tensions in a horizontal plane, to enlarge a movement idea, to use the off-vertical (of the woman's body) as a metaphor for danger and the assertion to overcome that danger. At the same time, however, if we probe underneath the surface of the final theme a little more, we suggest that this abstract relation of woman to the mass and to modernist forms can also be read analytically as a counterpoint to the historically perceived role of women as producers and consumers of denigrated cultural forms.

During the nineteenth century, women became increasingly associated with 'mass' culture, while real 'high' culture remained the privilege of men. Women were excluded from authentic high culture before the nineteenth century but, during the industrial revolution and cultural modernization, this exclusion took on new overtones. In the late nineteenth and early twentieth centuries, the idea of the threat of the masses 'rattling at the gate' led to cries of the loss of civilization and culture and the underlying view that it was the rise of mass culture (the masses) which had caused this decline. But there was yet another hidden subject underneath this – women. Women were also rattling at the gate, but their battle was with a male-dominated society.

As artistic realism gave way to aesthetic modernism, so the identification of woman with mass culture came to take on new dimensions. Time and time again, in the political and artistic discourses of the turn of the century, the woman was associated with mass culture, while 'high' modernist culture remained firmly in the privileged realm of the male. Ultimately, according to Huyssen (1986), mass culture as woman comes to stand as modernism's other. So, it is interesting that Choleric in Balanchine's work becomes the leader of the mass, a symbol of danger, which forms into strong, abstract, modernist-like configurations. In this instance, the mass, with a woman at its head, actively advances into the shape of modernism rather than adopting its prescribed role as modernism's denigrated other. We suggest that woman, here, as a metaphor for danger, is active, not passive, and not merely being supported.

Even in theme 3, one can see these features and effects: the colossal circlings of the legs one after the other taking the woman into the shape of a ship's prow, enlarged movement and shape enabled by the man's support. Or there are the high lifts with pointes pulling together underneath the woman, then shooting out arrow-sharp to the floor, a movement that contributes to the geometrical content of the apotheosis. Then, in the 'drag step', with the man reaching out and upwards, the effect of energy and work is increased by the woman clinging aggressively to his back. We do not read this as Daly does: 'the man literally carries the ballerina on his back'. Nor do we see her stretched legs and pointes pushing into the floor as 'lifeless, following after her like limp paws' (Daly 1987).

In the context of the whole ballet and the expressiveness derived from abstract features, we begin to read gender relations differently from Daly, and we would rather agree with Edwin Denby's (1986) observation of 'girls dancing hard and boys soft' in *The Four Temperaments*. Even in theme 3, the woman shows her own work: she is not simply the manipulated, passive woman. Elsewhere, women show rather than mask the power of pushing themselves upwards, as well as being supported into huge lifts. True, there are instances of women being manipulated blatantly like marionettes, turned and strummed like a cello in theme 3, for instance, but these are just brief touches of humour, not used to build a character, or to be fixed like a label to a dancer, and, in the same ballet, it is just as easy to find examples of men being mocked, played with, again as brief touches of expression. Just as often, too, women and men work together to produce image and effect.

Yet, still, like Davies, we do not feel that Balanchine is making any major point about gender, at least in *The Four Temperaments*. Gender is not really on his agenda either. He uses ballet's gender conventions as invisible conventions, fascinated by the particular content of ballet language, its emphasis on line, stretch and verticality and the extension of these features in doublework, and wanting to use that content for every expressive purpose other than to comment on gender relations.

Balanchine's comments, often chauvinistic comments, about women are famous. Several of his dancers have spoken in support of them. The ballet culture as a whole supports them. In one sense, he said too much. In another, he said far too little, but, then, he was not given to talking much at all, and certainly not to the sophisticated analysis of his work that would have placed his comments on women in a very different perspective. However, it is clear that many of his dancers, for example Merrill Ashley, Kyra Nichols, Suzanne Farrell and Darci Kistler, have invested their roles with quite different and wide-ranging representations of women, and possibly these dancers have done so in the light of changing representations of women in life around them. 'In spite of the choreography', Daly (1987: 17) suggests, referring to Ashley's autonomy in the *Symphony in C* adagio. We would suggest that the choreography has the formal richness and potential that have encouraged these interpretations, that it was a text created in dialogue with its original cast, and that is now a text that has an independent life from that of its creators. We refer again to the tripartite structure here, choreographer/dance/viewer, and bring the performer into the picture as well. We believe too that Balanchine dancers today might also do well to research their own image, beyond the immediacy of their own roles and in relation to the whole poetic context of a ballet.

We are not denying that Balanchine can be read as Daly reads him – only that there are many other possibilities, many yet to be discovered as new interpretations emerge, if we admit the poetic function of art. The picture becomes far more complex and, we think, more intriguing. We suggest that the same ideas can be readily applied to other ballet choreographers.

A richness emerges when we consider the interplay of both the poetic and semiotic perspectives. So often, work is examined from one or the other of these two perspectives, and analysis is only the poorer for this. We are open to the possibility of multiple readings on the basis of intertextuality (author(s)/text(s)/reader(s)) which post-structuralist and postmodernist approaches celebrate. However, we do not wish to suggest that any account will do, as is often the case in postmodernist and post-structuralist approaches which place stress on the relativization of accounts and a seemingly endless play of signifiers. Ultimately, both perspectives are structuralist in orientation, because they maintain that the world is made up of relationships between objects rather than the things themselves. Semiotic analysis, for example, is founded on the notion that there is an arbitrary relation between the sign and its referent, between the elements that comprise the sign, the signifier and signified, and an arbitrary relation between the signs which, by virtue of their difference from each other, make up the system of signs in question. Both perspectives together can now enhance our understanding of all kinds of dance, work that we feel questions traditional male/female roles as well as work that does not seem to do this.

Note

1 Daly's work draws on developments in feminist film theory, which incorporates semiotics and psychoanalysis. One of the reasons why the authors have chosen to focus on Daly's writing is that it has often been used rather uncritically by other writers who adopt a feminist stance. There is a chapter on Davies' work in Jordan (1992).

15

A TAPESTRY OF INTERTEXTS

Dance analysis for the twenty-first century

Janet Lansdale (formerly Adshead)

> *To see a World in a Grain of Sand*
> *And a Heaven in a Wild Flower,*
> *Hold Infinity in the palm of your hand*
> *And Eternity in an Hour*
> (William Blake, c.1803)

To begin a twenty-first century essay on dance analysis with an extract from a poem written at the very beginning of the nineteenth century, by the English visionary painter and poet William Blake (1757–1827), might seem to strain credulity, since dance research is very much a newcomer as a discipline, one which could hardly have existed at that time. Furthermore, Blake's spiritual convictions were strongly held in the face of the growing imperative of scientific rationalism, as his biographer, Peter Ackroyd (1995) illustrates, whereas at the beginning of the twentieth-first century this is no longer contentious (except in fundamentalist religious contexts), but rather the taken-for-granted *modus operandi* of everyday life, and of many disciplinary investigations.

Nevertheless, like most effective art, this poem might be seen as timeless: not only is it a well-known and evocative poem, it also speaks to the present as much as to the past. Blake's poetry, it has been suggested, carries a link to the present in its 'biblical motifs and images' (ibid.: 25).[1] That this is effective largely though metaphoric relevance, rather than factual connection, is a demonstration of the power of the image, whether visual, verbal, danced or musical, to speak across different aesthetic environments and time periods, even when the fundamental mode of rationality changes from a theological to a scientific one. Arts scholarship today inhabits a paradoxical position, evoking a history of images which, in turn, suggest other times and places, dealing with ideals and ideas in a mode which is imaginative and expressive, rather than scientific.

I suggest that this extract from William Blake's *Auguries of Innocence* (in Keynes 1966: 431) may be seen as a metaphor for the process of analysis of dance, bringing attention to the relationship between the single moment and the whole of an experience, in an act of interpretation, whether of life, of a dance or of a poem. The analogies that suggest themselves are several. Firstly, the poem points up the momentary nature of experience, highly relevant to the perception of dance, since the moment is all we can see. We cannot appreciate this time-based art all at once like a painting, so, like music, we observe (and usually hear also) a moment-by-moment shifting landscape – knowing full well that this is a fraction, a slice, a tiny part that fits within a larger whole of the dance (Adshead 1988). Each moment thus takes on the character of 'infinity in the palm of your hand', referring simultaneously to the significance of the moment and to the meanings of the whole. In each single moment we realise the dance as 'the world in a grain of sand' or, expressed another way, the entire dance becomes encapsulated in a single movement. Yet, as it is extended before our eyes, each moment presenting itself before us in turn in this physical, yet metaphorical way, each sequence followed by another, and another, the dance reaches towards infinity (or more prosaically towards the end). In the wholeness of the moment we see 'heaven', in the exquisite connectivity of elements, distinctively formed in *this* way in *this* dance.

Therefore, in looking at dance analytically, a notion that does not in itself exclude either interpretation or metaphor, we have to observe the single moment intently, to register its completeness while also seeing its movement toward something else – another moment – what it shares with the next, and how it differs. This accumulation of moments, marked by similarity and difference among and between them, culminates in wholes of varying sizes and ultimately in the 'dance', something that has a beginning and an end even if it is without conventional beginnings and endings.[2]

The ways in which we have conducted analysis vary through time. During the twentieth century, systems of dance analysis were built upon the thinking of earlier dancing masters and social commentators to construct classifications of movement, often articulating their codifications based directly on highly specific and deeply expressive needs of the dance of a particular time. Some elements dominate, capturing the imagination at certain times and others at other times, rising and falling in interest, in consequence of shifts in philosophical, cultural and art practices more broadly. The pull of a dancerly artistic moon is reflected throughout its history, drawing both practice and analysis closer to its theatrical shores at one moment and then to its abstract shores of line and colour as a visual or musical art at another.[3]

How might these classifications or codifications be characterised now, for the twenty-first century? It is vital to recognise the implications of the way dance is constituted both in verbal language and in its own 'dance languages', each of which have developed specific vocabularies and physical counterparts, for example in systems of dance notation, in the movements enshrined in a technique and in the language used to teach technique, repertoire and choreography and to write about it. This might entail the construction of an endlessly proliferating series of languages, but since all dance forms have some connection with elaborated movement, it is sometimes suggested that a single system, akin to Western musical notation and analysis, would be useful.

Indeed, Laban-based movement analysis is one such system that has been championed as universally useful; a tool capable of use in the analysis of all dance and movement forms. A shift can be seen from what might be called Laban's early-twentieth-century romantic organicism to the pseudo-scientific Labananalysis which his American followers subsequently developed, and which has been applied in many domains including therapy (Bartenieff *et al.* 1984).[4] But this context-free, apparently objective analytic framework, like all such models (even in science), is embedded in a particular contextual and conceptual environment. It is necessary to understand Laban's theories in these terms.

Thus to regard any one system of movement analysis as universally useful is to fail to recognise the strength of argument in the 1980s' development in dance studies towards understanding the conditions of production and reception of cultural practices and away from the 'excavation', as Desmond (1997a: 3) terms it, of the text. Even a single movement is not value or culture free.

Despite this, Preston Dunlop (1999), a key European inheritor of Laban's work, continues to promote a view of his work that downplays the significance of a particular kind of mysticism, as well as his possible Nazi involvement (Karina *et al.* 2004; Moore 1999). According to Moore, esoteric philosophy was a *crucial* underpinning for Laban's choreutic theories, while Kant argues that he was deeply implicated in the Third Reich.

Cultural studies encompass a myriad of approaches and subjects but most importantly it promotes a focus on political engagement and the analysis of power. It becomes obvious that any language of movement and dance, both the practical form and analysis of it, is embedded in a particular context: its own internal language constructed within the frame of its cultural and political ecology. Hence, in my view, the promotion of a Laban system of movement analysis reflects a now out-dated globalising and colonising tendency that cannot be supported in either political or epistemological terms, given the huge diversity of cultural expressions.

Concentrating now on the dance form, as the individual moments accumulate a structure also emerges, partly given by the dance, its internal codifications, and its positioning of movement, musical and visual materials, and partly by what the spectator brings to it. We should ask, however, whose structure this is in a more precise sense. In an earlier work (Adshead-Lansdale 2007) I draw out a discussion of narrating voices, or, put another way, of who is telling what kind of story. While this is an obvious area of interest in terms of the dance-maker and her/his collaborators, it is just as relevant in analysing a dance. The voices of the dance-maker and collaborators are important but they are not the only voices of interest in this debate. The reference to narrative voices in the plural reinforces two principles: firstly, that many stories can be told, with the corollary that none of them has a claim to be universal or all-embracing; and, secondly, that the story told will differ in consequence of the cultural position and individuality of the person who tells it.[5]

The idea of narrative rests on structure – they are interwoven, traditionally, in the sense that there is a beginning, a middle and an end, implying an evolution of events. While this is much challenged by postmodern dance-makers, it survives at least in the sense that a dance starts, a series of events follows, and some time later it stops. This series of events guides the reader, often in well-worn ways, to follow the 'story' or in the case of a less obvious narrative, to note the passing similarities and differences, in constructing a more abstract canvas. Interest in the regularities and disparities that appear in creating units larger than the sentence (a kind of equivalent to 'paragraph' dance structures) has led to theories of structure or of combining elements, that draw on literary theories of structuralism and semiotics and which, in turn, relate to the topic of discourse (Adshead-Lansdale 1999a). Knowledge of the conventions governing how links are made between elements and between small wholes and the wider context is a necessary condition of successful understanding. These conventions are the material underlying constructions of genre, and of discourse analysis, as my own extended intertextual analysis of Lloyd Newson and his company DV8s, *Strange Fish*, shows (Lansdale 2007). I use this powerful work, first shown on stage in England in 1992, and later made widely available on video (1993; televised in 1994), as illustrative material for my argument.

Although the 'text' (the dance and its accompanying sources) guides the reader it does not pre-determine the outcome of interpretation. A useful distinction can be made when we study a dance between 'authorial' and 'ancestral' voices, although the two are closely intertwined.[6] I use 'authorial' in the sense of the 'author' as historically constituted, as the original artist, but I also treat the construct of 'author' as equivalent to the 'reader' in the sense of a postmodernist 'creator' or 'constructor' of the work. On this basis, each of us has a 'voice' which becomes 'authorial' as we bring the work into existence. People engaged in making and performing the work, whether as performers, film makers, critics or theorists, speak with 'authorial' voices, just as much as those watching and writing, whether from academic disciplines or from experience in theatre practice. In the book referred to above, concerning Lloyd Newson's *Strange Fish*, I suggest that many such 'authorial' voices can be heard, arising from individual characterisations, from situations that develop, and in terms of the concerns being dealt with; that is, its subject matter and treatment.

In contrast I use 'ancestral' to refer to those traces of the past and of the pre-existing present which surround creative artists and writers and the ideas with which they engage. The term 'ancestral' allows me to reflect not only on specific antecedent texts and narratives that might affect an individual's response (whether as maker or reader) but also on those narratives enshrined in the history of dance and theatre. Prior modes of analysis are part of this. Both authorial and ancestral voices are important in the creation and understanding of any theatre or dance form. They are often highly significant as the basis of the genre coding of the text and it is an appreciation of genre that allows us to position a dance within a range of dances and to see how, and in what ways, it sustains existing ideas and develops new ones (Frow 2006).

Thus the answer to the question 'whose narrative, or whose analysis, is this?' is not simple. Lloyd Newson created one narrative for the stage and he collaborated with David Hinton in creating another one for the film of *Strange Fish*, which Hinton directed. Critics wrote about it, and I have created yet another. What is brought to the fore is my own purpose in carrying out this analysis, which, while not perversely in opposition to previous constructions, is nonetheless uniquely mine. And so the 'I' in the narrative of analysis can be exposed. As de Lauretis (1984: 10) observes, narrative acts 'to engender the subject in the movement of its discourse, as it defines positions of meaning, identification, and desire'.

In order to address this idea in greater depth and to argue the case for an intertextual reading it is necessary to present a brief theoretical aside on deconstruction, developing the idea of metaphor in relationship to close reading of the dance. Deconstruction and intertextuality are inherently related since together they raise underlying theoretical and value positions to a level of awareness where they can be examined in relation to the text.

Its key attributes lie, firstly, in its contribution to a sceptical and close reading of texts (a term in which I include dances and other cultural products); secondly, in its attention to the nature of metaphor; and thirdly, to metaphor in the context of political and ideological struggle. In Derrida's view of language there can be no one-to-one correspondence; the signifier does not yield up a signified directly, they continually break apart and re-attach in new combinations. If meaning is not immediately present in a sign, but 'scattered or dispersed along the whole chain of signifiers ... [it produces] a kind of constant flickering of presence and absence together'. To 'read' is to 'trace' this process. In turn, a 'trace' – a track or footprint – is an imprint of something absent, and by analogy each sign is inhabited by the trace of another sign, traced through all those that have gone before 'to form a complex tissue which is never exhaustible' (Sarup 1988: 35–6).

Dance analysis thus becomes a system which requires attention to the detail of the dance: its movements, the spatial orientation and dynamic inflection of each movement, its presentation within a visual and often musical environment, as well as its subject matters and treatments. But it is also, always, critically aware of the multiple possible significances evoked in this flickering fashion and of the connections between them – a complex tissue indeed – which then demands that the reader trace a particular route to arrive at an interpretation.

These notions of trace, absence and flickering presence are central to the construct of intertextuality. Whether the notion of intertextuality as used in literature (where it originated) is the same as that used in dance or music or film and media is something that needs debate. When used in music it seems to be a less open concept, where texts are linked from within to contextual information, as in 'intertextual correspondences'. This is closer to source criticism, where notions of influence continue to be evident (Worton and Still 1990). It is a version of intertextuality in which late works illuminate early ones and early works point to meanings in later ones. This can tend to become an extended literary analysis closely related to the written texts with which the music or dance connects – hidden analogies and correspondences – rather than the problematic juxtapositions arising from the direct engagement with the work, implied by the form of intertextuality that I use.

The music theorist Kofi Agawu explains intertextuality rather differently as 'forcing an engagement with other texts (musical, literary, as well as critical)' and in the sense of the play that is set up by Kristeva's codes. He asks how 'intertextual resonances interrupt and thus help to define narrativity',[7] showing that intertextuality makes for a less direct narrative – enriching, building 'an intricate web of relations around text and intertexts' (in Ayrey and Everist 1996: 237). This is more clearly in line with literary notions and with the account of intertextuality that I support.

It is my contention that theories and methodologies, or practices, of intertextuality can be used to demonstrate how different interpretations are possible, how a range of texts, and traces of texts might prompt them, and how viewers or readers can construct them. No two retellings of a story are the same, as Doniger (1998) points out in relation to the telling of myth and legend. This in turn leads to a demand that we understand how different readers are differently placed or situated and how they draw on historical and cultural accounts in order to create stories. The same person may construct different stories at different times, or if situated within another cultural group. We might ask if there are commonalities within groups – do gay men tell stories of relationships in a way that is common to them but different from that of gay women or heterosexual men or women? Labels such as these are treacherous in any case, since 'gay men' are not a heterogeneous group. But if the categories are refined, for instance to London-based 19–25-year-old male gays or heterosexual females, we begin to have a more precise specification of who is doing the reading. It may also be possible to ask what would be evident in a work such as *Strange Fish* that might tell the reader that those involved in its creation approached it from a specific gender perspective. Equally, one can ask how such identity positions might be reflected in a reading. Replacing the heterosexual world-view, like the colonialist world-view, with another world-view, does not make the reading any more valid, although it may be interesting or more fashionable, or challenging for readers in the early twenty-first century.

The construct of 'intertextuality', I argue, is helpful in several senses. Firstly, it is a method of tracing the interrelationships of actual people, hiding behind, and reflected in, the terms 'author', 'text' and 'reader'. Secondly, it can identify and clarify the potentially conflicting sets of genre coding that add other layers to the possible modes of interaction – as in the case I examined in detail, between the choreographer, the dance and the spectator of *Strange Fish*. Thirdly, intertextuality can reveal both what is present in these texts and what is absent, pointing to the traces that dominate and those that appear to retreat as we construct different readings. Since people interacting and dancing are inevitably embodied, the body itself becomes highly visible, although often through (paradoxically) its absence in critical writing and its metaphoric use elsewhere.[8] Fourthly, intertextuality focuses on the social and cultural representation of embodied human beings, since it looks outside the conditions of dance discourse to its interaction with other discourses.

Considering the interaction with other discourses, Desmond (1997a: 1) suggests: 'recent work ... is beginning to foreground theoretical concerns which ... focus on the ideological underpinnings of aesthetic practices'. Martin, similarly, is careful to insist that while politics and dance share 'movement', they have to be 'specified' as distinct cultural practices, and not collapsed one into the other. Through analysis of certain social scenes in *Strange Fish*, a 'theory of politics' can be made visible, if such a theory is understood as ways of treating 'participation generated through the gathering of bodies' (Martin 1998: 9). Certain scenes make identification with a 'particular political movement' prominent. It is possible to see how a 'sense of space and time is generated through social life' within a theatre piece (ibid.: 35). Translated into physical theatre, politics asks *what* is mobilised rather than *how* resistance operates, and, as Martin argues, this 'may be a more constructive framework ... in which to value and evaluate social change' (ibid.: 13).

It invites the construction of an intertextual web of methodological traces. In particular, *Strange Fish* seems to demand further analysis of this kind, since it hovers over the borders of expressionist theatre, even as it trespasses into postmodern territory. There are contradictory themes, which together render the work capable of generating, and allow the reader to construct, a matrix of free-floating, and only sometimes interlocking, interpretations.

From this challenge, however, flow a series of questions about how decisions are made about which kinds of theories, and from which domains, might be fruitful. As the preliminary statement in Graham Allen's recent text (Allen 2000) states, intertextuality is employed in structuralist, post-structuralist, semiotic, deconstructive, post-colonial, Marxist, feminist and psychoanalytic theories, and has been applied across a range of literary and cultural texts. Constantly at the forefront for me is the argument that theories and practices are in fact interrelated: they co-exist, infiltrate each other, are entailed one in the other through time. How they do this at particular moments and in response to, or in anticipation of, new art, is what is of interest as is what is explored in practice. As Meinhof and Smith (2000: 7) point out, 'the demarcation of the limits of the linguistic, symbolic or discursive realm cannot be quickly and comfortably settled'. Theories are intertexts, too.

Thus our ever-changing processes of structuring, as created through, and in, linguistic practice, serve to make life harder for the analyst. David Best (1974) describes the Wittgensteinian position on 'family resemblances' as useful for opening up philosophical debate in order to counter too rigid a drive towards 'defining' complex ideas – in this case, ideas of performance, movement and dance. But he also warns that a theory of family resemblances is not a 'universal panacea' (ibid.: 31), nor an excuse for lazy thinking, nor a means of avoiding difficult issues. Neither does he use it to support a modernist position where the arts can be detached from life. In a move that shares much with post-structuralist thinking, he also argues for an understanding of the arts as culturally embedded practices, both in conditions of their creation and in responses to them (Best 1992: xiv).

In consequence, the fact that many post-structuralist positions challenge a notion of a single truth, and open up multiple interpretations, does not relieve us of the responsibility to work at what such accounts might comprise, and how they might be (differently) constructed. It is not a fall into extreme relativity or subjectivity, but a recognition that there is more than one 'truth' and that the responsibility for constructing these truths lies directly with us. It follows that the moral or ethical implications of these positions, too, lie securely in our domain. The kind of rationality that this requires is interpretative and recognises its own presuppositions.

As Lyotard expresses it:

> most people have lost the nostalgia for the lost narrative. It in no way follows that they are reduced to barbarity. What saves them from it is their knowledge that legitimation can only spring from their own linguistic practice and communicational interaction.
>
> (Lyotard 1984: 41)

Between this 'meta' level of theorising and the immediacy of the dance, there is another structuring framework, which arises from the way academic disciplines are currently shaped. Disciplines themselves are subject to historic change and there have been many contenders over the years claiming relevance to the performing arts, from anthropology to zoology. Putting them into play together can, as Lyotard suggests, promote an argument that has the advantage of making visible the flexibility of its means, that is, the plurality of its languages and its character.

The intertextual point is that the texts relevant to any dance bear traces from the immediate present, as well as the supposedly dead past. If it is obvious that 'all texts contain traces of other texts', a more sophisticated version of this idea focuses on 'the interactions between texts, producers or texts and their readers' lifeworlds' (Meinhof and Smith 2000: 3). How the spectator, or reader, contributes his or her own intertexts to 'create' the work (in a highly specific sense) is also the subject of debate. My choices figure here: yours would change the narrative. In consequence, interpretations can be defended yet still be fluid. Paradoxically it allows the reader to 'create the text' and simultaneously to 'read the text as it wishes to be read' (Eco 1984: 9). Hence it is 'a tool which cannot be employed by readers wishing to produce stability and order, or wishing to claim authority over the text or other critics' (Allen 2000: 209).

In summary, the application of particular theories to analysis of dance, music and theatre is not without difficulty. Choice can appear to be arbitrary at one extreme, or to be an attempt to colonise an unsuspecting victim at the other. What the rationale might be for choosing any particular theory is exposed to question, requiring the writer to answer whether it is driven by random choice, historical tradition, an argument about theory, current fashion or personal inclination. The process of choosing, and the validity and appropriateness of choices made, in this treacherously open post-structuralist field becomes fundamentally the issue.

In parallel, the method employed in writing might then attempt to mimic the 'continuous centrifugal' and 'centripetal' movement towards, away from, and around both the dance, and the context or culture to which it refers (de Marinis 1993: 68). These shifts of position are sometimes in harmony, and often not, in the case of any particular reader. As Ruffini argues, in the spaces created between a multiplicity of texts and traces there is the opportunity – indeed, more strongly, the demand – that each reader should engage in this process of constructing meaning by unravelling what seems to be implied by the work, while simultaneously creating his or her own threads. O'Flaherty (1980: 3), in a rather practical and even prosaic way, provides a justification for raiding the 'toolbox' of theory in order to address specific problems appropriately, and in order to distinguish between how one goes about it and how one justifies what one has done.

The postmodern world recognises the existence of epistemological boundaries only in order to challenge them, leap over them and dissolve them. My own position is one of responding wholeheartedly to the idea that in these interdisciplinary or interstitial cracks lies the possibility for expansion of critical thinking and for the creation of new insights.[9] Thus, to 'see a world in a grain of sand' is a reflection of the depth of close examination in dance analysis, embedded within an imaginative tapestry of intertexts, and through this engagement, to 'hold infinity in the palm of your hand'. William Blake becomes entirely apposite since through this intense focus we experience an hour's dance in its entirety as indeed, an 'eternity'.

Notes

1 It seems a widely held view in many cultures that art of the past may speak equally, if differently, to other eras, but I speak here of a Western, Christian history.

2 In an earlier text contributing authors articulate a system of analysis of dances, which explains this process in greater detail (Adshead 1988).

3 See my analysis of Lloyd Newson's *Strange Fish* which I refer to in this chapter for a fully worked out example in contemporary dance. Foster's *Choreography and Narrative* (1996c) traces similar ideas through story ballets from early-eighteenth-century theatres through to ballets such as *Giselle* at the end of the nineteenth century.

4 Laban-based in this case, but the argument applies to other movement analysis systems.

5 A useful introduction to theories of narrative can be found in Porter Abbott (2002).

6 An interesting debate could be developed here about this interrelationship and the sense in which all authorial voices are to some extent ancestral, and vice versa.

7 In the *Nachtmusik*, Ayrey and Everist (1996: 235).

8 Such discourse can be unhelpful in so far as it sustains a distinction between minds/souls and bodies, as well as suggesting that they are somehow detached from cultural practices more widely, neither of which is tenable.

9 A pair of articles published in *Dance Chronicle* illustrates this point well. The struggle for respectability, as determined by scholars in other fields, against the relevance and value for an understanding of dancing and dances, forms the debate recently revisited by Ralph (1995) and continued by Adshead-Lansdale (1997).

16

LOOKING AT MOVEMENT AS CULTURE

Contact improvisation to disco

Cynthia J. Novack

In a made-for-television movie shown in Fall 1986, a woman dies ... or, at least, according to the doctors, she is 'body dead'. But somehow her brain remains alive, functioning normally. At the same time, a second woman is pronounced 'brain dead', but her body continues to breathe and function perfectly. In a miracle operation, doctors place the living brain of the first woman into the living body of the second woman. The ensuing TV drama explores the question of this new person's identity.

The doctors have no problems whatsoever with the woman's identity. Gleeful over their accomplishment, they reassure her that she really is her brain and that her body is essentially irrelevant to who she is. Her husband, however, resists this new body and is disturbed by the fact that the woman looks, moves and feels totally different; how can she be his wife? His rejection causes her to feel doubt and confusion as to her own identity. Further complications ensue: she is followed around by the husband of the woman whose body her brain now inhabits. She looks like his wife; she must be his wife, still alive somehow. Eventually, though, the miracle woman and her husband (that is, the husband of the woman whose brain survived) become reconciled to her new body as they both realize that, indeed, she is her brain, and they live, we assume, happily ever after.

This popular consideration of the mind/body split exemplifies some familiar attitudes toward movement. Like the doctors in the TV movie, many cultural observers and researchers ignore the body and its actions, seeing them as irrelevant trappings for the mind. They scarcely notice movement and do not consider its role or significance in human events; such omissions are common in accounts of cultural history and anthropology.

If researchers do pay attention to movement and the body, it may be only in order to see the mind which lies behind it. If gestures, for instance, can be translated into verbal messages, then they have been 'explained'. Cultural observers with this orientation look for the cognitive components of movement systems ('what does the movement stand for?' – a common approach in popular nonverbal communication theory) and/or the social structural implications of the body ('how do concepts of the body duplicate the social order?' – the approach of social theorists such as Mary Douglas). These translations of movement into cognitive systems can be illuminating, but sometimes they subsume the reality of the body, as if people's experiences of themselves moving in the world were not an essential part of their consciousness and of the ways in which they understand and carry out their lives.

On the other hand, researchers who wish to redress the imbalance of mind over body may react by positing the body and movement as the primary reality. Like the husbands in the TV story, they maintain the dichotomy between mind and body by emphasizing the body alone. Some researchers tend to look only 'at the movement itself' ('just describe what you see', they say) as if the body, movement and mind were independent entities, scarcely connected to social and cultural ideas and institutions. Indeed, much writing in dance history tends toward a simplistic, descriptive approach to discussing movement.

The problem here is that the division of mind and body (and the various attitudes toward movement this division suggests) dichotomizes aspects of experience which are not only closely related but which also reflect and refract upon one another. To detach one aspect from another for analytical purposes can contribute valuable insights into the nature of movement, but if one aspect is taken as the whole, distortion results. For, in fact, as sociologist John O'Neill (1985: 22) comments, '*Society is never a disembodied spectacle*. We engage in social interaction from the very start on the basis of sensory and aesthetic impressions' [original emphasis]. The body and movement are social realities interacting with and interpreting other aspects of the culture. Structured movement systems[1] such as social dance, theatre dance, sport and ritual help to articulate and create images of who people are and what their lives are like, encoding and eliciting ideas and values; they are also part of experience, of performances and actions by which people know themselves.

Since movement and the body are often opposed to words and the mind, it is interesting to look at the resemblances between movement systems and language. Both are cultural activities which have biological aspects. Even apparently simple and 'natural' actions such as walking or sitting are in part culturally constructed. Also, like language, movement is ubiquitous, a cultural given which people are constantly creating, participating in, interpreting and reinterpreting on both conscious and unconscious levels.

However, movement is unique. It precedes language in individual development, forming a primary basis for both personal identity and social relationships. It is kinaesthetic and visual, rather than aural, and, in many instances, movement is less specific (and therefore often more inclusive and ambiguous) than language. But while movement does not usually have structures which are analogous to the grammar that characterizes every language,[2] it has observable patterns and qualities which can be identified with particular cultures and historical periods. Any traveller knows the reality of these patterns; the 'natives' may walk with a different gait, may gesture more or less elaborately, may have a different rhythm and timing. The discomfort of being out of place and recognizable as a foreigner arises in part because of a difference in movement systems.

In order to observe and understand more about movement, one needs to ask what characterizes it in a given setting, how the characteristics form an overall impression, and what kinds of acceptable variations can exist. This requires careful analysis of the movement as it occurs. Understanding movement also involves asking what meanings and associations are embedded in and created by the experience of moving. Looking at movement alone, like examining any 'text', can reveal details of the techniques and structures of a movement system; but it cannot tell us how movement is interwoven with other aspects of the culture or what its implications or associations might be in any given circumstance. If we are to read the ambiguity as well as the pattern embedded in movement, we must investigate not only what the movement is like but also what its import might be and how different participants, audiences, and outsiders might understand it. Thus the movement system needs to be viewed as part of the cultural reality. It is patterned, yet it shifts and changes – as does all of culture.

Contact improvisation, an American dance form, provides an example of a structured movement system whose features are part of a shifting cultural landscape.[3] Theatre dancer Steve Paxton and a group of colleagues and students first developed contact improvisation in 1972 by experimenting with partners giving and taking weight improvisationally. The practice of contact improvisation achieved a richly varied, yet defined and identifiable, movement style. It spread to many groups of people in the US (and eventually in Canada and Europe), reaching its peak as a social and performance form in the mid to late 1970s, and is still practised by hundreds of dancers today.

People doing contact improvisation create a dance through collaborative interaction, basing their improvisation on the physical forces of weight and momentum. The dancers are supposed to be absorbed in experiencing the movement and sensing (largely through touch) the experience of their partners; in order to allow momentum to develop, dancers have to keep their energy freely flowing, abandoning self-control in favour of mutual trust and interaction.[4]

Contact improvisation as it emerged in the early 1970s was often learned in settings (jams) more akin to social dance situations than to theatre dance classes. Anyone could practise the form and, theoretically at least, perform it publicly. The experience of the movement style and improvisational process itself were thought to teach people how to live (to trust, to be spontaneous and 'free', to 'centre' oneself, and to 'go with the flow'), just as the mobile, communal living situations of the young, middle-class participants provided the setting and values which nourished this form. Dancers and audiences saw contact improvisation as, to use Clifford Geertz's phrase, a 'model of' and a 'model for' an egalitarian, spontaneous way of life (Geertz 1973: 93–4).

Contact improvisation has a history of development and change; it also has historical antecedents within both social dance and theatre dance forms. Rock-and-roll dance, a mass cultural form, was characterized by some of the same qualities in movement style and structure as contact improvisation (internal focus, ongoing energy flow, extemporariness) and the same values or concepts with which these qualities were associated (self-expression, freedom, egalitarianism, spontaneity). Theatre dance forms, practised by relatively small groups of people, shared some of the concerns of contact improvisation, investigating physical forces in dance and 'democratic' performance modes. As the contact improvisation movement arose and grew, it existed simultaneously with contrasting movement forms, such as disco dance; eventually, its style changed as technical developments ensued and as the circumstances of its practice and performance were altered.

Shifts and patterns can be perceived by tracing some of this history – noting the presence of some of contact improvisation's movement characteristics and ideas in prior American dance and performance forms, and looking at contact improvisation in conjunction with certain coexisting movement practices. This study illustrates some ways of looking at movement as culture, while at the same time it points to the complexity of the topic. Certain movement qualities appear through time, yet meanings suggested by these qualities subtly shift; contrasting movement styles exist simultaneously, sometimes embodying the same meanings and sometimes opposite meanings. Yet movement, which seems so elusive, can also be very concrete. Evoking the way a group of people move can call up the ambiance of a cultural time and place with clarity and immediacy.

The development of rock-and-roll in the late 1950s marked a major, widespread incorporation of dance and music from black communities into the mainstream of American popular dance and music. The powerful influence of black dance and music in shaping American culture has a long history, and the emergence of rock-and-roll dance and music is a key moment in that history.[5] Central to this development were social changes, most notably the civil rights movement, which challenged former boundaries between blacks and whites. Also key, and historically unprecedented, was the post-war media explosion of television, which consolidated rock-and-roll as a mass phenomenon.

The borrowed/incorporated movement qualities and structures from black dance traditions included extensive use of shoulders, head, hips and knees, often moving independently or in different directions at the same time. Emphasis tended to be on continuity of energy flow and on rhythmic impulses, rather than on the specific positioning of body parts, and on improvisation both by individual dancers and by couples.

By the mid 1960s, people in some communities had carried improvisational flexibility in rock-and-roll dancing to a point at which it was acceptable for dancers to go out onto the dance floor, alone or with a group of people rather than a partner, and move in highly individual styles. But although the 'steps' were not codified and most people felt they were being 'free', the dancing was still typified by certain structural and movement characteristics. Dancers improvised within a specific movement range. They tended to move with a focus inward rather than outward to a partner or to the environment, absorbed by the music and the experience of moving. They frequently danced with a sense of energy freely sent in all directions, creating an impression of abandon and literally giving up control.

These movement qualities were important components of the cultural environment of that time. Engaging in these ways of moving shaped feelings not only about the 'right' way to move and to dance, but also about the 'right' way to live. The movement style seemed natural, contemporary, free and not 'uptight'. Along with the rock music of the period, dancing both reinforced and crystallized an image of the self: independent yet communal, free, sensual, daring. This image of self would be central to contact improvisation.

The movement qualities of rock dancing were also associated with contemporary social movements and practices such as the civil rights movement, youth culture and drug-taking, and with values such as rebellion, expressiveness and individualism within a loving community of peers. Dancing encoded these ideas in a flexible and multilayered text, its kinaesthetic and structural characteristics laden with social implications and associations. Depending on the circumstances and cultural backgrounds of the participants or observers, different aspects of the dancing would emerge as primary.

For instance, because of its pelvic movements and open derivation from black culture, the twist (c.1961) was at once perceived by segments of the American public as overly sexual, as well as antisocial, because of the separation of one dancer from another. In 1962, one English journalist visiting New York wrote:

I'm not easily shocked but the Twist shocked me ... half Negroid, half Manhattan, and when you see it on its native heath, wholly frightening ... the essence of the Twist, the curious perverted heart of it, is that you dance it alone.

(Beverly Nichols quoted in Cohn 1969: 105)

To opponents, the twist was shockingly autoerotic and unwholesome. To those who danced the twist or enjoyed watching it, the movement had similar but more sanguine meanings – it was sexy, exciting, wild. In any given social setting, certain meanings became more prominent than others. For instance, for those who danced it in New York City's Peppermint Lounge, the twist was a symbol of the latest and the newest in hip social circles. But for some teenagers, forbidden to do the dance in schools or community centres, it was an act of rebellion against staid and repressive authority.

Rock dancing throughout the 1960s was given significance by dancers engaged in social action. For many members of the counterculture, the free-flowing, internally focused dancing was an integral part of giving up control and losing oneself in the drug experience. For more politically minded people, rock dance was a metaphor for political awareness. The extensive improvisation in rock dance enacted the rejection of explicit structures in New Left and feminist organizations. Being able to 'do your own thing' on the dance floor carried out a commitment to individualism and egalitarian ideals frequently voiced in 1960s' politics. The development of new music and dance forms by black artists was part of an identification with and pride in black culture fostered in the civil rights and black liberation movements. And the lack of differentiation between male and female movement, abhorred by rock's critics, was a positive emblem for some people of a rebellion against American gender roles.

As explicit political phenomena, the student movement, the civil rights and the black liberation movements, the antiwar movement and the women's movement found only tenuous moments of alliance with each other. But dancing, a multivocal and flexible sphere of social activity, could on occasion alleviate and even transcend political differences, emphasizing the shared ethos of these movements for social change.[6]

On the other hand, the experimental dance of the late 1950s and the 1960s was usually quite different from the social dance of the same time period. An obvious distinction is that rock-and-roll dance and music were large-scale social activities, while theatre dance was confined to a relatively small number of people clustered most noticeably in New York and other metropolitan and university centres. Most theatre dancers participated in social dance, but only a handful of social dancers performed theatre dance.

Movement contrasts were also evident. Rock dance tended to be exuberant and anarchically complex, while theatre dance was often pedestrian and minimal. The familiar joke summarized the situation: in the early 1960s, people would go to a dance concert to watch people stand around, and afterwards everyone would go to a party and dance.

At the same time, a fusion of aesthetic and social ideas was occurring. Merce Cunningham's aesthetic dictum that any movement could be considered dance proved a powerful concept for younger dancers engaged by re-emerging ideals of social equality and community. Those ideals were embedded in the experience of social dance, which required no formal training and was hence seen as 'democratic', but which was also clearly 'dancing'. According to choreographers Douglas Dunn and Trisha Brown, social dance has played a key role in changing conceptions about movement. In a conversation recorded in the late 1970s, Dunn commented, 'Before the sixties there was no consciousness of certain things as being dance.' Brown added, 'I think the "Twist" helped a lot in the sixties.' And Dunn replied, 'Rock dancing was a bridge between your daily life which was still unconscious perhaps and part of your classroom dance life which was not making available that possibility [of all kinds of movement]' (Brown 1979: 170).

At first, the bridge between daily life and theatre dance was explored by experimental choreographers through the conscious inclusion of 'pedestrian' and/or athletic movement. Like Cunningham, experimental choreographers in the 1960s were acting in part in opposition to the symbolism and drama of the modern dance tradition; this contributed to the emphasis on the 'purely physical' – the austere, the minimal in movement. Yet the ubiquitous rock music and dance, experienced by many young people as the quintessential expression of the times, affected these dancers as well, and the qualities experienced in rock dancing gradually began to appear more and more in theatre dance.

By the early 1970s, free-flowing movement, focus on the inner experience of moving, and energy thrown in all directions became prevalent in American theatre dance. They appeared strongly in contact improvisation and in the dances of choreographers such as Trisha Brown, Lucinda Childs, Laura Dean and Twyla Tharp.

Tharp, for instance, who was consciously influenced by black dance and social dance traditions, developed a style which has been described by movement analyst Billie Frances Lepczyk as freely flowing and internally focused. These qualities, she suggests, are 'least pronounced in ballet and in most previous major modern dance styles'; they 'create a loose, care-free, casual manner which makes the movement appear easy – as if anyone could do it' (Lepczyk 1981: 129–31). The movement style of social dance shaped in the 1960s and its implications – that it was loose, carefree, casual, easy – continued into the 1970s in theatre dance.

Contact improvisers amalgamated the sensual, free-flowing, inwardly experienced movement of 1960s rock dance with an 'objective' stance toward the physical capacities of the body typical of 1960s experimental dance. They borrowed movement exercises from aikido – the Japanese martial art – in order to create dancing that was not based on aesthetic choices. At the same time, a crucial new element was added: touch. If dancers doing the twist never touched, contact improvisers tried to maintain a constant 'point of contact' between bodies. The technical investigation of the give and take of weight coincided with the interest in touch so prominent among the therapeutic psychology movements of the early 1970s. Although contact improvisers were cautioned not to become involved in 'the gland game', as Paxton called it, the sensuality of the form was a major feature for participants and audiences. In this respect, contact improvisation can be seen as a culmination of opposition to post-war repression.

Early performances of contact improvisation in the mid 1970s have been described as being like 'a hot basketball game', with the audience gasping, laughing, clapping throughout. After performances, recalls Lisa Nelson, an early contact improviser,

> there would be a lot of dancing in the audience. People would be jumping all over one another. They would stick around and really want to start rolling around and want to jump on you. The feeling was of a real, shared experience among performers and audience, a tremendous feeling of physical accessibility between performers and audience.
>
> (Nelson 1983, personal correspondence)

The movement in contact improvisation and the social structure of its practice and performance were mutually reinforcing. At least through the mid 1970s, many of the participants lived in communal and/or transitory circumstances, organizing their dancing and their lives in the collective styles which had first emerged in the 1960s. Participants and fans saw the movement qualities, the improvisational process, and the practice/performance style of contact improvisation as embodying central values arising from the 1960s counterculture: egalitarianism, rejection of traditional sex roles, individualism within a group, and an opposition to authority.

However, the social structure of contact improvisation could not be maintained. By 1981, most participants had abandoned countercultural lifestyles and the institutions supporting dance had become less favourable towards informal performance. Nevertheless, participation in the dancing continued to foster countercultural values. Contact improvisation carried the meaningful aspects of 1960s' social dancing into the late 1970s, even after the environment in which the movement originated had changed.

One of the clearest indicators of the changing environment can be seen in a popular dance form coinciding with contact improvisation – disco dance. Whereas contact dancers partnered in any combination of male/male, female/male or female/female, with both people free to give weight or support at any time, disco dancers returned to the traditional form of social dance partnering in which the male led and directed the female. Disco dance was much more controlled than contact improvisation. It emphasized relating to a partner through sight and one-way manipulation, instead of touch and mutual control.

Disco dancers transformed rock dancing's focus on the self as an individual within a group into a display of the self with a partner of the opposite sex. Their movement style was much more outwardly directed and presentational, posed and controlled. Dancers tended to focus their energy in one direction at a time, often exclusively towards a partner.

The movement in disco dance encoded planning, control and heterosexual activity to a much greater extent than rock dancing or contact improvisation. One has only to think of the dances and story of the film *Saturday Night Fever* for illustration: John Travolta's character uses his showy, aggressive dancing to create a sense of self which is strong, competitive and sexy. He manipulates his partners physically and emotionally as he dances with them. He matures by realizing that he must exert some of that same control in his everyday life and make something of himself by leaving his working-class neighbourhood in Brooklyn for the possibility of upward mobility in Manhattan. Disco dancing becomes a metaphor for life, but, at the same time, it is a childish activity, best left behind. The aggressive 'macho' image of the dance must be tamed, not so that he can become a liberated man, but so that he can succeed in the real world of money and fame.

Over the past ten years in America, the movement trends evident in disco dancing have become even more prominent. The relaxation prized in the 1960s and through the 1970s in some communities gave way to 'stress management,' and 'looseness' gave way to the achievement of 'fitness'. Dancers participated in and often articulated these changes. Perhaps the most popular 'dance form' of the 1980s, aerobics, cannot be considered either a social dance form or a theatre form, but a kind of sports training which purports to help a person (usually a woman) gain control over her body and look good. Aerobic dancing focuses on self-control and on the appearance rather than the experience of the body and movement.[7] The ever-growing popularity of sports also seems notable, for the movement qualities and structures utilized in sports activities, although varied from one game to another, inevitably involve control and competitiveness.

The startling surge of interest in the mid 1980s in professional wrestling, a cross between sport and performance, contrasts ironically with the still-surviving practice of contact improvisation. Like contact improvisers, professional wrestlers perform and collaborate as partners through touch, but they do so in order to simulate violent competition – a 'spectacle', Roland Barthes (1972: 23) calls it, which in America represents 'a sort of mythological fight between Good and Evil'.

Ideally, contact improvisers carry on what they see as a sincere and intimate dialogue between two people through the interaction of their bodies, cooperating with the laws of physics and evoking images of camaraderie, play, nurturing, sport, sex and love. Wrestlers, too, must cooperate with the laws of physics, but the singular image they evoke is one of violation, violence and spectacle. Wrestlers engage in an elaborate choreography which they and their mass audiences know is fake but pretend is real. The pleasure of watching wrestling lies partly in the discrepancy between the brutality depicted, which the audience can passionately cheer, and the reality that no blood is spilled and wrestlers are seldom seriously injured. Movement here is a theatrical trick, an outward appearance, a conspiracy by the wrestlers with each other and the audience, which the savvy viewer can appreciate on more than one level.

It would be misleading, however, to think that contact improvisation has not also changed over time. During the early years of its development, contact improvisation was practised in slightly different ways by different people: some were more interested in performing, others in simply getting together to dance; some emphasized the aesthetic or athletic aspects of the form, others the therapeutic or interactive elements. In recent years, the unity of theatrical and social impulses embodied in the early years of the form has diminished greatly, a tendency created by changes in the technique of the dancing and, as mentioned earlier, by changes in the lives of the dancers and the circumstances of performing.

As technical skills among contact improvisers increased and the form became more clearly delineated, divisions between skilled and unskilled dancers became more evident. As skilled dancers turned more to performing, difficulties developed over how to maintain a non-presentational dance style as a theatrical form. This dilemma was both a technical problem – how to structure the dance without destroying its basic conception and ethos – and eventually a practical problem – how to compete in the increasingly competitive business of producing dance.

By 1983, many of the people who originally created and shaped contact improvisation reached a stage in their lives in which marginal living was no longer possible or desirable; as they stopped dancing or moved on to create professional careers, new contact communities could not form in the same way as they had in the early 1970s, because economic circumstances were so different.[8] Other professional dancers wishing to add contact improvisation skills to their repertoire of movement could do so more easily, and contact improvisation was treated by many as simply another dance technique.

As a result of all these changes, contact improvisation performances in the past five years have been rare, although the influences of contact improvisation on movement styles and techniques are widespread throughout theatre dance. Those contact improvisation performances I have witnessed have been highly skilled, characterized more by friendly and playful adeptness than by passionate unpredictability. The baseline movement characteristics were the same, but the dancers tended to move with greater control over the movement flow and a greater degree of outward focus. The audiences, while warm, were sedate and reserved, a marked contrast to the audiences 12 years ago.

Other theatre dancers have also articulated changes in recent years, opting in many cases for greater control and flashiness. It is not only younger choreographers like Michael Clark or Molissa Fenley who create these images. Even Martha Graham's company, with its Halston costumes and attention to body line and arabesques, seems more polished and visually spectacular. This is not to say that dancers conspicuously plan these changes; like all participants in a culture (to paraphrase Marx), they make their own dances, but within a set of rules they do not always personally create.

For example, in 1985 choreographer Bill T. Jones, who practised contact improvisation early in his career (1974–6), discussed reviving a duet he had made in 1978 called *Shared Distance*. The dance had been created originally with Julie West, who had also trained extensively in contact improvisation and had very little other dance experience.

> Julie and I were both involved in this kind of natural, free-wheeling, raw look when I made the dance. Now I'm working with a different dancer with no contact background and trying to understand how to change or revise the dance. When I push her through space, we [Jones and Arnie Zane] keep saying, 'Well, you should keep your legs together.' Before, Julie would just come off flying. Why do we suddenly feel that that's not appropriate now, that when I push her away, she should look designed in the air? These things are very real. My past and my future meet in this piece, and I'm trying to understand it. 'The messy look', 'cleaning up the act' – contact was about messiness.
>
> (Jones 1984, personal correspondence)

The sentiments of this choreographer are about very real things. How we move constitutes a part of our past and our future. The 'free-wheeling, raw look' is not a fixed definition for the movement characteristics of free flow and multiply-directed energy, but neither is 'messiness' (certainly the Polynesians, whose dance contains free flow and multiply-directed energy, do not define the movement in these ways). 'Free-wheeling', 'raw' and 'messy' are meanings which Americans fused with certain movement qualities in particular cultural and historical times. In 1978, Bill T. Jones saw free flow and indirectness as being natural and free-wheeling; in 1985, these same qualities seemed messy.

Structured movement systems can join meaning and movement for many years. But movement systems within any culture are not monolithic and static, nor are their relationship to social contexts always direct. Rock-and-roll dancers in the 1950s seem, at least in hindsight, to have anticipated cultural change through movement qualities adapted from black dance traditions. Rock dancers in the 1960s epitomized the counterculture and captured a range of social meanings in a variety of settings, while experimental dancers – a much smaller group of people within the same subculture – embodied some of the same social meanings within different movement styles and structures.

Contact improvisers in the early 1970s amalgamated movement qualities and social ideas from rock dance and the martial arts with aesthetic conceptions from experimental dance and a fascination with touch among certain educated, middle-class people. Contact improvisers in the late 1970s maintained movement qualities and social ideas in small communities after the supporting social bases for those ideas had disappeared, whereas some other theatre dancers adopted their techniques for use in choreography.

Disco dance and aerobic dance seem to be more direct expressions of the mainstream social and cultural milieu of the late 1970s and 1980s, often crossing class boundaries and providing metaphors for the way many American men and women see themselves.

Like other cultural phenomena, establishing laws of cause and effect for movement is neither probable nor advisable. What is of interest in the study of structured movement systems is the description and interpretation of the cultures which they stimulate. By looking at different dance forms, sport, theatre or everyday movement patterns as cultural realities whose kinaesthetic and structural properties have meaning, possibilities emerge for articulating and clarifying our experiences of who we, and others, are.

Notes

1 I take the term 'structured movement systems' from anthropologist Adrienne Kaeppler, who advocates its use as a more inclusive and fruitful way of conceiving of movement when doing cross-cultural studies and comparisons. For a concise statement of her ideas, see Kaeppler (1985).

2 A major exception is American Sign Language, which has a complete grammar. Also, movement systems such as South Indian or Tongan dance contain linguistic structures.

3 A complete ethnographic analysis of contact improvisation is made in 'Sharing the Dance' (Novack 1986). The discussion of contact improvisation in this article focuses on selected aspects of that analysis.

4 My discussion of movement characteristics throughout this article makes use of concepts drawn from Laban Movement Analysis (or Labanalysis) and choreographic techniques and devices.

5 Stearns and Stearns (1968) trace the development of black vernacular dance related to jazz music.

6 Dance does not always play a unifying role, of course. It can be used to distinguish one group from another, or to exert control by one group over another. See Spencer (1985) for an interesting discussion of this issue.

7 Sally Banes (1986) has suggested that the urge for control constitutes the central attitude towards the body in the 1980s.

8 Communities which practice contact improvisation exist, but their emphasis lies almost entirely on creating social interaction among members and on dancing as a means for interaction. The theatrical aspects of the form are absent.

17

GETTING OFF THE ORIENT EXPRESS

Shobana Jeyasingh

'The Dance is occasioned by no specific need. It has come into use because it creates beauty.'

(Bharata in the *Natya Sastra*)

An important part of the history of Bharata Natyam in the West is the methods and avenues through which the Westerner has striven to understand and respond to it. During the time of Uday Shankar and Ram Gopal in the earlier decades of the twentieth century, the general public, with some notable exceptions, flocked to see them as exponents of oriental or Hindu dancing and both these dancers were commercial successes presented by leading impresarios in big theatres. In the case of Uday Shankar, a young art student in London, Anna Pavlova had a greater influence on him as a dancer than any classical Indian technique and yet he was seen as the authentic voice of India speaking directly and immediately to us from 5000 years of civilisation.

The irony was, of course, that 5000 years of civilisation notwithstanding a few hundred years of colonial rule had, with other factors, brought about the demise of the classical technique through the alienation of the educated Indian from his fine arts and through the gradual erosion of the traditional sources of patronage – the court and the temple. And even as this review of Shankar was written in 1934 the fate of the dance in India seemed to be in the balance. It was still to be finally decided whether the Victorian social reformers (both Indian and English) who wanted the traditional community of dancers attached to the temples to be disbanded would triumph or whether the dance was to be rescued from its old setting and rehabilitated in the new centres of power, the cities of India. The two sides had locked horns in the press and a great war of words was in progress. The classical technique was largely available only through a few members of the old world of dancers and their teacher/choreographers who had to be systematically sought out. The dance itself waited to be given the stamp of general social approbation including a change of name. In this process of rehabilitation Rukmini Devi, the Indian wife of a leading English theosophist, was to play a dramatic part.

In 1934 she had yet to see the Bharata Natyam recital that would take her away from performing bits of *Swan Lake* under the banyan trees of the theosophical centre in Madras to becoming a dedicated pioneer in bringing about the large scale accessibility of the dance in India.

When the rehabilitation of the classical technique finally got underway, it judged Shankar harshly: 'Uday Shankar's dance, considered as some kind of dance, was tolerable. But considered as Indian dance, as Bharata Natya ... it was absolutely unconvincing except for the costume, the decor and the music' (Seshagiri in *Sound and Shadow*). 'Were Uday Shankar to stay in India for a few years and put himself to systematic training under a master ... [he] would not have striven in vain' (Ganadasa in the *Journal of Indian Renaissance*).

What Seshagiri failed to appreciate, apart from Shankar's genius for innovation and contemporary truth, was that in that magical place 'the Orient', a place invented by the West for its own amusement, costume, decor and music were very much of the essence. Here, 'virtuosity was in the tremor of an eyelid' (*New York Herald Tribune*) and 'where there was nothing more arduous than gathering flowers, nothing more troublesome than bees, nothing more frightening than "the sound of approaching footsteps" ' (*The Sunday Times*). Indeed a journey through its enchanted terrain provides countless diversions as in this description of its dance: 'The movement of the oriental dance is concentric. The knees almost instinctively come together and bend, the curved arms embrace the body. Everything is pulled together. Everything converges' (Andre Levinson quoted by Alistair Macaulay in *Dance Theatre Journal*). This movement is noteworthy for its striking contrast to the turned-out openness of Bharata Natyam and the stateliness of Kathak.

The post-war immigration of Asian people into Britain was the earliest death knell for 'The Orient'. When the sloe-eyed damsel moves into the semi next door she loses that most exotic of qualities – distance. And as the natives pondered on how best to assimilate these 'natives' Bharata Natyam, through a semantic somersault, became one of the 'ethnic' dances of Britain. Its separateness became the key to its understanding. 'Orientalist' gave way to the incessant clamour of 'What does it mean?' of the ethnicists, as Indian classical dance, forsaken by the impresarios of the Shankar/Gopal era, did its round of the smaller regional arts centres. Bharata Natyam came to be valued chiefly as an example of its culture and religion and Bharata Natyam dancers came to be valued as race relation officers, cultural ambassadors, experts in multiculturalism, anthropological exhibits – everything save as dance technicians. The general belief was that the dance itself could not be appreciated without a detailed study of the Hindu pantheon together with the proper decoding of the innumerable hieroglyphic hand gestures and eye-movements. Here they were probably helped along the road by those who saw the parading of seemingly obscure cultural and religious appendages as a measure of the dance's complexity and richness of heritage.

While it is undoubtedly true that a major influence in the formation of the dance was temple ritual (the others were court life and secular theatre), what is often overlooked is the totally different definition of religious activity that the West has. Here religious dance is strictly liturgical dancing where integrity of emotion takes dominance over exhibition of technique. In India, where to be religious in no way presupposes a rejection of the secular or indeed the sensual (as exemplified in Kajuraho), religious dance has no limitations. In Britain, however, the same term denies the dance not only the lively debate, the abundance of new choreography, the backstage rivalries that characterise the dance scene in India but, more importantly, it denies the central role that technique plays in the dance and it obscures the fact that, for the best part of the past sixty years, Bharata Natyam has been seen, like any other performance art, on the theatre stage.

The other danger that the ethnicists court in the constant quest for explanations is to make the dance nothing more than the sum of its literal meaning. As any opera-goer would agree, an ignorance of the language is no impediment to the enjoyment of the music. Similarly, the 'meaning' of the ballet *Swan Lake* does not rest with the acting out of the story nor is that the ultimate aim of the production. What is more significant is that the choice of stories from myth and legend illuminate the kind of truth that the dance addresses and which its technique serves. What motivates the ballet-goer is not the blow-by-blow account of the plot nor the literal understanding of its mime but, quite simply, the dance itself.

Similarly, Bharata Natyam is about dance, and the most pertinent quality of that dance is its classicism. This seemingly simple truth is yet one of the hardest to convey. The word itself has to be divested of its total Eurocentric bias before one can go along this more fruitful avenue of understanding. The Oxford English Dictionary firmly points towards Greece and Rome in its definitions of classicism. The organisation of material in dance books, the thinking behind the dance syllabus in educational institutions, the programming of dance festivals and the presentation of dance in the media, all derive from a categorisation that sees Dance with a capital D divided into classical (ballet) contemporary (Western), social, folk and ethnic. This is tantamount to dividing mankind under the headings European urban, European rural, Travellers and World Tribes. Internationalism in dance matters, more often than not, is a nod across the Atlantic. This subconscious evaluation was tellingly brought home to me in an interview for an important dance appointment where I was a member of the interviewing panel. Asked how the candidate regarded South Asian dance, his reply was that he himself had the highest regard for central European folk dance. Pressed further on classical dance he felt that the basis of all dance was ballet. As for classical dances from another culture the idea seemed to cause him genuine puzzlement.

The word 'classical' first and foremost implies a particular relationship with the past. It is a gracious acceptance of the past as a refining process and though one can in the present carry on that process it is done essentially in reference and in deference to what has gone on before. Classicism is often associated with certain golden periods of history where the ground rules were laid down, its aesthetic principles, manners and style are still associated with that art form. In ballet it is possible to see not only the Greek and Roman ideal of the human form but also the manners of the great European courts. Similarly, Bharata Natyam is the product of both the pan-Indian, Sanskrit culture which produced the *Natya Sastra,* (the handbook for theatrical productions in AD4) and the cultural achievements of the court at Tanjore in South India in the eighteenth and nineteenth centuries.

Bharata Natyam technique

One of the features of the past history of Bharata Natyam was the careful recording of it for future use in teaching and performance. The carvings of the dance poses in the great social and academic centres of those times, the temples, recorded in great detail the technical features of the dance. The numerous books and treatises dedicated to analysis of form, to the creation of an appropriate terminology, and to methodical codification of steps bear witness to the high esteem in which the correct rendering of technique was held. Indeed, a major role of the dance was to display the technique for its own sake as *Nritta. Nritya* on the other hand was the technique, together with stylised facial mime, in the service of drama.

The basis for the Bharata Natyam technique is the perception of the human body as a geometric ideal both in its static position (pictured as the straight axis around which a circle could be drawn) and its articulation through the dance (which explores all the harmonious geometric shapes possible from the central axis within the circle). Kapila Vatsyayan in her admirable book *The Square and the Circle of the Indian Arts* (1997) discusses fully how this geometric ideal not only connects all the classical Indian art forms from music to architecture, but in fact is the expression of the fundamental belief in Hinduism regarding the relationship of man to the universe.

The *natya-aramba* (the beginning of dance) position shows the body lowered along the central axis of the circle and divided along it through the *araai mandi* or *demi plié.* By so doing it creates a series of three equilateral triangles in space. To create this image the dancer has to centre the body by pulling in the stomach and pulling up the upper torso. There is a feeling of growing taller and expanding; this forms the base line of a triangle. To create a second triangle, turn out from the hips is essential (which forms triangle 3) since without this the base line of the second triangle will not be legible. The depth of the plié is crucial if there is to be harmony between triangles 2 and 3. These three triangles form the Bharata Natyam body picture and are the ideal that the dancing body aims for and which the classical sculptures show us. In post-colonial times the achievement of this uncompromising ideal is made harder by the fact that, while the dance itself has been successfully rejuvenated, we still need to retrieve that systematic body training which alone could have made those athletic temple poses possible.

When the body moves from the *natya-aramba* position it does so through four foot positions. Unlike ballet, the demi plié of Bharata Natyam is not an intermediary position from which the body moves. The Indian technique demands a muscular consolidation of this position by allowing the weight of the lower body to 'earth' it. The arms in *natya-aramba* in a semi-circular shape peculiar to Bharata Natyam create a three-dimensional effect to the circle and trace its curve.

A discussion of this primary position of the dance will not be complete without some indication of the philosophy or emotion that this technique implies. The placing of the body with the turnout and pulled up torso has the quality of openness and extreme stylisation in movement. Its relation to space is confident and secure and by virtue of its abstract quality it engenders a feeling of objective pleasure. There is a special quality to the pleasure that comes from technical achievements governed by strict rules where the achievements are ends in themselves. The rules of Bharata Natyam Nritta, by referring to purely geometric ideals, make it also a totally objective dance.

As befits a dance where expression equals the physical expression of the technique, the training process is devoted to shaping the body to suit the dance. One could almost call it an indoctrination. This may sound mechanical and uncreative but what Arnold Haskell says about the pirouette and the fouetté could equally well be applied to the steps of Bharata Natyam:

> These ... are the musical notes, limited in number, in themselves nothing. The effect depends on how they are combined and executed. It is this classicism that is helping the dancer to express herself, that leaves her so gloriously free, if only she is big enough.

The 'musical notes' in Bharata Natyam are the *adavus* – units of dance which contain in them the alphabet and grammar of the dance. Each *adavu* (and they are limited in number) is made up of stance (vertical with feet in parallel, demi plié or full plié), foot positions, arm lines and patterns for the hand. In execution an *adavu* usually spans 6 or 8 beats, produces a rhythmic phrase by foot-beats and requires the eyes to give focus to the lines created by the arms by following them. The corpus of *adavus* deal with all the movements possible including those that are static and those that allow the body to travel together with leaps and turns.

The nature of Bharata Natyam Nritta can be understood and appreciated by considering the following principles: *Clarity*. The principle of '*angasud-dha*' or correct and clean rendering of line is indispensable. Apart from the legibility of the three triangles as discussed earlier, the progression of the arms from one shape to the next has to be committed and firm. Without *angasuddha* the dance literally would not exist for that is what makes it visible. *Grace*. If there was to be only clarity then the dance would have a clockwork and mechanical quality. '*Lasya*' or grace is the vehicle through which Bharata Natyam's obsession with strong line is presented to the audience and the tension between the abstract and the physical is resolved. *Vigour*. As a dynamic *lasya* is seen as a complement to '*tandava*' or vigour. It points towards the strength and speed especially of footwork in the execution of the characteristic fast rhythms of the dance. *Precision* or *tala suddha*. This principle is linked to the special relationship that Bharata Natyam has to time. Through footwork it is possible to pattern time in such a minute and detailed way that on one level the dance is the percussive structure of the music. It is no accident that even the smallest joint in the body contributes to the movement; the neck joint and the wrist are all used to add percussive detail. Precision is at its most exciting when linked to speed and all *adavus* are therefore practised in three tempos. Speed is also a test of centredness because while the limbs move, *angasudha* or clarity can only be maintained if equilibrium and control are there in the centre. This quality of effortlessness, which is the communication of the quiet centre, is much sought after.

The choreographer of Bharata Natyam Nritta approaches his or her material very much as a ballet choreographer does. His or her artistry is seen in the imaginative combining of the *adavus* into *korvais* (literally an enchainment) and the changes he can ring within the received corpus of steps. The choreography is governed by principles of symmetry (for example, movements started on the right followed by movements to the left) and harmony (the arithmetical progression of rhythm). The fact that it follows the compositional rules of classical music heightens the formal and abstract quality of its structure. The display of virtuosity is often a built-in feature and traditional choreography gives ample scope for polished articulation of the technique at speed. Such passages are recognised and applauded by the audience just as happens in a ballet performance.

A rigorous definition of the salient features of Bharata Natyam Nritta (and for the purposes of this article I have not dealt with *nritya* or mime) does not necessarily consign it to a dance museum. Periods of conservation such as that immediately preceding and following India's independence are just as necessary as periods of development. The greatest strength of a classical dance lies in its objectivity when faced with the continuous flux of historical change. It alone has the tenacity to speak with confidence to the present without turning its back on the past.

18

BRIDGING THE
CRITICAL DISTANCE

Marcia B. Siegel

The following essay is adapted from two talks given at the conference of the Dance Critics Association which took place in conjunction with world dance performances at the 1990 Los Angeles Festival. They were published in slightly different form in Looking Out: Perspectives on Dance and Criticism in a Multicultural World *(ed. David Gere, New York: Schirmer Books 1995) and in* Ballett International, *July/August 1991.*

There have been some underlying themes of this conference, and one of those themes is fear. Fear of the Other is one form of it. And I don't just mean racist fear, which we've elaborated on quite a lot during the conference. I mean that in Euro-American culture many people think the business of a critic is establishing and protecting norms. To acknowledge high art in another culture is to threaten 'our' standards (i.e. whatever it is we endorse to our readers). And it also threatens how those standards are determined, which is something we don't normally examine. Where did we get them from? What are they based on? How much do they influence what we write? If we open ourselves up to the Other, on equal terms, we'll have to give up our position as standard-setters, because it means acknowledging that someone else has set some other standard that's equally ... standard.

When we step outside our Euro-American framework, we experience a desperate need for criteria. We demand formulas, rules, contexts, signs of the exceptional. We want to be responsible and not misinterpret, but we hate to give up what we see as our evaluative job. Understandably, we're nervous being out there on our own, confronting an immediate, unfamiliar experience and dealing with it inside ourselves, let alone playing judge over it.

And then we have to think and be interesting in 700 words.

It seems to me the matter of criteria is very problematic. For one thing, you can't always know what the criteria are. No matter how hard you try and how many people you consult, or how many times you've seen that dance form before, you can't always know what that culture is accepting as good or bad. (If you're in the Good-or-Bad business.)

And even if we could learn some of the basics of a culture, or of its cultural forms, are we really sure we'd know what the whole range is? Can we say that the dance we're seeing here in Los Angeles is *the* Javanese court dance? Is this the only way to perform that dance or style? Is this the only context in which that style is seen? In places with very strong cultural styles, like Java, everything from tourist performance to the most classical, private and high-context high art can use the same elements. These basics, in any culture, get manipulated by the culture and within the culture. We may see only one example of a given dance in our lifetime, so how can we say we know if it's characteristic?

Another fear, and it's related to that, is the sense that we ought to establish some sort of historical, aesthetic or stylistic authenticity for our subjects. When you travel, you realize what a huge variation there is among what seem to be the normative genres within any culture. Style, or technique, or form, isn't just one thing. Although it may be ever so much simpler for us to identify a classical style or a folk dance form that someone has conveniently researched, it's folly to expect that it will look exactly the same as the researcher described.

Western critics have hierarchies, though we may not admit it. Going from the bottom up, we esteem social dancing, pop dancing, jazz dancing, theatrical dancing, concert dancing, ballet. Classical ballet seems accepted as the crowning achievement of dance art in Western culture. And, within that hierarchy, we also tend to respect old work more than we respect new work, and an 'accurate' reproduction of an old work over a reinterpretation.

Now, even if these hierarchies are justified (I don't think they are), even if you were going to rank things by levels and categories, how do you figure out a comparable scale for some other culture? How do you discriminate the best dancing or whatever, without imposing an imagery that may not apply to it? And then, supposing you follow some guidelines issued by the local authorities, standards established by scholars or academies, can you be sure these most meticulously researched and preserved forms mean the same thing for all time and for everyone in that culture?

I find the interplay between preservation and inevitable change very poignant and very distressing. I also love old dances and I wish we could preserve old traditions and I know we can't. I think that is true in every single culture. It's true in ballet and modern dance. I've seen those two forms change drastically just in the twenty-five years I've been writing. And that's right in front of our eyes. So how can we talk about 'The Tradition' or 'the authentic' in a culture that's thousands of years old and has been undergoing change over all those years? Much of that change having been instituted from outside, by colonial powers as well as other forces like trade and technology.

I like the idea of reincarnation. The idea that to talk about change in culture is not to talk about terminality. It's not to talk about something being destroyed or something decaying, but something that's in a process. The natural process, the process of nature, is, yes, trees die, but other trees grow out of what dies, and everything is in a constant state of metamorphosis and rebirth.

Everything is authentic something. And if we weren't so diligently seeking out how this compares to some norm that we don't really know very much about anyway, we might really *look* at what is being done, and try to determine what that is.

I think this conference has concentrated quite a lot on traditional forms. Those high-art traditions, those codified stage forms that are culturally endorsed, the things that come here touring, like the Wayang Wong. We're very lucky to have it. But it alone doesn't represent Indonesia. It doesn't represent Java. It's one form, and a very high-art, officially sanctioned, intentionally visible form that is to some extent moulded in an image of what such art should be. I don't think they're going to bring some of the seedier forms over here, or the airport art, or the vernacular shows that people put on in the backyard, which for me would be just as interesting. As a matter of fact, certain governments apparently withheld funding for groups appearing at this festival because they considered them vulgar or lowbrow.

The emphasis on high traditional forms is easier for us critics because more interpretive and background material is made available to us about them. More scholarly writing and analysis has been done. They may superficially resonate with things we call 'classical' in our own system of values because they're likely to be linked to historical or religious phenomena, to have clear encoded vocabularies, sequences and musical accompaniments, and to emerge from rigorous training processes. But these 'classics' are changing, and they are much too complex and multifaceted to be matched against our equally complex but differently formulated traditions.

We also have a great fear of making a mistake. We might say the wrong thing, and I must say that a great deal of intimidating sanctions have been issued in the last four days from this platform along the lines of: Non-Natives Keep Off. I certainly take to heart everything that's been said, but it's not going to deter me from doing my work, with the most informed and open spirit I can bring. And it shouldn't deter you. Get the tools. Get the ability to look. Open your mind, and do it.

Although what we do has some similarities to ethnographic field work, we cannot be anthropologists. Any of us might want to go into one particular culture and immerse ourselves in it, and we could make that choice. But, realistically, that would eliminate other choices. To me, being a critic is a great privilege because I can see a lot of things. I can experience many different things and address them. And I don't want to sacrifice that, much as I might want to spend more time in cultures that I find especially congenial and learn more about them first hand. We just can't work intensively enough with any one thing to become anthropological experts.

An anthropologist is also going to try to get direct information from the doers, from the culture itself. As critics, we'd like to have that, but we don't. We usually have access to the artists only through their press representatives and their presenters. We get little useful information from them. And if we can get in direct contact and speak to the performers, the teachers, the choreographers, we have to surmount problems of language, problems of interpretation, problems of what is it that they really mean and do they understand what we really mean when we're trying to get this information.

But even if we could assume maximum accuracy and utility from our verbal sources, my best information is in the dance. My observation of the dance, which in a sense is my participation in the dance, allows me to connect the performance with my writing. I'm aware that it's controversial to assume we can learn something non-verbally from a culture whose deepest traditions we can't read. But I'm very unsure about the fashionable tendency to discard the idea that there might be 'universals' – qualities or expressive behaviours that all people share. I do know that physicality is universal. It underlies all performance, certainly all dance performance, and it contains basic information. I am fully aware that physicality always takes place in reference to a context and that the context is not universal. We can't ignore that context, if we have access to it in some form. But the performance itself is also a context.

I am Laban-trained and I certainly believe that Labananalysis and Choreometrics direct us to useful information. The Laban systems draw attention to dynamics, the use of space and time and weight, to phrasing, transitions, the shape of the movement, parts of the body used or not used, and to the performer's sense of the space through which he or she is moving. There are interpretive problems with Choreometrics, but its movement researchers, Irmgard Bartenieff and Forrestine Paulay, did come up with basic tools and ways of organizing observational data that would help us in these unfamiliar situations.

I would say that all of the Laban systems – Labanotation, Labananalysis and Choreometrics – though they are probably the largest body of analytical work anybody has ever done with movement, are Eurocentric. Laban theory centres on the body and conceives of movement from the performer's point of view, not from the audience's point of view. It doesn't really concern itself with choreography, with the overall form of a dance piece or the process of a performance. It doesn't address the group. It leaves out a lot of things that aren't paramount in Western choreography. So even though it's useful, I don't find it is everything. I'm going to suggest a few other things that I've been working with, that seem to encompass the performance as a whole experience.

The first one is *lexicon*. That is, if we take note of the actions, energies, objects, places, people, sounds that the dance immediately draws our attention to, we can come up with a sort of vocabulary belonging to that dance. The lexicon is like the raw materials of the dance. As soon as we consciously begin assembling a lexicon, we start to track how it gets manipulated, interwoven and elaborated on during the dance. We do this unconsciously always, I think, but looking for it more purposively leads us to structure, conventions, typical ways of moving that we might not be so clear about otherwise, or that we might overlook because they're unfamiliar.

The *beat and rhythm* are essential. I don't see how you can look at any dance form without understanding what its rhythm is and how that rhythm is expressed, musically, physically, spatially, its colour, its energy, its variety.

We in the West tend to see dance as a unified entity, where everything serves one choreographic end, or is meant to be in one form – Aristotelian if you will. Not all dance is like that, and we should discover what the *orchestration* is, how it works, what it serves. How are all the parts of the piece orchestrated? How do the individuals go together with the other individuals, the dancers with the music? What are the segments in the dance and how are they marked off? What are the changes, what triggers them, and how does the dance change from one section to the next, from the beginning to the end?

What are other *structural elements*? For example, is the dance a progression or is it a series of things that occur on an equal level all the way through? How is this structure or progression communicated? Who dictates when things change, and what does he or she dictate? Is the sequence learned on the spot? Is it spontaneous, or is it learned ahead of time and always repeated the same way, or does it blossom extemporaneously out of a set pattern?

What is the *performance practice*? Is it filled with artifice and how is artifice stated and where does it come from? Or is it very naturalistic? What are the patterns or conventions of visual focusing?

These things are all in play as we watch a performance. Out of all the possible ways to perform, they have been selected and refined by the culture which performs them, and their development during the course of the dance is a kind of text that we can read without extensive knowledge of the other texts out of which it arose. In many ways, we learn from the dance just what the dance is, and how to respond appropriately to it. I encourage you to be more confident of your ability to discern the workings of these movement texts. I think we have to recognize and compensate as best we can for our personal biases and lapses in information. We can't go to see one performance of something and understand it. Mark Morris may have gone and looked at one Kathak performance for a long time and 'gotten it'. But what he got he translated into some personal expression. Our job as critics is to communicate on behalf of those performers, not to express our creative fantasies. If you think you got it, you can only admit to the limitations of what it is you got, on one viewing. But express that. Describe that. Address that. Don't just sort of say, well, this is it.

Multiculturalism and eclecticism have been confused here. I don't think they're the same thing. For a long time in this country [the US] we considered ourselves a melting pot, and in that sense eclecticism is not at all new. It's not new for a dancer to appropriate from other cultures. The whole twentieth century has been doing it, from Ruth St Denis to Mark Morris. But recognize that when we're looking at their work, we're looking at a Western form, into which these elements have been inserted to make it more interesting, give it a twist or pay an homage to something that the artist has been taken with. I submit that, though benign and well-meaning, that's nevertheless a form of cultural imperialism. The end product is still ballet. It's still modern dance. No matter what Balanchine took from this culture and that culture, he still made ballet and we can recognize it as ballet. I'm not putting down ballet or Balanchine. I'm just saying, it's not multicultural, it's not intercultural. It's using cultural material to revitalize an ongoing form. I am dismayed by Arlene Croce's idea that multiculturalism and all the imperatives that surround it just now can be answered by the appropriation and subsuming of any culture's bric-a-brac into Western forms. And that that answers all our conscience problems about recognizing the rest of the world. It doesn't for me.

Art or dance, or however you want to define this experience we're looking at, is more than that, and can be more than that. I don't just mean it can have different colours or that it can have different cultural styles, I mean it can address other things, entirely, and still be wonderful, and still be worth our true attention and love. Western dance forms are built on individual creation, personality, the assertion of personal skills. They are theatrical, self-contained, mostly transitory events in proscenium spaces, they provide entertainment in a highly developed aesthetic tradition. We in this country have almost no knowledge of dance as ritual, dance as a spiritual lesson, dance as a historical memory, dance as a means of communal celebration – at least, our arts pages don't recognize them.

That doesn't put the multiculture out of bounds for us as critics, but, if we admit these possibilities, we will have to relinquish some of our accustomed critical behaviours. One reason multicultural performances are so popular is that they often aren't framed in closed, one-way presentational structures. They're often more inclusive and spontaneous, more participatory and personal. Even Western audiences find them accessible, not esoteric as ballet and modern dance can be for the lay person. They give us access, temporarily, to community, to spirituality, a longed-for social bonding that seldom occurs in a Western, high-art encounter.

Work on your editors; get them to see the expanse of non-theatrical spectator dance, participatory dance, ritual dance and all kinds of other venues and forms. Even if there are no imported companies touring through town, the public festivals and entertainments of transplanted minorities and indigenous non-Anglo populations are part of every city's culture today. Can't we write about them as vibrant performance activity and experience? Isn't that at least as important to us as sitting in a theatre and being constantly stunned with new tricks and new ideas?

One reason multiculturalism is such a tense issue now is that it is perceived as a major force in the weakening of Western high-art traditions. In a pluralistic, postmodern society, no monolithic art form can satisfy everyone, and even those of us who grew up on the high arts – I certainly did – may welcome other reflections of what has become a very complex lifestyle, other models for solving the confused ethical debates in which we're involved. I listen to Mozart; I also listen to gamelan and samba and West African drumming. Why not?

Ballet and modern dance as we've understood them seem to be going through a fallow period, and not only because of competition from the multicultural sector. We're seeing a lot of imitation, a lot of desperate clasping on to what remains of these older traditions, and not very much 'authenticity' of feeling about it, and certainly not very much creativity within those forms. The phase will undoubtedly pass, but I'm not so interested in looking at those mainstreams or writing about them at this point.

I don't mind if I get labelled an anthropologist, or a journalist, and not a critic. I've been interested in non-Western forms for a long time, writing about them since the early 1970s, and I find them more and more interesting, and more and more of a challenge. And very much to my surprise, some fascinating contemporary forms are getting invented – and they're not even forms. They're little ideas, poking up here and there, from people who have not been totally overcome by the massive infiltration of ballet and modern dance training around the world. Assimilating those and other influences, often recovering their own buried cultural heritage, some choreographers have come to a new resolution of dance identity for themselves, or are dancing out the colliding, still unassimilated elements of what is contemporary life for them.

I think the questions surrounding what is anyone's identity in anyone's culture are deep and affecting. They are going to result in creative work. I personally want to be around to see that work too, and to write about it, and I hope you'll be there with me.

Afterword

At the beginning of the 1990s, when this essay was written, I was thinking about the role of critics in a world of cultural change. I wrote from the perspective of a professional dance critic struggling to represent a performance scene that had eluded the categories of modern dance and ballet, high art and low art. I was looking for a way of outwitting the supposed critical imperatives – opinion, evaluation, labelling and rating – yet certain we wouldn't want to discard those subjective options entirely, even if we could. I was looking for ways of writing about the unfamiliar without applying the assumptions of the familiar. Two decades later many of the terms of this dilemma have shifted. But the challenge remains.

If the performance world was opening up in the 1980s and 1990s, it now seems to have entered a well-trod cycle. Stagnation leads to revolution, the conservative forces kick in, new norms get established, and when they start to congeal a new revolution germinates. In the aftermath of the multicultural avalanche of the 1980s, the categories have tightened again. Stylistic exploration has led to eclectic fusions that sometimes consolidate into new stylistic entities, like the post-Butoh work of Eiko and Koma, or the meditative modernism of Taiwan's Cloud Gate Dance Theatre. More often we see the styleless populism of contemporary dance, or the opportunistic eclecticism that can easily access modern dance, Tae Kwon Do, Capoeira, aerial dance, belly dance, rap, tap, Kathak, anything at all. Style is becoming less a signifier than a new shade in a limitless movement palette.

In the wake of *Riverdance* we've seen floods of polyglot commercial shows. Threatened world-dance traditions have been codified and protected by government-sponsored academies, with performing companies to project them on tour as staged emblems of national identity. In the US, dance has become a familiar presence as a component of sports events, 'reality' competitions and gym culture. Hundreds of dance bites are consumed every day on YouTube. So, while dance becomes as much a part of our life as music, its cultural and historical meanings grow less specific. Accustomed to smoothed out, historically sanitized dancing, we're less exposed to what's strange. Presenters aren't bringing us the great touring exemplars of Kabuki, Peking Opera, Kathakali. We've had few opportunities to experience the steady stream of smaller-scale pleasures – Chinese finger puppets, Burmese dance-drama, Balinese Wayang Kulit – since the splendid years of importations organized by Beate Gordon for New York's Asia Society. The great performers aren't traditionalists, like Balasaraswati, but modernists, emigrés, movie stars (Akram Khan, Vincent Mantsoe, Tamasaburo). The folkloric groups have all gone slick and Folklorico; or they've constituted themselves as urban villagers, absorbing the street beat into their Aboriginal or South African or South American roots.

In this country, economic stringencies and political correctness have toned down the discourse and the differences. Big ballet companies are programmed for the widest audiences, not the connoisseurs. There are fewer attempts to revive ballets from earlier periods; to do so would require an open-mindedness that the audience hasn't the patience for. In modern dance, world dance and small-scale ballet, diversity plays to specialized niche audiences. We have more dance to see now, but fewer mysteries.

The serious challenge of dance preservation and dance scholarship still lies in how we see, how we interrogate. And in how we write. The position of critics and the uses of the critical eye have been changing too, over the last decades. Daily and weekly newspapers, the natural home of those who report and review the ongoing cultural scene, have cut the space they allot to independent commentary, in favour of writing that promotes the personalities and aspirations of dance-makers on the immediate horizon. Many powerful American dailies have eliminated criticism as a regular item, or relegated arts reviewing to freelancers, who have to work with limited space, poor compensation and the tacit understanding that they're part of a marketing apparatus. More recently, newspapers themselves are migrating from print to electronic formats. Some dance critics have been able to make a transition to the Internet, but independent dance coverage is increasing in the blogosphere, where opinion is wide-ranging and there's a low priority for writing finesse.

If there's a place for a deeper perspective in dance, I believe it will be in extended critical studies. Scholarly research has often bypassed this perspective, but dance-based analysis and persuasive, non-political writing can enrich our knowledge of the field, as well as expand the general public's appreciation of what's too often a passing diversion. A first step into that future would be the incorporation and development, within the university dance studies curriculum, of observation, language, analysis and writing skills utilized by professional dance critics.

The American presidential election of 2008 holds great symbolic value for us. In choosing a leader who embraces not only his own multiculturalism but also the world's, we seem to be trying to erase the polarities that have constricted our thinking. Unity was Barack Obama's mantra throughout the campaign, and although the word 'art' has not been an overt part of his agenda, his thoughtful world view gives the arts community hope. If his administration brings about less fear and military aggression, and more dialogue with other nations, we may see a restoration of cultural exchanges on both the teaching and performing levels. Our country may ease restrictions on visas for visiting students and artists. I believe we'll see a greater inclusiveness, a higher degree of racial and religious tolerance. In an era like that, it's the writers who will be called to differentiate art from art-junk, to show us that dance has its uses beyond the marketplace and even beyond the theatre.

December 2008

19

TWO ANALYSES OF 'DANCING IN THE DARK' (THE BAND WAGON, 1953)

Richard Dyer and John Mueller

Richard Dyer

'I seem to find the happiness I seek'

Couple-dances in the MGM musicals of the forties and fifties play varia-tions on the construction of heterosexuality, but with a greater emphasis, compared with Rogers and Astaire, on both difference and female-on-male dependency. 'Dancing in the Dark' from *The Band Wagon* suggests an idea of a fusion of difference within heterosexuality, which then leads to a sense of enabling dependency. Fred Astaire and Cyd Charisse, entirely within the one number, 'Dancing in the Dark', reach a different-but-equal arrangement through 'a sense of the fusion of differences, achieved through both an accommodation to each other's (dance) style and a use of (dance) ground uncommon to both.

The dancers, as characters and stars, represent two different sets of values explicitly embodied in their dancing styles. He is the old Hollywood musi-cal, his dance based on vaudeville, his idea of the purpose of the thing 'pure entertainment'; she, with her background in ballet, represents the new Hollywood musical of the forties, with its infusion of American Ballet Theatre and its aspiration to be meaningful as well as entertaining. The film is very deliberate in its use of Astaire and Charisse and poses them the question of whether they can dance together (with all that implies). 'Dan-cing in the Dark' is the demonstration that they can. It follows a series of disastrous and quarrelsome rehearsals for the show they are both to appear in; having at last discussed the fact that they both feel inadequate in relation to the other, they go at his suggestion to Central Park to see if they are capable of dancing together. They walk through a public dance floor of couples and into a clear space. The setting is important. It is not the theatre, it is not professional dance of any kind, it is the recreational space and dance of 'ordinary people'. This both provides neutral territory for these two professional dancers and also suggests the idea of doing what they feel like, rather than what, as in rehearsal, they are being required to do. The joy, naturally, is that they discover that, when they are themselves and ordinary, they can indeed dance together.

To achieve this the dance has to give the impression of spontaneity and intuition. She initiates the idea of dancing by idly sketching an expansive, balletic movement out into the area, establishing it as a space to dance in. He initiates the idea of dancing together by then doing a nimble turn which ends up with him posed facing her. As characters, both are spontaneously trying out the possibility of dancing. There then follows a longish sequence of mirroring, moving from side to side facing each other, looking into each other's eyes. There is no sense of one being the reflection of the other: one does not start a movement a moment before the other; neither looks at the other's body. It is perfect intuition, pure transparency of understanding between them. The steps here and throughout are a combination of ballet and hoofing, equally shared, practically impossible to disentangle. In other words, the perfect fusion, through spontaneity, intuition and transparency, of difference.

As the number develops, there is an increase in mutual holding and her-on-him dependency positions. Out of the fusion of what they really are/want develops a new awareness of difference and dependency. The instances of the latter are enabling: he spins her out or pulls her up in ways that allow her to flourish, to extend exhilaratingly upwards or outwards, with an energy and expansiveness at odds with the contained and inward movement associated with pretty femininity in showbiz dance. This is not to say that her movements connote masculinity – they are far too graceful for that – but rather they suggest the ideal of womanhood confidently flowering in the ground of male support.

'Dancing in the Dark' accomplishes the movement from courtship (getting to know one another) to consummation (reaching a peak of passion) within one number.

John Mueller

Astaire Dancing

A hefty percentage of the musicals produced in Hollywood in the 1930s were of the backstage variety – musicals in which putting on a show provided the major impetus for the plot. Astaire's first film, *Dancing Lady*, was one of these, but, thereafter, except for *The Band Wagon* (1953), he avoided them. Although the setting for most of his films is show business in one form or another, almost all of his films are primarily love stories – romances about two people who happen to spend a great deal of time singing and dancing, usually with each other.

It was difficult to develop fully more than one plot line in the Hollywood musicals of Astaire's era, because the films were short and so much of their time had to be given over to musical numbers. Although most backstage musicals also involve a love story, the putting-on-a-show theme tends to dominate, the love story to become incidental. This happens in *The Band Wagon*, too, though the script is perhaps slightly more successful than most in giving each plot line its due. In part this is because both revolve around the Astaire character. He plays a washed-up Hollywood hoofer who is trying to make a comeback on Broadway in a new show written for him by his friends, played by Oscar Levant and Nanette Fabray. At first the show is a disaster, run by a director (Jack Buchanan) who insists on making it 'intellectual'. When it fails, Buchanan willingly turns things over to Astaire, who achieves success by excising the pretentiousness and stressing that the show should be 'fun set to music' – to borrow a line from an earlier Comden–Green fable, *The Barkleys of Broadway*.

The love story concerns Astaire and his ballerina partner in the show, played by Cyd Charisse. Wary of each other at the beginning, they gradually become attracted, and finally sink into a clinch at the end. In some respects it's unfortunate that the love story must be given subplot status, for the problems that beset the Astaire–Charisse romance are interesting and have considerable potential for development. The two are kept apart not by contrived plot devices like mistaken identity but for reasons that derive directly from fundamental plot premises: self-consciousness about the differences in their ages (Astaire was fifty-four in 1953, Charisse thirty) and about their different backgrounds (the high-art world of ballet, the lowly world of tap). In addition, Charisse is already 'taken' – she is the girlfriend of the show's choreographer, played by James Mitchell.

At first Astaire and Charisse have little interest in each other offstage and evince a considerable incompatibility during rehearsals. Eventually, however, they talk over their differences and, with tension reduced, resolve to see if they can dance together. The resulting romantic duet, 'Dancing in the Dark', is the film's highlight. Not only do they discover they can dance compatibly, but, in some remarkably ingenious choreography, they begin inadvertently to fall in love.

Charisse and Astaire meet at a party for the show's backers and he tries, without her noticing, to make sure she is not too tall for him. Although they soon find themselves arguing over his age and her artistic pretensions, Buchanan is able to dragoon them into the show.

Things do not go well at rehearsals. Astaire feels out of place and has difficulty managing the lifts and other feats urged on him by the show's high-pressure, patronizing choreographer, James Mitchell. Frustrated and furious, Astaire finally throws a tantrum and walks out. At the instigation of the choreographer, Charisse visits Astaire in his room at the Plaza Hotel and awkwardly tries to calm him down. In a scene that strains Charisse's acting ability to the limit, the two dancers finally talk things out and are able to smooth over many of their differences, most of which have been caused, they discover, by their defensiveness toward each other. Charisse asks, 'Can you and I really dance together?' To find out, they take a horse-drawn cab to Central Park where they seek out a place to dance.

Eventually they come across a secluded open-air dance floor. The music of the most famous Schwartz-Dietz song of all, 'Dancing in the Dark', wafts through the trees, and to its accompaniment they do discover, to no one's great surprise, that they can indeed dance together, and quite well.

This dance is often seen as a crucial metaphor for the central problem in the putting-on-a-show plot: the successful blending of the high art of the ballerina with the low art of the hoofer and ballroom dancer. This notion should not be pushed too far, however, since, after all, the show is not a success when Buchanan attempts to blend high art with popular art, but only when Astaire takes over and throws out all the high-art pretensions. Besides, the ballroom/ballet blend characterizes all of Astaire's romantic duets with ballet-trained partners: Vera-Ellen, Leslie Caron, the Charisse of *Silk Stockings*, even Audrey Hepburn. The duet is remarkable not so much for its ingenious blending of art forms as for the way it develops a subtle emotional transformation. Astaire and Charisse, now wary friends, set out with a task before them that seems straightforward: to discover if they can dance together even though they come from different worlds and different generations. In the course of the dance, however, something unexpected happens: quite contrary to their wills and intentions, they begin to fall in love. Two choreographic devices are used to trace this: an elaborate game of touching and partnering, and the use of stunned hesitations.

The progress of the romance in the dance is most clearly charted in the way the dancers touch each other. At first they are distant and reluctant to touch. However, as the dance, and the romance, build, the partnering gradually becomes closer and progressively more confident and joyous, and lifts and elaborate partnered spins are worked into the texture. Finally, the climax of the dance is reached during an elaborate progression across the floor in which Charisse makes a great, deliberate show of wrapping her arms around Astaire's back rapturously. Touching, in fact, is used neatly to mark out the emotional change in the scenes that frame the dance: as they ride to the park in the horse-drawn cab, Astaire and Charisse are steadfastly not touching – to emphasize this, Astaire has his arms folded across his chest; in the ride *from* the park, by contrast, they are holding hands.

At the same time, the second choreographic device is being developed. One of the most remarkable aspects of Astaire's dancing and choreography is his ability to alter and shade the tempo within a single phrase. In 'Dancing in the Dark' these modulations of tempo are used to dramatic purpose: several times the dancers sink to the floor and hesitate in apparent surprise and wonder at what is happening to them; then they are impelled back into the dance. Later, when romantic inhibitions have been overcome, the idea is reprised, altered now to suit the dancers' new relationship: the sinking and rising are done in cooperation – as if the pair are mocking their earlier uncertainty and hesitancy.

The arrangement and orchestration of the music, by Conrad Salinger, is quite beautiful: sensual and dramatic, avoiding the tendency toward sappiness or lugubriousness that so often prevailed in MGM musicals. Another special appeal of the number is its attractive, understated decor, which contrasts markedly with the gaudy excess of the Broadway show Buchanan is trying to put on. Especially impressive is the simple, becoming costume Charisse wears, a copy of a $25 dress that had been purchased from an Arizona supplier by costume designer Mary Ann Nyberg. It cost the MGM wardrobe department $1,000 to make copies of the dress for the dance number.

At the beginning of the number, Astaire and Charisse leave the cab to wander silently through Central Park in search of a place to dance. They cross a crowded ballroom floor (where a band is playing the contemplative 'High and Low' from 1930) and eventually come upon a secluded dance area. Their walk is sombre, reflective; they are obviously ill at ease with each other. They do not touch; Astaire, in fact, mostly keeps his hands in his pockets.

Entering the dance area, Charisse, without looking at Astaire, inserts a brief, swooning dance phrase into the stroll, by way of invitation. Astaire answers with a danced turn that causes him to pull his hands from his pockets. But then he realizes that he doesn't know what to do with his hands; he reaches out, splays his fingers and uncertainly pulls his hands back toward his body. Rather than touch her, he deliberately clasps his hands behind his back. In this tense and strangely restrained pose, the 'Dancing in the Dark' melody enters, and the dance begins.

In the first phrases the dancers flow sometimes with the melody (richly rendered by cellos), sometimes with the countermelody. Astaire's hands are finally freed in a turn, and he reaches out to touch Charisse – from a distance – and sends her into some quick spins. This leads to turns that begin with the dancers close but soon develop into a remote embrace. Separating, they glide back to the edge of the dance floor.

The music now returns to the opening phrase and the dancers repeat their reflective, musically intricate dance-walk, but with an important difference – Astaire is now loosely partnering Charisse, hand to hand. She turns in his arms, and they resume the walk in a tighter pose, with him partnering her from behind. Out of this emerges a partnered pirouette (the first of several in the dance), which Charisse ends by sinking to the ground. The dancers hesitate in this pose, in apparent bewilderment, and then return to the dance.

They sweep liltingly side by side around the floor, and then once again Charisse spins into a fall. This time the fall emerges not from a partnered pirouette but from a lift, and this leads to the second bewildered hesitation. They are again pulled back into the dance by the music and are soon moving across the floor, Astaire firmly partnering Charisse from behind. The themes of touching and of hesitancy are intricately linked here as Charisse's right hand slowly moves upward – as if it were being impelled, reluctantly, by an outside force – to take Astaire's hand.

Another partnered pirouette leads to the third of the fall-hesitations, and then, all hesitation gone, the dancers flow across the floor, their progress punctuated by a pair of exultant lifts. At the far end of the floor (after the first of the two camera cuts in the dance), there are more partnered pirouettes, now elaborated with shifts of direction and extensions of arm and leg. After the dancers separate briefly, Charisse sinks down on a bench, her back to Astaire. Unlike her previous falls, this one does not suggest bewilderment or uncertainty. She simply waits, proffering her hand with full confidence that Astaire will come around behind her, take it and pull her back into the dance. This he does, exactly as the orchestra returns full-throatedly to the main theme. He pulls her upward and then off the bench and into his arms.

After more partnered pirouettes comes the emotional climax, in a final progression across the floor that displays to advantage Charisse's remarkable arms. (It is of interest that, where other choreographers were understandably mesmerized by Charisse's long, shapely legs, Astaire saw the choreographic possibilities in her long, shapely arms.) Charisse turns in Astaire's arms and then locks her left arm around his neck. In that position she performs two voluptuous backbends. Then she pauses, leaning against him, and finally, with great deliberateness, wraps her other arm around his neck in an embrace that is at once dramatic and intimate as he presses her tightly to his body.

With that, the dance and the dancers have made their statement, and all that remains is to blend the dance back into the story. After a camera cut, Astaire and Charisse dart toward some stairs that lead up from the dance floor and spin their way up them – one of those difficult steps that look so easy in Astaire's work. At the top they form dramatic poses with diagonal arms, first in opposition, then together. Charisse sinks to the floor for a final mocking reprise of her earlier falls; where those were uncertain and bewildered, this one is confident and trusting. Astaire pulls her to her feet again, and they climb back into the cab – Astaire pausing to dance his re-entry. As the music fades, they settle back into the seat of the cab, contentedly holding hands. The thing that Astaire, not notably a sentimental person, remembered most about the duet twenty-seven years later was the trouble he had 'getting back into that dammed cab'. Salinger's musical arrangement at the end of the number is very fine: the 'Dancing in the Dark' melody for violins, and a bold, dramatic countermelody for brasses, blend effortlessly into some jaunty, quietly contented phrases for strings as the dancers reboard the cab and sit back.

In the hotel-room scene that precedes the 'Dancing in the Dark' duet, the scriptwriters had Astaire call 'human speech' the 'greatest means of communication'. Astaire delivers the line dutifully – and then calmly proceeds in this duet to show how much more richly dance can communicate.

Part IV

LOCATING DANCE IN HISTORY AND SOCIETY

As dance writers integrated their close attention to the dance work itself with an investigation of its engagement with broader social, political and economic concerns, they positioned dance in relation to its cultural and historical context. An attention to issues of representation and power characterizes much of the writing produced in the 1990s and 2000s. Dance writers have looked at dance as a social and political practice, applying these debates to a range of forms and historical contexts so that dance is understood as an integral part of the workings of societies.

Such an approach has dispelled the myths which have accrued to some periods in dance history such as the Romantic era. As Jowitt points out, ballet in Western Europe during the first part of the nineteenth century (predominantly between the 1830s and 1850s) was the site of considerable ambiguity. In those dance works which have become synonymous with the period, the ballerina was etherealized whilst her dance technique demanded more and more strength and concealed virtuosity. The ballet itself provoked poetic and impassioned response yet was also considered a less-than-respectable art. Women were put on a metaphorical pedestal but men would be enticed to the theatre so they could literally look up their skirts. In her exposition of the period, Jowitt locates ballet within the wider world of Romanticism, and her writing is significant for this breadth of perspective.

Jowitt's writing offered a fresh historiographic approach to the role of women in dance, thus reflecting (if not overtly claiming) the feminist perspectives which produced new ways of looking at cultural phenomena. The ways in which constructs of femininity are embodied in dance was central to these new visions. Inevitably, perhaps, the construct of masculinity then came under scrutiny. Ramsay Burt (1995) not only considers the cultural meanings inscribed on the body of the male dancer but also deals with theatre dance forms other than the oft-targeted classical or Romantic ballet. Here, examining Nijinsky and the Ballets Russes, Burt takes a broad approach to his subject, dealing with Nijinsky's persona as a performer and his choreographic *oeuvre*. He argues that Nijinsky's choreography was more radical than Fokine's not only in aesthetic terms but also in its representations of masculinity. Nevertheless, whilst his stage image presented 'a limited but contained expression of homosexual experience', choreographically the 'norms of traditional masculinity remained intact'. Nijinsky's appeal to a wide audience can partly be located in this ambiguity of persona; he conformed to images of male prowess yet, in his exotic, sensual and androgynous roles, subverted those very images.

Like Jowitt and Burt, Dempster explores the political implications of dance through a gender analysis. She considers the body in both its conceptual and corporeal form, tracing attitudes to, including the rejection of, the 'natural' body in ballet, modern and postmodern dance. Her historical trajectory is supported by analyses of dance works in which she focuses on how the body is constructed – and deconstructed – in performance. An examination of how women 'write the body' offers Dempster the methodological framework of gender, but this does not limit her to one critical allegiance or perspective. Although commonplace now, writings on women and dance in the 1980s heralded a new transdisciplinary approach which identified dance as a key performer in the construction and circulation of social hegemonies.

Similarly, Savigliano offers a gender analysis of tango, focusing not on the *femme fatale* stereotypically invoked in representations of the form but rather on the temporarily non-dancing wallflower. Shifting the idea/term from a noun (the wallflower) to a verb (wallflowering), Savigliano considers how, within the context of the *milonga*, the tango dance club, all women wallflower, albeit for greater or lesser stretches of time. Savigliano aligns the position of the ethnographer, as one who watches but is never fully integrated into a situation, with that of the wallflower, considering how both move between activity and passivity in the negotiation of their roles. In addition, Savigliano sketches out a series of indicative tango interactions through invoking a set of representative tango *figuras*, or movement sequences. Through this process, Savigliano examines the 'food chain' of the *milonga* and puts forward a theory of gambling, calculated risk-taking, that troubles conventional notions of gender.

Yatin Lin's entry, by contrast, looks less at gender than at national politics. Investigating several works by Lin Hwai-Min, choreographer and director of the Taiwanese contemporary dance company Cloud Gate, Lin argues that these choreographies signal changes in Taiwanese identity. Using concepts such as flexible accumulation and flexible citizenship, Lin examines Taiwan's complex history, constituted by multiple cultural layerings and a corresponding multiple 'layer[ing] of consciousness'. Such a framework allows Lin to explore changes in Taiwanese identity through several Cloud Gate pieces so that Lin Hwai-Min's oeuvre sketches out transitions from Chinese identification, to Taiwanese-ness, to an awareness of the issues at stake in urbanization. Cloud Gate's most recent works suggest a space for Taiwan in a globalised cultural sphere.

In the process, the dance work becomes a site where national identity is negotiated and refigured.

Juliet McMains examines national politics as mediated through categories of race. She explores the relationship between reality television and ball-room dancing, both of which offer 'the promise of personal transforma-tion'. In American television's *Dancing with the Stars*, one of many international spin-offs from the BBC's *Strictly Come Dancing*, celebrities are paired with professional dancers in competitive dance routines which are judged by 'experts' and viewers alike. Film footage of struggles in rehearsal, and subsequent personal success, become symbolic of what can be achieved through labour. Although at the heart of many cultures and political sys-tems, McMains argues that this ethos is central to the American Dream: equal opportunity for all. However, she argues that opportunity is only for those who conform, those who can reproduce an essentially white American way. This is exemplified through an examination of how the Latin American dances are presented and judged. These forms have been appropriated for white, Western cultures from the beginning of the twen-tieth century. As such, their manifestation within the ballroom bears little relation to their origins as popular dance in the vernacular context; the invisibility of this heritage and the ascription of value to contemporary derivations are problematic. It is only when 'the racial hierarchy embedded in its representation of Latin dance is exposed and dismantled' that the American Dream will be one 'that celebrates rather than erases the diversity and multicultural heritage of its believers'.

Pallabi Chakravorty also looks at nationalism and its relationship to intra-national hierarchies and categories of difference. Alongside this, she critiques global notions of inter-culturalism by injecting a discussion of power differentials into otherwise celebratory narratives of cultural exchange and cultural borrowings. Chakravorty argues that the revival of Indian classical dance forms emerged out of a problematic inter-culturalism, one cultivated by colonialism and orientalism. She addresses the complex intersection of nationalist discourse and gender ideology in the refiguration of the regional dances of India as national forms. Chakravorty argues that the emergence of Indian nationalism itself was itself a product of this unequal inter-culturalism, developing as it did out of the embrace of Western post-Enlightenment thought by indigenous elites. As such, Chakravorty signals the complex factors that are at stake in the reinterpre-tation of dance traditions, while also pointing to the imperialist agendas that implicate nations in one another's 'traditional' practices across geographical boundaries.

The issues engaged here – gender, nation, race and colonialism – do not exhaust the possibilities for a consideration of dance's intersection with politics. They do, however, suggest a range of inquiries enabled by the consideration of dance's relationship with power. Similarly, the examples

explored here – classical, popular, concert, mediated, historical and contemporary – indicate the broad applicability of such critical frames. The
expanding of these frames suggests further options for the field of dance
studies.

Further reading

Carter A. (ed) (2004) *Rethinking Dance History: A Reader*, London: Routledge.

Chakravorty, P. (2008) *Bells of Change: Kathak Dance, Women and Modernity in India*,
Kolkata: Seagull Books.

Gere, D. (2004) *How to Make Dances in an Epidemic: Tracking Choreography in the Age
of AIDS*, Madison: University of Wisconsin Press.

Grau, A. and Jordan, S. (2000) *Europe Dancing: Perspectives on Theatre, Dance and
Cultural Identity*, London: Routledge.

Malnig, J. (2008) *Ballroom, Boogie, Shimmy Sham, Shake: A Social and Popular Dance
Reader*, Champaign: University of Illinois Press.

20

IN PURSUIT OF THE SYLPH

Ballet in the Romantic period

Deborah Jowitt

A mortal man, consumed with passion for a supernatural creature, attempts to possess her. He loses her for ever. The subject enchanted Parisian audiences of 1832 and sparked a new trend in ballet. But although Filippo Taglioni's *La Sylphide*[1] seemed to strike like a flash of lightning, a number of practical inventions, decisions and developments facilitated the emergence of the aerial ballerina and her ardent partner in tales of gossamer and gloom. Less than a year after the July Revolution of 1830 installed Louis Philippe on the French throne, the Opéra ceased to be court property. Dr Louis Véron, as the new director of what was now a private enterprise with a government subsidy, wished quite naturally to make the Opéra's productions reflect both its new independence and the power of the bourgeoisie that had triumphed the previous summer. He wanted that confident middle class in his audiences. They were already flocking to the boulevard theatres to see fairy spectacles and pantomimes, to see plays that laid on Gothic horror – their effects rendered more magical by improved stage lighting and machinery. The astute Dr Véron could see that the public craved mystery and exoticism, that they would be thrilled to see on the Opéra stage the haunted German valleys and misty Scottish fens that they had long been reading about in ballads by Goethe or Heinrich Heine and in novels by Sir Walter Scott, to see vaporous, beckoning women – firing a man's imagination even as they chilled his flesh with long, pale fingers.

The magical *verismo* of these other worlds offered escape during a period of what must have seemed a dizzying succession of sweeping political changes, particularly in France. The present government's careful middle-of-the-road policies might as easily be swept away. Science was revealing more mysteries than it explained, and religion had lost much of its potency. On the one hand, instability and uncertainty as a condition of life; on the other, a complacent, plodding morality. No wonder that the Parisian public loved to see theatre that made enigma and restlessness thrilling, but at the same time tamed it and contained it through theatrical conventions.

Up-to-date lighting equipment transformed the ballet stage into a fitting habitation for sylphs and other ethereal creatures. According to ballet historian Ivor Guest, one of Véron's first innovations at the Opéra was the installation of oil lamps with large reflectors to soften and diffuse the light. For the moonlit cloister act of Meyerbeer's opera *Robert le Diable*, he ordered the house lights extinguished. In short, he did everything that could intensify the atmosphere of light and shadow and heighten the effects of trapdoors, wires, veils, explosive powder, smoke machines, waterfalls and other marvels of stage apparatus.

Gradual developments in ballet technique made possible what was generally considered a new style of dancing, one well suited to bring fantasies to life. From Marie Taglioni and other dancers, as gifted if not as innovative, came the lightness and mobility that not only made fantasy flesh, and vice versa, but created a symbol of the unattainable far more profound than most of the ballet plots that made it possible.

Several scholars have wondered whether what we call Romantic ballet was perceived in its heyday as a vital part of the Romantic movement that flourished in painting, sculpture, music and literature. Were the flittings of these dancers truly 'Romantic' in the sense of challenging academic traditions? Was ballet not, they argue, a 'juste milieu' phenomenon that, like some of the middle-of-the-road painting of the day, simply applied a patina of Romantic imagery to traditional theatrics and to the same dance techniques that served neoclassicism? They have observed that even the most ardent of balletomanes, Théophile Gautier, thought that 'dancing is little adapted to render metaphysical themes' (Gautier 1973: 17).

It is true that ballet choreographers that we consider Romantic exploited and developed a traditional vocabulary, but an arch-Romantic like Byron did not deviate from traditional poetic forms either. And the German poet Friedrich Schlegel viewed Romantic poetry as something that would open up 'a perspective upon an infinitely increasing classicism' (Rosen and Zerner 1984: 17). In all fields of art, it was only pointless academicism that was to be resisted – like the approved genres of painting, and ballet's traditional classifications of male dancers according to physique as *danseur noble*, *demicaractère*, or *caractère*. The choreographers' choice of particular steps within the classical vocabulary and the freer way dancers performed them did indeed 'increase' the range of classicism.

Certainly the general public did not attend the ballet for spiritual enlightenment, and it naturally lapped up spectacle and technical prowess. The *Petit Courrier des Dames* correspondent must have alarmed his Parisian readers when he described a sumptuous production of the colourful ballet *La Gitana* in Saint Petersburg in 1838. There were, he exclaimed, 500 people in the last act's masked ball, 5,000 candles, and 120 chandeliers: 'Is Europe saying the Opéra is no longer the first theatre of the world for art and splendour?' (PCD 1839: 31). When Giselle was first seen in London in 1841 in the form of a play – with dances, set to the original Adolphe Adam music, for those dangerous and alluring ghosts, the wilis – a poster advertised in huge letters what was obviously a major attraction: FIRST NIGHT OF THE REAL WATER![2]

Certainly the leaders of the Romantic movement in literature and painting – the fiercest balletomanes among them – looked down on ballet even as they delighted in it. It was, they understood, an excuse for watching pretty, lightly clad women disporting themselves. Yet everywhere their prose betrays deeper responses. Writing of *Giselle* in *Les Beautés de l'Opéra*, Gautier luxuriates in his description of the opening of Act II, when the heroine has become a wili: 'And the rising moon that shows through the slashes of the leaves her sweet, sad, opaline visage, does her transparent whiteness not remind you of some young German girl who died of consumption while reading Novalis?' (Gautier *et al.* 1845: 15). If some have considered Gérard de Nerval insensitive for remarking that Giselle died of loving dancing too much (Chapman 1978), what more poetic fate could await anyone: the artist dying of excess devotion to art? The Romantic imagery in these ballets goes quite deep, and, whether spectators of the day realized it or not, the dark and mysterious currents within the plots, the edge of morbidity, the hallucinatory visions drew them to the ballet as much as did the acrobatic feats of dancers and their personal charm.

Everyone may have thought, with Gautier, that ballet was suited to express only passion and amorous pursuit, but it is passion darkened by the Romantic preoccupation with the dichotomy of flesh and spirit. Many of the ballets express the despairing notion that a perfect union between man and woman is possible only beyond the grave. Few supernatural ballets ended happily. In Filippo Taglioni's *La Fille du Danube* (1836) and August Bournonville's *Napoli* (1842), the lovers are united on earth because they have proved their incorruptibility – never sullying their ideals, never swerving in their devotion to each other, no matter how many temptations or gorgeous lookalikes are strewn in their paths.

The heroes of nineteenth-century ballets behaved according to the Romantic ideal of the hero, of the artist. Customs wearied them, and they would brook no restrictions except those that they imposed themselves. Frequently they cast aside attractive women of the correct rank, amiability and certified humanness to pursue their chosen sylph, undine or even a fey and spiritual peasant girl (*Giselle*). The crucial test to which the hero is often put exemplifies a highly Romantic dilemma. Will he be steadfast to his ideal, his true love, and not be taken in by a beguiling facsimile? When young Rudolph in *La Fille du Danube* becomes demented because his beloved (whom he takes to be mortal) has thrown herself into the river, his friends attempt to distract him by a veiled double who dances almost as well as does his darling. Weathering this deception, he plunges into the river and into a lively throng of veiled naiads, who 'dance their mazy fascinations around him' (Heath 1977: 80). But his love has given him a posy, a talisman which helps him to distinguish between truth and illusion. In

Bournonville's *Napoli*, the faithful fisherman Gennaro, searching the grottoes of the sea for his supposedly drowned Teresina, is confronted with a bevy of beguiling sea nymphs, among whom sports his reluctant, magicked sweetheart. The stage image is a familiar one: the lone man threads his way through swirling flocks of identically dressed females, looking searchingly at each one. It persists through *Swan Lake* and *The Sleeping Beauty* into Balanchine's ballets and such modern fantasies as the scene in the 1937 movie *Shall We Dance?* in which Fred Astaire dances perplexedly down a line of fetching women in Ginger Rogers' masks.

True and false confront the ballet hero in subtler forms too. The tragedy of *Giselle* is often presented as arising from a nobleman's thoughtless dalliance with a peasant girl, but there is another possible interpretation: Albrecht and Giselle are soulmates, made for each other, but issues of class prevent him from recognizing this. Certainly the several great performances given in our time by Gelsey Kirkland and Mikhail Baryshnikov brought this to almost unbearably poignant life.

But, although the themes of truth versus illusion, ideal versus real, that pervade so many of these ballets link them persuasively to Romanticism, the choice of subject was not the crux of the matter. According to Baudelaire (Rosen and Zerner 1984: 22), anything could be viewed 'Romantically', and he cited as characteristics of such a vision, 'intimacy, spirituality, colour, aspiration toward infinity' – all of which distinguished Romantic ballet.

Realism, an instance of 'intimacy' and a feature of much painting, was an integral part of the Romantic ballet worlds too, especially those created by August Bournonville and Jules Perrot. Even in supernatural ballets, they prided themselves on the detail of their crowd scenes, the verisimilitude with which they evoked a Highland revel or a Naples dockside or a village festival. The admittedly theatricalized naturalism, with dances justified by parties or festivals, set off the spirit world where dancing was a given and a metaphor for the restlessness of spiritual longing.

The supernatural ballets also had connections with early-nineteenth-century landscape painting. Although the popularity of this genre of painting reflected the desire to turn to nature as a constant in a bewildering world, the painter – imbuing nature with his own feelings – brought out its mysteriousness, its changeability. The play of light and shadow over a field could suggest conflict among the powers of nature. The mysterious landscapes of Caspar David Friedrich are tranquil, yet disturbing; Hugh Honour (1979: 78) has pointed out how Friedrich occasionally 'painted the foreground in great detail, but sank an immeasurable chasm between it and the distant, almost visionary, horizon, tantalizingly out of reach, creating an uneasy mood of yearning for the unattainable'. And in Turner's sensuous vortexes of light, nature itself becomes a shimmering dreamworld.

The air, earth, fire and water spirits of ballet awakened their lovers to the beauty of the natural world, to that landscape glinting beyond the window. In the second act of *La Sylphide*, the sylph flies to a treetop to bring down a nest for James's inspection and offers him spring water in her cupped hands. The scene must have seemed to contemporary spectators almost a visualization of Victor Hugo's popular poem 'La Fée et la Péri' in which a fairy tries to win the soul of a dying child by promising to reveal nature's secrets.

In considering how these ballets were perceived in their day, one must – as always – allow for individual sensibilities. When Hans Christian Andersen saw the 'Ballet of the Nuns' in Act II of *Robert le Diable* at the Paris Opéra in 1833, he was overwhelmed by the thrilling atmosphere of death, misty female sensuality, forbidden pleasures and religious blasphemy:

> By the hundred they rise from the graveyard and drift into the cloister. They seem not to touch the earth. Like vaporous images, they glide past one another. Suddenly their shrouds fall to the ground. They stand in all their voluptuous nakedness, and there begins a bacchanal like those that took place during their lifetimes,
> (Aschengreen 1974: 15)

But for every Andersen, there was undoubtedly a Fanny Appleton (later Mrs Henry Wadsworth Longfellow), who remarked in a letter that the members of the corps de ballet 'drop in like flakes of snow and are certainly very charming witches with their jaunty Parisian figures and most refined pirouettes' (Guest 1980: 112).

Marie Taglioni's style of dancing, so enchanting to audiences, was the result, not just of her sensibility, but of changes in ballet technique. The manual of classical dancing produced in 1828 by the La Scala teacher and choreographer Carlo Blasis shows how the turnout of the hips had increased since the eighteenth century, making it possible for dancers to raise their legs higher, to execute more brilliant beats, to change directions more rapidly and more fluidly. Although dancing of the 1830s would probably not strike us as particularly expansive, it would have seemed to nineteenth-century balletomanes much freer and larger in scale than what they had seen around the turn of the century.

In this development, fashion played a role. When the *ancien régime* was toppled, with it fell the ponderous, ornate and constricting clothes that went with rank and power. The soft slippers and light, loose-fitting dresses and Grecian draperies that came with, or just after, the French Revolution enabled women dancers to increase the range of their movements significantly. By the time corsets returned, the dancers had already changed, and they never looked back. Even before *La Sylphide*, Taglioni was dancing onstage in simple light dresses similar to those her mother made for her to practise in. As historian Marian Hannah Winter (1974) has remarked, fashion freed dancers' thighs. Ecstatic reviews of the way Taglioni bent from side to side confirm that it made possible some freeing of the torso as well.

Pointe work, so crucial to the image of the supernatural female, was not a new technique in 1832, although it wasn't standard equipment for all female dancers when Taglioni came to the Paris Opéra. (The 1830 edition of Blasis's manual doesn't even mention it.) Geneviève Gosselin, people remembered, had danced on her toes in 1815, maybe earlier, and 'grotesque' (meaning acrobatic) dancers of both sexes did pointe work. It was viewed more as a feat than anything else – and often seems to have been performed as one. Engravings of the little company that Filippo Taglioni assembled for the Opéra in Stuttgart later in the 1820s show all the women on pointe. It is during those years that his daughter must have worked on perfecting her own approach – discovering ways to strengthen her feet and rise onto her toes without apparent effort.

Some of the impetus for pointe work might have come from the elaborate 'flying' techniques developed by Charles Didelot. His *Zéphire et Flore* astounded London balletgoers in 1796, Saint Petersburg audiences in 1804, and Parisians in 1815 (when Mlle Gosselin reputedly stood on her toes). It was still a favourite when Taglioni performed it in Paris with Jules Perrot in 1830. Didelot didn't simply fly down some heavenly personage on a cloud to clinch the plot. Any of his dancers might fly by means of individual wires and harnesses. They could take to the air, or be carefully lowered until only the tips of their toes touched the stage floor. For imaginative choreographers and ambitious dancers, it must have seemed natural to wish to echo that effect in passages where it wasn't possible to attach someone to a wire.

Circumstances, then, conspired to produce a style of dance and stage machinery ideal for supernatural subjects. Marie Taglioni's own attributes, her classes with Auguste Vestris in Paris, and her father's taste and inspired coaching defined that style. Not all dancers copied her purity, her coolness or her de-emphasis of athleticism, but they studied her delicate attack, her simplicity, the fluidity of her arms and torso. For example, it was remarked – as if it were a novelty – that she often held her long arms down, gently curved, instead of flourishing them about; one characteristic of the style that August Bournonville perpetuated in Copenhagen is just such a *port de bras* for jumps. It tends to make dancers look lighter and to focus the audience's attention on their nimble feet.

*

Dancers have always been praised for 'lightness', but from the 1830s until late in the century, variants of the term saturated the metaphors and similes of writers on ballet. Light as weightlessness, light as luminosity; in English the same word serves both meanings. But even in languages where the words differ, the meanings intertwine in descriptions of ballerinas. *The Times* in London described Adèle Dumilâtre's dancing as being 'so ethereal … that she almost looked transparent' (Guest 1984: 92). The delight caused by airy and seemingly effortless dancing, set off by mysterious lighting and gauzy, billowing skirts, seems related to the century's uneasiness about the flesh. Praising the lighting for Perrot's Eoline, Gautier raved that it gave the illusion that 'Eoline is only the envelope, the transparent veil of a superior being, a goddess condemned by some fate to live among men' (ibid.: 311). The 'condemned' is telling, and it's interesting that it comes as if automatically from the pen of a cheerful hedonist like Gautier. Insubstantiality, then, is close to godliness.

Lightness in the sense of airiness complements the notion. The buoyancy of the female dancer helped her to embody a spiritual aspiration; the lightness of a male dancer suggested the hero's desires to transcend the limits of the flesh. It could also stand for the winging of his soul as he took on some of the qualities of the sought-after dream. Even the constant motion, the restlessness for which dancers were admired, can be seen as a dissatisfaction with present existence and a yearning for realms beyond. Also, in the Romantic era, the artist-as-rebel was a favoured image. By their apparent denial of gravity, the sylphs and their kin prettily demonstrated their exemption from laws governing human behaviour. So female dancers were enthusiastically compared to birds, butterflies, balloons, feathers, moonbeams, shadows, and criticized for showing too much vigour or attack. Male dancers, generally disprized during these years, succeeded the more they resembled the women in terms of style. It was 'the aerial Perrot, Perrot the sylph, Perrot the male Taglioni' (ibid.: 57).

The lithographers intensified the public's fantasies of supernatural heroines. The ballerinas – even when depicting real if exotic women – seem unstable, elusive. They hover on one improbably dainty toe, not in perfect equilibrium, but leaning slightly forward as if they're just passing through the pose. When shown in midair, their bodies are softly curved, legs barely apart – less as if they'd leapt than as if they'd been blown upward. Some of the poses may be artistic conventions rather than ballet reality but the conventions were dictated by the artists' perceptions of the ballets. And, as refinements of dance technique helped create the airborne images onstage, techniques in lithography developed as if in response. As Charles Rosen and Henry Zerner have pointed out, 'drawing on the surface of the stone made possible subtle nuances of tone and images that vanish at the edges' (Rosen and Zerner 1984: 79). The dancer becomes the glistening focal point in an evanescent and cloudy world.

She may have been an abstraction, but she was unmistakably female. In expressing the ambiguous tensions they felt between reality and spiritual longing, the ballet librettists and choreographers – almost without exception male[3] – revealed confused emotions in regard to women. On the one hand, almost all the stories were told from the hero's point of view; on the other, the ballerinas dominated the stage. Even in ballets where the hero dreamed the heroine, she was clearly superior to him – enchanting, evasive, unrestricted by his codes, and able to drift about on her toes. Yet she flew into his arms of her own accord. In the thrilling, much-discussed dream sequence in *La Péri*, Carlotta Grisi leaped from the framed platform that contained 'her world' and was bravely caught by Lucien Petipa. The audience marvelled over his strength, but was more excited by her daring, and *The Times* critic commented on some lifts in the same ballet: 'She is supported by Petipa, but seems as if supported by air alone' (Cohen 1976: 85).

Only occasionally in these ballets does a male character obviously dominate a female one. Jules Perrot, a compelling performer as well as a brilliant choreographer, created intriguing demonic roles for himself in several ballets. August Bournonville, working in Copenhagen relatively isolated from Parisian fads, refused to cater to the general dislike of male dancers; like Perrot, he was a good dancer and wanted to perform. The fairy worlds were, as a rule, unbalanced in their populations. Gautier (1845: 17) explained that Myrtha, the Queen of the Wilis, had only female subjects, since men were 'too heavy, too stupid, too in love with their ugly hides to die such a pretty death'.

These rather liberated creatures imagined by men stood opposed to the respectable middle-class wife and mother (also, to some extent, a male creation). In *La Sylphide*, James's betrothed, Effie, a woman of real weight and substance, with sensible shoes and domestic talents, is far less vivid than her rival. Despite their supposed purity, the supernatural creatures are *femmes fatales*, representing all that is erotically potent and compelling about women. They offer a double message, beckoning the hero both as the incarnation of an ideal and as a temptress luring him from the straight and narrow. It isn't for nothing that Erik Aschengreen (1974) called his fine monograph on Romantic ballet 'The beautiful danger'.

Balletomanes were awed by the effort it took to appear effortless. In 1839, when Lucile Grahn first performed *La Sylphide* in Paris, the house held its breath to see if she would do Taglioni's 'terrible pas' of Act II, which Elssler had cut: 'C'était une question de vie où de mort' (PCD 1839: 207). And what applause when she triumphed in it! Because the preferred steps for spirits were bounding ones, the labour that went into becoming ethereal was considerable: the quantities of ballottés, brisés, temps-levés, emboîtés, assembles, cabrioles, sauts de basque and ballonés that packed the dances required strong ankles and good wind. It was thanks to Arnalia Ferraris's 'supple and sinewy foot' that she was able to 'beat the *entrechat huit* to perfection' (Beaumont 1938: 225).

In the days before the blocked pointe shoe was perfected, hovering on tiptoe required immense strength. Today's dancer, wearing a blocked and stiffened slipper, stands, in effect, on her toenails, on the very tip of her toe. The vertical equilibrium is so secure that, once up there, she is almost at rest. The ballerina of the mid-nineteenth century was stepping as high onto the toe pads as possible, and could stay there only by exertion of all her leg muscles and a tremendous lift in the body. Yet in 1846, in *Paquita*, Carlotta Grisi thrilled balletomanes by fancy hops 'on the tip of the toe with a turn of dazzling vivacity' (Guest 1980: 254).

In addition, female dancers, along with the men, had to be skilled at balancing on the flat foot or half-toe for extended periods of time. The choreography of the day featured elaborate *adagio* sequences that are uncommon now except in the Bournonville repertory. Standing on one leg, the dancer would revolve smoothly, make one pretty pose metamorphose into another, bend forward or back – all without wobbling. Taglioni is said to have worked for two-hour stretches three times a day with her father while preparing for her debut. Léopold Adice's syllabus of 1859 lists a barre in which exercises are performed one hundred times each. Bournonville dancers hoisted their legs in *grands battements* a total of 320 times. To be secure in *adagio*, a dancer might work at holding one leg in the air for a hundred counts, as Marie Taglioni did. Louise Fitzjames had her maid stand on her hips to increase turnout, and Carlotta Grisi said sourly that those times Jules Perrot stood on her hips while she lay face down on the floor with legs spread were the erotic high points of their liaison. Beginners forced their turnout by standing in a box with braces that could be adjusted via a series of grooves. (No wonder Marie Taglioni was easily able to pass off one of her pregnancies as knee trouble.)

The prose devoted to ballerinas during the heyday of Romanticism makes it clear that spectators found the paradox of a real, and probably available, woman playing an incorporeal nymph a titillating one. Gautier lingers lovingly over descriptions of ballerinas' knees, ankles, breasts, noses and chins. Fanny Cerrito 'knows how to curve and soften her plump arms like the handles of an ancient Greek vase' (Chapman 1978: 33). Classical allusion aside, the sentence is unabashedly sensual.

Besides the enraptured accounts, a beguiling detritus of poems, lithographs, curios and sheet music attest to the fervour dancers inspired. Portraits of the most famous ballerinas of the day assumed curious forms. A 1984 exhibit presented by the Theatre Collection of the Austrian National Library included the following mementoes of the wildly acclaimed Fanny Elssler: a porcelain cast of her left hand, her right foot sculpted in marble, portrait medallions naming her 'Terpsichore's Darling' and images of Fanny and her sister Therese as sylphides painted on a cup and on a pipe. In terms of the souvenirs and verbiage they generated, dancers – female ones, at any rate – were the rock stars of the nineteenth-century bourgeoisie.

For the unearthly heroines of the ballets, physical union with a mortal posed usually fatal danger. The sylph lost her wings and expired. Alma, the 'daughter of fire', a statue who comes to life by day, faces a vexing dilemma: if she falls in love, she will become a statue for ever. (Seldom was an audience more tantalized by the prospect of a lovely idol falling off her pedestal.) By these standards, the women dancers of the nineteenth century were not very sylphish offstage. Salaries for all but the stars were not high; a well-to-do protector, not hard to come by, was considered by many to be a necessity. Members of the Jockey Club frequented the green room and backstage areas of the Paris Opéra; at Her Majesty's Theatre, the bloods of London could obtain seats in the 'omnibus boxes' on the sides of the stage – the better to ogle, and perhaps to pinch and pass messages. Benjamin Lumley, the director of this theatre when *Ondine* was premiered there, related that backstage one evening when Fanny Cerrito was dancing the lovely 'Pas de l'Ombre', frolicking on the seashore with her newly acquired shadow, Adeline Plunkett aimed a kick at Elisa Scheffer, her rival for the favours of the Earl of Pembroke, missed, broke the cord holding the 'moon' lamp, and temporarily extinguished Cerrito's dance (Guest 1969).

Sometimes, of course, dancers married other dancers or formed liaisons with them – as did Jules Perrot and Carlotta Grisi, Arthur Saint Léon and Fanny Cerrito, Fanny Elssler and (briefly) Anton Stuhlmüller. However, these relationships in no way exempted female performers from the solicitations of others. Young corps dancers were particularly anxious to secure wealthy protectors or husbands. Out of their meagre salaries – often made even smaller by fines levied for various infractions – they had to pay for classes, obtain practice clothes, scheme for advancement. Many came from poor families. In *Les Petits Mystères de l'Opéra* (1844), Albéric Second's satirical look at the backstage world of the Paris Opéra, one *petit rat* wears a capacious pocket under her sylph costume, into which she packs useful objects she's picked up, including a pack of cards, five or six cigar butts, a squeezed half lemon, some cheese, a scrap of soap, and a necklace. Furthermore, she says, the bulging pocket gives her a 'Spanish shape' pleasing to the gentlemen in the stalls. The same girl relates how the dancing master Cellarius lures coryphées – who rank above the girls of the quadrilles – to come to his place the three times a week when they're not performing and partner gentlemen who are ostensibly learning to waltz: five francs to dance with a chair, ten to dance with a *figurante* at the Opéra. Supper on the town afterward, where a girl can gorge …

Given the lack of birth control, it's not surprising that many female dancers became mothers. Ballerinas often danced well into their pregnancies. Sometimes their offspring accompanied them on their numerous tours or guest appearances. More often, the babies were brought up by grandparents or aunts or friends. 'Well, Fanny, send the brat to me', Elssler's English friend Harriet Grote wrote cheerfully, when Fanny decided not to take her seven year-old Therese to America. It was four years before Fanny retrieved her daughter (Guest 1972: 67).

The nineteenth-century female dancer would probably not have struck us as looking ethereal, considering her diet, childbearing and the kind of muscles she had to develop. Fanny Elssler, to judge from her pink satin and black lace 'Cachucha' costume, was a woman of medium height with a trim, but not tiny waist and a full, curving bust. A sylph could hardly be ethereal enough in her dancing, but the woman who played her could be too ethereal to suit public taste. Gautier couldn't abide shoulder blades that stuck out ('two bony triangles that resemble the roots of a torn-off wing' – the analogy is revealing). Poor Louise Fitzjames was constantly criticized for her thinness. A caricaturist presented her as a dancing asparagus, and Gautier (1973: 21) said that she wasn't 'even substantial enough to play the part of a shadow'. Being substantial enough to play a shadow ... it might be considered the mission of the Romantic ballerina.

Such ballerinas were among the first to embody abstract qualities, which not all of the spectators who flocked to adore them recognized. These performers didn't *represent* Beauty or Music or Fecundity as had their counterparts in earlier centuries, yet their light, fleeting, ardent dancing could suggest something larger than their stage personas and more ineffable than the roles they played.

Most of the supernatural ballets of the early nineteenth century – along with a host of other ballets of the period – have perished. The only works in this genre that can be experienced today are *Giselle* and the Danish August Bournonville's version of *La Sylphide*, his *Napoli* and *A Folk Tale* (in the last two, the heroines were not supernatural, but were temporarily in thrall to supernatural forces). All have been altered to some degree, and the *Giselle* we see today was largely rechoreographed by Marius Petipa in 1884. The poetic image of a mortal man lured by a filmy female vision into a magical world didn't perish with the decay of Romanticism, however. Transformed by new ideas and new styles in dancing, it bloomed again in Saint Petersburg, and years later in London and New York City. It is with us still.

Notes

1 See original text for fuller discussion of this ballet.
2 Playbill for Sadler's Wells Theatre, week beginning 23 August 1841.
3 Some of the exceptions are Lucille Grahn, Fanny Elssler's sister Therese; and Marie Taglioni, who choreographed *Le Papillon* in 1860 for her protégée, Emma Livry.

21

NIJINSKY

Modernism and heterodox representations of masculinity

Ramsay Burt

Male prowess in Nijinsky's roles

A much reproduced drawing by Jean Cocteau shows Nijinsky in the wings after *Le Spectre de la Rose* (1911). Like a boxer between bouts, he lies back exhausted on a chair holding a glass of water while Vassili, Diaghilev's valet, fans him with a towel. In the background, looking concerned, are Diaghilev, Bakst and Misia Edwards (later Sert) and her husband. Part of the mythology about Nijinsky concerns his incredible leap out through the window at the end of this piece and, in general, the extraordinary agility and elevation of his jumps. Michel Fokine, however, talked down Nijinsky's leap (Fokine 1961: 180–1). Anton Dolin claims that he had danced most of Nijinsky's roles either with the Ballets Russes or subsequently and with many dancers from the original casts. In his opinion Nijinsky's roles were not that demanding technically. This is perhaps to miss a crucial point about the attitude towards technical feats shared by Nijinsky, Pavlova, Fokine and other dancers of their generation from the Imperial Theatres. They disliked the *tours de forces* performed by the older generation of ballerinas and male dancers, feeling that these looked mechanical and were unsympathetic to the creation of an artistic feeling in performance. (But the younger dancers had all been trained to perform and all did perform the virtuoso roles in the Petipa repertoire.) Nijinsky's sister Bronislava, in her *Early Memoirs*, gives us several very detailed accounts of her brother's performances and how he prepared for them. She tells how his daily practice was geared towards developing his strength and that he would practise much more difficult feats than were needed for his roles. She also says that he would practise to minimize the preparations for jumps, and that he worked at finding how to land softly afterwards, so that when he was on stage his performance would appear effortless and flowing.

The description that Rebecca West gives us of the effect, is echoed in many other accounts:

> The climax of his art was his jump. He leaped high into the air, and there stayed for what seemed several seconds. Face and body suggested that he was to mount still further, do the Indian rope trick with himself as rope, hurl himself up into space through an invisible ceiling and disappear. But then he came down – and here was the second miracle – more slowly than he had gone up, landing as softly as a deer clearing a hedge of snow.
>
> (quoted in Buckle 1975: 390)

It would seem that Nijinsky did possess extraordinary strength and agility but that this was accompanied by hard work at creating an illusion of effortlessness. As Nijinska remarked: 'Do you remember how many transitions, how many nuances there were during the course of his leap? These transitions and nuances created the illusion that he never touched the ground' (Nijinska 1986: 86). What all this amounts to is that, whatever Dolin may have believed, Nijinsky did produce a spectacle of famed and mythologized agility on stage. While it was Diaghilev who commissioned these roles, it was Fokine who came up with the steps. As Lynn Garafola (1989) points out, Fokine is a transitional figure between the nineteenth-century ballet tradition and twentieth-century modernism. Judging by survivals like *Le Spectre de la Rose*, or from descriptions of ballets like *Narcisse* (1911), as far as the steps of Nijinsky's solos are concerned, these were fairly traditional. Compared with Nijinsky's subsequent innovations, Fokine's choreography is conventional, in phrasing and use of space: aided by Fokine's and Nijinsky's musicality, jumps and effects coincide with appropriate musical climaxes, while spatially there are circles that boldly encompass the stage, and strong diagonals to give Nijinsky the appearance of mastering the space. These are devices for displaying traditional male virtuosity. The film theorist Steve Neale (1983: 15–16) has proposed that 'women are a problem, a source of anxiety, of obsessive enquiry; men are not. Whereas women are investigated, men are tested. Masculinity, as an ideal, at least, is implicitly known. Femininity is, by contrast, a mystery.' The evidence suggests that in these virtuosic roles, Nijinsky passed the test. Fokine himself was keen to dance Nijinsky's roles himself in 1914 after the latter's break with Diaghilev and the company. Fokine's male solos clearly conformed to conventional expectations of male strength and prowess, and supported the notion that the Russian male dancers were less tainted by civilization and more in touch with 'natural' masculinity than their Western contemporaries.

Nijinsky as genius

Nijinsky was not just famous for his strength, agility and for his exceptional skill in partnering a ballerina. He was also hailed for his extraordinary expressiveness and the uncanny way he 'got into' his roles. His performance as Petrouchka is the prime example of this. Nijinsky's role contained both dynamic dancing and demanding mime. His sister records:

> When Petrouchka dances, his body remains the body of a doll; only the tragic eyes reflect his emotions, burning with passion or dimming with pain ... Petrouchka dances as if he is using only the heavy wooden parts of his body. Only the swinging, mechanical, soul-less motions jerk the sawdust-filled arms or legs upwards in extravagant movements to indicate transports of joy or despair ... Vaslav is astonishing in the unusual technique of his dance, and in the expressiveness of his body. In *Petrouchka*, Vaslav jumps as high as ever and executes as many *pirouettes* and *tours en l'air* as he usually does, even though his petrouchkian wooden feet do not have the flexibility of a dancer's feet.
>
> (Nijinska 1981: 373–4)

It was for his dramatic expressiveness in roles like Petrouchka and the sensuality of his performance of roles like the Golden Slave in *Schéhérazade* (1910), as well as for his technical abilities, that Nijinsky was acclaimed as a genius. As Christine Battersby (1989: 74) has argued, the idea of genius has sometimes been invoked to allow male artists to give expression to emotions that, over the last two centuries, have been characterized as feminine. In Nijinsky's case, the description is, in the hands of some writers, a back-handed compliment. Prince Peter Lieven, for example, suggested:

> I think the neatest and at the same time the truest estimate of Nijinsky's intellect was given me by Misia Sert, one of Diaghilev's best friends. She called him an 'idiot of genius'. This is no paradox. In our enthusiasm over the 'entity of genius' our admiration goes to the dancer's creative instincts and not to the conception of his brain, as for example, his role in *Petrouchka*.
>
> (Lieven 1980: 89)

Alexandre Benois is even more dismissive of Nijinsky's intelligence. For him Nijinsky was someone who only came alive for the stage: 'Having put on his costume, he gradually began to change into another being, the one he saw in the mirror ... The fact that Nijinsky's metamorphosis was predominantly subconscious is in my opinion, the very proof of his genius' (Benois 1941: 289). They are surely both putting Nijinsky down retrospectively. Both disapproved of the radicalism of his choreography, and are writing with benefit of hindsight, knowing of his subsequent mental illness. But the idea that Nijinsky was a genius in his dancing and in his on-stage creation of roles such as Petrouchka is a comparatively safe and unthreatening one. It can easily be recuperated within conservative definitions of masculinity.

Nijinsky's heterodox roles in Fokine's ballets

Nijinsky's roles were nevertheless transgressive. Most of them presented a spectacle of male sexuality. This raises the question of whom this spectacle was intended for, as gender ideologies enforce that the dominant point of view is male, presuming that men are attracted to the spectacle of female sexuality but repelled by the male body. Heterosexual male norms are generally maintained through keeping male sexuality invisible. Any explicit expression of male sexuality was against the conventions of nineteenth-century middle-class gender ideologies. How far therefore did Nijinsky's roles in ballets such as *Narcisse*, *Schéhérazade*, *Le Spectre de la Rose* and his own *L'Après-Midi d'un Faune* (1912) break with the nineteenth-century tradition, and to what extent were they still open to acceptable interpretation as essays on classical or 'oriental' themes?

Many contemporary descriptions of Nijinsky ascribe androgynous qualities to his dancing, stressing its male power and strength but female sensuousness. Richard Buckle quotes several descriptions of Nijinsky's performance of the Golden Slave in *Schéhérazade* including Fokine's comment that 'the lack of masculinity which was peculiar to this remarkable dancer … suited very well the role of the negro slave' (Fokine 1961: 55). Fokine then likens Nijinsky to a 'half-feline animal' but also to a stallion 'overflowing with an abundant power, his feet impatiently pawing the floor'. Alexandre Benois, who wrote the libretto for this ballet, described Nijinsky's performance as 'half-cat, half-snake, fiendishly agile, feminine and yet wholly terrifying' (Buckle 1975: 160). It has already been pointed out that, within the technical range of male ballet dancing of his day, Nijinsky was considered to perform considerable technical feats. His roles often therefore allowed him to express sensuality and sensitivity (conventionally feminine) with extraordinary strength and dynamism (conventionally masculine).

None of the descriptions of Nijinsky suggest that he was actually effeminate. Moreover, according to Anton Dolin (1985: 50), Diaghilev disliked obvious homosexuality and hated any signs of effeminacy. Garafola (1989: 56) suggests that the androgynous quality of Nijinsky's dancing may have related to the image of the androgyne in the work of many homosexual visual artists of the Aesthetic movement at the end of the nineteenth century. The androgyne presented the image of a graceful, innocent, often languid youth, unspoilt by the world. Emmanuel Cooper (1986) has suggested that many homosexual artists of the Aesthetic movement saw in the androgynous male a positive image of the homosexual as a third sex. According to the 'scientific' explanation of homosexuality initially proposed by Karl Ulrichs, homosexual men were women born in men's bodies, and constituted a third sex. Those homosexuals who subscribed to the notion of a third sex saw this as a slightly effeminate 'in-between' man or woman (see Dyer 1990).

The role of Narcisse which Nijinsky created in Fokine's *Narcisse* can be interpreted as a straight piece of classical mythology, but is also open to interpretation as an image of the third sex. The figure of Narcissus is an image that has a history of use by homosexual artists that goes back to Caravaggio. Nijinska's description of Narcisse exemplifies all the qualities associated with the Aesthetic androgyne – grace, innocence and unspoiltness:

> His body of the youth in love with his own image emanated health and the athletic prowess of the ancient Greek Games. It could have been dangerous to portray in a dance the sensual and erotic Narcisse, driven to ecstasy by his own reflection in the water. Vaslav had so interpreted this scene that all such implication disappeared, dissolved in the beauty of his dance. Each pose on the ground, each movement in the air was a masterpiece.
>
> (Nijinska 1981: 366–7)

Alternatively the vigorous classicism of Nijinsky's presentation of the role might be interpreted from another, different homosexual perspective that looked back to Classical Greece as an example of a robust, manly culture in which male homosexuality was normal (see Dyer 1990: 22–5).

What made *Narcisse* acceptable to straight audiences, apart from its classical origins, was the fact that it is a moral fable that warns against the dangers of self-obsession. For transgressing social norms, Narcissus is punished. On another level he also has to be punished for being the erotic subject of the (male) spectator's gaze, as must the Golden Slave in *Schéhérazade*. In the Slave's case the discourse through which Nijinsky's highly ambiguous and exotic roles might nevertheless have appeared acceptable was that of Orientalism. As Edward Said (1987) has pointed out, for the nineteenth-century European (and by implication for the Ballets Russes's audiences) the Orient was associated with the freedom of licentious sex. In the Romantic imagination, Mario Praz (1967) identifies a literary and artistic tradition which combined the imagery of exotic places, the cultivation of sadomasochistic tastes, and a fascination with the macabre. *Schéhérazade*, with its orgy and subsequent execution, is clearly an example of this. All of this is within the discourse of Orientalist art, with the qualification that Nijinsky, the Golden Slave, could, as a Russian dancer (though actually Polish by birth), claim to be part 'oriental'.

Those involved in the Ballets Russes, as Russians, were ambiguously both of the East and West. Peter Wollen points to the ambiguous nature of the identity of the Russian ballet: it was a fusion of French ballet traditions and indigenous Russian Orientalist traditions. Drawing on dancers and visual artists from Saint Petersburg, it was part of European Russia in contrast to more 'eastern' Moscow. 'Yet by a strange reversal the trend was turned around and, in the form of the Ballets Russes, Paris (cultural capital of Europe, the "west") began to import Russia, the "east", in a deluge of exaggerated Orientalism' (Wollen 1987: 21).

The Ballets Russes never performed in Russia and both Diaghilev and Nijinsky were dismissed from the service of the Imperial Theatres. Bakst, Benois and Roerich never worked for the Imperial Theatres after 1909, Fokine leaving in 1918. After 1911, Nijinsky was unable (or Diaghilev may have encouraged him to believe he was unable) to return to Russia because he had defaulted from his military service. Yet these artists claimed, as Benois put it, to be presenting Russian ballet to Europe, making new works that would embody 'all the beloved old with a fresh and stimulating manner of presentation' (Benois 1936: 194). One can therefore conclude that the project of the artists and intellectuals in Diaghilev's circle was to define through the ballet their identity as Russians, in ways that were impossible within and oppositional to the hegemonic Russian establishment.

For Diaghilev and Nijinsky as homosexual men, this marginal position also enabled a limited but contained expression of homosexual experience. Nijinsky's homosexuality was signified primarily through ambiguities within the stories, and through qualities of costume and decor. It was not signified by the virtuosic solos for which he became famous. In the case of the Golden Slave, Fokine's innovatory methods of combining mime and dance into expressive movement (Garafola 1989) were a vehicle for expressing a transgressively sensual and eroticized male image, but in a context within which transgression was seen to be punished. Punishment in the form of the violent ending of Schéhérazade might be appreciated as an erotic spectacle, but was made acceptable by being displaced from 'normal' Europeans onto 'oriental' 'Others'. The status quo of norms of traditional masculinity thus remained intact. It is only through the modernism of his own choreography that Nijinsky actually challenged and disrupted conservative gender ideologies.

Nijinsky's ballets and gender representation

Nijinsky's Jeux has not survived, and can only be glimpsed through descriptions, from the evidence of photographs and from drawings by Valentine Gross. It was the first 'modern' ballet to take a modern theme (tennis and a triangular relationship) and use a modern set and costume. Nijinsky was interested in Gauguin's paintings while working on Jeux (see Nijinska 1981: 442). Buckle (1975: 339) points to ways in which the surviving drawings and photographs of *Jeux* resemble the monumental, sculptural qualities of Gauguin's compositions. But Nijinsky's attraction must also surely have been thematic. Gauguin rejected the sophisticated social mores of nineteenth-century Europe in preference for what he saw as the innocent freedom of social and sexual relations in Tahiti. In doing so Gauguin contributed to the European myth of the 'primitive'. To the Western 'orientalist' imagination 'primitive' people were less inhibited about sexuality. *Jeux* was set in the present, and its theme was surely modern, uninhibited social and sexual relationships. His other ballets at the time, *Faune* and *Sacre*, deal with similar themes and are both set in the 'primitive' and mythic or mythological past.

Nijinsky's *L'Aprés-Midi d'un Faune* is set to Debussy's *Prelude à l'Aprés-Midi d'un Faune* of 1894 that was itself inspired by Mallarmé's poem of 1876. The poem presents the reveries of a young Faune. These include an encounter with two beautiful nymphs which may be recollected from a dream, a fantasy or a real event. Mallarmé was one of the poets that Verlaine dubbed 'les poètes maudits', pure of heart but despised and rejected by both mother and society, and accursed (maudits) by God. Nijinsky's amoral interpretation of the poem is surely within this tradition. The ballet's first performance provoked heated debate in the French press, and charges of indecency (ibid.: 284–9). These largely concern the ballet's ending. The Faune, having surprised a group of nymphs, carries back to his rock a veil that one of them has dropped. As it is usually performed now, the Faune stretches out on top of the veil while making a couple of pelvic thrusts, jerks his head back in pleasure and then lies still. The first performance may have been more sexually explicit than this, or, as Richard Buckle suggests, he may have been lying on his right arm and thus appear to be masturbating (ibid.: 284). According to *Figaro* the ending was changed after the first performance, thus eliminating the 'indecency'.

As a classical male role, the Faune superficially resembles the title role of Fokine's *Narcisse*. The difference, however, is in its attitude towards morality. Underlying the myth of Narcissus is a warning about unnatural behaviour – being unmoved by the love of Echo, being obsessed with personal appearance. The Faune, however, is 'pure', 'natural' and innocent. The movement style of the ballet is simple walking steps and jumps, dance stripped of every vestige of balletic style. This exquisite surface thus, by being outside of balletic convention, created an ideological space for the ballet that was outside of social convention. The Faune, as Nijinsky shows him, is amoral, and the piece a deliberate provocation to society to condemn such spontaneous sexual behaviour, as if he were saying only a depraved mind could see anything depraved in this. It was surely Nijinsky's homosexual point of view that allowed him to produce a representation of 'natural' masculinity that ran so strongly against convention. As Sokolova, who danced in the ballet with Nijinsky, recalls,

> Nijinsky as the Faune was thrilling. Although his movements were absolutely restrained, they were virile and powerful, and the manner in which he caressed and carried the nymph's veil was so animal that one expected to see him run up the side of the hill with it in his mouth.
>
> (Sokolova 1960: 41)

Nijinska's (1981) description of his other ballet for Diaghilev, Sacre, also stresses the animality of the male dancers. In the reconstruction that Millicent Hodson produced for the Joffrey Ballet the men look bestial. They characteristically make their entrances leaning forward; their postures are like those of the figures in the famous nineteenth-century Russian painting of The Volga Boatmen by I. Repin (1844–1930). The angle at which the men in Sacre lean, and the slightly pointed hats they wear, make them look as if they are about to jump forwards and upwards, and penetrate into one of the massed groups of women. In the first act men fight each other in the Games of the rival clans. The Ancients, in the second act, wear bear skins with the animals' heads fitting on their own like hoods. Grouped with other men round the circle in which the Chosen One is trapped and will dance herself to death, they perform a dance sequence which includes a movement where they drag their left foot across the floor like an animal pawing the ground. Throughout the Chosen One's sacrificial solo, they wait for her death spasm, the signal for them to rush in and grab her, hoisting her high in the air. All these are instances of the bestial quality in the male roles in Sacre.

Sokolova recalled the heat on stage every time Sacre was performed (Sokolova 1960: 44). Millicent Hodson (1985: 41) suggests this may have been partly due to the ritualistic nature of the movement – circle dances that generated altered mental states. It must also have come from the effort expended by both sexes in jumping, throwing themselves on the ground and straight away springing back up again, running, stamping. Within this, the male dancers have more dynamic leaps and jumps than the female ones. These are the sorts of movement for which Nijinsky himself was famous in his roles in other men's ballets. In Sacre, rather than hiding effort and exhaustion, these are if anything exaggerated. There is no way that the male dancers in Sacre could have been thought of as effeminate. If Faune presented a pure, 'natural' masculinity, in Sacre Nijinsky has stripped this of its acceptable classical setting, to produce a representation of masculinity at its nastiest and most abject. The first performance of Sacre on 29 May 1913 at the Théâtre des Champs-Elysées has gone down in history for the disturbance that split the audience. That what split them was the revolutionary character of the choreography and not the music is proved by the fact that the latter was ecstatically received when performed on its own in a concert in Paris early in 1914. It was Nijinsky's choreography, including the ways in which masculinity was represented in the ballet, that surely caused the most offence.

Modernism and the male body

Jacques Rivière (1983) argued that the difference between Nijinsky's work and that of Fokine was a new focus on the body: Fokine was too artful, vacillating and vague, but Nijinsky did away with artificiality in 'a return to the body'. Fokine had nevertheless, in his roles for Nijinsky, expanded the range of male dance to include both sensitive and sensual movement, and strong and dynamic expression. Fokine's ballets might hint at aspects of male sexuality whose expression had not previously been acceptable, but these occurred within exotic, 'oriental' or classical settings that were far enough removed from contemporary, modern European ones to defuse any potential threat. In addition Nijinsky as a dancer was so dynamic and skilful that he was hailed as a (male) genius. This in itself was a convenient excuse for any eccentricities. Thus although Fokine may have been introducing types of representation that were new to dance, they could nevertheless be fitted into existing conservative gender ideologies.

It is these two aspects of Nijinsky's star persona – the dynamic solo and the homoerotic spectacle – that left an active legacy for much of the twentieth century. First, the myth of Nijinsky's leap has fascinated many male ballet dancers and set a standard to which they have aspired. Second, photographs and drawings of Nijinsky in revealing costumes were a prototype for a genre of homoerotic images of male ballet dancers.

It is only in the last few years that Nijinsky's contribution to radical dance practice has been rediscovered by dance historians. *Sacre* can now be seen to have revealed the division in the audience for early modernism – between liberals and radicals who were sympathetic to changing social mores and those conservatives who responded to the anti-bourgeois sentiments of modernism. If the re-emergence of the male body in dance and ballet at the beginning of the twentieth century can be seen as a disruptive force, it was neither through the renewal of bravura male dancing nor the founding of a homoerotic tradition but through the radicalism of early modernism. By denaturalizing and destabilizing the representation of gender in theatre dance, Nijinsky was using the kinds of deconstructive strategies that are more familiarly associated with the work of the postmodern choreographers.

22

WOMEN WRITING THE BODY

Let's watch a little how she dances

Elizabeth Dempster

Major innovation in dance has occurred largely outside the ballet academy. The radical redefinition of concert dance which began at the turn of the twentieth century was a movement initiated by women artists working independently of traditional structures to develop new languages of physical expression. The early modern dance was a repudiation of the tenets of nineteenth-century ballet, including its emphasis on spectacle and virtuoso display. It was an avowedly female-centred movement, both with respect to the manner in which the body was deployed and represented and in the imagery and subject matter employed. The early-modern dancers were asking that the body and its movement, along with the place and context of dance, be looked at in new ways. They inherited no practice; the techniques and the choreographic forms they developed were maps and reflections of the possibilities and propensities of their own originating bodies.

In the early 1900s dancers such as Isadora Duncan, Loie Fuller, Maud Allen and Ruth St Denis constructed images and created dances through their own unballetic bodies, producing a writing of the female body which strongly contrasted with classical inscriptions. These dancers, creating new vocabularies of movement and new styles of presentation, made a decisive and liberating break with the principles and forms of the European ballet. The modern dance genre is now most closely identified with the choreographic output of the second generation of modern dancers – Mary Wigman, Doris Humphrey, Martha Graham – and the training systems they developed. It is to this body of work that the following discussion refers.

Modern dance is not a uniform system, but a corpus of related though differentiated vocabularies and techniques of movement which have evolved in response to the choreographic projects of individual artists. Common to these contrasting styles of dance – and it is this that allows us to group otherwise disparate works under the banner of 'modern dance' – is a conception of the body as a medium and vehicle for the expression of inner forces. The spatial and temporal structure of these dances is based on emotional and psychological imperatives. The governing logic of modern dance is not pictorial, as in the ballet, but affective.

For the modern dancer, dance is an expression of interiority: interior feeling guiding the movement of the body into external forms. Doris Humphrey described her dance as 'moving from the inside out' (Cohen 1972); for Graham (1950: 21–2) it was a process of 'making visible the interior landscape'. This articulation of interior (maternal) spaces creates forms which are not, however, ideal or perfected ones. The modern dancer's body registers the play of opposing forces, falling and recovering, contracting and releasing. It is a body defined through a series of dynamic alternations subject both to moments of surrender and moments of resistance.

In modern dance the body acts in a dynamic relationship with gravity. For Humphrey the body was at its most interesting when in transition and at a moment of gravitational loss, that is, when it was falling. Modern dance has often been termed 'terrestrial', that is, floor-bound and inward-looking. As such it has been negatively compared with the ballet and the aerial verticality and openness of that form. But, as Graham has stressed, 'the dancers fall so that they may rise'. It is in the *falling*, not in being down, that the modern body is at its most expressive.

The modern body and the dance which shapes it are a site of struggle where social and psychological, spatial and rhythmic conflicts are played out and sometimes reconciled. This body – and it is specifically a female body – is not passive but dynamic, even convulsive, as Deborah Jowitt sees it:

> In many of [Graham's] important works of the forties and fifties, you felt the dancing shuddering along in huge jerks, propelled by the violently contracting and expanding bodies. When I first saw Graham in 1955, I was stunned by the whiplash of her spine; by the way, as Medea in *Cave of the Heart* she writhed sideways on her knees – simultaneously devouring and vomiting a length of red yarn.
>
> (Jowitt 1977: 72)

Jowitt concludes that Graham's dancing was like no other she had witnessed, 'a body language consisting solely of epithets'.

Modern dance posits a natural body in which feeling and form are organically connected. Graham, for example, conceived the body as a conduit, a responsive channel through which inner truths are revealed. The body has a revelatory potential and technique is the means by which the outer manifestations of the body are brought into alignment with the inner world of the psyche.

> Through all times the acquiring of technique in dance has been for one purpose – so to train the body as to make possible any demand made upon it by that inner self which has the vision of

what needs to be said. No one invents movement; movement is
discovered. What is possible and necessary to the body under the
impulse of the emotional self is the result of this discovery.

(Graham in Cohen 1974: 139)

The function of technique in modern dance is, as Graham has described it,
to free the socialized body and clear it of any impediment which might
obscure its capacity for 'true speech'. Ironically, perhaps, this concept of
the 'natural' body was expounded in support of highly systemized
and codified dance languages and training programmes which inscribe
relationships – necessarily conventional and arbitrary – between the body,
movement and meaning.

Modern dance's valorization of the 'natural' and its positing of an individualized presymbolic subject are not features of the classical system of
training. Ballet training shapes, controls, improves upon and perfects the
body's given physical structure; in this process both the natural body and
the individualized subject are erased. As the principles of modern dance
have become progressively codified into systematic techniques, the concept
of a 'natural' body, pre-existing discourse, can no longer be sustained.
Modern dance, now distant from its creators' originating ideas, is passed on
through highly formalized training programmes; and, like the classical
system, this training involves erasure of naturally given physical traits and
processes of reinscription.

How are the body and 'the feminine' inscribed by the female-devised languages of modern dance? Graham's dances sacralize and mythologize the
female body, a body shown to be subject to forceful emotional, unconscious
and libidinal impulses. In Foster's reading it is the body of the hysteric:

The action begins in the abdomen, codified as the site of libidinal
and primitive desires. The symbolic contents of the abdomen
radiate through the body, twisting and empowering the body with
their message. Graham's characters seem to be subject to the psychological mechanism of repression. The powerful message from
the unconscious makes its way only with difficulty through
the emotional and intellectual centers of the person and into the
world. Graham depicts the tense conflict between corporeal and
psychological elements.

(Foster 1986: 81)

Graham's location of 'the feminine' may seem uncomfortably close to the
space traditionally ascribed to the body, women and dance within patriarchy.

Her choreographies, however, represent the inner world as a dynamic,
outward-flowing, conflictual force; 'the feminine' is not passive but volup-
tuously and sometimes violently active. It is a force which shapes the outer

world. Graham's work reflects the psychoanalytic preoccupations of her time, but the public and performative nature of Graham's articulation of these concerns, and the power she ascribes to the female body, significantly distinguish her representation of the feminine from that associated with clinical practice.

As early as the 1930s Graham and her fellow artists were presenting a newly defined dance practice in the public arena and in so doing they created spaces for dance and for women which had not existed before. But this form of dance, once an oppositional practice, is now offered as a second language supplementing classical ballet in the training of the professional dancer. In my judgement modern dance's gradual codification, its identity as a formularized technique, has rendered it susceptible to colonization; and it is this codification rather than any inherent ideological complicity which permits elements of modern dance to be subsumed into the ballet.

Lincoln Kirstein, the founding father of the New York City Ballet, has cursorily dismissed modern dance as the 'minor verse' of theatre. He considers it timebound, nostalgic and lacking the 'clear speech acts' and universal legibility of the ballet. He is one of a number of critics who have argued that ballet is the only enduring Western concert dance form (Kirstein 1935). In Kirstein's view, ballet's pre-eminence is assured because modern dance has failed to produce a stable lexicon and is therefore lacking in consequence.

But modern dance has clearly developed vocabularies and syntactical conventions; and Kirstein's perceptions are misplaced. He would be less inaccurate if his subject had been postmodern dance. The postmodern is not a newly defined dance language but a strategy and a method of inquiry which challenge and interrogate the process of representation itself. Once the relation between movement and its referent is questioned, the representational codes and conventions of dance are opened to investigation. Analysis, questioning and manipulation of the codes and conventions which inscribe the body in dance are distinguishing features of the postmodern mode.

In the 1940s Merce Cunningham had already begun to demonstrate that dance could be primarily about movement. In contrast to the expressionism of modern dance, in which movement is presumed to have intrinsic meaning, Cunningham choreographies emphasize the arbitrary nature of the correlation between signifier and signified. In his deconstruction of existing choreographic codes Cunningham challenged the rhetoric of 'the natural' which surrounded modern dance. The political dimensions of this deconstructive project have been addressed more directly in the work of some of the later postmodern choreographers.

Susan Foster defines two stages/modes of postmodern dance practice: objectivist and reflexive. The first is the precondition for the second, but the two modes were coextensive in the 1960s and 1970s and together constitute the genre. Foster differentiates the two stages of postmodern dance as follows:

> Objectivist dance focuses on the body's movement, allowing any references to the world to accrue alongside the dance as a by-product of the body's motion. The reflexive choreography ... assumes that the body will inevitably refer to other events, and because of this asks how those references are made. Whereas objectivist dance has laid bare the conventions governing representations to allow the body to speak its own language, reflexive choreography works with these same conventions to show the body's capacity to both speak and be spoken through in many different languages.
>
> (Foster 1986: 188)

Like Cunningham, the postmodern choreographers emerging in the 1960s distinguished themselves from both the classical tradition and the then firmly established modern dance in that their focus was on the fundamental material and medium of dance, the moving body itself. The body was no longer to be trained to the task of interpreting or illustrating something other than its own material reality. Postmodern dance does not present perfected, ideal or unified forms, nor bodies driven by inner imperatives, but bodies of bone, muscle and flesh speaking of and for themselves.

> The dances are about what they look like. Because [objectivist dances] simply present individual people in motion, the dancers clearly do not presume to represent idealized experience or experience that might be common to all people.
>
> (ibid.: 185)

In *Work 1961–1973* Yvonne Rainer (1974) writes of her 'chunky' body not conforming to the traditional image of the female dancer. Elsewhere she recalls a Boston reviewer, writing in the 1960s, disdainfully commenting on the 'slack' bodies of (the later-termed) postmodern dancers (Brown and Rainer 1979). A democratization of the body and of dance was heralded in the postmodern work of the 1960s and 1970s. Whilst Cunningham pursued a deconstruction of choreographic conventions through technically trained bodies – bodies which maintained the 'look' of the dancer – postmodern works of this period featured both trained and untrained performers, in short 'any-old-body'. Widely used choreographic devices such as rule games, task-based and improvisational structures provided a frame for the perception and enjoyment of bodies in action – trained or untrained, old or young, thick or thin, male or female.

The play of oppositions and the gender stereotyping embodied in the ballet and perpetuated in modern dance traditions were systematically de-emphasized in the postmodern work of this era. Within the selection, structuring and performance of movement strong contrasts and oppositions were reduced or eliminated. Rainer speaks here of *The Mind is a Muscle, Trio A* (1966):

> The limbs are never in a fixed, still relationship and they are stretched to the fullest extension only in transit, creating the impression that the body is constantly engaged in transitions. Another factor contributing to the smoothness of the continuity is that no one part of the series is made any more important than any other. For four and half minutes a great variety of movement shapes occur, but they are of equal weight and are equally emphasized.
>
> (Rainer 1974: 67)

The postmodern dancer's range and style of movement were not determined by gender, and sex-specific roles were rare – notable exceptions being a number of works by Yvonne Rainer in which issues of gender, sexual identity and seduction in performance were addressed directly (ibid.). The early postmodern focus on non-hierarchical and non-genderized use and organization of the body and its movement continues in current postmodern dance.

Postmodern dance, as Foster has indicated, also involves the reworking and reassessment of earlier forms of bodily inscription – drawing from, quoting, subverting and manipulating classical and other lexicons. Referring to Rainer's *Trio A* (1966) and Trisha Brown's *Accumulation* (1971), *With Talking* (1973) and *Plus Watermotor* (1977), Foster has noted the tensions which arise when (at least) two disparate modes of representation are juxtaposed or brought into dialogue (Foster 1986: 186). In these works the body is present as an instrument concerned simply with physical articulation, but at the same time it also alludes to other discourses: Rainer's *Trio A* contains references to earlier dance forms and Brown's dance presents speaking and dancing as simultaneous but independent texts. The play of contrasting discourses and the use of quotation in postmodern compositional process produce layered and complex dance works open to multiple readings. Yvonne Rainer, in conversation with Trisha Brown, discusses this effect in Brown's *Glacial Decoy* (1979):

> The costumes bring in another dimension ... of, not exactly a persona, but an association with personae created elsewhere and earlier, somewhere between *Les Sylphides* and *Primitive Mysteries*, maybe even *Antic Meet*, which has that take-off on *Primitive Mysteries*. And it is the dress that produces this association. There's a recurring, fleeting transformation from a body moving to a flickering female image. I think that because the dress stands away from

the body the image is never totally integrated or unified, so one goes back and forth in seeing movement-as-movement, body-inside-dress, dress-outside-body, and image-of-woman/dancer, which is not the same thing as seeing or not seeing your work in terms of your being a woman. Femaleness in *Glacial Decoy* is both a given, as in your previous work, and a superimposition.

(Brown and Rainer 1979: 32)

The process of deconstruction and bricolage commonly associated with postmodern dance also describe an attitude to physical training. The development of what might be termed the postmodern body is in some senses a deconstructive process, involving a period of detraining of the dancer's habitual structures and patterns of movement. The dancer brings intelligence to bear on the physical structure of his or her body, focusing close attention upon the interaction of skeletal alignment and physiological and perceptual processes. Through this process the dancer reconstructs a physical articulation based on an understanding of what is common to all bodies and what is unique to his or her own. Our bodies evolve in dialogue with a complex physical and social world, so training systems which have informed postmodern dance are based on a conceptualization of the body as an organism in flux. The postmodern body is not a fixed, immutable entity, but a living structure which continually adapts and transforms itself. It is a body available to the play of many discourses. Postmodern dance directs attention away from any specific image of the body and towards the process of constructing all bodies.

If postmodern dance is a 'writing' of the body, it is a writing which is conditional, circumstantial and above all transitory; it is a writing which erases itself in the act of being written. The body, and by extension 'the feminine', in postmodern dance is unstable, fleeting, flickering, transient – a subject of multiple representations.

23

GAMBLING FEMININITY

Tango wallflowers and femmes fatales

Marta E. Savigliano

Tango often evokes fatal men and women caught in a somewhat dangerous dance, where obscure desires (forbidden liaisons, provocation, transgression, betrayal, revenge, jealousy) become spectacularly stylised. Depictions of tangos in narrative cinema, tango choreographies conceived for the stage, tango portrayals and tango metaphors in advertisement and literary fiction, and to some extent tango lyrics have contributed to this by now worldwide well-established cliché. As an ethnographer of the *milongas* (tango clubs) and as an aspiring *milonguera* (tango dancer) I became increasingly puzzled with the presence of wallflowers and the absence of femmes fatales in the every-night tango scene of Buenos Aires.[1] This paper, then, situates wallflowers and more precisely the act of wallflowering at the centre rather then at the outskirts of the *milongas*. (Readers should be aware of the manoeuvring I am exerting here by setting the wallflower into motion, that is into wall-flowering. The story starts with the limits of translation. In the *milongas* women wallflower [*planchar* is the slang Argentino-Spanish for this activity]. There is no corresponding noun to this verb applicable to the *milonga* setting. [*Planchadora*, as the one who *plancha*, would immediately bring to mind someone who presses or irons clothes for a living. It is a profession of sorts, with no relation to the dancing/non-dancing economy that I am addressing here. *Planchar* – and this is a wild guess – has been assigned to this active 'waiting to be asked to dance' perhaps as an association with the unintended 'ironing' of the garment on which the aspiring dancer sits for extended time.] Therefore, while *wallflower* [in English] ascribes a rather set identity to those who don't dance – meaning they probably never will because of who they are – *planchar* designates a [lack of] activity – not dancing – into which some aspiring dancers happen to have fallen under certain circumstances. *La que plancha* [the one who wallflowers] is not as stuck in the character as 'the wallflower': One wallflowers; the other is a wallflower. This picture does not include those who, whether inside or outside of the dance club or dancing situation, choose systematically or circumstantially not to dance. The lack of desire to dance immediately situates them outside of the rules of the game [the economy]. I am proposing the idea that a full tango experience is impossible without the presence of wallflowers and without the threat of wallflowering as the potential dancers enter the tango club. And I wish to clarify that wall-flowering is a traumatic, intense, trying, unpleasant state to go through. Since all women in the *milonga* scene wallflower to a certain extent, wallflowering is both despised and admired for reasons I will soon explicate.

Given that *milongueras* often wallflower more than they get to dance at tango clubs, and that they (we) endure rather than enjoy this rather humiliating position, I have wondered why and how women wallflower and what is at stake in this act of passivity. Why do women attend the *milongas* night after night, persistently undergoing this enhanced state of anxiety that compromises their self-esteem? Unwilling to settle for a facile explanation in terms of heterosexual sado-masochistic dynamics (as in: 'Women enjoy submission; they like to suffer'), I will entertain the idea that *milongueras* are irredeemable gamblers of their own femininity.[2]

Before discussing this idea, however, I wish to backtrack to the wall-flowers so that you know more precisely who are these tango characters that have become my obsession and specifically what it is that they do. Along the way you will notice their invaluable contribution to rethinking the role of the dance scholar, and, in particular, to the ethnographic technique of participant-observation. (My references to wallflowers and wall-flowering frequently shift from the position of the observing wallflower [the ethnographer] to that of the wallflowers being observed [the *milongueras*]; and the wallflowering ethnographer here evoked is a self-reflexive type. My goal in so doing is to capture the state of confusion that characterizes participant-observation, 'native' ethnography and auto-ethnography, on their own and combined.)

The ethnographer as wallflower

(Readers less interested in ethnography than in wallflowers should skip to the next section.)

The following sections have the double purpose of introducing some paradigmatic tango *figuras* (movement sequences) while generating reflection on some paradigmatic ethnographic techniques. The tango embrace, hooks, spins and so on are described in order to call attention to the practice of description in itself. The result is a counter-transparent effect in that the dance ethnographer is caught in the work of ethnographising, recurrently interjecting observations and interpretations. The dilemma of ethnographic participant-observation – of assuming alternately active passivity and passive activity – is thus highlighted in terms of a 'problem' impossible to solve given that it condenses the very possibility of the production of anthropological knowledge.

The ethnographer, in this case a dance ethnographer, will be presented attempting to capture the signs and the signification of ephemeral chor-eographed movements. She is both an intruder in the dance scene, and a necessary presence for the dance to actually occur. She is a troubled observer obsessively preoccupied by her desire to participate in the dance, while that desire strongly informs her renderings of the dance. The dancers' own desires are reported through her own, her desire pouring into them. Observing and unable to fully participate in the tango world, or at least to participate the way in which 'they' do, she includes herself as a victim of scholarly observation. Alternately, she discovers the power of her gaze, capable of not only observing but actually also creating the dance through interpretation. Looking for empathetic understanding while simultaneously generating a report to the academy, the dance eth-nographer resorts to her familiar horizons of meaning – such as feminist theory and politics – in order to figure out (and thus disfigure) the dan-cers' stakes in the dance. She asks: Does the tango present a fatal, 'macho' man or does it stage a femme fatale? Is *she* a self-defeating, manipulative woman trying to make a dent in the male homosocial tango world? Is *he* a traitorous seducer in need of maternal reassurance who mistreats those he seeks to fulfil his fantasies? Who is the victim of the tango, and who the victimizer? And whose questions are these, the tango dancers' or her own?

Neither tango nor the dancing bodies in themselves should be credited for provoking this complex ethnographic situation. The most down-to-earth cultural practice or artefact participates in a similar ethnographic knower/known dynamic. Bodies are not intrinsically more mute than nations and dancing is not necessarily more elusive than economics. The difficulty of the scholarly enterprise becomes more noticeable, however, because until recently dance as a field was left at the margins of the trodden paths of modern disciplinary knowledge. It is the lack of investment in developing a discourse to account for bodies performing seemingly unpro-ductive movements that allows these reflections on the ethnographic predicament to be revisited.

Speculations of (from) a wallflower (position)

(The actual performance of the wallflower starts here.)

I am pleased to introduce you today to an often invisible and mistakenly shameful character of the dance scene: the wallflower. These speculations are intended as a vindication of the wallflower. And I must confess that in doing research on tango I have frequently identified with this character. So, in speculating about 'her', I have engaged in reflections about my own eth-nographic undertakings. In order to elicit your sympathy, however, in a less self-indulgent tone, I will address both the dance ethnographer and the wallflower as if they were a (third person) 'she'.[3]

Haunted by an itch to tango the dance ethnographer sits restless at the computer screen, performing her scholarly duties. She wants to dance but she is accountable mainly as a wallflower. Wallflowering, she observes, wedges a speculative space between dance spectatorship and dance performance that allows her to observe, participate, interpret and write. The figure of the wallflower highlights the performance of ethnography and the production of ethnographies of performance. *She writes*:

'In performance and cinematic studies much effort has been devoted to the conceptualization of the production/emission and consumption/reception of cultural representations. (Note: Cite Laura Mulvey 1988a and 1988b; Herbert Blau 1990; Bill Nichols 1981; and others.) A wallflower potentially condenses the role of a hyperactive audience, who could but will not deliver the act of dancing; and of an ultra-marginal and passive performer who can inadvertently slip away from the dance scene (ethnographic field) at her whim, running away with the best gossip of the evening. That is, if she can overcome a sense of melancholia, a tendency to believe that others and not herself determine her lonesome fate. The wallflower's viewpoint complicates the dualism entrenched in these performance–audience oriented epistemologies. Through participant-observation and observant-participation wallflowers contribute to cultural construction from a position that, although not free of *resentment*, embraces the productive side of performative failure.' *She leaves her desk and starts rolling around sitting on her desk chair while explaining*:

This wallflower, then does not take on an identity but rather assumes a position[4] that revindicates an active aspect of some seemingly inactive undertakings, calling attention to an activity that takes place somewhere else – not exactly *on* the dance floor nor completely away from it. Wall-flowering is somewhat like plotting. The wallflower is characterized by a profound knowledge, investment and even training in a performance genre, coupled with a view from the margins, as an engaged spectator of that which she is ready to perform – and yet she does not. Her unpopular, often denied, but vastly practised doings capture the embodied learning anxieties of the dance ethnographer with a specificity that the role of a 'participant-observer' so elegantly covers up. *Still sitting and rolling, she adopts extravagant positions*:

Marginality, misfitness, naïvety, awkwardness, patience beyond the call of duty and frustration with a smile are some of the very corporeal experiences to which a wallflower/ethnographer is and accepts to be submitted to in the course of fieldwork. The passivity involved in learning from others' activity will eventually deliver the strategic production of knowledge. Actually, wallflowering is somewhat prescribed by the participant-observer technique in that the desire to go native or to become totally involved in a given 'culture' should be persistently frustrated by the demands of objectivity or, at least, of maintaining the distance required for the production of anthropological interpretations. But anthropologists are wallflowers with a vengeance. The tense marginality of the expert in the midst of a participatory project metamorphoses into a manipulative work of representation and interpretation as soon as the institutional, discursive field of anthropology is regained. *She stops rolling around, sits tall and still, and adopts a preachy tone in saying*:

The wallflower position is more often imposed on women than it is self-elected by us. And arguably anyone who wallflowers, that is, who obsessively observes action while actively remaining passive, becomes feminized. It is from this feminized but not submissive position (the one of the wallflower who does not give up and eventually transforms the dance scene) that these performative speculations choreocritically address women's positions in the sensuous production of the tango. *She mimics the activities she orally describes*:

Sitting uncomfortably at the edge of her chair, clutching and stretching her toes captured in ankle-strapped high-heels ('you can't leave Buenos Aires without your tango shoes!' said Rivarola, her dance teacher–informant), the wallflower/ethnographer intensely watches the tango scene. She looks for the intentionality hidden in every move. She knows that there is more to it than what she can see. Her hands, placed on the small table in controlled relaxation, long for a note-pad where she would record that today, Friday 22 March 1996, she sits at *la milonga* El Tugurio, in downtown Buenos Aires. Her manipulative work of interpretation is about to start. *The tango couple enters under a spotlight, while she continues on her chair, at a small and round table. The tango couple follows her instructions*:

La Salida ('Departure' or beginning of a tango dance)

As handsome as he can be, not because of his physical attributes but rather cultivating a handsome-like attitude, *el milonguero* stands at some edge of the dancehall (against a wall, behind a column, next to the bar's counter, by the hall that leads to the entrance door) monitoring the *milonga* scene. His gaze wanders distractedly through the tables until it locks, abruptly, with *la milonguera*'s look. She has been sitting there, quietly conversing (not laughing) with her female friends since the last dance-set was over. He interpellates her with an intense nod, just one quick reverberating stroke that raises his chin and runs up through his face, lifting his eyebrows. She might deflect his invitation to dance, flashed through the room by quietly continuing her visual search, or she will immediately move her chair to the back, stand-up and, after a brief pause, start walking towards her new tango partner as he moves towards her. An instant is enough (and usual) for this intensely engaging exchange. The wallflower wonders, taking quick head-notes, 'How did it happen?' She would have missed it for sure. Yet they are already meeting at the dance floor.

The tango music starts. They converse for a few music times, weighing their words, getting ready to carry each other's bodies. This is the only opportunity for verbal or even visual exchange among tango partners, until the tango is over. They embrace.

The tango embrace grows rather than happens. It is carefully crafted by the two, taking hold of their entire bodies. He initiates the embrace, already a movement without displacement, by placing his upper arm under hers, pushing upwards, seeking for the weight of her embracing arm. The torsos move slightly towards each other as the heads search for contact, turned towards the hands that clasp and extend the arms that will lead the dance trajectory. The tango bodies stretch both from the waist up and down as if pulled from both ends along a slightly tilted axis, joining at the top. The balls of the feet look for groundness. Well planted, although she is already brought to raise her heels in tension. They sense each other's balance wondering how much challenge they can give and take in the movements they are about to perform. They quickly calculate the possibilities opened up by this firm, tight, yet flexible embrace that will structure the tango moves without asphyxiating their unmatching, improvised steps. The wall-flower watches the construction of the tango embrace taking place in what feels like suspended but not empty time. Suddenly, gravity seems to pull the bodies down, the knees bend for an instant to a tango rhythmic slash, and they slide without bouncing into a tango walk.

They just walk.

Walk together. Walk as close as necessary. So close that, at a certain point, the differences between the two of you will become essential. The need to master the other is irresistible. The resistance to being engulfed is hysterical. Keep on walking. You cannot give up. It is beyond your control. Just try to make it beautiful. Perform. Do not hide your fear, just give it some style. Move together but split. Split your roles. Split them once and for all. One should master, the other should resist. And forget that you know what the other is going through.

The interpretations of the wallflower slip into the tango scene. (Her desire?) The dance moves her imagination. Too invested in the tango to be a mere spectator, the wallflower actively spectacularises the dance. The tango takes three rather than two: a male to master the dance and confess his sorrows; a female to seduce, resist seduction, and be seduced; and a gaze to watch these occurrences. The male/female couple performs the ritual, and the gaze constitutes the spectacle. Two performers, but three participants, make a tango (cf. Savigliano 1995). The wallflower/dance ethnographer scribbles, annoyed by her self-reflections. *The dancers follow her instructions.*

El Ocho (the figure eight)

In the midst of a seriously firm embrace, holding tender torsos together, the *milonguero*'s right hand exerts a pressure on the back of his dancing partner, slightly above her waist, with a swaying movement: a wave that strikes, delicately, first with the base of the palm of his hand, signalling to cross her legs 'that way' and immediately after, with the tip of his fingers, another small push, indicating the next crossing over, this time 'this way.' That way and this way, again, rubbing knee against knee, she slides one foot, almost sticking to the floor, obliquely forward; she gyrates, tip-toed, from the hip down, *quebrando*, that is, braking the waist, her torso always facing his, only to repeat exactly the same movement, with the other half of her body – as if a mirror had sliced her in half. She brings her feet together, stretches her knees and waits, tense, for the next *marca*, the next indication, the next gentle push, the next musical time. *The tango dancers freeze; the wallflower continues illustrating with arms, torso and head movements.*

The double curving lines that intersect and twist the dance trajectory complicate the structurally smooth paths of logic (thinking patterns) that should lead her to a conclusion. As the *milongueros* repeat the figure eight, the wallflower/ethnographer paraphrases their intricacies and doubles her understandings in entangled contradictions. Tango's figure eight (*el ocho*) assaults her with the impossible image of two victimizers and no victims dancing: a deadly woman and a fatal man, oblivious to the presence of a victim. *The wallflower freezes.* Who is the victim if not the most engaged spectator? The wallflower swallows and sweats. *The tango dancers turn their heads and look intently in her direction. They resume dancing.*

Ganchos (hooks)

The *milonguera*, about to complete another figure eight, pivots on her right foot as she slides her left foot in a diagonal, full thrust initiated at the thigh. Her intentions are thwarted by a slight pull he exerts on her back, motioning in the opposite direction. Startled for a split second she recovers her balance and, facing away from her partner, redirects her free leg in a high-speed kick aimed at striking the void he has created by bending his knee. Her leg hooks dangerously onto his thigh and falls immediately back to the ground. Flashy! No wonder Madonna adopted the *ganchos* as paradigmatic tango figures in her portrayals of a defiant Evita, notices the wallflower. The *milonguero* is now the victim, she asserts with relief. *The tango couple dances distractedly, bored.* The tango-woman expresses her anger ... when the tango-man gives her the space. Whose timing was it? And how will this situation develop? *The wallflower shows excitement. The dancers start following mechanically her indications.*

El Giro (the spin)

Taking slightly broader strides than during the tango walk, the *milonguera* encircles her partner describing a quadrangular floor pattern. The embrace slackens, and the tension moves into their erected spines. The *milonguero* indicates a displacement that he will not follow. Nailed on one spot of the dance floor, making himself light on the ball of one foot while playfully ungrounding the other, then crossing it behind so as to turn in a twist, the *milonguero* provides the turning axis for *el giro*. It takes her exactly four steps to go around a full circle: legs crossing way up at the thighs, one; uncrossing, two; crossing behind, three; and free again, four. Mechanically perfect. How can anyone see passion in this tango machine, the wallflower wonders. For an instant she saw the sacred circle and the ringmaster, at the centre, trotting his favourite tamed animal in the arena. *The dancers perform a fast tango walk in a diagonal and initiate a 'cradle'. The wallflower runs after them carrying her chair, and sits down again.*

El Ultimo Compás (the last beat)

With the last music time, the perfect ending. Sharp. A full stop placed on the dance floor exactly when the music turns into silence. The tango is over. The tango bodies have been anxious all along, awaiting this trying moment. A retrospective interpretation of the whole danced tango will follow. Evaluating the corporeal communication between the dancers in the midst of a tango is a hard task. The fast exchange of challenging entangle-ments erupting in between tense walks, the rhythmic juxtapositions played by the feet, the arms turning from a solid to a warm embrace all amount to an undecidedly harmonious/disharmonious effect. In the end, however, regardless of the raucous or serene nature of the tango's sequential meta-morphosis, the moment of dramatic effect should be marked in unison. Two high-heeled slippers facing two laced, pointy shoes, four stretched knees almost in contact, the embrace suddenly grows tighter and a quiver-ing movement ripples down the *milonguera*'s spine until it falls from her tail-bone, in a straight line, right down to the floor. The music ends. The two torsos release a breath. Two complicit smiles signal the aftermath. They interrogate each other with ironic remarks: 'That was not too bad.' 'No, not so bad.' They might take the tango risk, jointly, again. *The wallflower leaves her chair and walks to her bed, located a few steps away.*

Wallflowering gone wild

(Warning: Readers allergic to poetic prose should skip this section.)

Growing wild images, creeping on the walls of the dance hall, the wallflower exudes the fragrance of all failed performances. On edge, at the verge, from the fringes, observing marginalia the dance scholar as wall-flower witnesses and records the dancing event. Wearing spiky rimmed glasses – rather than spiky high heels – the tango wallflower half-sits on a chair, by the non-dancers' side of the dance floor, skirting the *milonga* scene. She attentively watches the evening developments. She is ready to dance; she has been practising, she knows all the rituals: the glances, the nods, the walks, the entangled figures. And yet her performance is that of a knowledgeable spectator who fails to perform desired embodied steps. She scribbles, she interprets, she produces ethnographic writings.

At the verge, she nervously waits to be asked to dance and she does not want to be asked, so that she can continue performing, to the point of perfection, in her daydreaming, following the movements of the actual dancers, obsessively fixing, correcting, embellishing every embrace, every posture, every step strategically interpreting. She pours drama into her writings. Utterly gendered, the scholarly wallflower (who according to the Oxford English Dictionary is 'a lady who keeps her seat at the side of a room during dancing, whether because she cannot find a partner or by her own choice') engages in choreo-writings: the spec(tac)ular trafficking of corpo-traces that enter the heteronormative academic floor.

The wallflower I have in mind sits perky, alert, awake and unnoticed. She is smart. No typical melancholy wallflower but her evil twin sister – the one who might or might not walk on spiky high-heels but certainly watches my and your steps through spiky-rimmed glasses.

The art of wallflowering: a gambling theory

As a matter of fact, all women who approach the *milonga* scene must learn, sooner or later, that every time they enter a *milonga*, they will do so as a wallflower. Unless she arrives with her set dancing partner, every woman wallflowers (and to a certain extent, so do men). Nobody enjoys it, and some are better at it than others. In tango, wallflowering is an art.

A woman's wallflower position will be tested every single night at the *milonga*, no matter how good a dancer she is. The events of the night, some of which are more easily predicted than others, will bring her, more or less successfully, out of this position and closer to its opposite ... that of the dancing femme fatale. Dancing certainly makes the difference. At the *milongas* most habitués aspire to dance and they dream of dancing all night long. If and whenever this occurs, *milongueras* leave the scene as goddesses of the *milonga*. And very few attain this position on any given night.

The wallflower (a dancing loser) becomes a successful *milonguera* (a winner of the tango dancing game) by dancing a sufficient quantity and quality of dances. It is not enough to get to dance a lot; you have to learn to be choosy. Dancing with the best *milongueros* available at the club is crucial. *Milongueras* must learn how to discriminate among potential dancing partners. And, after spotting the best, they must carefully plot how, when and with whom they will show off their dancing skills so as to call the attention of those potential best male partners. Accepting all invitations to dance, regardless of the partners' qualifications, are a sign of desperation and thus of low self-esteem. In addition, *milongueras* are judged in terms of how they get to dance to start with. Women who ask men to dance or who approach *milongueros* and start long conversations in hopes they will be asked to dance, definitely lose points. Issues of dignity cannot be overemphasized in what is considered to be a successful *milonguera*.

In order to move out of the wallflower position, you must become an object of desire, more precisely, of tango dancing desire. An object of a doubly, interwoven desire that includes the promise of becoming a potential vehicle for attaining the passionate tango state (that ephemeral sense of being bodily connected against all odds), as well as of generating desire on the part of those who watch the possibly sublime tango take place. For the men and women present at the *milonga* are the prospective femme fatale's witnesses and the men among them, her future dance partners. In their arms, tango after tango, the *milonguera* (or aspiring *milonguera*) will move from wallflower to goddess of the *milonga*.

Here is where I should tell you about her elaborate tricks, her ways of going about generating collective desire. But I will not. (I am contemplating writing a Handbook for Aspiring *Milongueras* where these secrets would be revealed. This however would amount to betraying not the *milongueras* (they mistrust their competitors anyway, and needless to say the wall-flowering ethnographer) but a longstanding *milonga* tradition, according to which you learn how to play the tango dancing game as you go. Verbal instructions or conversations on these matters are rare among true *milon-gueras*; it is expected that aspiring ones will learn through observation and experience.) For now, I will briefly address the nature of her fatale-ness or irresistible dance-appeal. She might or might not be beautiful, but she must act and move with the confidence of a beautiful dancer; she must dance tango well (which does not necessarily coincide with the former); and she must necessarily be a smart risk-taker. (As I noted before, a savvy *milonguera* chooses her partners carefully and studies beforehand their dancing skills. She will not decline dancing with all neophytes [it is understood that the *milonga* food chain needs them for the sake of reproduction] and she will avoid impoliteness and cruelty [watchful *milongueros* might avoid approaching her for fear of being subjected to the same embarrassing treatment]. But she will deliver what each of her partners deserves. Investing too much focus and too many skills in dancing with a worthless partner is unwise. Again, the *milonguera* loses points.) Her fascination resides in how she combines intelligence and dancing skills. She is the master of her own body's seductive dancing powers, so reassured of her mastery that she can give it away at will. A *milonguera* could be thought as fatal when, after making herself vulnerable by accepting to be in a subservient wallflower position (sitting by herself in a highly visible spot, for example, is taken as a sign of admirable courage), she succeeds in becoming an object of collective, tango dancing desire (a sure sign of possessing a highly competitive gift for intelligent manipulation). A *milonguera* who is a winner at the tango game is a talented manager of her own resources. Sweet revenge, murmurs the dancing femme fatale of the night, knowing (and this is a sure sign of *milongueras'* wisdom) that she will fall back into wallflowering as soon as she steps into the next *milonga*.

In the tango milieu, fatale-ness amounts to dance-appeal, and in that sense men are more likely to achieve that position than women. Dancing skills, attitude and manipulation are required of both, but men are not subject to the same wallflowering requirements and judgments. *Milongueros* are in charge of asking women to dance and although a woman may refuse to accept the offer it is unlikely that a man will spend the night *rebotando* (bouncing). In addition, when men are not dancing it is assumed that they are resting and getting ready to make their next choice of a dance partner. They are choosing; women are waiting to be chosen. For *milongueras*, becoming a dancing femme fatale is a harder and an endless job that involves not solving but rather manoeuvring complex paradoxes concerning their feminine constitution.[5] The *milonguera* makes a puzzle out of herself. She enters the *milonga* as a (desiring) subject – she wishes to dance.[6] At the same time, in order to fulfil her desire, she must work at becoming an object (of desire) as she sits to wait for a dance. In doing this, *milongueras* often suspend (place between parenthesis) who they are and what they do in their daily lives, and adopt a nocturnal feminine identity. This amounts to a *milonguera*'s identity. They ready themselves for playing the tango dancing game that requires, as a gaming rule, to risk waiting for a male dancer to identify them as desirable. This is the liminal state of the wallflower that, as I have attempted to show throughout this paper, is a very active take on passivity. Once she is asked to dance, and as she dances more and more in the course of the evening, her status as a (desiring) object of desire rises. In other words, her status as an object loads up to a point at which she is able to exert fatal feminine will over others. At this point, *milongueros* become her playthings, her objects of desire, and she can pick and choose with whom, for how long, and in what ways she wishes to dance. She is still an object of desire, but with strong desires of her own, and plenty of desiring subjects ready to become her desired dancing objects. At this point, her status as a female subject has recomposed at a different, exhilarating level when compared with the one she experienced before entering the *milonga* – that flat and often compromised feminine agency she performs in everyday life.

The *milonguera*'s feminine identity is taken apart each time she enters the *milonga* scene and it is laboriously reassembled in the course of the night.

The outcome is unpredictable, although experience, tango gambling experience, helps. Her passion for tango is a dangerous addiction that entails putting at risk, again and again, the quality of her everyday femaleness and her skills at gaming nocturnal femininity. The *milonguera* is more than a dancer whose presence is necessary for the reproduction of the tango world. She is, simultaneously, a (dancing) workaholic and a compulsive gambler, hooked up into both, the heavy labour of building femininity and a game called tango in which her femininity is at stake.

Milongas' politics of pleasure are puzzling and they are often misunderstood when considered according to modern, bourgeois and, I dare to say, daily daytime standards. *Milongas* are fantasyscapes of that parallel dimension that is the night, when nocturnal identities come out with the wildest ambitions and the most fearless desires to risk. Within this milieu, *milongueros* and *milongueras* gamble with and through each other by dancing tango. They cultivate a multiplicity of social transgressions. They enjoy crossing over socially accepted borders of age, social class, status and even partisan ideologies. It is most definitely a gendered and heterosexual game, but the terms are quite unconventional. *Milongas* offer a space for unruly behaviours, out of which odd (and rather unstable) heterosexual couples result. When judged according to modern everyday bourgeois standards, true *milongueros/milongueras* do not fit heterosexual gender prescriptions. Men are patriarchal and authoritarian, but are also often economically dependent and obsessed with their looks and seductive skills. Women are frequently wealthier, better educated and more entrepreneurial than their partners, but forgiving and blinded by romance – until they become fed up and leave the men for a better catch or a more restful existence. *Milongueros* confirm their theories about the female of the species and await freshly arrived prey in the *milonga* niche. *Milongueras* tend to abandon the scene altogether with a telling tango story of wallflowers and femme fatales, often with a twist: the true femme fatales of the *milonga* are actually men. *The wallflower leaves the writing scene on this taunting note, betting on the tangoesque allure of delivering always less than it seems you could.*

On a projected computer screen rolls the following list of maestros y maestras, danzarines y bailarinas, milongueros y milongueras *whom she wishes to thank de todo corazón:* Lidia Ferrari, José Luis Lussini, Enriqueta María Palencia, Susana Cannataro, Raúl Bravo, Omar Correa, Eduardo Capussi, María Edith, Juan Carlos Muiño, Ana Postigo, Ana Gómez, Dina, Brenda, Cinthia, Blanquita Carozzi, Lawrence Leetz, María Teresa, Eduardo Aguirre, Ernesto Guerrero, Jorge Gallo, Angel Cristaldo, Bocha y Lidia Migale, Esther 'Pichi' Pinelli, Liliana, María Emilia, Pedro y Ana Monteleone, Eduardo Arquimbau, Graciela González, Celia Blanco, Juan Carlos Copes, Verena Voucher, Carlos Copello, Gustavo Naveira, Héctor Chidichimo, Puppi Castello, Guillermo Cunha Ferré, Alejandra Quiroz, Brigitte

248 MARTA E. SAVIGLIANO

Winkler, Nicole y Ricardo, Omar Vega, Suzzana, Nicolás, Danel y María, Jessica, Esteban, Carlos, Antoñito, Toto, Cacho, Susana Miller, Marcelo Pareja, Hans Muller, Fernando, Walter, Héctor, y Natalia Gómez Gil.

Notes

1 I have been attending *milongas* in Buenos Aires since 1989. I formally assumed a conflictive 'insider/outsider' position ('Am I here to dance or am I doing research?') between 1994 and 1997, when I decided to undertake 'fieldwork' in order to write an ethnography of the contemporary *milonga* scene. Since then, as some of the *milongueros* have pointed out to me, I am not really a *milonguera*. My investments as a full dancing participant have been compromised by my 'interests in living things in the *milonga* in order to write about them' (Eduardito, informal conversation, August 1996).

2 Zoning on the tango 'world', sexed identities and sexual matters are unavoidable. Pleasure and its sexual/sensual intricacies (tango practitioners insist on this enigmatic differentiation) motivate its producers/consumers and mark the form 'tango' as practice and representation. Thus scholars, artists (choreographers, filmmakers, dancers, writers), and to a certain degree practitioners, with and without feminist preoccupations, have faced the 'woman's question' in tango. More frequently than not, women's participation in the tango scene, curiously despite differences in terms of historico-cultural background or setting (not to mention ideological, economic, or political positions) is explained in terms of (universal) sado-masochism. (See Elizabeth Grosz 1990 for a discussion of feminist debates on femininity in psychoanalysis.) 'Explain' here is a euphemism for 'labelling and stopping' reflection, placing a familiar 'plug' onto the subject (and subjects) under scrutiny. Women who participate in the tango scene are tempted to accept these clinical views of themselves. They recognize their subservient position in most of the things they undertake in life. A certain discomfort, however, is enhanced when tango is at stake because they participate in the *milongas* at their will and for the purposes of pleasure. (Alternatively, I could claim an 'active', phallic-like, powerful masochistic role for *milongueras* following Gilles Deleuze's (1991, 1996) decoupling of the Freudian SM dynamic). However, Deleuze's analysis vindicates the masochist as a man who produces and controls his [male or female] figures of inflictment. This would apply to the *milongueros*, if their portrayal as 'femmes fatales' (which I advance toward the end of this paper) would be accepted. Culturalist explanations rush in: This is Latin America ... so the answer lies on machismo. (I have undertaken an analysis of machismo and its politico-cultural dimensions elsewhere; Savigliano 1995.) How to step aside of sado-masochism and its shadows? Are there any ways to address heterosocial and heterosexual women's pleasures that do not immediately prompt interpretations in terms of victimization? I am trying to go beyond the comforts of compulsive repetition ('women are specially adept at it'; 'women don't know any better'). I am especially concerned about the application of pathological explanations interwoven with culturalism. When women's presence in the tango world is explained (away) through *machista* sado-masochism (a specifically 'Latin' and more resistant strain of the universal patriarchal virus), the often female and feminist researchers provide the diagnosis once they are safely back in their home laboratories (or, to put it in other words, once fieldwork is completed and they are back at their academic or creative desks.) There is little contemplation for the intelligence of those other women, the 'genuine' ones such as the

milongueras , who continue enduring and enjoying that world under study that has been taken as a source of insightful inspiration.

Benevolent expressions of concern and desires to salvage other female victims of culturally residual, backwards patriarchies are also rather suspicious. There seems to be no legitimate space to place those women uninterested or unresponsive to accusations of victimization. It is assumed, by default, that they are stuck paddling in the deep waters of (self-selected?) victimization. These interpretations in fact show little 'intercultural' gyno-sociality at play. There is little investment in learning from other 'native' women the secrets of the worlds in which they live, including their survival tactics and their concepts of pleasure. Researchers and artists often arrive in the tango world either with a preconceived idea of what it is all about or informed by tango men. They enter into dismissive competition with the *milongueras* for the favours of the *milongueros*, using their privileged positions as 'non-natives' to the *milonga* scene. I grant that the nature of the tango world aids this effect. (Like the film industry or academia, the tango world is a macho/boys world where women play their reproductive, accommodating and resistive tricks.) Thinking of the *milongueras* as irredeemable gamblers does not quite do the work of depathologizing their nocturnal doings and inclinations. Gambling, in the sense of taking unnecessary risks, is an unproductive and often addictive enterprise (see Walter Benjamin 1969b: 177–80 and Jacques Derrida 1995). However, gambling one's femininity evokes more active and less doomed images than the Freudian masochistic framing of feminine inclinations.

3 On pronoun 'shifters' see Roman Jakobson (1960).
4 See note 1.
5 I am not following here a Freudian or Lacanian psychoanalytic approach. I am borrowing the vocabulary that is available, and twisting its conceptual connotations so as to fit the particularities of the tango world. Gender and sexuality, in my view, are culturally specific and fluid constructs. A particular economy ruled by a shared theory of value organizes the traffic of desire, its subject and object positions, and establishes 'worth' assessments. Desire thus becomes tangible: participants (think they) know what they desire. Women in the *milongas* are not interested in proving their femininity; that is, so to speak, a given – what I call here an everyday 'flat' femininity. They are seeking (desiring) to become goddesses of the *milonga*: a goddess for a night. That amounts to femininity with a difference, and for a short amount of time, conditioned to a specific social space (the *milonga*). Therefore the feminine identity I am trying to analyse here falls into the particularities of what I am choosing to call nocturnal 'identities' constituted in dialogue with (and in opposition to) everyday sexed/sexual politics.
6 For a discussion of the uses of the concept of the 'subject' at the intersection of psychoanalysis and Marxism see Stephen Heath (1991).

24

CHOREOGRAPHING A FLEXIBLE TAIWAN

Cloud Gate Dance Theatre and Taiwan's changing identity

Yatin Lin

The repertoire of Cloud Gate Dance Theatre of Taiwan and its founder/ artistic director Lin Hwai-min reflects the changing status of Taiwan over the past three decades. Lin Hwai-min's early work, *Tale of the White Serpent* (1975), embodied two sources of influence: Martha Graham's modern dance technique and Peking Opera movements. In 1978, due to the emergence of a Taiwanese consciousness, Lin created *Legacy* – an epic dance piece depicting the history of Taiwan's early immigrants from China. By the 1980s, Cloud Gate's choreographies contemplated the rapid urbanization of Taipei. *The Rite of Spring, Taipei, 1984* (1984) constitutes a commentary both on the original choreography to Stravinsky's music by Vaslav Nijinsky, as well as that by Pina Bausch. Recently, Cloud Gate's dances have been influenced by taichi and other Chinese martial arts. Starting with *Moon Water* (1998) and followed by the Chinese calligraphy-inspired *Cursive Trilogy* (*Cursive* 2001, *Cursive II* 2003 and *Wild Cursive* 2005), Lin Hwai-min re-examines the aesthetics of modern dance. Amid a continuing quest for Taiwanese identity, where there is a constant struggle between global/local and modern/traditional, Lin and Cloud Gate's dancers continue to amaze audiences with the theoretical power of the moving body.

This research grew out of my long-time interest in Cloud Gate Dance Theatre, one of the most productive dance companies in Taiwan, and its changing repertoire over its first three decades. I have selected a few examples out of more than seventy dance pieces by Lin Hwai-min, its founder and artistic director. I read his choreographies as critiques upon the social and political phenomena of the corresponding eras.

My approach follows the model of allowing dance and various theories from cultural studies, post-colonial studies and globalization discourses to converse. I seek to trace the connections between Cloud Gate's artistic initiatives and the changing identity of Taiwan. In my analysis of the dances, I incorporate issues of race and ethnicity in the inquiry of 'Chineseness' in the first place, while, in subsequent sections, issues of the mainstream *vs* the

vernacular culture, and class differences that arise from Taipei's urbanization process in the 1980s, are discussed. In looking at more recent works,
I focus on global and transnational studies as they elucidate Taiwan's status
in relation to mainland China and the world.

Overview

First, I will lay out some theoretical discourses deployed in this paper. The
overarching theoretical framework here is the concept of choreographic
flexibility. My thoughts regarding flexibility first arose through readings on
globalization, as in the writings of David Harvey (1989), Aihwa Ong (1999)
and Arjun Appadurai (1996) among others. Harvey observed the concept of
flexible accumulation in late-twentieth-century economic models, which is
different from the Fordian economics of the first half of the twentieth century. Flexible accumulation values mobility, such as the distribution of
workers to different worksites, based on specific needs. As for Ong's study
of the overseas Chinese in South-East Asia, she depicted how the characteristic of flexibility enabled these mostly upper-class businessmen to
capitalize on their networking (*guanxi*) skills from their countries of origin,
while at the same time obtaining a second passport from a first world
nation (such as the United States, Canada, Australia or New Zealand), in
order to expedite their travel and business ventures. Ong argues that in
these cases of 'flexible citizenships', these businessmen mostly obtain their
second passports for pragmatic purposes, such as allowing their children to
live and study legally in English-speaking nations so as to gain a more
competitive edge in the globalized world. Another anthropologist,
Appadurai (1996: 33) presented the concept of 'flows', such as the flow of
people, information, technology, capital and ideology in his study of the
cultural dimensions of globalisation. It is due to such mobility of
these flows of ethnoscapes, mediascapes, technoscapes, financescapes and
ideoscapes that flexibility can be attained by individuals.

Each of these scholars elaborates on a distinctive notion of flexibility in
relation to the disciplines of economics and anthropology, yet none focuses
on performance in general, nor dance specifically. I was inspired to contemplate this notion of choreographic flexibility towards contemporary
Taiwanese dance partly because of the corporeal flexibility of the human
bodily movement that is so valued by dancers. Especially since the mid-
1990s, Cloud Gate's company members began practicing a new hybrid form
of *taichi* training introduced by Mainland Chinese immigrant martial arts
master Hsiung Wei in Taiwan, called *taichi daoyin*. Unlike the more well-
known *taichi* practices, which emphasize set poses and exercises sequences
along with the function of self-defence, *taichi daoyin* emphasizes the flow of
qi (vital energy within one's body) and its unobstructed travel from the
lower abdomen area (*dan tian*), up through each vertebra of the spine and

into the extremities. In order for the *qi* to flow smoothly, the foremost criteria are for the various joints in one's body to be flexible and unhindered. Hsiung's *taichi daoyin* often begins with exercises that rotate the joints in a three-dimensional spiral route. How might this practice of cultivating bodily flexibility dialogue with discourses in globalization and even further theories of economic and cultural flexibility?

Other than the corporeal understanding of flexibility, which serves as a starting point, my second interpretation of flexibility comes from the field of Taiwan studies. With its history of colonization, Taiwan's ability to adopt different identities is a response to various political, historical, social and economic situations. A former offshore territory of China, Taiwan is located on the western edge of the Pacific Ocean, lending itself to foreign inhabitation. Following settling by the indigenous Austronesians in Taiwan, Portuguese sailors in the sixteenth century gave this island its first non-Asian name: Formosa, from 'Ilha Formosa', meaning 'beautiful island'. By the seventeenth century, Spanish and Dutch colonial powers vied for control of Taiwan, mostly due to its strategic geographical location as well as its natural resources. The Spaniards took hold of Taiwan's northern port of Tamsui, while the Dutch governed the southern city of Tainan. It wasn't until 1663 that a Chinese expatriate Cheng Chen-kung (also known as Koxinga) gained control of Taiwan. In 1895, Taiwan was handed over to Japan as part of the Shimonoseki Treaty signed after China's defeat in the Sino-Japanese War, marking the beginning of Taiwan's Japanese colonial era. By the end of the Second World War, Taiwan was returned to China, as the Chinese Nationalist Party (or KMT for KuoMingTang) led by Chiang Kai-shek took over control of the island. After Chiang lost the Chinese Civil War to Mao Tse-tung's Communist Party in 1949, his regime retreated to Taiwan, in hope of reconquering mainland China. Since then, these two 'Chinas' have existed in rivalry, even up to today's current ambiguous situation of economic ties between the Taiwan Straits, but no official political interactions, other than via civilian organizations from both sides. Due to these various political shifts, Taiwan's cultural identity has undergone various waves of identity crisis. Thus, I refer to the concept of 'cultural flexibility' to interpret the shifting identity of Taiwan through the years, as it has undergone multiple waves of colonization and hybridization processes accordingly. To summarize, I argue that due to the unique geographical location and historical circumstances of Taiwan, Cloud Gate's dancers have formed their own unique bodily aesthetics based on the long-term hybrid training of ballet, Western modern dance techniques, Chinese martial arts and Hsiung's brand of *taichi daoyin*. It is this versatile and intelligent 'Cloud Gate body' that allows Lin to create works which embody the multiple waves of influences from within Taiwan and abroad, reflecting the cultural flexibility of Taiwan on a choreographically grounded level.

Scholar Leo T. S. Ching (2001), in his study of one of Taiwan's literary pioneer Wu Cho-liu's *The Orphan of Asia* (*yaxiya de gu-er*), adapted the concept of 'double consciousness' from Paul Gilroy's *Black Atlantic* into a 'triple consciousness' of Taiwan's post-colonial subjects. Also known as *Go Daku-ryu* in Japanese, Wu wrote this novel in secrecy between 1943 and 1945, depicting the tragedy of a colonized subject Hu Tai-ming (or 'Ko Tai-mei' in Japanese), who journeys from colonial Taiwan to imperial Japan and war-ridden China.

Wu's novel depicts the psychological turmoil of a colonial subject in search of a sense of belonging. Similarly, in diasporic studies, the notion of 'home' involves a complex set of factors. This search for a home, or the renegotiating of affiliation with Taiwan through changing historical periods, is also the focus of this study on the changing repertoire of Cloud Gate. Re-examining the cultural identity of Taiwan from the late twentieth century to the turn of the millennium, vestiges of these three layers of consciousness – Chinese, Japanese and Taiwanese – still exist. In addition, I would also include a fourth layer of consciousness via the cultural hegemony from the West, predominantly referring to the influence on Taiwan from the United States since the Cold War.

Dance and cultural identities: Lin Hwai-Min and Cloud Gate's changing repertoire

Chineseness in Tale of the White Serpent (1975)

Based on these insights, my study maps four stages of Lin Hwai-min's repertoire. First, his exploration of Chineseness in *Tale of the White Serpent* (1975); second, his embodiment of Taiwanese cultural awakening in *Legacy* (1978); third, his reflections upon the urbanization process of cosmopolitan Taipei in his *Rite of Spring, Taipei, 1984* (1984), and finally marking a space for Taiwan in the globalized twenty-first century with *taichi*-inspired works such as *Moon Water* (1998) and *Cursive* (2001). However, a brief description of the local dance scene prior to the emergence of Cloud Gate may add to the understanding of the significance of this first professional dance company's influence in Taiwan.

During the Japanese colonial period, when Westernization indirectly influenced Taiwan due to drastic changes since the Meiji Restoration, many Taiwanese upper-class (especially doctors') families were introduced to ballroom dancing or European-style physical culture as a way to improve their bodily postures.[1] Taiwanese dance pioneer Tsai Jui-yueh's early beginning in teaching and choreographing dance upon her return from Japan during the post-war period showed traces of such Western/Japanese-influenced mentality. For example, in her choreography titled *New Construction* (1949) to percussion music in the style of German

Ausdruckstanz ('dance of expression', indicating the influences of Tsai's Japanese mentor Ishii Baku), dancers each represented a nut or a bolt in a larger mechanical machine, working toward modernization.

After the Chinese Cultural Renaissance Movement proposed by the Chinese Nationalist Government in the mid-1950s, Japanese cultural vestiges were consciously erased, to be replaced with hegemonic Chinese culture. Under the leadership of the *Minzu Wudao* Committee led by General Ho Chih-hao, Chinese 'national' dance was being invented. Based on vague memories as well as the creative imagination of émigrés from mainland China, various Chinese dance repertoires began to take shape and eventually got standardized as choreographies taught in various dance departments founded by these pioneers. Some 'classic' examples include the *Miao Girl's Wine-Cup Dance* (1959), later revealed to be invented by Tsai herself instead of an 'authentic' reconstruction from the Miao minority group from south-western China.

Under the rule of the Chinese Nationalist Party led by Chiang Kai-shek, Peking Opera became elevated as the 'National Opera' (or *Guo-ju*), due to its Mandarin lyrics; movements from Peking Opera were also deemed the main source of Chinese classical dance accordingly. Yu Ta-kang, a Chinese scholar of the classic texts and Peking Opera expert promoted this performing art form enthusiastically to the younger generation, including choreographers and dancers such as Wong Yen-lu, Lin Hwai-min, and others. During the Cold War decades of the 1960s and 1970s, various American modern dance companies including those led by Alvin Ailey, Jose Limon, Merce Cunningham and Martha Graham toured to Taiwan under the sponsorship of the US government. Yu felt that with these Western dance influences, these young artists could enliven Peking Opera through incorporating various elements of it into modern choreography. One such result was Lin's *Tale of the White Serpent*, which drew on Chinese Opera tradition, but with a new twist from the technique and theatrical style Lin learned from Graham while studying at the Graham school in New York City in the early 1970s, as well as upon her company's tour to Taiwan in 1974. After all, Graham is known for drawing upon the interior landscape of her protagonists in works such as *Cave of the Heart* (1946), *Night Journey* (1947) and *Clytemnestra* (1958).

During this period of early diaspora for the Chinese mainlanders in Taiwan, their mentality was to renew the essence of 'Chineseness' with a flair for contemporary aesthetics. Even though Lin Hwai-min himself was a Taiwanese of Min-nan (or Southern Chinese) heritage, as a member of the post-war generation, his education was moulded through the ruling Nationalist party's 'Chinese' ideology, emphasizing its legitimacy as the inheritor of Chinese civilization and ethics. 'Taiwaneseness' as a consciousness was still suppressed during this time. Thus, it is not surprising that the founding slogan of Cloud Gate in 1973 was 'composed by Chinese, choreographed by Chinese, danced by Chinese, for a Chinese audience'. The notion of 'Chinese' at that time was not differentiated from 'Taiwanese'. In fact, most of the Taiwanese people during the period of Chiang Kai-shek's rule from 1949 to 1975 were indoctrinated to identify themselves as 'Chinese'.

Lin Hwai-min's twenty-minute long quartet, *Tale of the White Serpent*, is based on a popular Chinese legend of two snake spirits who transform themselves into women and fall in love with an innocent scholar. The opening section depicts the trio's first encounter while sharing an umbrella on a rainy day and the women's rivalry over the Scholar's attention. Based on her charm and magical power, White Snake wins over the Scholar and on the eve of their wedding night, Green Snake is deeply tormented, as depicted through Green Snake's solo which incorporates various Graham contractions in her abdomen repeatedly while rolling with agony on the dance floor.

Thus, due to the reliance on a popular Chinese plot, Chinese traditional long gown costumes worn by the White Snake and the Scholar, props such as the wooden umbrella and the folded fan, and Chinese percussion instruments from Chinese Opera accompaniment although composed in a modernist style, not to mention movements such as the typical 'orchid fingers', waist-initiated turns and other trembling hands gestures from Chinese classical movement, altogether these show clear signs of the dominance of 'Chineseness' in Lin Hwai-min's choreography during this early stage.[2]

Taiwaneseness and Legacy (1978)

The late 1970s marked a clear transition in terms of the rise of Taiwanese consciousness. Circumstances such as the switching of diplomatic allegiance by many nations to Mao Tse-tung's People's Republic of China alerted Taiwan's young intellectuals of the reality that Chiang Kai-shek's Republic of China 'temporarily' in exile in Taiwan was losing its hold in the international political arena. Nativist *Hsiang-tu* (literally 'homeland soil') writers and artists began to focus on the plight of the less fortunate, including peasants, labourers and prostitutes. For example, writer Huang Chun-ming's well-known short story *Days by the Sea* was adapted into film, as well as into dance by Cloud Gate's Lin Hwai-min. Taiwanese intellectuals and artists could no longer endure the suppression of their vernacular culture, especially at a time when the existence of the Republic of China was being questioned internationally. Gradually, the more indigenous cultures of Taiwan's Austronesians and early wave of Chinese Min-nan immigrants from the south-east coastal provinces of Fujian in China – dating back to the seventeenth century – were used to indicate the uniqueness of Taiwan in contrast to China. This transition towards vernacular interest is evident in Lin's work of the late 1970s, including choreographies such as *Days by the Sea* (1977), *Legacy* and *Liao Tien-ting* (1979) – the 'Robin Hood' of Taiwan during the Japanese colonial era. Folk singers from this era such as Chen Da, a wandering bard from southern Taiwan were 'recognized' by European-educated ethnomusicologists from Taiwan such as Shih Wei-liang and Hsu Chang-hui, who brought him to the capital city of Taipei to record albums to preserve this 'dying' singing style. Chen Da's epic songs about Taiwanese immigrants laid the blueprint for Lin's *Legacy*, with Chen's hoarse voice inserted as interludes between dance sections. Through such narrative and musical associations, the transition from identifying with an 'imaginary' home in mainland China – where many Min-nan Taiwanese or the post-war generation of mainlanders had never even set foot – to a new 'home' based on a relationship with the land of Taiwan was being proposed via *Legacy*.

Based mainly on movements associated with physical labour such as pulling the mast, clearing the field, planting and harvesting rice, *Legacy* vividly depicted for the first time on stage the hardship these early pioneers experienced as they risked their lives in search of a brighter future. Premiered in 1978 on the eve of the US announcement that official diplomatic ties would be formed with Mao's China instead of Chiang's regime in Taiwan, *Legacy* provided a force of stability at a time of great anxiety. Furthermore, the clear decision to search for movement originating from the local land and its people also marked a significant shift towards vernacular, Taiwanese consciousness. In other words, this epic dance-drama marks an important transitional awareness in the Taiwanese community, awakening them to the notion that they now have to acknowledge that this land on which they lived would be their new 'home'. Chinese mainlander immigrants eventually identified with Taiwan, despite cultural differences between themselves and the Taiwanese, caused by historical circumstances, and no longer deemed Taiwan as a temporary site of refuge.

Cosmopolitanism and Rite of Spring, Taipei, 1984 (1984)

By the 1980s, Taiwan, and especially its capital city Taipei, had undergone rapid urbanization. Construction of major public roadways and facilities were well under way. Furthermore, with Westernization as part of the process, the sense of dislocation and alienation was intensified, especially for labourers who relocated to Taipei in search of better jobs. In other words, Taiwan's cultural identity was taking a rapid turn towards modernization. This transition is evident not only through large governmental construction projects; it is also depicted in various art forms such as urban planning, architecture, literature and film. Chinese cinema scholar Yingjin Zhang (2000) points out the different phases in the cinematic mapping of Taipei. For example, in the 1960s and 1970s, Taipei was configured as an icon of urban modernity to support the KMT government's drive to build Taiwan as part of a modern 'Chinese' nation. By the 1980s, Taipei was refigured in New Taiwan Cinema as a site of distinctly Taiwanese experience; a site of cultural hybridization where the Chinese influence is shown to be merely one among many competing cultural forces in the formation of Taiwan's new identity. Furthermore, Zhang pointed out that the change from 'China' to 'Taiwan' and later to 'Taipei' seems to dovetail with the movement from modernization and nationalization, to globalization and hybridization in the age of transnational capitalism. Here, instead of applying the more often used concept of hybridity as proposed by post-colonial scholar Homi Bhabha (1994: chap. 4) (a result of the colonial subjects' act of mimicry which necessarily involves a slippage), Zhang borrows from Jan Nederveen Pieterse's concept of a 'continuum of hybridities', where 'on one end, an assimilationist hybridity that leans over towards the centre adopts the canon and mimics the hegemony; and at the other end, a destabilizing hybridity that blurs the canon, reverses the current, subverts the centre' (Zhang 2000: 2).

Without doubt, Lin Hwai-min's works are products of hybrid cultures, be it between Graham technique and Peking opera movements as in *Tale of the White Serpent*, or Taiwanese peasant labouring movements and Chinese acrobatic feats in *Legacy*. However, by the 1980s, more confident of his artistic experimentations, Lin began challenging himself by confronting the canons of the West. Lin perhaps felt a need to prove himself in relation to the new 'priestess' of Western concert dance – Pina Bausch, artistic director of the Tanztheater Wuppertal – as he too choreographed his version of the *Rite of Spring, Taipei, 1984* to the same original score by composer Igor Stravinsky that Bausch used in 1975. But, rather than an unspecified setting/location as in Bausch's *Rite*, Lin clearly locates his version in the time and place of contemporary urban Taipei. In other words, from the depiction of early Taiwanese immigrants' 'uplifting fighting (*pa bia*, an expression in local Min-man dialect) spirit' shown in *Legacy*, to those of factory workers and prostitutes in the dark and forgotten corners of Taipei's alleys, Lin was broadening his concern to address all walks of life within the city of Taipei, including the underprivileged class often left out of dance repertoires. Furthermore, Lin also incorporated various Tanztheater aesthetics such as the use of collage, popular songs, wide spectrum of movements ranging from everyday poses to social dance, as well as closer attention and experimentation regarding stage design. In addition, by renaming Cloud Gate Dance Theatre as Taipei Contemporary Dance Company while touring abroad in the 1980s with *Rite*, Lin attempted to revamp the image of his ensemble into an urban, contemporary group without the cultural baggage of Chinese cultural heritage.

New 'Eastern' aesthetics in the age of globalization

By the turn of the twenty-first century, economic and cultural globalization became unavoidable, especially with China and Taiwan both eventually becoming official members of international organizations such as the World Trade Organization (WTO) in 2001 and 2002 respectively. Cultural theorist Stuart Hall defines globalization as 'the processes, operating on a global scale, which cut across national boundaries, integrating and connecting communities and organizations in a new space–time combination, making the world in reality and in experience more inter-connected' (Hall 1992: 299). For some theorists, globalization marks the end of nationalism, since national boundaries are gradually losing significance. However, others view globalization as working hand in hand with nation-states, subtly substituted for 'inter/nationalism' – the other side of nationalism (Iwabuchi 1994: 10) In the case of Japan, according to scholar Koichi Iwabuchi's article 'Complicit Exoticism: Japan and Its Other' (ibid.), the decrease of the *Nihonjinron* discourse – a theory of Japaneseness complicit with Orientalism and self-Orientalism – which emerged in the 1930s and fell out of favour by the 1980s, was gradually substituted by the *kokusaika* (or 'internationalization') discourse, which evokes nationalist sentiment while encouraging people to become internationalist. In other words, *kokusaika* could be viewed as a Japanese version of the globalization discourse.[3]

Likewise, with the expanding global competition and market, Taiwan's dance community also has to find its unique bodily aesthetics in order to carve out its own space in the international dance stage. Such was one of the reasons for the emergence and popularity of the so-called 'Eastern bodily aesthetics' dances choreographed by several Taiwanese dance artists beginning from the mid-1990s. Using Asian-based bodily trainings such as *taichi, chi kung*, yoga and butoh, many Taiwanese choreographers were able to acquire invitations from curators of the Western dance world, securing their place among dance artists from other parts of the world who are also working to create a synthesis of tradition and modernity based on their own dance practices.

Certainly not the first to experiment with such 'Eastern' corporeal trends, Lin Hwai-min received the widest success both in Taiwan and abroad after he premiered *Moon Water* in 1998, a dance derived from *taichi daoyin* training, a form of synthesized *qi-gong* from master Hsiung Wei. One of the reasons for the popularity of this dance is due to the interest in the West regarding 'Oriental' movement practices, found to be both exotic and fascinating. For example, when performed at the Lyon Dance Biennale in 2000, Cloud Gate's *Moon Water* and Taiwanese female choreographer Lin Li-jen's *Anthem to the Fading Flowers* (2000) were voted respectively as the critics' and audiences' favourites. However, what distinguishes the long-term success of Cloud Gate's *Moon Water* and their later *Cursive* trilogy (2001, 2003, 2005) from other Taiwanese choreographers also using Eastern bodily training is the dancers' solid *taichi*-derived movement foundation, which serves as a base for Lin Hwai-min's bold experimentation.

Cursive is inspired by the art of writing Chinese characters on rice paper with brush and ink. German-based American choreographer William Forsythe also envisioned bodies as writing in space and time in another theoretical model. In a CD-ROM titled *Improvisation Technologies: A Tool for the Analytical Dance Eye* (Forsythe 1999) he demonstrated a system of writing with various parts of the body in space. The goal is not to create decipherable shapes and forms, but to use this as a method of improvising new movement vocabulary. For example, Forsythe demonstrates techniques called 'U-ing' and 'O-ing', and how different dots in space can be linked into lines using various parts of the moving body. In *Cursive*, Lin Hwai-min also asked his dancers to improvise in response to projected and enlarged scripts of Chinese calligraphies. However, there is a distinct difference between the two approaches, which both draw from the art of writing. Forsythe's focus seems more on the shape and forms of writing, while Lin's emphasis is on the shared use of the *qi* (energy) that is required of calligraphers, martial artists and dancers alike. As described in ancient texts on the pedagogy of creating the different strokes in Chinese calligraphy, the essence lies in the use of flow and its abrupt gathering of energy at the end (the concept of the Chinese word *so*). It is this similar characteristic as adapted in dancing *Cursive* that distinguishes it from the endless elongation and expansion characteristic of many Western dance forms. In other words, the differentiation lies in Forsythe's insistence on space as pure and abstract, and not historically specific, while Lin's aesthetics preserves and synthesizes a new Sino-culture-based identity which draws on an ancient Chinese tradition and gives it a new location and embodiment. This allows Cloud Gate to stay connected to a specific place and history while at the same time entering a global circulation of dance practices.

In this age of globalization, cultural otherness sells. As scholar Kevin Robins (1991: 31) puts it, globalization 'exploits local differences and particularity'. Asian-American scholar Shu-mei Shih (2003: 146) proposes that 'in view of the tension with China, for Taiwan to have an increasingly globalised economy ... and to have a more globalised culture is to displace Sinocentric influence and invent new forms of trans-culture'. In other words, she believes that globalization may be Taiwan's survival strategy. Lin Hwai-min is well aware of the unique situation of Taiwan, which Shih described as 'partak[ing] of an ethnic Sino-Chinese heritage without having to be part of China' (ibid.: 149). She further refers to the example from Taiwanese female visual artist Wu Mali's proposal of 'cultural inauthenticity' as 'a theoretical basis for a new culture in Taiwan that creates itself out of the destruction of cultural authenticities by reshaping them into a unique entity' (ibid.). Lin Hwai-min is also presenting new bodily aesthetics in works such as *Moon Water* and the *Cursive* trilogy, based on the unique hybridization of *taichi daoyin* martial arts practice and contemporary Western dance. Furthermore, Lin's ballet *Smoke* (2002), in which the techniques of Western ballet have been influenced by the dancers' *taichi* training, was even exported to the Zurich Ballet in 2004 and performed by their dancers in Europe, the birthplace of ballet. This reverse phenomenon has been viewed as an 'eastern invasion' by Taiwanese dance scholar Chen Yaping (2005).

To summarize the different aesthetics displayed by Cloud Gate's representative works over these three decades, I argue that its newfound choreographic practice based on the principle of corporeal flexibility ties in with the metaphorical concept of flexibility in our current globalized era. Expanding upon the use of flexibility as proposed by Emily Martin in her study on human bodies and immunization, I suggest that Cloud Gate incorporates this strategic spirit in its march onto international concert stages. Even from the example of global corporate models, expanding itself into various different sectors, in 1999, Cloud Gate Dance Theatre Foundation added a second dance ensemble for younger dancers: Cloud Gate 2, encouraging a new generation of Taiwanese choreographers to create and perform with their own style. More interestingly, the Cloud Gate Dance School enterprise was also founded a year earlier in 1998, offering creative movement exploration classes for children, adults and senior citizens. As of 2009, twenty-one Cloud Gate branch schools have opened all over Taiwan, and have brought in profits for this well-run organization, even expanding into collaborating with organizations in Hong Kong.

With the rest of the twenty-first century ahead, what will emerge as Taiwan's new cultural identity? The recent aggressively promoted and highly visible culture of the Hakkas – another ethnic Chinese minority from China's coastal province of Guangdong – in addition to the various indigenous groups in Taiwan, the large influx of immigrant labourers from South-East Asia, and even the 'imported brides' from mainland China and neighbouring Asian regions have all increased significantly, entering the mix of Taiwan's ever-changing demographic. As Lin Hwai-min and the dancers of Cloud Gate continue to think through Taiwan's various historical, social and political issues with their bodies, I believe more interesting experimentations will continue to be created.

Notes

1 See *Viva Tonal*, a documentary which lays out the popular songs and dance practices of Taiwanese during the Japanese Colonial Era, including waltzes, foxtrots, and so forth (Taipei: Public Television Service, 2003).
2 'Orchid Fingers' refers to a popular hand gesture often seen in Chinese dance, where the thumb gently touches the joint of the extended middle finger, while the other three fingers also point outward, like petals of the orchid.
3 In terms of the concept of 'self-Orientalism,' Iwabuchi (1994: 3) refers to Carol Gluck's observation of how the real West was irrelevant to the Japanese. 'What had mattered was the idea of the West that the Japanese had created for the purpose of self-definition.' See Gluck 1985: 137.

25

REALITY CHECK

Dancing with the Stars and the American Dream[1]

Juliet McMains

Even before *Dancing with the Stars* premiered in 2005, reality television and ballroom dancing shared a powerful narrative – the promise of personal transformation. Whether the goal is to transform the physical body and its presentation as in *America's Top Model* or its internal character as in *Survivor*, reality television foregrounds personal growth. The American ballroom dance industry is likewise powered by a similar promise of personal transformation that I have elsewhere called Glamour (McMains 2006: 1–9). As a reality television show about ballroom dancing, *Dancing with the Stars* doubles the power of this promise. Crucial to the fantasy is the assurance that anyone can imagine him or herself into the protagonist's role, which is why *Dancing with the Stars* contestants, although celebrities, are carefully balanced to represent a wide range of races, ages, body types and backgrounds. *Dancing with the Stars*, which has captured the hearts of over twenty million Americans who tune in each week to see non-dancing celebrities perform ballroom routines with their professional ballroom dance partners/teachers, appears to be affirmation of the American Dream. Anyone, regardless of size, age, race or physical limitations, can overcome obstacles to achieve success. Who cannot be inspired watching Heather Mills, who wears a prosthetic leg, out-jive her two-legged competitors? As they witness football linebacker Jason Taylor learn to waltz with the grace of Fred Astaire, many viewers begin to believe that they too might conquer the most unlikely challenges.

These fairy-tale stories do not, however, require the magic of wizards or fairies. Transformation is possible, the viewer is assured, through hard work. A video montage of rehearsal bloopers – stumbles, kicks to the face and tears – is aired before each polished performance, reminding viewers that perseverance in the face of difficulty yields success. The promise of equal opportunity upon which this quintessentially American ideal is based, however, does not allow for the multicultural difference that the show's multi-racial cast appears to celebrate. As I will demonstrate through a critique of *Dancing with the Stars*' representation of Latin dance, this particular iteration of the American Dream is dependent on assimilation.

African Americans are encouraged to enter the competition as long as they dance like Caucasians. Latin dances are included in the repertoire only after they have been redefined by Euro-American taste. The power of ballroom dance to enable personal growth is open to anyone, provided he or she is willing to conform to rules and aesthetics that were created by white people. As a white person myself, I don't mean to imply that there is anything wrong with white American culture. What I do wish to suggest is that there is something troubling (and even wrong) with promoting white culture at the exclusion, erasure and devaluation of other cultural expressions. I will explore how *Dancing with the Stars* produces this assimilationist model of cultural difference and suggest possible means of redress, if not for the television producers, then at least for knowledgeable viewers.

The winning formula

A cross between a game show and talent show, *Dancing with the Stars* pairs national celebrities (usually actors, singers or athletes) with professional ballroom dancers in a series of elimination-style dance competitions. Each week, the star non-dancers learn one or two new routines to be performed on live television. Each couple can only progress to the next round by winning high marks from the professional judges in the television studio *and* from the home television audience, who vote by phone or Internet. This formula was first introduced in the UK with the show *Strictly Come Dancing* in 2004. BBC Worldwide had developed versions in twenty-nine countries across Europe, America and Asia by 2007. Because Britain has been exporting its style of ballroom dancing and its corollary competition format since the late 1920s, export of the television show was relatively easy. Similarly trained English-style (renamed International Style in the mid-twentieth century) ballroom dance professionals well versed in DanceSport (competitive style ballroom dance) were already teaching around the world. Since every country has its own cadre of B-list celebrities eager to boost sagging careers by allowing television cameras to film them tripping as they attempt to tango, an international patchwork of programmes derived from *Strictly Come Dancing* emerged virtually overnight.

The American version, broadcast on ABC, had run seven seasons by the end of 2008, ranking among the top ten television shows nearly every week since its initial run in the summer of 2005. While *Dancing with the Stars* is not the first American show to feature amateur social dancers (shows from the 1950s like *The Arthur Murray Party*, *American Bandstand* and *The Buddy Deane Show* all included teenagers performing the latest social dances), nor the first to present ballroom dance competitions (*Championship Ballroom Dancing* enjoyed a successful twenty-year run on PBS in 1980–2000), it is unquestionably the most popular. Before exploring its representation of Latin dance, I will examine some of the reasons why *Dancing with the Stars* is so successful. While my analysis is based on the American version, given the similar format of each national adaptation, I suspect that my explanation of its popularity will resonate with viewers of this show in many other countries as well.

Ballroom aficionados have long suspected that their beloved dance form was ideally suited to television. The minute and a half competition routines often read like condensed soap operas – scenes of lust, betrayal and euphoria melting into one another in fleeting tableaux of romantic courtship. Such accelerated melodrama seemed custom-made for the short attention span of the spectacle-driven television viewer. So too was the rapid succession of picture-perfect poses that in competition were selected to snatch the judges' attention away from other couples. Such moments when dancers suddenly suspend their movement in poses that are arresting in display of dexterity and control could be translated into 'jolts' (emotional rushes for audience members), satisfying the high 'jolts per minute' standard in American television programming. The format of DanceSport competitions, however, where at least six (and upwards of twenty-four) couples dance simultaneously, weaving in and out of empty spaces left by their competitors, has always been a stumbling block for television crews. Eager for the close-up, the cameras dart and cut from the legs of one couple to the face of another, resulting in a dizzying jumble of shots that fail to engender cohesion or sustain interest. Television producers longed for a competition in which couples danced in succession rather than simultaneously. Without the ability to follow a single couple through an entire routine, television had trouble building audience investment in the success or failure of any one couple, and thus failed to establish DanceSport fan bases who would argue at the water cooler about the judges' calls and the merits of their favourite teams.

Dancing with the Stars has overcome this barrier, presenting each couple dancing solo on their live broadcast and generating heated debate the following day by loyal fans. Not only does the camera crew have the luxury of focusing on only one couple, but the benefit of a rehearsal where the best camera angles for each move can be selected, transforming a dance form that is made for in-the-round viewing to one that is captivating in two dimensions. Whereas the ballroom dance industry has been unwilling to compromise its multi-couple judging system to satisfy the needs of television, made-for-television competitions are not bound by the rules of DanceSport. *Dancing with the Stars* hosts do not, in fact, ever use the word 'DanceSport', preferring the more commonly recognized term 'ballroom dancing'. So, although the event is clearly presented as a competition in which athleticism, a rigid physical training regimen and psychological discipline are key to success, it is not framed as a sporting event. *Dancing with the Stars* is instead presented as entertainment for the whole family, including sports heroes and competition for men, chivalry and elegance for

women, clear gender roles with which kids can identify, and revealing costumes for everyone to enjoy the well-chiselled bodies of the professional
dancers. *Dancing with the Stars* has made ballroom dancing 'cool' to just
about every American, even macho heterosexual men, apathetic teenagers
and African Americans (who had until recently predominantly shunned the
form). Studios across the country report nearly doubling of enrolment in
ballroom dance classes and entries in competitions since *Dancing with the
Stars* debuted.

I believe one key to the success of *Dancing with the Stars* is the celebrity/
professional dance partnership. Since the beginning of the twentieth century when exhibition ballroom dancers emerged from crowds at cabarets
to perform more intricate versions of the popular dances of the time,
performance of ballroom dance has always depended on viewers feeling a
sense of intimacy and kinship with the performers (Tomko 1999: 27).
Contemporary DanceSport, however, has been abstracted so far from
social forms that the unwavering lines of a professional dance couple are
too polished for the general public to be able to imagine themselves into
the story. Because beginning dancers are featured, television viewers can
follow them through the learning process, discern their improvements and
mistakes and envision that they too could be undergoing the transformation from non-dancing mortal to ballroom diva. Two amateurs dancing
together, however, would be unlikely to produce television-worthy spectacle, which is why one member of each partnership in this hit show is a
professional dancer. But not just any amateur will do. The 2005 TLC
reality series *Ballroom Bootcamp* that paired 'average Joes and Janes' for
competition with professional dance partners was pulled before the first
season concluded. Joes and Janes could not sustain our attention. But
celebrities, who are used to being in the spotlight, performing under
pressure, and above all entertaining, are able to hold their own while
dancing grapevines and lock steps live on national TV. Even those celebrities with limited dance talent manage to entertain through their charisma
and sense of humour.

In addition to clever partnership pairings, there are several other key
factors that have helped to ensure the success of *Dancing with the Stars*,
including use of highly skilled specialists, audience participation and
witty improvisational dialogue. The professional dancers featured on the
show are among the most highly skilled DanceSport competitors in the
country. Aside from the advantage of being able to showcase professionals dancing with each other in slick production numbers peppered
throughout the show, producers also benefit from their teaching and
choreographic expertise. The American ballroom dance industry is organized around pro-am (professional–amateur) competitions, events in
which professional dance teachers compete in partnerships with their
students. Thus, most of the professional dancers appearing on *Dancing*

with the Stars are already expert teachers and choreographers who know not only how to coach a neophyte dancer to performance level, but are also experienced in crafting choreography that allows the professional to do 90 per cent of the work, enabling the students to appear much more skilled than they really are.

In the age of participatory television in which consumers shape programming content, the use of home viewers as judges to select winners has been a key component of this show's winning formula. Use of the audience alone, however, would not have been sufficient. Not only do scenes of contestants biting their lips in anticipation of the judges' scores create necessary drama, but the judges educate viewers on how to evaluate a ballroom dance competition. Judges offer not only numerical scores, but vital commentary and critique, providing home viewers with the vocabulary they need to be able to discuss the merits of each performance with their friends: Clyde's frame was weak; Marie missed too many heel leads; Mario's jive had no foot articulation. By offering viewers the opportunity to share such informed knowledge as a means of performing their social capital, the producers are also increasing the value of *Dancing with the Stars* by integrating it into the daily formation of social bonds.

Finally, I credit host Tom Bergeron for keeping the mood light. Perhaps because they've shied away from direct reference to sport, *Dancing with the Stars* never approaches the solemn intensity of a real DanceSport competition. Bergeron's continual volley of jokes, some scripted and many off the cuff, keeps in check any threat of the competition tension escalating beyond playful jockey. When English judge Len Goodman starts to sound as if he would like to rescind the treaty ending the American Revolution because the audience has failed to agree with his critique of the foxtrot, Bergeron calls him 'Cranky Pants'. The camera cuts back to a shot of Goodman laughing good-naturedly at this characterization, and the show is reaffirmed as light-hearted entertainment. Ironically, it is precisely because no one on the show is allowed to treat a missed heel lead with the same gravity as a mistake in air traffic control that the power of dancing becomes evident to the viewers.

Dance, this show teaches, offers anyone the satisfaction of personal growth through overcoming adversity. Dance is hard both physically (viewers are regaled with tales of sore muscles, occasional trips to the hospital and continuous weight loss) and emotionally (contestants are represented being pushed to perform routines that are sexier, funkier or more elegant than their daily personae). Those who persevere through the pain are rewarded with newfound confidence and strength that will outlast the glitter ball trophy presented as first prize. Thus, although only one couple each season is crowned *Dancing with the Stars* champion, the benefits of personal transformation are awarded to all worthy contestants.

Brownface

Precisely because this show is so successful (and because I myself enjoy its inescapable seduction), I feel it is important to critically examine some of its unintended messages. In my book *Glamour Addiction* (McMains 2006) I have written about the ways in which the Latin dances performed in ball-room dance competition enact a racial discourse that perpetuates negative stereotypes of Latin culture and people. I have called this performance of Latinness 'brownface', referring to the body paint worn by ballroom dance competitors, particularly in the Latin division. Brownface is required of *Dancing with the Stars* contestants as well, even those whose skin is by nature melanin-rich. The embrace of brownface even by African American contestant Monique Coleman, who appears in one of the on-show inter-view clips saying, 'even I got a spray tan. I've been sucked in – I'm a black girl!' illustrates that brownface is not merely about prepping pale skin for the harsh lens of television. It is also about donning a mask of Latinness that might free the dancer to step outside his or her own culturally accep-table range of expression. While, on the one hand, the alter-ego assumed even by Latino contestants when performing Latin ballroom dances may allow them to garner audience votes for shimmying and grinding without jeopardizing their 'respectable' reputations, such acts of brownface simul-taneously erase and displace traditions of Latin dance by Latin peoples. In this essay, I will highlight some of the ways in which *Dancing with the Stars* extends and even exacerbates this troubling practice.

For at least a century, Europeans and North Americans have appro-priated and redefined dances from Latin America for inclusion in ballroom syllabi, studios, parties and competitions. Through a process closely linked to imperialism and colonialism, the dances of rumba, cha cha cha and mambo from Cuba, samba from Brazil and tango from Argentina were reinterpreted by ballroom dance teachers. Rhythms were simplified, improvisation was minimized, and aesthetics from ballet, including straight legs, vertical posture and extended limbs sustained in poses, were incorporated into these revised Latin dances.

Tango was the first Latin dance widely embraced in Europe and the United States, enjoying its first surge of popularity in the early 1910s (Savigliano 1995). As the oldest Latin dance to be taken up by Europeans and Americans, the tango has been rechoreographed more often than any other Latin dance, each nation's version departing radically from Argentine styles. Tango choreography in *Dancing with the Stars* has also been singled out more often than any other dance for criticism by the judges. English judge Len Goodman consistently praises the dancers for performing what he calls 'proper tango' and chastises them when they dance steps that others might call 'authentic,' that is, tango from Argentina. Although Goodman never defines his use of 'proper', it is a thinly veiled euphemism for

'English tango', which would hardly be considered proper in Argentina. The English tango substitutes sharp jerks of the head for the risqué intertwining of the Argentine legs and an outward extension of the torsos for the intimate inward lean of the South American dancers' posture. Given that dance traditions sharing the name 'tango' differ so radically, one might expect a short history lesson to reduce audience confusion. Despite the fact that many episodes of *Dancing with the Stars* include brief clips of professionals executing the dance about to be attempted by the contestants overlaid with a list of steps or techniques to watch for, never has the history of tango been addressed. Nor have any Argentinian tango masters been invited to perform in the many professional showcases featured on results night. By failing to recognize the existence of Argentinian tango and repeatedly referring to English tango as 'proper tango', *Dancing with the Stars* implies that the Latin American version is improper and inferior to the European style. Such language reaffirms the Eurocentric chauvinism by which the ballroom industry has operated for the past century.

When Judge Carrie Ann Inaba advises contestant Heather Mills to take ballet classes as a critique of her samba performance, South American viewers might be puzzled. Ballet trains the body in a vertical posture that is lifted and static throughout the torso; whereas Brazil's many iterations of samba require quite the opposite – loose and free hips and ribs jostling atop steps on bent knees (Browning 1995). This paradox is easily resolved by the revelation that this is not a competition in dances from Latin America, but a ballroom dance competition. Despite the moniker 'Latin', ballroom Latin dances share little with popular dances in Latin America. While ballet classes would not help Heather dancing *samba de roda*, they would help her in a ballroom dance competition where movements inspired by Latin American dances (e.g. torso isolations, shoulder shimmies, hip rolls) are combined with steps from ballet (e.g. *battements, arabesques, pirouettes*). Judging a Latin dance by the aesthetic priorities of ballet, however, reinforces the dangerous misconception that balleticized Latin dance is a more evolved (i.e. superior) expression of the 'cruder' Latin form. Such discourse reinforces ethnic and racial hierarchies that imply the Latin Americans who developed 'primitive' Latin dances are inferior to the North Americans and Europeans who 'refined' them. I do not mean to single out the judges alone as guilty of racism. Had I been asked to judge, I too would have faulted Heather Mills on her lack of mastery over skills that, although developed in ballet, are now essential to a successful ballroom dance performance. The danger of *Dancing with the Stars* is not merely the language used by any of its on-air personalities, but the way in which its composite representation of Latin dance perpetuates racist ideologies.

Western reinterpretation of Latin dances has never been confined to the moves. The music has likewise been altered for inclusion in European and

North American ballrooms. Latin rhythms were simplified, tempos standardized, instruments subtracted and added so that Western consumers could relate more easily to the foreign sounds. Although ballroom dancers have been guilty of separating Latin dances from the music for which they were named for the past century, *Dancing with the Stars* accelerated this practice to the point of absurdity. In an apparent attempt to appeal to the musical tastes of their audience, the producers mismatch the dances and the music so severely that even ballroom dancers are baffled. Such incongruous music selections, however, are never made for the dances of European or American origin such as waltz, foxtrot or quickstep. It is always for the Latin dances that non-traditional music is chosen. Dancers have been required to perform mambo to rap and dancehall reggae, cha-cha to R&B and rock, and samba to disco and hip-hop. Occasionally Latin music is selected, but even then integrity of the dance-music complex is rarely maintained. When the Brazilian hit 'Mas Que Nada' was played, contestants were asked to dance a mambo, not a samba. In assuming that the dances can be separated from the music for which they were named, the show's creators are assuming that Latin dances are defined by their moves. In its culture of origin, however, each Latin dance is primarily defined by its relationship to a specific musical tradition. Many ballroom dancers have likewise been guilty of this misconception, but *Dancing with the Stars* has trumped even the most egregious examples in the ballroom industry.

All Latin dances and the musical genres from which they take their names were born through a blending of elements from European, African and (to a lesser extent) indigenous culture. Thus, to object to further hybridization of Latin dance in Western ballrooms through incorporation of elements from Western dance would be to ignore the tradition of transculturation out of which Latin dance emerged. I love DanceSport's version of rumba – the languid walks onto long legs as one hip snakes behind, the vacillation between passionate embraces and abstract shapes, and the sudden suspension of whirling turns in lines that dissolve and twist into ever-expanding images of surrender. I also love the Afro-Cuban rumba – the lively, angular steps, the playful chase between a bragging man who is thwarted by a woman's perpetual rejection of his sexual advances, and the interplay of the pulsating feet, hips, rib cage and arms as they lock onto the clave rhythm. *Dancing with the Stars* audiences, however, only get to enjoy the former, the exclusion of Afro-Cuban rumba further perpetuating a common misconception that it is less evolved than the 'refined' ballroom style.

My objection is not that DanceSport rumba is being showcased on television, but that it is being presented without any recognition of the Cuban dance from which it borrows its name, leading many viewers to falsely conclude that they are indeed watching a Cuban dance. Perpetuating such confusion is troubling in the aftermath of European colonial rule, enduring racial inequity in both South and North America, and American intervention in Latin America. Just as Europeans and Americans have for centuries extracted resources from Latin America for their own advantage, Euro-American versions of Latin dance enable Westerners to define and represent Latin America for their own use and benefit, largely ignoring the needs or interests of Latin Americans and further excluding Latin America's marginal populations.

Furthermore, the omission of actual dances from Latin America on *Dancing with the Stars* potentially exacerbates black/white racial tension in the United States. Although such an accusation of racism may seem unfair, especially when the producers clearly make an effort to recruit African American celebrity contestants each season, the aesthetics rewarded on the show represent a racial hierarchy. Each Latin dance that was adapted for ballroom competition developed in black communities in its country of origin. Thus, it is hardly surprising that the Latin American iterations of these dances share many techniques and aesthetics with other African diasporic dance forms, including bent knees, anterior pelvic tilt, flat feet, lower centre of weight, polyrhythmic movement of the torso and the centrality of improvisation (Gottschild 1996: 8–9) In contrast, the ballroom Latin dances foreground straight legs, neutral pelvic alignment, higher centre of weight, unified torso movements and pre-determined choreography. Thus, judging Latin dances by Euro-American ballroom standards without recognizing the corollary beauty of the Afro-Latin forms teaches viewers to privilege European over African aesthetics, and, therefore, white over black. This hierarchy is also reinforced when the only judge who is a ballroom dancer (the other two judges are theatrical dancers) harshly criticizes the inclusion of steps clearly drawn from black culture, like krumping or the butterfly.

Redress?

Is it the television producers' responsibility to redress a century of appropriation and misrepresentation of Latin dance, or at least to educate the audience that these are not actually Latin dances, but hybrid creations of the ballroom dance industry? To their credit, they hired top ballroom dancers and rarely asked them to venture outside their field of expertise, usually keeping the selection of dances within the canon of contemporary American and International style competition dances. Granted, they do invent a few rules for the purposes of this show that don't exist in ballroom dance competitions, like the frequently broken mandate not to break hold in the middle of the tango. Overall, however, they take great pains to accurately represent the ballroom dances as they are currently practised in the ballroom dance industry. So why do they make no effort to explain the radical disconnect between ballroom Latin dances and Latin dances enjoyed by people in Latin America? Do the ratings of the substantial American Latino population not interest ABC?

The inclusion of Latino contestants suggests that they do, as long as appeals to Latino viewers don't alienate non-Latino viewers. When Chilean celebrity contestant Cristián de la Fuente advanced to the finals, he appeared to be breaking protocol when he slipped in a brief Spanish plea for Latino viewers to vote. Such exceptions underscore the assimilationist model of diversity that is portrayed in *Dancing with the Stars*. Asian, black, Latino, white and mixed-race contestants are all invited to participate, as long as they speak English and aspire to the aesthetic values of Euro-American culture. Although the expectation of assimilation applies to all minorities and immigrants, I believe the representation of Latin dance on this television show both reflects and contributes to heightened American anxiety specifically about Latino immigration. Although the majority of professional dancers on the programme are themselves immigrants from Eastern Europe, their use of non-English language is not as closely monitored as was evidenced when ABC unwittingly aired rehearsal footage of one of the professional dancers swearing in Russian at his celebrity student. In a climate of intensifying public debate about illegal immigration from Latin America and predictions that Latino refusal to assimilate will destroy national cohesion (Pettus 2007), *Dancing with the Stars* is modelling assimilation for its Latino viewers.

Although my focus is specifically the American television show, I will briefly discuss the impact of its implicit racial discourse in other national contexts. Whereas I have argued that *Dancing with the Stars* teaches its viewers that success requires relinquishing ties to racial and ethnic heritage by conforming to dominant Euro-American aesthetic values, the message to viewers in other countries might be less explicitly about racial assimilation than assimilation to a dominant Western cultural ideal. For example, by accurately performing English ballroom dances, contestants on the Russian, Bulgarian or Japanese shows can prove their mastery over Western culture. Thus, these programmes might suggest to their citizens that success requires conforming to Western rules and values.

Whereas most European and East Asian versions of *Dancing with the Stars* are very similar to the American format, South American and Indian programmes incorporate their own local and national dance forms. So, in addition to dancing waltzes and cha-chas, contestants will dance Bollywood in India, *samba de gafiera* and *forró* in Brazil, and *chacarera* in Argentina. Although the more localized adaptation is partly due to a less well-established ballroom dance industry in these countries, I believe it also signals a resistance to American/British cultural dominance. Turning the tables on the Euro-American stereotype of Latin dance as oversexed, the Argentinean *Bailando por un Sueño* recently added the most overtly sexual dance style included in any version of the show – North American pole dancing. Such a tactic, I believe, counters the pervasive American stereotype that led one professional dancer on *Dancing with the Stars* to instruct his partner to get into character for her Latin dance by portraying a 'skanky hoe'. 'Who is the skanky hoe now?' the Argentineans seem to be saying by representing North American dances as more sexual than their own. Although such moments of resistance within international versions of the television show may be encouraging, their broadcasts rarely reach American and European audiences. Thus, I return to the American *Dancing with the Stars* to contemplate how the programme or its viewers might re-envision it in such a way that does not reinscribe racial, ethnic and national hierarchies.

Although its directors may not believe they bear responsibility for educating audiences, *Dancing with the Stars* embeds extensive educational content within its entertainment format. Millions of viewers who did not know the difference between a foxtrot and a cha-cha two years ago can now evaluate the technical merits of both, at least as danced in the ballroom dance industry. *Dancing with the Stars* has promoted awareness about disability by including a deaf contestant as well as one with a prosthetic limb. It has extended the upper age limit and size acceptable for women flaunting their sexuality on television by including older women of varying body types on the show. It has greatly reduced stigma endured by men who dance, and it has consistently recruited African American celebrity contestants to compete in a sport that has almost no African American participation. Why then is the representation of Latinos through this discourse of brownface never questioned?

I expect that *Dancing with the Stars* is daunted by the admittedly formidable task of educating the public about a century of misrepresentation of Latin dance. It is, however, a job they are ideally situated to undertake now that they have mobilized the American public behind ballroom dancing. A first step at recognizing the multiplicity of interpretations of Latin dance might be to invite expert Afro-Cuban rumba dancers, Argentinian tango performers or Brazilian samba *blocos* to perform in the guest spots during results shows. Would it be too difficult for a few of the comedy sketches, such as the one in which Jimmy Kimmel appears giving a 'rumba' lesson by jumping up and down with his parking lot security guard (who is dressed in drag), to include some actual education in dance history?

While I have little power to change the content of one of America's most successful television programmes, I can encourage educated viewing. Even if *Dancing with the Stars* continues to represent ballroom Latin dance as if it were the refined, superior and more cultured version of dance invented by so-called primitive people, we can counter this misrepresentation through education. I encourage everyone to read histories of specific Latin dances (Browning 1995; Daniel 1995, 2002; McMains 2006, 2008; Savigliano 1995), to watch examples of a variety of Latin dance forms on the Internet, and to visit dance halls where Latin Americans are themselves dancing. Our goal should not be to expose the ballroom Latin dances as false, but to bring them into respectful dialogue with Argentinian, Cuban and Brazilian dances. I hope that the encounter will result in equal appreciation of both the weighted, improvisational play of the Afro-Latin forms and the lifted, geometrical design of the Euro-Latin forms, the products of distinct but contemporaneous modern cultures. Not until the racial hierarchy embedded in its representation of Latin dance is exposed and dismantled will *Dancing with the Stars* endorse a twenty-first century American Dream, one that celebrates rather than erases the diversity and multicultural heritage of its believers.

Note

1 This article is based on a paper I delivered at the 'Re-Thinking Practice and Theory' conference in Pantin, France, June 2007. I would like to thank my fellow panellists Jennifer Fisher, Roxane Fenton and Julie Malnig, each of whose work stimulated my own thinking about the role of dance in reality television.

26

FROM INTERCULTURALISM TO HISTORICISM

Reflections on classical Indian dance

Pallabi Chakravorty

At the MTV awards show in September 1998, Madonna performed a spiritual song in a transparent white T-shirt with three Indian *Odissi* dancers in their classical regalia. Within two days of this event a representative of a Hindu religious sect, the Vaisnavs, condemned Madonna for debasing Hinduism and Indian women. A significant intercultural event, which had been generating pride for some sections of the Indian–American community, had once again exposed the lack of context and historicity in interculturalism. *Odissi* is not merely an aesthetically pleasing dance form from eastern India; its history is embedded in various ancient fertility cults tied to ritualistic Hindu temple worship by women dancers known as '*maharis*'. The dance was also performed by young male dancers known as '*gotipuas*', who performed outside the temple. Frederique Marglin (1985) traces *Odissi* to the powerful cult of Chaitanya (a Vaisnavite saint reformer) in the sixteenth century. She explains that, like many indigenous dance forms, it was simply called *nacha* before its revival in the 1950s by dance scholars and male teachers. Thus, the dance is a product of a complex mix of Hindu nationalism, regional chauvinism and national revivalism and is embedded in patriarchal views of the role and function of women in society. Madonna's commercial interculturalism failed to take note of this: by trying to glamorize an exotic tradition she, unsurprisingly, offended the self-appointed bearers of that tradition.[1]

Interculturalism is an important concept for analysing cultural systems in this time of cultural globalization. My intention here is to uproot interculturalism from its location in Euro-American metropolitan centres and restore it to historical specificity within the context of the formation of the Indian nation-state and national identity. Without question or scrutiny, Western dance and theatre circuits have generally adopted and accepted the notion that Indian classical dances serve as quintessential representations of Indian authenticity. It is rarely acknowledged that the present representations of classical Indian dance are extensions of the nationalist discourse of post-colonial and colonial India. However, since the 1980s a steady stream of scholarship has shed new light on the traditional temple dancers of India, connecting their artistic practices to colonial and post-colonial Indian history.[2] Avanthi Meduri, for instance, has analysed the complex intersection of national and international events that transformed 'Sadir' dance to Bharatanatyam (1996). My argument (which draws on Meduri's work) emphasizes the intersection of 'East' and 'West' in the context of dance revival for refashioning a linear progressive history for the Indian nation-state.[3] Thus, this essay will attempt to relocate interculturalism to the historical juncture of nationalist discourse in India; the purpose is to reflect on its implications for the post-colonial context of dance/ performance as well as cultural and gender identity.

Interrogating interculturalism

Interculturalism is a hotly debated issue within the contemporary discourse on culture. The idea of interculturalism evokes its postmodern moorings, particularly its intimate association with the avant-garde in Euro–American culture. Commonly explained as cultural borrowing, interculturalism poses serious questions of cultural appropriation when located between unequal relations of power, such as between the Western nations of advanced capitalism and the developing world. To be more precise, as Andrée Grau notes:

> It would be naive to see interculturalism as an overriding global phenomenon that transcends the differences of class, race and/or history. The implications for interculturalism are not the same for people in impoverished countries as for people in technologically advanced societies.
>
> (Grau 1992: 17)

India is well represented in writings on interculturalism, beginning with the early influence of Grotowski and later taken up by Eugenio Barba, Richard Schechner, Philip Glass and others.[4] Marranca points out that, despite having culture as its central ethos, interculturalism (in relation to performance and theatre) emphasizes aesthetics of form rather than a sense of the 'historical–cultural–social–religious' context of the performance traditions (Marranca et al. 1991: 21). In a similar vein Rustom Bharucha (1990) argues that interculturalism is an ahistorical appropriation of Indian cultural forms in the West, where the forms have been abstracted from their original context to be used as performance models in Euro-American cultural centres. In his strident critique of interculturalism, Bharucha argues that Grotowski's version of interculturalism, reflected in his search for primal, pre-cultural communion with human beings, ignores the specificities of history and cultural context. Similarly, he writes that Barba's 'theatre anthropology', by focusing on scientific laws and principles in analysing the body, celebrates transculturalism rather than specific histories (ibid.: 4). Bharucha contends that Glass's version of interculturalism reflected in the opera about Gandhi (Satyagraha) is 'unrealistic' and 'showy' and reveals more about American theatrical tradition than about Gandhi (ibid.: 93). His most fervent critique of interculturalism is aimed at Schechner, whose representation of religious festivals like Ramlila, within the postmodern categories of performance ritual, promotes 'cultural tourism' by ignoring the socioeconomic reality of India (ibid.). Articulated in this way, interculturalism appears to be subsumed under the master narrative of capitalism, to be showcased in the Western 'metropolitan supermarket' (Ahmad 1992: 128). Perhaps the eclectic use of a variety of dance styles from different cultures (often associated with postmodern dance) highlights the availability of all cultures of the world for consumption under the same roof.[5]

In this essay I view interculturalism as the ideological starting point for a critical elaboration of classical Indian dance. I look at the historical emergence of interculturalism in the context of the unequal cultural exchange between the colonizer and colonized, in this case Britain and India. My point of view is one of location – from the periphery looking at the centre – rather than the more standard opposite. I do not start from the view of interculturalism as an eclectic and progressive cross-cultural exchange or its ahistorical appropriation in Euro-American performance models; I look at it in the context of the Indian nation-state, not Euro-American centres. My objective is to historicize the process of cultural production – in this case, the discourse on interculturalism – as it relates to the construction of national and gender identity, classical dance, history and power. In short, I try to show, following Edward Said, that 'every cultural document [here, classical Indian dance] contains within it a history of a contest of rulers and ruled, of leaders and led' (Said 1987: 59).

Indian classical dance: a product of East and West

Dance historian and theorist Uttara Coorlawala writes:

> Say that Indian dance (classical) is an image reflected in two mirrors opposite each other – the 'East' and 'West.' As the image multiplies into variations of itself, it becomes impossible to determine which mirror it is in. When one image is exclusively selected, it usually reflects the perspective and the image of the one who is looking.
>
> (Coorlawala 1992: 147)

In many respects, my article is an extension of Coorlawala's view, only I contend that the 'East' (in this case India) and the 'West' (which includes the advanced industrialist nations in Europe and America) are connected by a history of power relations where the notion of 'reflection' is subsumed under the larger discourse on imperialism.

One of the obvious examples of this unequal discursive formation is evident in the cultural appropriation of the 'eternal' Orient as the repository of exotic customs and spiritual mysticism. Here, I have in mind (among other themes) the popularity of the Eastern dancing girl in Western ballets such as *La Bayadère* or *Nautch Dance*. The former, initially choreographed by the Italian master Filippo Taglioni, was taken up by the famous French choreographer and dancer Marius Petipa in 1877; great figures like Anna Pavlova, Tamara Karsavina, Rudolf Nureyev and Margot Fonteyn appeared in this ballet.[6] The *Nautch Dance* was choreographed by Ruth St. Denis, one of the pioneers of modern dance in America. She, along with Ted Shawn, created an entire spectrum of dance productions on Indian themes, from *The Nautch*, *The Dance of the Black and Gold Sari*, *The Cobras*, *Yogi* and *Radha*, to Shawn's *The Cosmic Dance of Shiva* (Jowitt 1988; Coorlawala 1992; Khokar 1997b). In fact, according to Coorlawala (1992: 123), both Shawn and Walter Terry had remarked that Ruth St. Denis's visit to India in 1926 and her non-authentic Indian dance were instrumental in reawakening interest among Indians in the 2,000-year-old heritage. Interestingly, in such dance creations India was repeatedly represented as a fantastic land of snake charmers, dancing girls and spiritual mystique – a predominantly Hindu land with very little heterogeneity. But, even more important, a rather complex result of intercultural contact (more appropriately termed colonial imposition, in the guise of European enlightenment) is evident in the production of an indigenous elite during nationalism. In an instance of true interculturalism, this elite group embraced the Western ideals of rationalism and historicism to define the incipient Indian nation-state (Chatterjee 1986; Kaviraj 1994). This is a critical argument. The revivalist and reconstructive movement of Indian classical dance cannot be viewed outside the context of the formation of national ideology in India. The discourses on 'East' and 'West' interwove to form the national ideology of India, and Indian classical dance was an extension of the same discourse.

Construction of the dancing woman in nationalist thought

During the nationalist phase in the early twentieth century, the revival of Indian classical dance came to be associated intimately with the construction of India's national identity. The concept of a common heritage provided an umbrella under which all the different regional dance styles were assembled. The dances came to embody the 'spiritual' roots of the past.

A close parallel is the emergence of folklore in Europe in the eighteenth and the nineteenth centuries;[7] Turner (1995: 337–42) expresses a similar view in her discussion on Balinese dance. In *Imagined Communities*, Benedict Anderson (1983) argues that 'nation' was not an essential concept but a historical construct. Partha Chatterjee (1986), in *Nationalist Thought and the Colonial World*, illustrates the complex relationship between nationalist discourse and colonial domination in the formation of the Indian nation-state. Chatterjee shows how 'nationalism' itself, being part and parcel of European discourse, was incorporated into the Third World struggle for self-determination. Thus, Indian leaders, after being exposed to Enlightenment philosophy (by virtue of an English education, which the colonizers saw as necessary for their own administrative purposes), appropriated the ideals of liberty and political equality to achieve independence. Moreover, through traditional cultural practice, such as dance and music, the nationalist discourse revived the essential spiritual identity of the East. The sole bearers of this spiritual identity, they proclaimed, were the (upper-middle-class and upper-caste) Hindu women. Chatterjee explains:

> The material/spiritual dichotomy to which the terms world and home correspond, had acquired ... a very special significance, in the nationalist mind. The world was where European peoples, by virtue of its superior material culture, had subjugated them. But the nationalist asserted it had failed to colonize the inner essential identity of the East which lay in its superior culture.
>
> (Chatterjee 1989: 624)

Thus, in addressing the 'woman question' in nationalist thought, Chatterjee employs the dialectics of public/world and private/home to formulate his idea of material/spiritual dichotomy. He argues that the woman in the nationalist discourse represents India's inner spiritual identity, which, in the nationalist view, is an authentic classical identity. In this way women's identity becomes synonymous with Indian tradition and the sanskritized Hindu doctrines of ancient India. This ideology is crystallized in the writings of Ananda Coomaraswamy, a renowned art historian and aesthetician, whose books are still required reading in many courses on Indian culture in Western universities. As he has written:

> Even in recent times, in families where the men have received an English education unrelated to Indian life and thought, the inheritance of Indian modes of thought and feelings rests in the main with women; for a definite philosophy of life is bound up with household ritual and traditional etiquette and finds expression equally in folktale and cradle-song and popular poetry, and in those Puranic and epic stories which contribute to the household

Bible literature of India. Under these conditions it is often the case
that Indian women, with all their faults of sentimentality and
ignorance, have remained the guardians of a spiritual culture which
is of greater worth than the efficiency and information of the
educated.

(Coomaraswamy 1957: 100–101)

These sentiments are not very different from those expressed in 1882 by
Bhudev Mukhopadhyay, another important intellectual figure, and a
nationalist like Coomaraswamy:

It is human aversion to the purely animal trait that gives rise to
virtues such as modesty. ... further within the human species,
women cultivate and cherish these Godlike qualities far more than
men. Protected to a certain extent from the purely material pursuits of securing a livelihood in the external world, women express
in their appearance and behavior the spiritual qualities that are
characteristic of civilized and refined human society.

(in Chatterjee 1997: 125)

Thus, in moving from the real to the discursive, Indian women became
symbols of culture and tradition.[8] The revival of classical Indian dance and
the construction of Indian womanhood are both reflections of this essential
Hindu identity. In the process, the dance itself was removed from its original practitioners like the *devadasi* and *nautch* dancers – who were not all
Hindus and certainly belonged in the public domain.[9]

It is interesting to consider the example of Rukmini Devi Arundale, a key
figure in reviving classical Indian dance; Meduri (1996) has documented her
pioneering work in creating the modern national dance of Bharatanatyam.
Rukmini Devi not only spearheaded the world mother movement launched
by the Theosophists (such as Annie Besant) in 1925, but also was instrumental in making the revival of dance and the arts an integral part of the
Theosophical agenda. She choreographed various dance dramas with
Sanskrit mythological themes in order to highlight the spirituality of the
dance form. In her words, this was a 'novel way of bringing religion to
people' (*Kalakshetra Quarterly*, quoted in Meduri 1996: 377). Rukmini Devi,
then, represented the ideal confluence of the ritual traditions of ancient
India and the emancipated sensibilities of a Western-educated, upper-
middle-class woman. In fact, she was hailed as 'world mother' in eulogies
such as this: 'the woman as she was in ancient India, not as she is today, the
woman who was the warrior, the true mother, the priestess, the ideal for
the world' (Ransom 1938: 486, quoted in Meduri 1996: 293). In her we see
the idealized confluence of mother, goddess and dancer, the complete
Sanskrit Hindu woman.

Nationalist discourse: history, nation, and dance

In the previous section I explained how the 'dancing woman' in classical Indian dance is a reflection of an essentialised identity of the Orient. I also explained how the dichotomous project (material/spiritual) in nationalist discourse helped to construct an ahistorical and orientalist view of Indian classical dance. Once again, I will refer to Chatterjee (1986) to demonstrate that the 'object' in nationalist thought was consistent with the Western notion of Orientalism and followed the same objectifying procedures of knowledge constructed in the post-Enlightenment era of Western science. This is most evident, as Chatterjee illustrates, in the work of Bankim Chandra Chattapadhyay (1838–94), a Bengali novelist and satirist. The latter, whom Chatterjee identifies as one of the key nationalist thinkers, situated his polemics in the essential spirituality of the East (represented by classical Brahminical India) as distinguished from the West (represented by the Enlightenment ideal of progress). Nationalists appropriate the privilege of writing history (all nations must have a history) for explaining social and cultural formations.

I argue that, following the same logic of linear, progressive history, dance revivalists and historians, such as Krishna Iyer, Rukmini Devi Arundale, Ananda Coomaraswamy and Kapila Vatsyayan, delved deep into India's past to invent an unbroken dance tradition. However, I should add here that Vatsyayan's more recent works (1989, 1995) have moved away from merely constructing linear histories and claiming pristine purity and antiquity for classical dance repertory. This is evident also in her historical analysis of Kathak dance, a classical dance form from north India, where she traces the dance to Sufi dervishes of the thirteenth and fourteenth centuries, rather than to immutable Vedic sources of ancient India (Vatsyayan 1982: 89–90).

The rewriting of dance history by the nationalist elites and revivalists obliterated in one sweep the history of the *devadasi* and *nautch* dancers from the national history of India.[10] This deliberate act of erasure is intricately connected to the social reform movements of the time. Specifically, it is a direct result of the anti-*nautch* movement of the 1890s, which began as a purity movement for national regeneration. English missionaries and Hindu social reformers led the crusade against the traditional dancers, which had a devastating effect on the *nautch* and *devadasi* institutions. They not only lost their traditional patrons, but the dancers were also ostracized from society with no alternative means of livelihood; many were driven to prostitution. The ideas of purification, reform and national regeneration prompted the English-educated elite to hark back to the 'spiritual roots' of the nation's past, which they argued resided in the traditions of arts, aesthetics and culture of the Vedic times. Thus, while the *devadasi* and *nautch* dancers were condemned as 'sinful', their artistic practices were revived as repositories of spirituality.

The revival of classical dance in the 1930s marked the historic moment when the Western-educated bourgeois elite appropriated the dances of traditional practitioners. The various regional dance styles began to be codified, textualized and canonized as authoritative knowledge and were elevated to classical status. Consequently, the nationalists and dance revivalists presented to the world and to themselves a linear and continuous dance tradition uninterrupted by historical variations. Hence, the revivalism of classical Indian dance as an extension of the nationalist discourse indicated to the colonizing culture the independence and integrity of Indian culture, free from colonial encroachment, and at the same time gave the young nation historicity. Classical dance came to represent the authentic sanskritized Hindu spirit of India's past, one that had been maligned by colonial rule.

This image of the essentialized, spiritual Orient continues to inform classical Indian dance. To prove that the antiquity of classical dance forms a seamless history, scholars, dancers and educators continue to refer to the 'sacred' text of Natyasastra, which originated in Vedic times, and thereby to inscribe the classical dance genre with an unshakable Brahminical world view. This representation of the Orient is not only evident in the classical dance idiom, but also in its representation of the ideal Indian woman. The renowned dancer Chaki-Sirkar (1993) writes that, even today, Indian classical dance resonates with patriarchal, Hindu themes in which sexually passive Radha longs for her beloved Krishna, who incessantly indulges in amorous and unfaithful adventures.

The iconization of Sanskrit heroines (nayikas) and gods and goddesses such as Radhha, Shakuntala, Nataraja, Shiva, Durga, Rama, Sita and others continues to dominate the classical dance repertory. The formal presentation of the classical repertory includes invocations to Lords Krishna, Ganapati and Vishnu or goddesses Saraswati, Durga and others to inscribe the performance within the spiritual space of the temple.[11] In reality, the actual production space is the competitive market and the modern secular stage. Thus, this static, fossilized and Orientalist view of Indian classical dance is not merely an ahistorical representation in the Euro-American centres of power, as one often finds under the rubric of interculturalism, but is dominant in the metropolitan centres in contemporary India. Bharucha (1990: 51) conceptualizes this phenomenon as 'festival culture', which he equates with Hobsbawm's 'invention of tradition'. According to Bharucha (1990: 10), this practice of reifying Indian tradition that harkens back to Sanskrit sources to create an aura of antiquity and authenticity underscores a 'system of power that promote(s) cultures on the basis of political exigencies, fashion and the demands of the international market'. The situation is eloquently summarized by Shobana Jeyasingh, who is a contemporary dancer based in London:

> The fiction of 'the Orient,' so beloved in the West as a place of simple spiritual certainties, exotic maidens and colourful rituals,

had to be reinforced once again to the viewers in their sitting rooms in London and New York. ... This stifling, historically inaccurate and ultimately life denying concept of the East is not an isolated example. It is very much a symptom of a more general, unequal power relationship between East and West. The West is the eternal anthropologist with the resources to observe, research and 'explain' all those exotic cultures. It is a kind of colonization through categorization and as such an exercise of power.

(Jeyasingh 1997: 31)

I should add, however, that in recent years a handful of dancers have continued to rearticulate Indian dance in contemporary terms. Dancers such as Chandralekha, Kumudini Lakhia and Manjushree Chaki-Sirkar have pioneered a nascent movement toward new directions in Indian dance.[12] Kumudini Lakhia was one of the earliest choreographers in India to reinvent Kathak as a dance vocabulary to be used in expressing contemporary thoughts.[13] Her choreographic works have represented ordinary, everyday women, rather than the 'ideal types' portrayed in classical dance forms. The clear straight lines of the Kathak idiom mark her compositions. She uses simple costumes and distinctive colours to create subtle yet dramatic shifts from the traditional ethos of Kathak. Her *Sam Samvedan* portrays a lone man's attempt to integrate with society, while *Atah-Kim* symbolically explores the drive for power and greed that forces man to compromise his values in life (Lakhia 1995).

Manjushree Chaki-Sirkar has reimagined the Indian dancing body as capable of creating versatile movements, thus breaking the rigid boundaries of classical vocabulary. Her works have been inspired by Tagore and his vision of dance as a vehicle for reflecting social concerns. Her dance style is called Nava Nritya, or new dance, and draws on classical dance and martial art forms. In works such as *Tomari Matir Kanya (Daughter of the Earth)*, for instance, based on Tagore's 'Chandalika', she addresses issues of women's human rights (Chaki-Sirkar 1994).

In her radical composition *Angika*, Chandralekha revamps the traditional technique of Bharatanatyam by presenting it as stark, geometric patterns in space, devoid of ornamentation. In this work she explores the origin of dance by demonstrating its cosmic, material and martial energies. Her other works, such as *Shree* and *Lilavati*, are deliberately provocative and challenge the ideal feminine body in dance.[14] There are many other dancers in India and elsewhere who are currently engaged in pushing the boundaries of the classical sensibility into exciting new territories. Although this new dance has yet to claim a collective political or ideological agenda, these dancers are united in disregarding the past patriarchal and feudal order, and to reclaim dance for their own individual self-expression.[15]

Summary

As I have argued, the term 'interculturalism' needs some reformulation in contemporary dance and theatre studies. As voices from the margin (including my own as a 'native' anthropologist) claim a hearing at the centre, the centre needs to be more self-conscious about the histories of power relations embedded in the margins. By locating the cross-cultural exchange associated with (Indian) interculturalism outside the Western centres of power, this paper has historicized this exchange in the context of the formation of the Indian nation-state. I have discussed and reviewed several arguments concerning how Indian womanhood became synonymous with Indian tradition and culture and how the revival of traditional cultural practices, such as dance, came to represent an authentic Indian identity, which resided in idealized Hindu gender identity. My central argument analyses how the discourse of 'East' and 'West' fused to form both the dominant ideology of classical Indian dance and a nationalist reconstruction of a linear progressive history for the incipient Indian nation-state. The idea of an ahistorical, static Orient, and its ideal representative, the spiritual Hindu woman of the classical tradition, still captures the imagination of the West; Madonna at the MTV awards is its latest incarnation. With the increasing visibility of Indian exports to the West, such as classical music and dance, a more self-critical intercultural dialogue needs to be generated within the Western centres of knowledge production.

Notes

1 A modern, partisan Hindu group, a branch of an older sect called Vaisnavs, claimed the tradition of Odissi as their own for political purposes. Interestingly, the Vaisnava sect was tied to the Bhakti movement in the medieval period of Indian history; it was known for its progressive anti-caste and anti-Brahminical position. The central tenet of Vaisnavism, which includes worshipping Vishnu and his popular incarnation Krishna, is based on the doctrine of Bhakti philosophy (see Tharu and Lalita 1991: 56–60).

2 See Marglin 1985; Srinivasan 1985; Kersenboom-Story 1987; Coorlawala 1992; Meduri 1996; Allen 1997; Iyer 1997; O'Shea 1998.

3 See Chakravorty 1998.

4 See Marranca et al. 1991.

5 See Ahmad (1992) for an elaboration of this idea in his critique of cosmopolitan culture. Trinh Minh-ha, a Vietnamese American filmmaker, explains interculturalism as 'sharing a field (that) belongs to no one, not even those who create it'. She marks this process as 'intercreation', where, she argues, the very notion of 'artist' is a simplistic and reductive concept (quoted in Grau 1992: 18). It has been pointed out to me that the association of interculturalism with postmodern dance is mostly an American situation. In the UK, for instance, postmodern dance is a 'monocultural' discourse; the interest in bringing genres together has been initiated by Indian and African diasporas (see Iyer 1997 in this context, and also Jeyasingh 1995: 193–7).

6 See Khokar 1997a.

7 See Giurchesu 1990, and Giurchesu and Torp 1991.

8 For construction of Indian womanhood, see Chowdhury 1998 (17–19) and Bagchi 1990.

9 In fact, the traditional temple dancers or the *devadasis* could belong to any caste and were symbolically married to the temple deity. This meant that they remained unmarried throughout their lives and often had multiple sexual partners (see Marglin 1985). Moreover, in northern and eastern India, many *nautch* dancers were Muslim girls, since Kathak was essentially a court dance patronized by the Mughal and Hindu royal courts of India.

10 For the effects of the anti-*nautch* campaign on the *devadasi* institution in south India, see Srinivasan 1984, 1985 and Meduri 1996. On *nautch* dancers of India, see Chakravorty 2000.

11 On the other hand, in other cultural spheres such as theatre, painting and even music there are and have been radical departures from the so-called traditional scriptures of the past. During the revivalist phase, dancer Uday Shankar (a contemporary of and collaborator with Anna Pavlova) tried to bring modernism to Indian dance, but he failed to institutionalize or make permanent his brand of modernism. His disciple Narendra Sharma continues to produce the most radical experiments in the Indian dance scene (Nritya Natika or National Ballet Festival or Uday Shankar dance festival are some of the cultural festivals in India that include classical and contemporary choreographers). The attempt by Rabindranath Tagore to create a modern dance language by combining various classical and folk styles remains limited to Bengal. In fact, what we know today as 'Rabindra nritya', or Tagore dance, is a hackneyed replication of Tagore's visionary creations.

12 The names on this list appeared in *The Telegraph*, the English daily newspaper in Calcutta (see Venkataraman 1990).

13 In 1971 she choreographed Duvidha in which she presented a woman torn between traditional and modern values.

14 See Bharucha 1997.

15 Here I am concerned only with urban India. In rural India, regional dances are performed during seasonal and other auspicious occasions in non-commercial surroundings. There is a continuous effort to claim national–classical status for regional dance styles to keep them from dying out. For example, recently two regional dance forms from eastern India, Gaur dance and Chhau dance, have demanded classical status. In urban India, classical dance now works as symbolic cultural capital for the lower-middle classes, who are being indoctrinated into the classical idiom through various state-supported programmes, workshops and television (see Chakravorty 2000). (For details on new dance, see Coorlawala, 1994; for an attempt at categorizing contemporary Indian dance, see Sirkar, 1997).

Part V

DEBATING THE DISCIPLINE

Texts that raise questions about the nature of dance studies and that consider the key methodological impulses within the field have a more recent history than the other modes of writing considered here. As a relatively young and almost inherently interdisciplinary academic field, dance studies has only recently begun to overtly consider and contest the relationship between dance and its constitutive methodologies. Similarly, it is only relatively recently that authors have considered the relationship of dance to other disciplines. This explicit attention to methodological concerns characterises the 'new dance studies' approach that developed in the 1990s and is continuing. This ongoing attention to methodology and debate suggests that 'new dance studies' cannot be pinned down as a single approach or set of approaches but that scholarly dialogue will continue to redefine the parameters of the field.

Susan Foster's text grapples with the concerns of historiography. Alerting us to the significance of the corporeal body and its cultural construction, Foster points to its neglect in Western scholarship. She also uses the body as metaphor in order to make problematic the historiographic project. Issues addressed include the notions that the historian (the body that writes history) intervenes in the creating of the past, that the corpus of history seduces us by its authority into believing in its stability, and that theoretical structures are necessary in order to produce meaning, but theories cannot accommodate all phenomena. What, asks Foster, is the relationship between past history and the mode of recording it? That is, between experience, especially the untranslatable experience of dance, and the written word? The historian cannot replicate history, but must create it. Foster likens the interchange between the bodies of the past, bodies of historians and the body of knowledge to a choreographic process – never static, conspiratorial and creating mutual signification. Furthermore, she was one of the first to stretch the conventional writing style of scholarly discourse as the words of different 'voices' dance along in compliance with their subject matter. In her final section, Foster's imagination takes flight in an extended analogy of the apparent polarities between rhetoric (the spoken word) and movement, or the dancing body. Two muses duet: Clio, the muse of history, who 'realises the need to bring movement and fleshiness into historiography' and Terpsichore, the muse of dance, who 'senses the need to rationalise choreography as persuasive discourse'. Foster's analogy is apt, for, being a dance rather than a fight, the duet calls for cooperation rather than competition, and, like the advancement of all knowledge, any resolution is only temporary.

Phillipa Rothfield considers, and contests, another set of relationships, that between philosophy and dance. Rothfield examines an interest among dance writers in applying phenomenology to dance, investigating the philosophical discourse's usefulness for looking at the moving body – its attention to the sensate body – while also flagging up the pitfalls of its emphasis on subjectivity. Drawing on examples from feminist and sexuality studies, on the one hand, and bioethics on the other, Rothfield demonstrates that the very notion of what it is to have a body, or to live as a body, is differently constituted depending on factors such as gender, ethnicity, culture and historical moment. Likewise, she considers how phenomenological studies of dance can obscure differences in practices of dancing as they create particular bodily subjects, engaging with specific moments of (dance) history. However, she does not reject phenomenology entirely but rather considers whether phenomenology can move away from generality and towards multiplicity and to what extent this manoeuvre can inform the study of dance. As such, she suggests that as much as post-structuralism has offered dance studies a means of characterising a socially, culturally and historically specific body, a critical phenomenology tells us 'what it's like to live as that historicized, normalized, bodily subject'.

Jens Giersdorf considers less the relationship of dance with other methodological moves and more a range of disciplinary manoeuvres within the field itself. Looking at three examples – Theaterhochschule 'Hans Otto' Leipzig, the University of Surrey and the University of California, Riverside – Giersdorf considers the methodological strategies undertaken to establish dance studies as an academic field within different national contexts (East Germany, the United Kingdom and the United States). Giersdorf lines up three approaches to dance studies – archive, analysis and choreography – and indicates how their central preoccupations grapple with contrasting versions of national self-definition, national parameters for higher education, and changing economic structures for and within universities. Thus these three approaches intersected with national concerns so that the archive engaged with East German nation building, analysis with the status of the UK as a post-imperial power, and choreography with the global US hegemony. Giersdorf mobilises such a claim in order to suggest that dance studies investigate the economic and institutional interests at stake in its disciplinisation.

Theresa Buckland illustrates the changing role of ethnography in dance studies. Buckland investigates the crisis of representation in conventional anthropology, tracing the turn away from the culture concept in post-modern anthropology and examining the accompanying embrace of ethnography by disciplines in the humanities. Considering the tenets of ethnographic field research, Buckland identifies a set of concerns common to the social sciences and the humanities-based fields that use ethnography. These include an attention to the experience and point-of-view of participants in, or 'insiders' to, the event being observed, an attention to collective, rather than individual, perception or understanding, and the use of participant-observation. Investigating political critiques of anthropology as well as a more general influence of post-structuralism on scholarly production, Buckland notes that ethnographic study moved from a technique for studying an 'exotic Other' to a device for understanding a range of practices, including those associated with a scholar's own community. She indicates the extent to which, despite challenges to anthropology, ethnography remains a key device for understanding dance as an integral part of social life.

Sherril Dodds likewise signals the importance of a scholar's direct experience for dance studies, in this case for the study of popular dance. She opens her investigation of the place and status of popular dance in academic research by noting the dislocation between her own teenage experiences of social dance and the fields of knowledge she encountered at university. She observes the way that slam dance which 'intentionally barges into and knocks about fellow participants' can be used as a metaphor for the way recent studies in popular dance have necessitated shifts and responses in the field of dance studies, spinning it off in new directions. Dodds sets the emergence of popular dance as a valid field of study against its exclusion in the constructed canon which has traditionally focused on Western theatre forms. She notes the slippery nature of any categorisation of 'popular dance'. However, it is the very richness of the field and the crossovers between this and 'conventional' art practices which produce new kinds of activity and help to expand dance studies not only in terms of its content but also its methodologies. Its fluid and unstable nature makes it difficult to treat the dance(s) as 'text' so critical strategies which cohere around this kind of analysis are, as a totality of approach, inappropriate. Arguably, any examination of what people do in a vernacular context necessitates an engagement with the people who do it, produce it and consume it, in relation to the systems which intersect all of these acts. In other words, scholars need to consider not just text or product, but agency. As such, 'academics must get to grips with the material realities of popular dance practice' which will allow 'for a reframing of its position within the academy from out of the margins and into a position of intellectual and embodied worth'.

Although philosophy has historically been awarded a more legitimate place within the academy than popular dance, its attention to dance has been scant, with the traditional mode of conceptual enquiry seeming at odds with the corporeal. Nevertheless, as the instability of knowledge is now recognized and the search for any definitive wisdom has been argued as futile, Betty Redfern demonstrates how traditional conceptual analysis can expose many of the assumptions buried in both scholarly and every-day discourse. Tackling the concept of art and exemplifying her argument with dance, Redfern raises issues which cohere around the nature of the activity: what kinds of movement, by whom and where count as 'dance' – and who says so? Other issues concern the nature of the debate itself. For example, does the singular form of the question 'What is art?' (or 'What is dance?') preclude a pluralistic response? Is the traditional quest for a defi-nition one that is doomed from the start? Exploring these issues through a model of logical argument, Redfern acknowledges the socio-historical construct of art but suggests that it is the very question of 'what is art', and the essentially complex and contested nature of art, which sustains the construct. It is the instability of 'art' which accommodates variation and change in practice and in theory; discourse does not solidify but remains, always, on the move.

The questions posed here – regarding the relationship of dance to his-tory, philosophy, ethnography and popular culture studies – as well as the exploration of different, strategic methodological moves within dance stu-dies signal the importance of explicit disciplinary debate within the field. Methodologies are, in themselves, invested with meaning and values; dis-ciplinary choices are political choices as well as intellectual ones. Dance studies, as a relatively new field and an interdisciplinary one, has been more willing to encourage such debates than older fields. Nonetheless, the field still requires that scholars query its central disciplinary and thematic con-cerns as these will inevitably change over time. A methodological decision may be strategic at one historical juncture but it may lose its force as the concerns of its surrounding society change. As such, the disciplinary exchange and methodological debate that characterised 'new dance studies' and that appears in a newer format here should carry forward as the field develops and reworks itself.

Further reading

CORD (2009) 'Dance, the disciplines, and interdisciplinarity', *Dance Research Jour-nal*, Congress on Research in Dance, special issue: 41:1 (Summer).

CORD/CEPA (2009) *Proceedings: Global perspectives on dance pedagogy – research and practice*, Congress on Research in Dance/Centre of Excellence for Teaching and Learning in Performing Arts, Special Conference, de Montfort University, Leicester.

SDHS (2007) *Proceedings: Thirtieth Annual Conference: Re-thinking Practice and Theory/ Repenser pratique et théorie*, Centre National de la Danse, Paris, France, Society of Dance History Scholars joint conference with CORD.

——(2008) *Proceedings: Thirty-first Annual Conference: Looking Back/Moving Forward*, International Symposium on Dance Research, Skidmore College, Saratoga Springs, New York.

27

CHOREOGRAPHING HISTORY

Susan Leigh Foster

Manifesto for dead and moving bodies

Sitting in this chair; squirming away from the glitches, aches, low-grade tensions reverberating in neck and hip, staring unfocused at some space between here and the nearest objects, shifting again, listening to my stomach growl, to the clock ticking, shifting, stretching, settling, turning – I am a body writing. I am a bodily writing.[1] We used to pretend the body was uninvolved, that it remained mute and still while the mind thought. We even imagined that thought, once conceived, transferred itself effortlessly onto the page via a body whose natural role as instrument facilitated the pen. Now we know that the caffeine we imbibe mutates into the acid of thought which the body then excretes, thereby etching ideas across the page. Now we know that the body cannot be taken for granted, cannot be taken seriously, cannot be taken.

A body, whether sitting writing or standing thinking or walking talking or running screaming, is a bodily writing. Its habits and stances, gestures and demonstrations, every action of its various regions, areas, and parts – all these emerge out of cultural practices, verbal or not, that construct corporeal meaning. Each of the body's moves, as with all writings, traces the physical fact of movement and also an array of references to conceptual entities and events. Constructed from endless and repeated encounters with other bodies, each body's writing maintains a non-natural relation between its physicality and referentiality. Each body establishes this relation between physicality and meaning in concert with the physical actions and verbal descriptions of bodies that move alongside it. Not only is this relation between the physical and conceptual non-natural, it is also impermanent. It mutates, transforms, reinstantiates with each new encounter.

Today's creaking knee is not yesterday's knee jogging up the hill. The way one reaches towards that knee, as much a metaphor as any attempt to name or describe the knee, already presumes identities for hand and knee. But during their interaction identities for hand and knee become modified. Together they discover that the knee feels or sounds different, that the hand looks older or drier than yesterday. Comparisons between past and present knees provide some sense of continuity, but the memory is also unreliable. Was it a year ago that the knee started creaking that way? Did it cease to make that noise during running, or after stretching? Why did it hurt yesterday and feel fine today? The body is never only what we think it is *(dancers pay attention to this difference)*. Illusive, always on the move, the body is at best *like* something, but it never is that something. Thus, the metaphors, enunciated in speech or in movement, that allude to it are what give the body the most tangible substance it has.

Organized collections of these metaphors, established as the various disciplines that scrutinize, discipline, instruct and cultivate the body, pretend permanence of and for the body. Their highly repetitive regimens of observation and exercise attempt to instantiate physical constants. Thousands of push-ups, pliés, or Pap smears later, the body appears to have consistent features, a clear structure, identifiable functions. If one is willing to ignore all subtle discrepancies and to uphold the statistical averages, one can almost believe in a body that obeys nature's laws. But then it suddenly does something marvellously aberrant: it gives out, comes through or somehow turns up outside the bounds of what was conceivable.

This is not to say that the body's latest unanticipated gestures occur beyond the world of writing. On the contrary, the body's newest pronouncements can only be apprehended as *bricolages* of extant moves. A sudden facility at physical feats figures as the product of past disciplinary efforts to render the body faster, stronger, longer, more dexterous. The onset of illness signals deleterious habits, psychological repression, a cleansing process. Any new sensation of sex issues out of an expanded, but not alternative, sensorium. These new writings, even as they jar perceptions with their arresting inventiveness, recalibrate, rather than raze, bodily semiosis.

How to write a history of this bodily writing, this body we can only know through its writing. How to discover what it has done and then describe its actions in words. Impossible. Too wild, too chaotic, too insignificant. Vanished, disappeared, evaporated into thinnest air, the body's habits and idiosyncrasies, even the practices that codify and regiment it, leave only the most disparate residual traces. And any residue left behind rests in fragmented forms within adjacent discursive domains. *Still, it may be easier to write the history of this writing body than of the pen-pushing body. The pen-pushing body, after all, bears only the thinnest significance as an inadequate robotics, the apparatus that fails to execute the mind's will.*

What markers of its movement might a bodily writing have left behind? But, first, which writing bodies? empowered bodies? enslaved bodies? docile bodies? rebellious bodies? dark bodies? pale bodies? exotic bodies? virtuoso bodies? feminine bodies? masculine bodies? triumphant bodies? disappeared bodies? All these genres of bodies first began moving through their days performing what they had learned how to do – these bodies' mundane habits and minuscule gestures mattered. These 'techniques of the body', as named by Marcel Mauss and John Bulwer before him, bore significance in the way they were patterned and the way they related with one another. Each body performed these actions in a style both shared and unique. Each body's movement evidenced a certain force, tension, weight, shape, tempo and phrasing. Each manifested a distinct physical structure, some attributes of which were reiterated in other bodies. All a body's characteristic ways of moving resonated with aesthetic and political values. The intensity of those resonances are what permit genres of bodies to coalesce.

Yet each body's movements all day long form part of the skeleton of meaning that also gives any aberrant or spectacular bodily action its lustre. Those everyday patterns of movement make seduction or incarceration, hysteria or slaughter, routinization or recreation matter more distinctively. The writing body in the constant outpouring of its signification offers up nuances of meaning that make a difference. The writing body helps to explicate the blank stare of the black man in the white police station, the raised shoulders and pursed lips of the rich woman walking past the homeless family, the swishing hips and arched eyebrows of gay men as a straight couple enters their bar, the rigid stance and frowning forehead of the single woman waiting at the bus stop next to the construction site. Or put differently: the writing body helps to explicate the blank stare of the black man in the white police station, the blank stare of the rich woman walking past the homeless family, the blank stare of gay men as a straight couple enters their bar, the blank stare of the single woman waiting at the bus stop next to the construction site. Each body's distinctive pronouncements at a given moment must be read against the inscription, along with others, it continuously produces. A blank stare does not mean the same thing for all bodies in all contexts.

How to get at this skeleton of movement's meaning for any given past and place? Some bodies' quotidian movements may have been variously recorded in manuals — ceremonial, religious, educational, social, amorous, remedial, martial – that instruct the body, or in pictures that portray it, or in literary or mythological references to its constitution and habits. In their movements, past bodies also rubbed up against or moved alongside geological and architectural constructions, music, clothing, interior decorations ... whose material remains leave further indications of those bodies' dispositions. Insofar as any body's writings invited measurement, there endure documents from the disciplines of calculation addressing the body's grammatical makeup – its size, structure, composition and chemistry – that tell us something about what shape a body was in.

These partial records of varying kinds remain. They document the encounter between bodies and some of the discursive and institutional frameworks that touched them, operated on and through them, in different ways. These documents delineate idealized versions of bodies: what a body was supposed to look like, how it was supposed to perform, how it was required to submit. Or they record that which was non-obvious, those details of bodily comportment construed as necessary to specify rather than those deemed self-evident. Occasionally, they reflect patterns of bodily deviance, whether ironic, inflammatory, inverted or perverted, from the expected. Whatever their take on bodies, these documents never produce an isolatable and integral single physical figure, but instead stock an antiquarium storeroom with the sharded traces of bodily movement across the cultural landscape.

A historian of bodies approaches these fragmented traces sternum leading, a sign *(in the West since, say, the eighteenth century)* that his or her own body is seeking, longing to find, the vanished body whose motions produced them. Yes, the historian also has a body, has a sex, gender, sexuality, skin colour. And this body has a past, more or less privileged, more or less restricted. This historian's body wants to consort with dead bodies, wants to know from them: What must it have felt like to move among those things, in those patterns, desiring those proficiencies, being beheld from those vantage points? Moving or being moved by those other bodies? A historian's body wants to inhabit these vanished bodies for specific reasons. It wants to know where it stands, how it came to stand there, what its options for moving might be. It wants those dead bodies to lend a hand in deciphering its own present predicaments and in staging some future possibilities.

To that end historians' bodies amble down the corridors of documentation, inclining toward certain discursive domains and veering away from others. Yes, the production of history is a physical endeavour. It requires a high tolerance for sitting and for reading, for moving slowly and quietly among other bodies who likewise sit patiently, staring alternately at the archival evidence and the fantasies it generates. This physical practice cramps fingers, spawns sneezes and squinting.

Throughout this process historians' own techniques of the body – past practices of viewing or participating in body-centred endeavours – nurture the framework of motivations that guide the selection of specific documents. One historian's body is drawn toward domestic labour and the panoply of sexual practices. Another responds to etiquette, fashion and dance, but ignores training for sports and the military. Whatever the kinds and amounts of bodily references in any given constellation of practices, they will yield versions of historical bodies whose relation to one another is determined as much by the historian's body history as by the times they represent.

In evaluating all these fragments of past bodies, a historian's own bodily experience and conceptions of body continue to intervene. Those bodies of the past were 'plumper', 'less expansive in space', 'more constricted by dress' than our own. They tolerated 'more pain', lived with 'more dirt'. The 'ankle was sexier', the face 'less demonstrative', the 'preference for vertical equilibrium more pronounced', than in our time. Even the space 'between' bodies and the codes for 'touching' and 'being touched' signalled differently from today.

These comparisons reflect not only a familiarity with corpo-realities but also a historian's interpretation of their political, social, sexual and aesthetic significance. Any of the body's features and movements – the space it occupies, its size and dispositions, the slowness, quickness or force with which it travels, a body's entire physicality – reverberate with this cultural significance twice over: physical actions embodied these values when the body was alive and kicking, whatever documentary apparatus registered its actions then re-evaluated as it reinscribed the body's semiotic impact. But if those bodies of the past incorporate a historian's bodily predilections, its political and aesthetic values, they also take shape from the formal constraints imposed by the discipline of history. Historians' bodies have been trained to write history. They have read widely among the volumes that compose the discourse of history and from them learned how to stand apart in order to select information, evaluate its facticity and formulate its presentation in accordance with general expectations for historical research. From this more distant locale, they work to mould the overall shape of historical bodies by asking a certain consistency, logic and continuity from the many and disparate inferences of which they are composed. They have also listened to authorial voices within histories that strive to solidify themselves so as to speak with transcendental certainty. From these voices they have learned that pronouncements about the past should issue in sure and impartial tones. They have deduced that historians' bodies should not affiliate with their subjects, nor with fellow historians who likewise labour over the secrets of the past. Instead, those voices within past histories teach the practice of stillness, a kind of stillness that spreads across time and space, a stillness that masquerades as omniscience. By bestilling themselves, modestly, historians accomplish the transformation into universal subject that can speak for all. But dead bodies discourage this staticity. They create a stir out of the assimilated and projected images from which they are concocted, a kind of stirring that connects past and present bodies. This affiliation, based on a kind of kinaesthetic empathy between living and dead but imagined bodies, enjoys no primal status outside the world of writing.[2] It possesses no organic authority; it offers no ultimate validation for sentiment. But it is redolent with physical vitality and embraces a concern for beings that live and have lived. Once the historian's body recognizes value and meaning in kinaesthesia, it cannot disanimate the physical action of past bodies it has begun to sense.

Tensing slightly closed eyelids, some bodies dimly appear: glancing, grasping, running in fear, standing stoically, sitting disgraced, falling defiantly, gesturing enticingly. In that dream-like space that collects filmed or performed

reconstructions of the past, visual images from the past, and textual references to past bodies, historical bodies begin to solidify. *The head tilts at an
angle; the rib cage shifts to the side; the writing body listens and waits as fragments
of past bodies shimmer and then vanish.*

If writing bodies demand a proprioceptive affiliation between past and
present bodies, they also require interpretation of their role in the cultural
production of meaning: their capacities for expression, the relationships
between body and subjectivity they may articulate, the bodily discipline and
regimentation of which they are capable, the notions of individuality and
sociality they may purvey. The facts as documented in any recorded discourses, however, do not a body's meaning make. They substantiate the
causal relationship between body and those cultural forces that prod, poke
and then measure its responsiveness. They substantiate only bodily reaction. They lie askew from a body's significance and in its wake. And even a
historian's movements among them cannot draw them together so as to
fashion meaning for a past body's candid stance or telling gesture. The
construction of corporeal meaning depends on bodily theories – armatures
of relations through which bodies perform individual, gendered, ethnic or
communal identities.[3]

Bodily theories already exist embedded in the physical practices with
which any given historian's body is familiar. Each of his or her body's various pursuits elaborates notions of identity for body and person, and these
conjoin with the values inscribed in other related activities to produce
steadier scenarios of who the body is in secular, spectacular, sacred or liminal contexts. Any standardized regimen of bodily training, for example,
embodies, in the very organization of its exercises, the metaphors used to
instruct the body and, in the criteria specified for physical competence, a
coherent (or not so coherent) set of principles that govern the action of that
regimen. These principles, reticulated with aesthetic, political and gendered
connotations, cast the body who enacts them into larger arenas of meaning
where it moves alongside bodies bearing related signage.

Theorics of bodily significance likewise exist for any prior historical
moment. Circulating around and through the partitions of any established
practice and reverberating at the interstices among distinct practices, theories of bodily practices, like images of the historical body, are deduced
from acts of comparison between past and present, from rubbing one kind
of historical document against others. In the frictive encounters between
texts, such as those expressing aesthetic praise, medical insights, pre-
scriptive conduct and recreational pursuits, theories of bodily significance
begin to consolidate.

The first glimmerings of body theories put meaning into motion. Like the
shapes that pieces from a puzzle must fit, theories contour bodily significance within and among different bodily practices. Theories allow inter-
polation of evidence from one practice where meaning is specified to

another where it has remained latent, thereby fleshing out an identity for bodies that informs a specific inquiry and also the larger array of cultural practices of which they are a part. Theories make palpable ways in which a body's movement can enact meaning.

Not all writing bodies, however, fit into the shapes that such theories make for them. Some wiggle away or even lash out as the historian escorts them to their proper places, resisting and defying the sweep of significance that would contain them. In the making of the historical synthesis between past and present bodies, these bodies fall into a no-man's-land between the factual and the forgotten where they can only wait for subsequent generations of bodies to find them.

I gesture in the air, a certain tension, speed and shape flowing through arm, wrist and hand. I scrutinize this movement and then feel my torso lift and strain as I search for the words that would describe most accurately this gesture's quality and intent. I repeat the movement, then rock forward insistently, pressing for a conversion of movement into words. A sudden inhalation, I haven't taken a breath in many seconds. I am a body yearning towards a translation. Am I pinning the movement down, trapping it, through this search for words to attach to it? This is what we thought when we thought it was the subject doing the writing. We thought any attempt to specify more than dates, places and names would result in mutilation or even desecration of the body's movement. We gave ourselves over to romantic eulogies of the body's evanescence, the ephemerality of its existence, and we revelled in the fantasy of its absolute untranslatability. Or else, and this is merely the complementary posture, we patted the mute dumb thing on the head and explained to it in clearly enunciated, patronizing tones that we would speak for it, thereby eviscerating its authority and immobilizing its significance.

It is one thing to imagine those bodies of the past, and it is another to write about them. The sense of presence conveyed by a body in motion, the idiosyncrasies of a given physique, the smallest inclination of the head or gesture of the hand – all form part of a corporeal discourse whose power and intelligibility elude translation into words. Bodies' movements may create a kind of writing, but that writing has no facile verbal equivalence. In commencing to write a historical text, discrepancies between what can be moved and what can be written require of historians yet another form of bodily engagement and exertion. Yes, the act of writing is a physical labour, rendered more vividly so when the subject of that writing is bodily movement resurrected from the past by the imagination.

But to construe bodies' movements as varieties of corporeal writing is already a step in the right direction. Where bodily endeavours assume the status of forms of articulation and representation, their movements acquire a status and function equal to the words that describe them. The act of writing about bodies thereby originates in the assumption that verbal discourse cannot speak *for* bodily discourse, but must enter into 'dialogue' *with* that bodily discourse. The written discourse must acknowledge the grammatical, syntactical and rhetorical capacities of the moved discourse. Writing the historical text, rather than an act of verbal explanation, must become a process of interpretation, translation and rewriting of bodily texts.

How to transpose the moved in the direction of the written. Describing bodies' movements, the writing itself must move. It must put into play figures of speech and forms of phrase and sentence construction that evoke the texture and timing of bodies in motion. It must also become inhabited by all the different bodies that participate in the constructive process of determining historical bodily signification. How could the writing record these bodies' gestures towards one another, the giving and taking of weight, the coordinated or clashing momentum of their trajectories through space, the shaping or rhythmic patterning of their danced dialogue?

And what if the bodies I am writing about spring off the page or out of my imagination, I don't know which, and invite me to dance. And what if I follow and begin to imitate their movements. As we dance alongside one another – not the euphoric dance of the self-abandoned subject, not the deceptively effortless dance of hyperdisciplined bodies, but, instead, the reflexive dance of self-critical bodies who none the less find in dancing the premise of bodily creativity and responsiveness – I'm not leading or following. It seems as though this dance we are doing is choreographing itself through me and also that I am deciding what to do next. Dancers have often described this experience as the body taking over, as the body thinking its own thoughts … but this is as inaccurate as it is unhelpful; it is merely the inverse, again, of the pen-pushing body.

At some point, historical bodies that have formed in the imagination and on the written page can seem to take on a life of their own. The historical inquiry takes on sufficient structure and energy to generate meaning and to narrate itself. Its representational and narrational determinants, infused with their author's energy and with the vibrancy of dead bodies, begin to perambulate on their own. When this transformation in the nature of the inquiry occurs, a corresponding redefinition of authorial function also takes place: The author loses identity as the guiding authority and finds him or herself immersed in the process of the project getting made. *This is not mystical; it's really quite bodily. Rather than a transcendence of the body, it's an awareness of moving with as well as in and through the body as one moves alongside other bodies.*

The transformation in authorial identity shares nothing in common with the appearance of modest objectivity that the universal subject works to achieve. The universalist voice, even as it strives not to contaminate the evidence, not to neglect any point of view, none the less treats the historical subject as a body of facts. Similarly, the partisan voice, fervently dedicated to rectifying some oversight and to actively exposing an area of deficiency in historical knowledge, approaches the past as fixed sets of elements whose relative visibility needs only an adjustment. If, instead, the past becomes embodied, then it can move in dialogue with historians, who likewise transit to an identity that makes such dialogue possible.

In this dancing out of all the parts that have been created, historians and historical subjects reflect upon as they re-enact a kind of improvised choreographic process that occurs throughout the research and writing of history: as historians' bodies affiliate with documents about bodies of the past, both past and present bodies redefine their identities. As historians assimilate the theories of past bodily practices, those practices begin to designate their own progressions. As translations from moved event to written text occur, the practices of moving and writing partner each other. And as emerging accounts about past bodies encounter the body of constraints that shape the writing of history, new narrative forms present themselves.

To choreograph history, then, is first to grant that history is made by bodies, and then to acknowledge that all those bodies, in moving and in documenting their movements, in learning about past movement, continually conspire together and are conspired against. In the process of committing their actions to history, these past and present bodies transit to a mutually constructed semiosis. Together they configure a tradition of codes and conventions of bodily signification that allows bodies to represent and communicate with other bodies. Together they put pen to page. Together they dance with the words. Neither historian's body nor historical bodies nor the body of history become fixed during this choreographic process. Their edges do not harden; their feet do not stick. Their motions form a byway between their potential to act upon and be acted upon. In this middle ground they gesture toward one another, accumulating a corpus of guidelines for choreographic signification as they go, making the next moves out of their fantasies of the past and their memory of the present.

Bodily musings

I can see them now, Clio and Terpsichore, costumed in their combat boots and high-top sneakers, their Lycra tights and baggy trousers, a leather jacket, a vest under which can be glimpsed unshaven armpits, perhaps even a bow tie or some plastic bananas as a hairpiece … I can feel them spinning, lurching, sidling and smashing up against one another, laughing knowingly as they wipe the sweat off foreheads and from the skin between lips and nose; in a standoff, carefully calculating the other's weight and flexibility, careening towards one another, rolling as one body and then falling apart, only to circle around for a fast-paced repartee, trading impersonations of past historians and choreographers they have inspired. Wickedly realistic details of one caricature set the other muse in motion. These simulated bodies pop out of theirs, a kinetic speaking-in-tongues, only to be displaced by other corporeal quiddities. Finally, they run out of steam, collapse on the ground, adjust a sock, scratch an ear. But these pedestrian gestures, infused with the natural reflexiveness of all muses, doubly theatricalized by the attentive gaze of the partner, commence yet another duet: the crossing of legs in response to the lean on an elbow, a tossing of hair in response to a sniffle. This duet rejuvenates itself endlessly. It has an insatiable appetite for motion.[4]

But where are they dancing, Clio and Terpsichore? in what landscape? what occasion? and for whom? No longer capable of standing in contemplative and gracious poses, no longer content to serve as the inspiration for what others create, these two muses perspire to invent a new kind of performance, the coordinates of which must be determined by the intersection of historiographies of dance and of body. But what will they claim as their dance's origin? How will they justify their new choreographic/scholarly endeavour?

Sifting through images of originary bodies, Clio and Terpsichore stumble upon an account of the origins of dance and also of rhetoric, the discipline that, after all, spawned that of history, iterated in the introductions to several handbooks on rhetorical practices written after the third century AD and up until the Byzantine period. These mytho-historic anecdotes focus on the city of Syracuse at a moment when the tyrants Gelon and Hieron rule with savage cruelty. In order to ensure total control over the populace, they forbid Syracusans to speak. Initially, citizens communicate with the rudimentary gestures of hand and head that index their basic needs. Over time, however, their gestural language, now identified as *orchestike*, or dance-pantomime, attains a communicative flexibility and sophistication that leads to the overthrow of the tyrants. In the elated confusion that follows, one citizen, a former adviser to the tyrants, steps forward to bring order to the crowd. Integrating gestural and spoken discourses, he organizes his arguments into an introduction, narration, argument, digression and epilogue, the fundamental structural categories of rhetoric, the art of public persuasion. In this account, the tyrant's eradication of speech – a levelling gesture that sweeps across public and private spaces – puts all citizens, male and female, those with expertise in logos and those who excel at chaos, on the same footing. From this common place, the rebellious bodies of the citizens slowly infuse movement with linguistic clout. They circulate around the tyrant, conspiring on a tacit and circumspect kinegraphy that not only indicates their expressive and physical needs but also a reflexive awareness of their predicament. Eventually, their collaborative subversion prevails, and the tyrant is overthrown. In this moment of political liminality *(and taking precisely the amount of time necessary to leap an epistemic fault)* the dancing body, forged in subversive communality, feeds/bleeds into the rhetorical body, a public and powerful figure. The reinstantiation of speech, however, does not return the community to speech as formerly practised.

Instead, the speaking body attains new eloquence, a new fascination, a new and seductive hold over its listeners.

What seems so promising about this story, beyond its delicious obscurity or its singular pairing of dance and rhetoric, as an originary pretext for Clio and Terpsichore's duet? They are not immediately sure, for it takes the two muses hours of negotiation (danced and spoken) to arrive at an interpretation they can agree upon: Clio initially refuses to believe that the rhetorical body, once originated, had retained any resonances of the dancing body. Terpsichore sulkily retreats into silence, gesturing with dignity and disdain the absolute untranslatability of her art. Clio, attempting to dialogue, praises the primordial status of dance, mother of all the arts. Terpsichore, infinitely bored by this guilt-ridden and misguided tribute, accuses Clio of inspiring only desiccated, static drivel. Now they're mad: they stomp; they shout; they hyperbolize; they posture; they pinch their faces, hunch their shoulders, and spit out the most absurd and hurtful provocations, then feign distress, victims of their own drama. But in the ensuing silence, the choreography of their combat in its full rhetorical glory stands out. Embarrassed by their excesses, but intrigued by the aesthetics of their anger, they cannot resist a candid glance at one another. Biting their lips to keep from laughing, they determine to continue their deliberations.

Terpsichore senses the need to rationalize choreography as persuasive discourse, and Clio realizes the need to bring movement and fleshiness into historiography. They both agree that they cannot help but admire the immense power in the resistive wariness of those bodies that have tangled with the demonic character of a tyrant. And they sense the strength of a choreographic coalition composed of multiple constituencies. They desire bodies capable of troping, that can render or depict, or exaggerate, or fracture, or allude to the world, bodies that can ironize as well as metaphorize their existence. Troping bodies do not merely carry a message or faithfully convey an idea, but also assert a physical presence, one that supports the capacity for producing meaning. Irresistibly, such bodies retain no authority over some transcendental definition of their being, but instead remain entirely dependent on their own deictic gestures to establish identity.

Clio and Terpsichore have watched this troping body emerge in their own collaborations. They believe in this body that fuses dance and rhetoric, but they also sense, just as the story predicts, its sinister potential. It can become powerful enough to sway other bodies, or even fix them in its hold. It cannot command such power if other bodies have learned the choreographic and rhetorical conventions through which meaning is conveyed. As long as every body works to renew and recalibrate these codes, power remains in many hands. But if any bodies allow this body of conventions to overtake them unawares, then the tyrannical body gains the upper hand.

Determined to keep such tyrants disembodied, *Clio and Terpsichore finish their coffee, roll up their sleeves, and begin to write (or is it dance?).*

Postscript

The claim for a writing–dancing body, formulated in response to political exigencies of this specific moment, dates itself in the kind of inscription it undertakes to make apparent. At another moment and given different political circumstances, the metaphor of a bodily tropology might well prove reactionary rather than resistive. At such a time Clio and Terpsichore might agree instead to reinvent a separation between body and writing so as to preserve the powers of both rhetoric and dance. In a world, for example, beyond script, one consisting only of screens of simulacra that invite us to don virtual reality gear and dive through ever-unfolding windows of images, what could give the body's presence or its vanishing urgency over other visions?

Notes

1 Roland Barthes opened up for consideration this approach to bodily writing most palpably through his attention to the physical circumstances surrounding his own profession as a writer in, among other writings, his autobiography (Barthes 1977).

2 The concept of kinaesthetic empathy is inspired by dance critic John Martin's conception of inner mimicry (Martin 1965).

3 The *Oxford English Dictionary* identifies two meanings for the archaic word 'theoric', one pertaining to the theoretical and the other to the performative. In resurrecting this term, I am trying to gesture in both directions simultaneously.

4 Cunningham's influence on this duet between Clio and Terpsichore is explicated more fully in my book *Reading Dancing: Bodies and Subjects in Contemporary American Dance* (Foster 1986).

28

DIFFERENTIATING PHENOMENOLOGY AND DANCE

Philipa Rothfield

Introduction

This paper is concerned with one kind of philosophical practice – phenomenology – and its ability to engage with kinaesthetic forms of corporeality. Its aim is to explore the extent to which phenomenological work can deal with questions of corporeal and kinaesthetic difference. Phenomenological philosophy has historically oriented itself towards questions of subjectivity, in particular through exploring self-world and subject–object relationships. Any extension of its thinking towards dancing will inevitably be concerned to explicate the subjective dimensions of movement and its perception. The lens of subjectivity offers a point of connection with movement practices through its felt dimension – the lived body.

However, the realm of subjectivity is no longer taken to furnish a ground of knowledge adequate in itself. As the many critics of consciousness argue, the subject is a false universal. This has implications for phenomenological thought which emerged well before the critiques of anti-humanism. The point is that the tendency towards universality which characterizes phenomenological thought represents a risk. The risk is that phenomenological analysis, in its universal incarnation, will fail to achieve the requisite generality. We have seen this occur more generally with respect to enlightenment discourses which covertly assume particular forms of gender, sexuality and ethnicity.

One response to such a danger, mooted by social theorist David Hoy and attributed to Merleau-Ponty, is to keep phenomenological description 'thin' (Hoy 1999: 7).[1] In this case, the risk of illegitimate universalization is minimized through the exercise of caution. The idea behind Hoy's proposition is to safeguard the phenomenological moment of analysis whilst juxtaposing a Foucauldian genealogical perspective. According to Hoy, it might be possible to impose Foucault's genealogical differentiations upon Merleau-Ponty's rather minimal account of subject–object relations within perception. Foucault functions to remind us that the 'putting into play' of universal structures is always socio-historically specific (Foucault 1984: 335). This sort of approach purports to retain a certain sort of universalism whilst recognizing a differential field of manifestation. There are two requirements according to this model. One, a valid, universal phenomenological analysis, and, two, an understanding of the factors which influence the putting into play of universal structures. These will differ according to the situation. If phenomenology were to make the envisaged contribution, then it would need to fulfil its universal promise however 'thinly'. To what extent is this possible? How plausible is it to develop a skeletal universalism which is nevertheless explicable in terms of historical complexity?

Phenomenology and difference

Merleau-Ponty's philosophy demonstrates a commitment to the view that *the world is refracted through our bodily sensibilities.* Although Merleau-Ponty recognized human corporeality as the means by which the world is understood, the whole relationship is articulated in the most general of terms: concerning *the* body rather than, for example, *this* body. The residual universalism of phenomenological analysis urges a breadth of analysis which is not always achieved. Consider the following examples, one concerned with phenomenological views of sexuality, the other, with phenomenological approaches to bioethics.

Although Merleau-Ponty's (1962) *Phenomenology of Perception* is generally pitched at a very abstract level, its attempt to give an account of the sexual character of human being can be said to exhibit the usual distortions of sexual indifference (Irigaray 1985: 69). Judith Butler (1989) has argued the case, criticizing Merleau-Ponty both for failing to specify the kinds of bodies and sexualities he was phenomenologically analysing and for the unacknowledged intrusion of his own sexually specific understanding of the matter. Butler's charge was that Merleau-Ponty did not consider *whose* bodies and *which* sexualities were at stake; nor did he acknowledge his own corporeal complicity in the way in which he viewed the subject. Thus, despite his intention to describe certain moments in the general structure of human, sexual being, Butler alleges that Merleau-Ponty's analysis was both partial and skewed.

Even the attempt to limit the scope of phenomenology to particular settings is liable to problems of difference. Phenomenological bioethics aims to analyse the experiential nuances of the doctor–patient exchange. It does so through rejecting the biomedical perspective as both objectifying the patient's body and undervaluing his or her corporeal experience of illness. Phenomenological bioethics values the patient's embodied understanding of the medical encounter as a crucial component in the medical exchange. The patient's perspective is said to be available to doctors because they share with patients a common basis of experience (Cassell 1985: 46).[2]

However, experiences of illness and even death vary. Jon Willis writes:

> ... the issue is not simply to modify elements of palliative care so
> that cultural differences in belief and practice are accommodated,
> but to recognise that different cultures 'do death' in different ways,
> and that institutions for the provision of palliative care are bound
> up in the 'way of dying' of the culture in which they originated.
>
> (Willis 1999: 427)

Willis's work addresses the particular needs of indigenous Australian central desert peoples. He argues that it is not possible to provide for what he
calls an 'acceptable death' unless that care recognizes and accommodates
the specific 'way of dying' of Australian Pitjantjatjara Aborigines as a cultural aspect of these peoples' lives. Willis's point is two-fold: firstly, that, in
the words of Ceres Victora, 'people know their bodily facts in different
ways' (Victora 1997: 170), and, secondly, that this needs to be recognized by
healthcare institutions. In Willis's view it is not possible to presume that
the one healthcare model can simply be tweaked so as to incorporate all
forms of difference. If Victora and other multicultural theorists are right,
there is no common corporeal basis for understanding which obtains in all
interactions between doctor and patient. If there is no shared corporeal
sense of understanding, then the 'exchange' of understanding between
patient and doctor cannot proceed from some common corporeal
denominator. The matter challenges the conception of a universal body as a
starting point for this kind of phenomenological analysis.

The situation is further complicated by the existence of institutional
norms which condition the medical encounter.[3] Dorothy Roberts (1996)
has drawn attention to the differential treatment women of colour receive
from doctors in the US compared with white women. Roberts found that
prejudicial treatment ensues from doctors' attitudes to their patients as well
as the institutional norms governing patient care. Gunaratnam (1997) has
also addressed the question of institutional norms by tracing the ways in
which culturally hegemonic understandings of order and good management
apply within palliative hospice care in the UK. Gunaratnam's work speaks
to the cultural and corporeal specificities of patients as distinct from their
doctors. It also strives to make visible the dominant cultural values
enshrined within medical institutions, and the ways in which these sites
contribute to ethnocentric forms of discrimination. Where there is a cultural, corporeal difference between the patient and the doctor/institution
which is characterized in terms of dominance, the patient is liable to suffer.
A phenomenological framework predicated upon an underlying sameness
between all peoples cannot deal with the impact of these differences.

What do these examples suggest regarding the plausibility of universal
thinness in relation to the phenomenological approach? The situation is not

one of logical impossibility.[4] There is nothing self-contradictory in the notion of a universal corporeal structure within phenomenological analysis. The question has more to do with what is at stake in the pursuit of which kind of analysis. In the case of phenomenological universalism, there is an ethical danger that corporeal forms of difference which occur within networks of domination will be elided; that the desire to achieve universality will blind itself to the discriminations performed in the name of sameness.[5] For example, Australian assimilation policies in the greater part of the twentieth century were used to justify taking Aboriginal children from their families with a view to erasing their blackness via forced relocation (Wilson 1997). Put bluntly, in the context of universalism, difference can manifest as a *problem*. Hoy imagined a skeletal phenomenological universalism able to be fleshed out in a differential historical manner. The concern expressed here is that universalism is liable to overstep its brief, that the *desire* to universalize is itself vulnerable to corruption.

There may be those who wish nevertheless to pursue the phenomenological enterprise as an 'unfinished project'.[6] In my view, a great deal depends upon its shape and form, that is, upon how that project would be constituted. In light of the many forms of social inequality inherent in social life, it appears that the universal impulse is all too readily co-opted towards hegemonic forms of utterance and appearance. In these instances, the universal becomes homogenized, and difference is thereby effaced according to dominant norms of articulation. A critical difference concerns how one approaches Merleau-Ponty's sense that the world is refracted through our bodily sensibilities. Is there one means by which refraction occurs or are there many? Whilst phenomenology could simply reassert its universalism, it seems to me that it has the potential to work through difference by approaching lived bodies according to their lived situation.[7] The resultant pluralization of the lived body would allow for the concept to stand as an index of differential corporeal circumstance – 'lived body' becoming lived bodies.

What if phenomenology were to relinquish the ideal of universalism, recast the lived body in pluralized terms, and aim instead for a regional series of understandings? The purpose of this paper is to see how that might occur in relation to one field, that of dance. This is neither an attempt towards a phenomenology of dance nor the positing of dance as an object of phenomenological knowledge. The intimacy of dance and phenomenology attempted here arises through the corporeality of this particular writing body, and is therefore inevitably informed by the author's kinaesthetic and corporeal understandings. As I will argue, the theorist's corporeality plays a part within phenomenological articulation.[8] It functions as a nexus for the development of phenomenological insight. But, like other realms of face-to-face, body-to-body relations, it is also a field of vulnerability. The descent of phenomenological discourse into the terrain of social and historical articulations is also its entrance into the ethical and political complications which characterize social life. The proposal to relinquish universalism in favour of complex specificity represents a shift towards the particular or, as Foucault would have it, towards the sense in which universal structures are taken to be inextricably bound up with the 'concrete determinations of social existence' (Foucault 1984: 335). The rejection of universalism is simultaneously a relinquishment of anthropological universals (Foucault 1994: 317).

In what follows, I attempt a modification of the phenomenological approach through reviewing its central moves. I shall approach phenomenological questions regarding dance via the work of Maxine Sheets-Johnstone. These issues will then be taken up via the notion of somatic attention as it emerges within ethnographic fieldwork. Somatic attention allows for a differentiated, cultural understanding of body-to-body relationships. The ensuing discussion will suggest that, although somatic attention is a way into understanding bodies as they are found within culture, it is also subject to the vicissitudes of power and dominance. The final part of this paper will be occupied with these questions as they relate to situations of kinaesthetic exchange.

The phenomenology of dance

Maxine Sheets-Johnstone's seminal work on dance and phenomenology, *The Phenomenology of Dance*, was an important contribution towards the field of dance scholarship (Sheets-Johnstone 1966). Sheets-Johnstone begins this work by stating:

> It is the lived experience which is of paramount significance. Through the lived experience we arrive at not only the sense of any particular dance, but also at the essence of dance.
>
> (Sheets-Johnstone 1966: 4)

According to Sheets-Johnstone, the lived experience of dance is immediate. It precludes reflection, criticism and evaluation. The phenomenological enterprise thereby requires the analyst to repeatedly return to the immediate encounter with dance, whether in the studio or in performance (ibid.: 7).

The disjunction between immediate, lived experience and the reflective realm is sustained throughout Sheets-Johnstone's analysis. Put simply, the action of reflection nullifies lived experience. This is because reflection transforms the experiential event into an object of thought. The dichotomy between immediate experience and reflective analysis resonates in the distinction between the implicit and the explicit, which is also at play in this work. The underlying factor is this: nothing is objectively constituted in lived experience. For dancer and audience alike, the lived experience only affords an implicit and not an actual awareness of anything in objective terms. Once awareness, for example of the body, becomes explicit, the moment of its experience evaporates. Thus, the audience could shatter the creation of dance by constituting the dancer as an object, by breaking down the action into its corporeal moments or by analysing it (ibid.: 38). Similarly, the dancer cannot reflect upon herself or her body apart from the dance. She is not conscious of creating dance, of the dance itself nor of her actions in creating it. If she construes her body as an object, she is not dancing (ibid.: 39).

The attempt to keep all objective thought implicit and not explicit occurs in part because of the view that phenomenology's aim is to characterize the subjective constitution of the world in lived experience. Only after that can we speak of the objective world. Sheets-Johnstone writes:

> To approach dance as a phenomenal presence is to presuppose nothing in advance of the immediate experience of dance. Because nothing is taken for granted, *dance is looked upon as a totality whose structures are intrinsic to it* [my emphasis]. To discover just what this global phenomenon is, constitutes the main project of this book.
>
> (ibid.: 8)

According to this view, dance offers itself as a singular object of phenomenological study. It is a holistic phenomenon having an essential structure. That essence appears throughout its manifestations. The essential structure of dance is to be discerned within experience, within the immediacy of lived experience. The phenomenological analyst has access to the essential character of dance through experience. His or her job is to pick out from (immediate) experience what is essential and therefore universal to the phenomenon. Inasmuch as dance expresses itself as a totality, its essential character persists through time. It persists historically as does the subject's ability to discern that essence.

To what extent is the phenomenological project independent of history? In the Preface to the 2nd edition of her book, written 13 years after its initial publication, Sheets-Johnstone noted the emergence of a new form of (post)modern dance, one which consists of movement *qua* movement. The existence of a contemporary form of dance, which is neither symbolic nor expressive, is at odds with certain assumptions made about dance in her book. Sheets-Johnstone's response is to signal the need for certain revisions in her work, some of which she alludes to in her own subsequent publications (ibid.: xii–xiv). Sheets-Johnstone could not possibly have known the turn that (post)modern dance was to take towards the kinaesthetic investigation of movement. What does this say about the 'totality' of dance? Is it 'essentially' unaffected by historical development? If so, then in principle Sheets-Johnstone could have provided for the subsequent turn towards kinaesthetic investigation; the job was flawed but feasible. On the other hand, if history impacts upon essence, then we are returned to the Foucauldian formulation: that the 'putting into play of these universal forms is itself historical' (Foucault 1984: 335). In such a case, each and every experience of structure will be particular, contingent and inextricably caught up in its conditions of articulation. According to this view, there is no moment where structure reveals itself. Rather, its 'appearance' is always affected by its conditions of articulation. This makes the task of its analysis difficult to say the least. How to draw out some essence when its appearance is inextricably historicized and it is experienced by a subject who is herself historical?

The belief that structure is consistently discernible over time parallels the view that the field of immanence is constituted apart from the transcendent. According to this position, the subjective realm of immanence is unsullied by an empirical reality which can be bracketed, thus allowing the essential characteristics of a phenomenon to shine forth in experience. Hence, the importance of protecting the immediate experience of dance from the polluting action of reflection, criticism and so forth. Postmodern, post-structural and post-colonial forms of discourse dispute the notion that the immediate is prior to and analytically separable from the influence of the external world, suggesting instead that the sphere of subjectivity is constituted through discursive and representational practices. They take the view that experience is 'always already' mediated, that there is no zone of immanence available to the subject. Taken corporeally, the point is that experience occurs in a body which is thoroughly marked by history. According to this position, Sheets-Johnstone's historical 'omission' was not a lack of eidetic vision on her part but an indication of the (limited) means by which movement is experienced. This concerns the ability of the phenomenological analyst to apprehend the global phenomenon of dance, by assuming what Donna Haraway (1988) calls 'the God's eye view'.

According to phenomenological doctrine, it doesn't matter who does the phenomenological investigation. The point is to focus upon phenomenal presence and its essential components rather than upon the specific orientation of the analyst. But experience occurs in a body. In a footnote to her own analyses, Sheets-Johnstone wrote:

> These terms describe the qualitative structures of the total illusion of force. As far as is known, they have never before been used. *They emanate from the author's own experience of movement as a revelation of force* [my emphasis].
>
> (Sheets-Johnstone 1966: 50)

As these remarks indicate, movement experience lies at the heart of phenomenological analysis. It is the corporeal means by which phenomenological insight can be gained. But, contrary to phenomenological belief, this experience is partial, depending upon its specific context of movement practice and corporeal engagement. Sheets-Johnstone's analysis grew out of her own experience of movement which occurred within a particular historical, intellectual and artistic context. That movement experience predated certain shifts in (post)modern dance – where an ethics and aesthetics of kinaesthetic investigation replaced expression-based forms of movement. To acknowledge these developments in the 2nd edition of the book is also to admit an inherent limit to the experiential basis of the work. Time is not indifferent to the corporeal sensibilities of the phenomenological analyst. These sensibilities are temporally, aesthetically and ethically located. They enable, or shape, certain kinds of approach, certain modalities of apprehension.

For example, Sheets-Johnstone (1966: 65) dismisses kinaesthetic response on the part of the observer as outside the proper, immediate experience of dance: 'Lived experience of the dance is ineffable: it has no kinaesthetic equivalents any more than it has any verbal equivalents'. The strength of this observation lies in the conviction that the immediate, lived experience of dance is concerned with symbolic form and virtual force.[9] However, once a field of practice is admitted which combines aesthetic value with kinaesthetic feeling, an observer steeped in or familiar with such an aesthetic may well apprehend, indeed privilege, the kinaesthetic register of movement. The point is that the experience of dance, so-called immediate and immanent, is shaped by the various fields in which it occurs, and the corporeal specificity of its observers. One way of putting this is to advocate Foucault's emphasis on the conditions, practices and relations which shape 'the historicity of forms of experience' (Foucault 1984: 334). Another might be to lay claim to the sense in which dance practices are governed by diverse imaginary fields which organize dancing bodies, choreographic practices and their corporealized perceptions. In either case, the view is that subjects and their lived experiences are situated within history.

Dance is not a phenomenal presence whose totality can be apprehended in the immediate and particular instance. It is a heterogeneous, emergent field of practice and performance which is encountered by a range of subjects in a variety of ways. Sheets-Johnstone's experience of movement as a revelation of force was embedded within a particular kinaesthetic context. This is not a deficiency but rather an indication of the corporeal means by which dance is known. In other words, experience is not a pure zone whose analysis can reveal a set of structures whose totality expresses the phenomenological essence of dance. But it is an important aspect of the practice of dancing and its perception. The experiential aspect of dance, which we might call its perception, is an embodied corporeal act, one which is embedded in the conditions of its articulation.

Somatic attention

The bodily act of perception has been described as a form of somatic attention by the ethnographer and cultural phenomenologist, Thomas Csordas. I have adopted and adapted the notion of somatic attention in order to differentiate the corporeal experience of movement. In its original context, it has been used to signify that there is no universal, invariant bodily self. The recognition that bodily subjects are always culturally specific does not merely apply to the cultural other as an object of ethnographic knowledge but also extends to the knowing subject. It pertains to the corporeal means by which a knowing subject apprehends the specificity of the other, via what Csordas calls the exercise of somatic attention. Somatic attention is characterized by Csordas (1993: 138) as those 'culturally elaborated ways of attending to and with one's body in surroundings that include the embodied presence of others'. There are two salient features of somatic attention: first, we attend with or through the body, and second, such a body's mode of attention is culturally, socially and intersubjectively informed. In other words:

> ... neither attending to nor attending with the body can be taken for granted but must be formulated as culturally constituted somatic modes of attention
>
> (Csordas 1993: 140).

For Csordas, having a culturally specific body means also that one perceives and understands the world in a culturally specific manner. I understand what is happening in my own and others' bodies through my own body. The cultural differentiation of somatic attention marks the descent of the phenomenological subject into the terrain of Foucauldian inscription:

> ... descent attaches itself to the body. It insinuates itself in the nervous system, in temperament, in the digestive apparatus: it appears in faulty respiration, in improper diets.
>
> (Foucault 1977b: 147)

The culturally specific body is not just an artefact, it is our means of experiencing the world, through involving the exercise of certain kinds of sense and sensibility (Csordas 1999: 155). The concept of somatic attention signals lived corporeality as the manner by which one person engages with another. Csordas acknowledges the role which somatic attention plays within embodiment-oriented, that is, phenomenological research. In his view, it implies that 'the body [is] now understood as a tool for research' (ibid.: 149).

In order to illustrate the exercise of somatic attention, Csordas draws upon his own fieldwork in relation to spiritual forms of healing, comparing the work of Catholic Charismatic healers with that of Puerto Rican spiritist mediums. Csordas depicts the bodily commonalities and differences according to which each group practises spiritual healing. Whilst nuanced in terms of the somatic attentions of the spiritual healers, no mention is made by Csordas of his own attentions. His monograph on charismatic healing, *The Sacred Self* (Csordas 1994), deals with people's somatic experiences as verbally reported rather than somatically apprehended on the part of the researcher.

The work of Robert Desjarlais, to whom Csordas refers, gives a better sense of the epistemological role of the researcher's own lived corporeality. Desjarlais studied healing amongst the Yolmo Sherpa people of Nepal, whilst apprenticed to a shamanic healer, Meme. Desjarlais wrote of his experiences of trance, healing ceremonies and everyday life over a period of eighteen months. Desjarlais claims that it is through living in the everyday manner of a people that one can come to understand their social and spiritual sensibilities, for the domain of cultural sensibility is to be found in everyday life:

> ... everyday actions are rooted in local sensibilities; this rootedness forces us to rethink how we talk of moralities, bodies, pain, healing and politics. For Yolmo wa, the aesthetic values that govern how a person dresses in the morning or talks with a neighbour constitute a tacit moral code, such that ethics and aesthetics are one. In Helambu, values of presence, balance and harmony are embodied, sensible ones, and thus, contribute to the force and tenor of human sentience. Yolmo sensibilities influence how and why villagers fall ill, how they heal, and what moments of pain and comfort feel like.
>
> (Desjarlais 1992: 248–9)

By sensible, Desjarlais means the corporeal and kinaesthetic sensibilities according to which Yolmo people live their daily lives. It includes 'how to eat a bowl of rice with style or greet an elder with grace'. It also embodies the rituals of drinking salt-butter tea, telling stories, warming oneself by the fire and smoking cigarettes. Desjarlais concludes that:

> By participating in the everyday life of a society distinct from one's own, an ethnographer confronts and slowly learns (often tacitly but always partially) patterns of behaviour previously unfamiliar to his or her body.
>
> (Desjarlais 1992: 19)[10]

These patterns of behaviour are consonant with the ethics, aesthetics and kinaesthetics of Yolmo life.[11]

The ethnographic scenario straddles situations of social and cultural difference with the ethnographer seeking to apprehend and find expression for the cultural other. The ethnographic divide is subject to differential power relations which lead to problems of representation as depicted by Gayatri Spivak (1985) in 'Can the subaltern speak?'. Their effect is to provide the ethnographer with a greater representational means by which to depict the cultural other. To that extent, the subaltern may never get to bring her somatic attentions to light except and insofar as the ethnographer represents them. It is no accident that Csordas's insights have tended towards the somatic modes of attention of the observed rather than those of the observer, that is, most of his ethnographic examples offer illustrations of the exercise of somatic attention in cultural others rather than indicate the somatic means by which the research itself was conducted. The danger of this situation is that differences in somatic attention may be missed. Who is to say whether a mode of corporeal attention is appropriately exercised in relation to its object, and who will approve the articulation of that apprehension?

Critical implications

We are now returned to Sheets-Johnstone's own corporeal attentions in relation to dance. If we no longer believe in the 'phenomenal presence' of the global phenomenon of dance, then the question of who perceives what and how comes to the fore. As does the question of their representational means. Inasmuch as the researcher's body is a site of investigation, that is, inasmuch as understanding is refracted through the researcher's own experiential and corporeal sensibilities, there is a problem of knowledge which does not attend Foucault's discursive, genealogical studies. This is the problem of the phenomenological subject, or, rather, the phenomenologist as subject. The phenomenologist's corporeality is the medium of investigation, at once a filter of data and the means of its revelation.

The implicit ambivalence of phenomenological corporeality is reminiscent of Derrida's reading of the *pharmakon* in Plato's work (Derrida 1981). Derrida's discussion centres upon an equivocation implicit in the notion of *pharmakon* which is elided if it is translated simply as remedy apart from its other meanings such as 'poison', 'recipe', 'drug' or 'philtre' (ibid.: 71). On the one hand, phenomenological corporeality is a means to the epistemological terrain of intercorporeal understanding. This is its role as remedy, the knowing subject as facilitating the process of phenomenological analysis. On the other, it also represents a limit, according to which the object of analysis may be known. This is the sense in which phenomenological corporeality is inevitably a prejudice, a form of partiality, a drug or poison.

Representational approaches to dance may wish to avoid the problem through bypassing the minefield of subjective apprehension. Such an approach would occupy itself with the conditions of emergence of phenomenological corporeality, the shaping of its sensibilities, rather than its exercise. But subjective apprehension is part and parcel of dance appreciation, observation, criticism and evaluation. It is important to pay attention to the exercise of corporeal sensibility, particularly when that sensibility is placed in a position of authority over other expressions of kinaesthetic value. For example, funding bodies depend upon expert testimony and judgement for their decision making. This is not reducible to matters of individual perception (that is, mere taste) but concerns the authorization of certain *forms* of perception to formulate critical judgements. Who gets to decide what is good work, and on what basis? What conditions the perceptions of 'expert' judges? If we recognize that kinaesthetic values are inherent in the exercise of somatic attention, then the question arises regarding the attribution of value to one form of perception over and above another.

Nowhere is this felt more than where there is more than one kind of work at stake, that is, where a situation of (kin)aesthetic difference exists. For example, in Australia, ballet occupies a primary and definitive position with regards to dance training, funding and appreciation. Its dominance is well established within institutional practices, audition criteria, curriculum development and what Dempster (1999: 16) calls, 'the perceptual disposition of the dancer'. Many Australian dance training institutions audition via ballet although their syllabus allows for subsequent specialization. This form of gate-keeping presumes that balletic skill underlies all dancerly facility. In order to acquire state funding, dancers and choreographers are also required to demonstrate dance ability. In a situation where access to the lineage of modern and postmodern dance is limited and offshore, ballet has come to occupy a position of dominance (ibid.). There are many instances in which a balletic sensibility had functioned to dismiss modern dance practice as not dance, unskilled and lacking in virtuosity because it is blind to the kinaesthetic values which underpin that practice – a blindness which derives from its own kinaesthetic specificity.

The effect of this scenario is that there are those in positions of critical authority who are unable to recognize certain forms of postmodern dance practice which they perceive as 'not dance'. The aesthetic values of muscularity, control and extension inherent in ballet have become normalized according to a somatic mode of attention which fails to recognize its own specificity. Power relations thereby underwrite the ability of certain perceptual sensibilities to function as universal and impersonal. As Libby Dempster writes:

> It [ballet] marks deeply not only the neuromusculature but also the perceptual disposition of the dancer. As Russell Dumas has remarked; 'Techniques like ballet put railway tracks through the

sensibility'. Dumas' point is that there is an intimate connection between perception and practice.

(ibid.)

The connection between perception and practice is important, for it signals the sense in which kinaesthetic sensibilities are embedded in forms of practice. This is Desjarlais's point about the link between the embodied rituals of everyday life, ethics and aesthetics. It also refers to the sense in which the practice of dance-funding decision making is complicit with particular kinds of corporeal sensibility. Here, in relation to expert testimony and judgement, it is a question of applying a specific framework of perception as if it were universal and unmarked by particularity.

The critical issue is that kinaesthetic values can become institutionalized, remain unconscious of their specificity, whilst functioning as the measure of dance literacy. The Australian choreographer Russell Dumas is particularly sensitive to the dominance of balletic values in Australia for it affects the way in which his work is perceived and evaluated:

> I believed it was important to show work there because it was really only in New York where there were critics who could recognize a lineage from Trisha Brown and Twyla Tharp ... I mean you worked in Australia, you did performances. The work was seen by five hundred people who usually had no ability to contextualize it. So the work was not perceived in the context of the traditions which informed it
>
> (Dumas 1998: 1–2)

Dumas's being informed in this context means working in both Brown's and Tharp's companies. It means dancing with those choreographers, rubbing up against them as it were, emulating and embodying those specific kinaesthetic values which constitute their work. This incorporates what counts as choreographic work, through what forms of investigation, sedimentation and modification, according to what kinds of ethical, corporeal relationship.

The above example does two things: it firstly fleshes out the sense in which perception may be embedded within a particular field of practice. In this case, it refers to the 'perceptual disposition' associated with classical ballet, its particular combination of kinaesthetic, muscular and spectacular value. Secondly, it looks to the 'application' of that particular sensibility with regard to fields of practice which are not part of the classical tradition, to its blind spots and their consequences. This latter state of affairs is not confined to an Australian context.

Francis Angol, a UK-based artist making contemporary African dance, also referred to the perceptual tendencies of audiences. Angol spoke at a one-day conference for artists working in African, Caribbean and African-American dance forms, *Ad Lab*, held at Chisenhale Dance Space in conjunction with the Association of Dance of the African Diaspora, in September 2003. Having shown a section of a work-in-progress, Angol lamented the fact that his distinctive jumping movements were perceived as *jetés* with some arms on top. My own experience of watching Angol dance was to observe an arched spine with incredibly deep hip flexion leading into jumping. The flow, rhythm and energy of the movement was unfamiliar, very possibly having origin or reference to certain African dance forms. Although the audience was told by one speaker (Funmi Adewole) that rhythm is central to African dance, and that, once established, its absence is also pertinent, I could not ascertain what rhythms may have been referenced in their absence nor the energetic consequences of these nuances. The problem expressed by several participants was that people lacking in literacy were not aware of that lack but exercised their own kinaesthetic sensibilities mixed with certain essentializing notions of African dance. These problems were also felt to exist at the level of state funding, evaluation and criticism. The lack of literacy in African dance in this context meant that many nuances were not just lost but were distorted.[12] Put generally, these difficulties represent the danger of reducing kinaesthetic difference to the conditions of visibility of the observer's mode of somatic attention.

The above discussion serves to illustrate the sense in which the perception of dance is inherent in practice, embedded in institutions and liable to hegemonic forms of normalization and domination. Both situations represent the occlusion of a dance practice by the imposition of a different and dominant kinaesthetic sensibility. The elaboration of kinaesthetic sensibility in relation to context, perception and practice signifies its differential 'descent' into those intricate modes of constitution that mark particular forms of work. This is the experiential level at which modes of perception, sense and sensibility take shape. Merleau-Ponty's term for this, the lived body, is a portal to a critical formulation of the phenomenological enterprise, one which requires a hermeneutics of suspicion, an ethics and politics of representation as well as a careful elaboration of its own forms of practice.

Post-structuralist work on the body is more likely to cite the social, cultural and historical processes which *shape* bodily experience, than to dwell upon their felt results. And, whilst Foucault may well enunciate the workings of society on the individualized body, we still want to know what it's like to live as that historicized, normalized, bodily subject, if only to test whether experience bears out genealogy. Phenomenology signals a high regard for the experiential aspect of corporeality. The terrain of lived corporeality may not be epistemologically reliable – its 'findings' remain provisional, its authority limited. But it is ontologically pertinent. Dance is one of those realms of ontological pertinence. Phenomenology represents a field, a domain, an axis of corporeality framed in relation to subjectivity. The differentiation of that field represents an epistemological complication, a reformulation, a multiplication. Not a rejection of its adequacy, just a sense of its being slightly out of reach, requiring a stretch, a shift of weight, a roll, perhaps a fall.

Notes

1 The term 'thin description' was originally used by the anthropologist Clifford Geertz in an attempt to distinguish between general statements (thin descriptions) and culturally loaded statements (thick descriptions). See Geertz (1973).

2 According to Cassell, 'Persons taking histories should use themselves and their own experiences with their bodies as a reference for what they hear.' (Cassell 1985: 46); see also (Toombs 1992: 98).

3 This has bearing upon Willis's second point regarding the functioning of healthcare institutions.

4 Lyotard (1984) did not 'prove' the sceptical turn toward grand narratives, nor did Foucault 'deduce' the impossibility of trans-historical objectivity. Foucault worked through engaging in specific historical analyses, showing the conditions of emergence of particular forms of 'objectivity' and their truth-effects. In other words, the postmodern assault on universalism has generally proceeded either by pursuing questions of difference or by claiming indifference towards totalization.

5 It is possible to characterize this kind of practice in relation to logo- or phallo-gocentrism, see (Grosz 1989: xix–xx).

6 Such was Habermas's response to Lyotard's critique of universal 'narratives', see (Habermas 2001).

7 By 'situation' is meant the contextualization and diverse manifestation of lived bodies.

8 Deleuze notes: 'A theorising intellectual, for us, is no longer a subject, a representing or representative consciousness ... Who speaks and acts? It is always a multiplicity, even within the person who speaks and acts ... Representation no longer exists; there's only actions – theoretical and practical actions which serve as relays and form networks' (Deleuze and Foucault 1977: 206–7).

9 The terms 'symbolic form' and 'virtual force' hail from the work of Suzanne Langer. For a detailed discussion of their historical and kinaesthetic significance, see (Dunagan 2005).

10 Cf. also Bateson's notion of 'kinaesthetic socialisation' (referred to in Desjarlais 1992).

11 For example, Desjarlais describes the way Yolmo men smoke cigarettes in muddy fields, crouching on their haunches, cupping burning embers with their hands. For Desjarlais, this practice and its postures resonates with Yolmo views about the body as a compact system of energies. Similarly, Yolmo people value what Desjarlais calls kinaesthetic attentiveness, being in the sensible present, rather than dwelling in the past or future. The importance of corporeal attentiveness is reflected in the way in which people feel themselves to be unwell through its absence.

12 In Angol's case and over the course of the conference it emerged that contemporary African dance was assumed to involve a conjunction of (contemporary dance) + (traditional African dance), an essentializing gesture which

confines all innovative possibility to Western art forms. Angol explained that after 15 years working in an African dance form, he felt able to move that work into a field of experimentation, not import a bit of London contemporary into a 'traditional' lexicon. Adewole also spoke on the history of Nigerian dance practices which had to adapt in relation to secularization, urbanization and nationalist agendas, thus contesting any simple notion of 'tradition'.

29

DANCE STUDIES IN THE INTERNATIONAL ACADEMY

Genealogy of a disciplinary formation

Jens Richard Giersdorf

Prologue

For the past thirteen years, I have been travelling to the United States from my home country of Germany, first as a graduate student in California and later as a professor in New York. Every time I pass through immigration I am asked a series of questions regarding my final destination and my occupation. The latter always leads to some confusion because my accent seems to turn 'dance history' into 'dentistry'. Forced by phonetics to use the term 'dance studies', I inevitably embark on an explanation of what 'dance studies' might be. Usually I avoid a long-winded, defensive clarification by comparing dance studies with one of its neighbouring disciplines: 'It is like art history, just writing about dance instead of paintings.' That does the trick, but it leaves a foul taste in my mouth.

Dance permits and requires a different set of theoretical and practical tools for its study than for instance a painting or a sculpture. I was a dancer at a time and in a country in which dance and other performative forms were powerful regulators of public discourses, as well as tools to resist censorship. I embarked on a career in dance studies because I wanted to think about the constructive powers of a form I appreciated as a practitioner. I also wanted to understand the relationship of the political to dance's aesthetic principles and techniques.

The collapse, in 1990, of my country, the German Democratic Republic (GDR), and with it the socialist educational system in which I had begun my studies in Leipzig, forced me to move to two countries that had a firmer history of dance studies in the academy and that consequently dominated international discourse in our discipline. At the University of California, Riverside, where I studied for my PhD, I found myself surrounded by an eclectic group of international dance scholars. Their diverse comprehension of dance and the theoretical focus of the programme at Riverside broadened my studies, by including considerations of identity constructs and cultural studies. My subsequent employment at the University of Surrey, Guildford, in Great Britain exposed me anew to a nationally regulated dance curriculum and posed new questions about dance studies as a discipline inside a national academic discourse. My recent transition to a small liberal arts college in New York City with a vocationally oriented dance department has heightened my awareness of the schism between vocational training and academic discourse inside dance departments. The following reflection on these stations of my trajectory in the academy offers a dialogue on the function of dance studies in the increasingly international and corporatised university and college education, its disciplinary and institutional structure and status, and its relationship to other disciplines.

Introduction

Among the presentations during the First National Ballet Conference in East Germany in 1977, a talk by Kurt Petermann, the late director of the GDR Dance Archive, stands out. Unlike the other presentations, there is no discussion of ballet practice. Rather, Petermann advocates the creation of dance studies as a discipline inside the academy (Petermann 1980). The strategic placement of Petermann's elaborations amid presentations on the development of ballet at this highly visible conference in East Germany revealed the growing importance of Petermann's effort to the East German government. Nine years later, the first students were admitted into the *Tanzwissenschaft* diploma course at the College of Performing Arts in Leipzig, creating the first dance studies course in Germany. Similar dance studies programmes launched around this time in the United Kingdom and the United States. This concurrent emergence of dance studies in the international academy begs the question, what social and academic developments gave rise to the disciplinary inquiry into dance? How does dance studies situate itself in relation to national, institutional and disciplinary demands? Answering these questions will help position dance studies in shifting academic landscapes and possibly provide suggestions for future developments.

Addressing these questions requires a dialectical approach that considers the relationship between intra-disciplinary and inter-disciplinary concerns. As such, I discuss for dance studies what Foucault calls the 'discursive formations' of disciplinary objects and sub-fields in conjunction with Bourdieu's understanding of the academic habitus of a discipline for the production and sustaining of cultural capital (Foucault 1972, Bourdieu 1988) in larger academic and national structures. My transnational position points at the transition from nationally demarcated knowledge production to an increasingly globalised vision for dance studies.

An important part of this negotiation is the increasing corporatisation of university education through its disengagement from the production of national and humanist subjectivity (Readings 1996). Bill Readings describes various shifts in the function and focus of university education, leading to the currently dominant corporate structure. Readings defines the modern university coming into being through the production of knowledge based on Immanuel Kant's concept of reason (Kant 2005). Kant's departure from empirical knowledge and towards an understanding of knowledge as a form of critical reflection on its own production paved the way for Friedrich Schiller and Wilhelm von Humboldt's concepts of education, leading to *Bildung* as the cornerstone of university education.[1] The German idealist process of *Bildung* provides the humanist subject with the capacity to interpret and influence social structures. The main component for such *Bildung* is, in Schiller's terminology, *ästhetische Erziehung* (aesthetic education) as a regulatory perspective and object of education (Schiller 2000). It is regulatory because culture functions as a controlling mechanism in human development to avoid negative side effects, such as the destruction of nature or civilization. Culture in this discourse is nationally demarcated and as a result universities (and, in many European countries, theatre) are major state institutions supporting the construction of national identification and the bourgeois citizen as national subject.

Readings sees a waning of this role with the erosion of nations through globalisation and argues that universities are turning into global corporations. His view is confirmed by current analyses of the growing reliance on adjunct and student labour (Berry 2005, Bousquet 2008, Aronowitz 2000), labour disputes for the acknowledgement of graduate students as employees in the University of California system in 1998 and national strikes in England regarding adjustment of faculty salaries to national inflation in 2006. These signal the erosion of the tenured professor's position as a personification of university culture and a move towards administrative power – a shift that impacted many disciplines through reduced funding, a product-oriented concentration on excellence and assessments of learning outcomes, and a focus on education as career development and not on the process of learning. I situate my discussion of the three graduate programmes in dance studies in relation to this transition from the university as a national institution whose mission is *Bildung* to a global corporation concerned with accountability.

To understand the impact of this shift and the formation of these programmes in relation to the differing national and academic structures, I compare the *Tanzwissenschaft* programme in Leipzig with the Dance Studies curriculum at the University of Surrey, Guildford, and the Dance History and Theory curriculum at the University of California, Riverside. The three programmes share a pioneering effort in establishing dance studies as an independent academic – and decisively theoretical – discipline. My main concern here is the evocation of disciplinary genealogies in the Foucaultian sense that highlights the tensions between existing discourses

(Foucault 1984). I am interested in establishing the national and disciplinary contexts of a programme and considering how a programme structured itself in relation to its matter of inquiry: dance, choreography and corporeality. All three programmes share a focus on dance and a struggle to define themselves in relation to other disciplinary discourses and the way dance was studied previously; their different visions for dance studies as an academic discipline makes them constructive case studies for intra-disciplinary and inter-disciplinary concerns in dance studies.

The programmes in Leipzig, Surrey and Riverside championed archivisation, analysis and choreography, respectively. These foci were articulated by the founding figures of these departments, yet they were also determined by a corresponding struggle for a national identity, the rethinking of nationality in a post-colonial world, and the altered understanding of national and other identity constructs in a globalising economy. The timing and scholarly agenda of these programmes make them an interesting case study because they allow an understanding of issues specific to the discipline of dance studies, yet they are also indicative of disciplinary discourses in academia and society. There are many other programmes, visions and individual attempts to define dance studies in these three countries and elsewhere. My focus on these three programmes neither tries to erase these other valuable discourses nor set them up as antagonistic to these three approaches. Rather, my essay should be read in relation to other analyses and should be seen as opening a dialogue with them.

The focus on the three programmes situates the investigation in the 1980s and 1990s, which allows for an understanding of shifts in dance studies in relation to changes in academic institutions. Such contemporary histories of dance studies can be analysed in relation to earlier developments of dance education in academia and performance culture. A body of valuable literature describes the beginning of dance education in the three national contexts (Adshead 1981; Barthel and Artus 2007; Gitelman 2003; Hagood 2000; McFee 1992, 1999; Ross 2000; Tomko 1999; Winkler and Jarchow 1996). Physical education, modern dance, women's liberation and the hygiene movement were important influences on the development of dance studies. They laid the groundwork for existing divisions of intellectual and manual labour as a central aspect of dance education. An investigation into these divisions of labour has to be extended towards rethinking the split between vocational- or conservatory-style training on the one hand and a humanities-based exploration, in the sense of *Bildung*, on the other. The split between 'practice' and 'theory', which occurred differently in all three countries, originates in part in the nineteenth- and twentieth-century history of education, especially in a transformation of the university that geared some institutions of higher education towards professional training.

Germany kept the distinction between universities that provide *Bildung* and the *Fachhochschulen* providing vocational training. Contemporary professional dance training still occurs mostly in conservatories. The British system distinguished universities from polytechnics and conservatoires as well yet dissolved some of the distinctions with the transformation of polytechnics into universities. Depending on the focus of a particular department, dance departments in Great Britain often have a more equal balance between studio classes and classroom instruction, yet there are still vocational institutions or conservatories almost solely focused on professional training (Adshead 1991). These conservatories have established partnerships with university programmes to gain degree-granting rights. The United States, which took British educational structures and German disciplinary concerns as models, introduced dance through teacher training and physical education (Hagood 2000: 19–101). Yet most contemporary university dance departments in the United States aim to train the dancer, choreographer, pedagogue and/or administrator.[2] In these departments, dance studies positions itself in service to this main objective.

This hierarchy between the manual labour of training and the intellectual labour of theorisation/historisation is more complex than it appears. Training is intellectual labour and an increased attention to the physicality of theorisation has challenged the ephemeral nature of thought (Foster 1995). The category of labour in relation to dance incorporates ludic and aesthetic considerations (Franko 2002: 2). Yet, when dance training is situated in universities or colleges, it often communicates only to a certain extent in technical or scientific terminologies and establishes itself more often in descriptive categories, such as excellence or competitiveness. Thus training-oriented dance departments struggle to prove that their applied knowledge is economically beneficial for a professional career while also justifying their place in the university structure that focuses on *Bildung*.

Similarly, vocational dance departments often define themselves in opposition to the seemingly theoretical educational value of dance studies curricula, unless they are structured in service of the dance training – which in most cases takes shape as traditional dance history or dance ethnography courses (Manning 2006). Most notable is the way the historical and the cultural situate themselves in relation to dance practice. Traditional dance history objectifies dance as a product, whereas cultural investigations are able to consider the practices of choreographing and dancing. So-called cultural investigation in dance might also include a self-reflexive integration of choreographic structures into its methodologies. Such practice could potentially challenge the division between dance education as *Bildung* and vocational dance training, something that dance history as it exists in many dance departments cannot. Dance studies programmes – educating future professors for vocational departments – need to address this issue; the Leipzig, Surrey and Riverside took different routes.

Archivisation, analysis and choreography – the three approaches of dance studies in Leipzig, Surrey and Riverside respectively – are also methodologies in dance studies. However, I am not providing an investigation of methodologies and methods in dance studies. Such work has been done in all three national contexts (Dils and Albright 2001; Foster 1986; Adshead 1981, 1988; Carter 1998; Buckland 1999b; Brandstetter and Klein 2007). I am interested in the three programmatic visions as overarching approaches that determine the methodologies and methods used in each institution. The 'discursive formations' articulating these visions are in no way complete, logical and chronological but instead define 'a field in which formal identities, thematic continuities, translations of concepts, and polemical interchanges may be deployed' (Foucault 1972: 126–7). It is important to understand the tensions between these different approaches and institutional/national structures to envision possible directions and strategies for the future of our discipline.

Theaterhochschule 'Hans Otto' Leipzig

Kurt Petermann founded the dance archive in Leipzig in 1957 primarily as a collection of folk dance material. This focus aligned itself with the socialist government's effort to utilise concepts of folk for the creation of a uniquely East German national identity. Founded in 1949, the GDR struggled to distinguish itself as a decisively socialist, yet distinctly 'German', nation. Folk material from geographical areas inside the East German territory provided socialism with a much-needed localised connotation. The folk, and hence folk dance, foregrounded Marxist–Leninist definitions of cultural production by establishing the people as the most important productive force behind any artistic output (Giersdorf 2008).

This utilisation of folk extended early-twentieth-century anthropological and archival projects in Germany and France. As Inge Baxmann shows in her research on the Archives Internationales de la Danse, founded in 1931, such a focus on the collection of native and foreign movement forms went hand-in-hand with an extensive theorisation of choreography's social impact on, and reflection of, different cultural structures (Baxmann and Cramer 2005: 17). This approach to archivisation as living knowledge and theorisation with an emphasis on national identity determined other archival projects throughout Europe.

The dance archive in Leipzig extended its collection into other forms of dance in order to provide an understanding of the entire socialist society that was struggling to define itself. The archive documented larger ballet companies, amateur dance performances and national as well as international dance competitions. Collections from the endowments of famous dancers, choreographers and dance historians, such as Mary Wigman, Rudolf von Laban, Gret Palucca, the controversial dance critic and scholar Fritz Böhme and the folk dance scholar Erich Janietz, extended the collection. Archival publications under Petermann's editorial guidance included the *Documenta Choreologica* – reprints of historical dance literature – and a comprehensive *Dance Bibliography*. The bibliography amassed information on every publication in the German language on dance from the fifteenth century to 1963, the year of the bibliography's inauguration. The structure of the *Dance Bibliography* speaks to the all-encompassing endeavour and, at the same time, emphasises the preservationist focus by freely mixing categories defined by kind of publication, kind of dance, contexts for dance and contributing elements of dance productions, with dance history.

Petermann's 1977 vision for a dance studies curriculum in East Germany emphasised the preservationist endeavour as well, yet he aligned it with other disciplines and thus followed the model established by the Archives Internationales de la Danse.[3] Evoking Schiller's famous statements on the importance of history in education, Petermann set out to establish *Tanzwissenschaft* as one of the main tools for an 'objective understanding' of social structures (Petermann 1980: 50). He lamented the exclusion of dance studies from this intellectual project and cited the historical reasons for this exclusion: dance, in his words, is 'an oral culture' (ibid.: 49). Still, he demanded that *Tanzwissenschaft* move beyond a simple historical and aesthetic consideration of movement. Petermann divided *Tanzwissenschaft* into three areas: fundamental studies of dance, historic subjects and choreology. The main problem with dance for Petermann is its non-materiality and his efforts were geared toward the construction of a tangible object, which then could be categorised and stored for future analysis.

Peterman offered three options for the establishment of *Tanzwissenschaft* in the academy. He favoured the one that would see *Tanzwissenschaft* as a specific area of study within the department of choreography at the School of Performing Arts in Leipzig. In his opinion, this combination would allow a strong connection between training and research. Petermann didn't live to see the first students enrol in the new course in 1986; he died in 1984. Yet his understanding of *Tanzwissenschaft* as an academic discipline, modelled after German disciplinary structures and in the service of the preservation of dance, was reflected in the curriculum of the *Tanzwissenschaft* programme in Leipzig.

The curriculum engaged with an ongoing debate about the cultural status, pedagogy and preservation of *Ausdruckstanz* (German modern dance) in East Germany. An increasing number of dance practitioners pressured the government to preserve Palucca's – and *Ausdruckstanz*'s – contribution to dance in East Germany and socialist society in general. The founding of the *Tanzwissenschaft* curriculum at Leipzig, with considerable input from modern dance, was supposed to create scholars qualified to notate and archive the waning *Ausdruckstanz* tradition for future generations in East Germany and thus preserve the national culture.

To cultivate a significant knowledge of dance techniques, *Tanzwissenschaft* students in Leipzig were grouped with students in choreography and pedagogy tracks. Thus, when I started the *Tanzwissenschaft* course in 1988, we trained for nearly two years in ballet, modern dance, German and Hungarian folk dance, medieval dance, improvisation and jazz dance. In addition we had to take classes in performance analysis, *Kinetographie*, the history of ballet, *Ausdruckstanz* and modern dance, dance criticism and *Tanztheater*, as well as serving as dramaturgical assistants for one semester at one of the main dance companies. Music education took up another sizable chunk of the curriculum, with music theory and specific courses on the history and theory of ballet music, as well as introduction to composition, piano, music analysis and aesthetics. Dance and music education was supplemented by Marxist–Leninist philosophy, psychology, cultural studies and aesthetics, as well as art history. Additional classes in theatre studies were historical in orientation.

Overall, the curriculum focused on the accumulation of empirical knowledge and training in dance, with the goal of providing the dance scholar with the information and methods necessary for understanding dance as a finished product. Classes in improvisation and aesthetics raised epistemological concerns in relation to dance and interrogated methods and methodologies regarding dancing and choreographing as processes. This focus on the process of dancing and choreographing, and with it an attempt to utilise dance practice as a structural device, eventually shifted more into the centre of the curriculum. With the opening of the Berlin Wall and the end of the GDR as a national entity – and the erasure of the East German educational structure – West German educational standards affected our course of study. The prescribed curriculum changed into a modular approach. We moved away from the choreography and pedagogy curriculum into theatre studies.

This meant a stronger exposure to Rudolf Münz's work on theatricality and, with it, a utilisation of theatrical practice for the historicisation and theorisation of theatre (Münz 1989). Münz defines theatricality as a relationship between four different occurrences of theatre in society. The first occurrence is the theatre as an institution with its historical elements, such as location of theatre and its buildings, approaches to acting, costumes, stage designs and dramatic texts, if available. This was complemented by a survey of theatre of the everyday.[4] To understand and expose these two occurrences of theatre – especially the often-disguised theatre of the everyday – as utilised by dominating power structures, one needs to consider what Münz calls 'anti-theatre'. This is theatre that is deliberately artificial, and Münz uses the examples of *comedia dell'arte* and the harlequin to understand the purposeful visibility of representation in 'anti-theatre'. 'Anti-theatre' reveals theatre as artificial representation by emphasising the theatrical apparatus-technique, role-playing, mask – as commonly disguised elements in institutional theatre and in the theatre of the everyday. Finally, one also needs to consider any prohibition or censorship of theatre (Münz 1989: 70).

Münz's definition of theatricality as a relationship between these four occurrences provides a theorisation of relations between theatrical practice and social systems similar to that provided by US 'performance studies'. Münz moves beyond a simple broadening of theatre into other realms of society by demanding that the methodologies for the study of all four occurrences of theatre have to be rethought in dialogue with specific practices. This avoids a construction of theatre as an object of study and shifts the focus to processes and practices that denaturalise theatre. The shift also rethinks established academic hierarchies in which a tangible object in the form of a score or written drama takes precedence over seemingly ephemeral practices, such as choreography or improvisation.

Exposure to Münz's denaturalisation of theatre through the display of its artificiality and an emphasis on everyday theatricality allowed us to question the preservationist focus of our previous *Tanzwissenschaft* curriculum. Münz rethought theatre, which in its institutional form was one of the main vehicles of a bourgeois German national identity. Archivisation of national culture in *Tanzwissenschaft* likewise supported the creation of a distinct East German national identity. Exposure of both theatre and archivisation as part of an ideological state apparatus forced me to rethink Petermann's approach to *Tanzwissenschaft* and to look for alternative models for dance studies in the academy. My employment at the University of Surrey in England provided me with an alternative national model.

University of Surrey

In *The Study of Dance* Janet Lansdale addresses the difference between theorising dance and dancing: 'The person who develops theoretical structures which underlie the process of studying dance has an aim which is broader than "how to do a plié" ' (Adshead 1981: xiv).[5] Throughout her career, Lansdale has maintained that dance is an object of academic investigation. The distinction between dance theorisation and practice informed dance analysis and education in Britain and internationally; it contributed to the creation of dance studies as an independent discipline in the United Kingdom with clear disciplinary boundaries.

The Study of Dance, in conjunction with the publication *Dance History: A Methodology for Study* co-edited by Lansdale and June Layson (Adshead-Lansdale and Layson 1983), became guiding texts for and chronicles of the establishment of dance studies in the UK. *Dance Analysis: Theory and Practice* co-authored and edited by Lansdale (Adshead 1988)[6] determined the theoretical focus of dance studies at the University of Surrey and – occasionally dominating competing visions – in the UK.

The Study of Dance provides a history of the development of the fields of dance and dance studies in the United Kingdom; it also establishes

Lansdale's focus on epistemological concerns in dance studies. She defines an academic discipline through the coherent collection of ideas, objects and/or experiences which justify interest and close examination.

> This examination might be theoretical (in making statements about), practical (in learning how to make, create or perform) and/ or evaluative (in learning how to criticise, appraise, make judgements about). A discipline with these features contains notions of standards applicable to understanding theoretical structures and revealed in the ability to apply principles of procedure in practice, and in making judgements within the framework of the activity.
>
> (Adshead 1981: 11).

Applying this definition of a disciplinary field to dance, Lansdale translates the investigation of ideas, objects and experiences into the categories of making (choreography), performing and appraising (appreciating) dance (Adshead 1981: 78). Choreography incorporates the ability to create dances and the knowledge of underlying principles of dance production. Performance is defined as 'skill involved in bringing the dance into existence' (techniques) and the ability to interpret a given choreography (ibid.: 81). Appreciation means critical enquiries such as 'description, analysis, interpretation, and evaluation' (ibid.: 82). Lansdale envisions the execution of all three categories both in 'theoretical studies' and 'practical demonstrations'. Finally, she situates her inquiry in a historical, spatial and social context, which allows her to propose models for establishing dance studies as an academic discipline in the British academy.

Lansdale emphasises that a dance form itself determines how it should be studied (ibid.: 108). As simple as this statement may seem, it nevertheless clearly defines dance studies as its own discipline governed by its object of investigation. Thus, following Lansdale, approaches to the disciplinary enquiry have to engage not only with the content of dance as a social, ritual or artistic form, and with their historical and spatial contexts, but also must mirror the structure of dance in its differing aspects and manifestations. The importance of this position becomes clearer in Lansdale's opening to *Dance Analysis*, in which she states that: 'a satisfactory analysis which starts from the dance has yet to be fully worked out' (Adshead 1988: 13). She establishes dance analysis as the 'central core' of the emerging dance studies discipline, which, in 1988, existed at BA, MA and PhD level in Britain (ibid.: 6). Other disciplinary discourses, such as anthropology, history, psychology and sociology contributed to an understanding of dance's place and function in a social context. Yet, as Lansdale argues, 'a deep and informed response to *the dance itself*' was still missing (ibid.: 6, emphasis in the original) and with it an 'understanding of the making of the dance and the results of that process – the dances as objects in their own right, to be appreciated for their own sake'. Lansdale sees this as a 'refining of the skills of appreciation' (ibid.: 7).

An interesting shift thus occurred between *The Study of Dance* and *Dance Analysis* – a modification that constructed dance as an object, and analysis as central to dance studies. Whereas *The Study of Dance* identifies choreography, performing and appreciation as equivalent in value for dance studies, *Dance Analysis* elevates appreciation as the central component of dance studies. This shift is important because it marginalises choreography and performance in academic investigation. Even though analysis pertains to choreography and performance, only analysis establishes dance studies as 'academically viable' (ibid.: 6).

The predominantly theoretical construction of analysis becomes clear when Lansdale establishes description, contextualisation, interpretation and evaluation as its components. These activities define the dance scholar as a highly informed and educated spectator looking at dance as an object of study. The scholar is knowledgeable of structural specifics of dance as well as of cultural and historical circumstances. These skills situate analysis in a social context – something that Lansdale not only insisted on in her early publication; but that was also mirrored in the structure of the programmes at Surrey.[7] Lansdale is aware of the necessity to extend investigation beyond a historisation of Western forms into a theorisation of non-Western dance. Yet, it is not always clear how the distinct structures and functions of non-Western forms are reflected in an appropriate approach to analysis, given that the dance as the object of investigation should dictate the form of analysis.

Attempting to define what structures disciplines, Michel Foucault (1972: 46) investigates the relationship between the object of a discourse and the structure of the discourse. He points out that we might be tempted to define a disciplinary inquiry by its object, but, in the course of the discursive practice, we restructure the object as needed and in alignment with the artificial rules of the discourse. Ultimately, such colonising practice might be less concerned with an understanding of the object itself but more invested in the institutional power gained through the establishing of the discourse as a field. It is worth considering Foucault's inquiry in the context of the University of Surrey and larger social structures in the UK.

Due to continual reductions in governmental funding, many universities in the UK are increasingly run like corporations. University structures are often determined by administrative and financial needs, and departments are treated as product or clients. During the nearly five years of my employment, the University of Surrey restructured itself three times. Financial motives, not academic needs, were the justification for restructurings that shifted the dance department into other governing bodies and aligned it with different disciplines. New hires of administrators outdid the number of hired academics and the pay scale reflected this as well. Departments rent their space from the university, which, because of the dance department's large demand for space per student, proved expensive (though it must be noted that such a practice is not at all common to all institutions in the UK). Such corporatisation revises the traditional function of the university as a nationalising institution. However, to hold on to some of the national importance and its former function as a creator of citizen subjects, the educational system in the UK is nationally controlled, with guidelines on benchmarks and assessments of learning outcomes. This colonial hold over the national supervision of a corporate structure (such as East India Company) is poised for change, as the UK comes to more rigorously reflect on its colonial power in the current post-colonial world, which will force a rethinking of the category of the citizen (Gilroy 2004: 121).

The focus on analysis as the main approach of dance studies reflects these struggles. Dance studies establishes itself as a discrete and viable discipline inside the corporate university because it provides a distinct object of study and a discourse that is informed by this object. Even though the object of investigation seemingly structures analysis, a predominant reliance on analysis actually restructures the object, thus administering power over the object without always acknowledging this reflection of a colonial taxonomy.[8] Rather than denouncing analysis in the name of its problematic characteristics, we should continue to recognise and theorise the possible hegemonic power of analysis, to enable a reflection on its function in the academy and in society.[9]

University of California, Riverside

Well into the requestioning of choreography and dance that took place within postmodern dance in North America, Susan Leigh Foster inserted her voice through the publication of *Reading Dancing* (Foster 1986). Influenced by her dance training and choreographic practice, cultural criticism and Hayden White's investigation into the underlying narrative structures of history, Foster categorises four contemporary approaches to choreography, technique, training and dancing. Her analytic categories allow her to rethink dance at different points of its structure. Picking up every aspect of dance production, she disentangles it from convention and its cultural referents. This move owes much to a structuralist approach that theorises language and texts as cultural products, allowing for the interpretation of the underlying structures of social systems. The construction of dance as text and the emphasis on logical and scientific categories denaturalise the process of dance-making. As a methodology for dance studies, this approach gives the discipline a framework for an equal status in the academy, one comparable to that of art history or theatre studies.

As much as Foster focuses her reading of dance on dance as a sign system, her framework does not lose sight of the political and cultural potential of dance. This attention to the historical and social is informed by post-structuralist critiques of structuralist universalising practices.[10] It entails a critical evaluation of the position of the dance scholar as well as a rethinking of dance history from a genealogical perspective. This focus on how knowledge is created in relation to sign systems shifts the focus of dance studies away from interpretation and historiography towards a field fundamentally informed by choreographic processes.

Foster and her colleagues proposed a PhD in dance history and theory at the University of California, Riverside, in 1991. The programme promised 'a formal and academic base for advanced research in the emerging field of cultural and historical studies of dance' (Foster 1991: 5). It strove to be interdisciplinary, culturally inclusive and exclusively theoretical. At the same time the proposal purposely omitted discourses that were often of importance to dance departments, such as kinesiology, ethnology, aesthetics and therapy.[11] This choice moved the programme away from the training of dancers, choreographers and dance pedagogues and towards a purely academic endeavour focused on 'research and writing about dance' (ibid.: 10).

The degree highlighted historical and reconstructive components in its proposal and drew parallels to art history as a study that did not rely on training in artistic practices. This again identified dance studies at Riverside as a theoretical discipline that emphasised the translation of dance into writing and the reconstruction of dance out of its sources as key issues for the PhD. The actuality of the programme, which admitted its first students in 1993, shifted this focus away from analysis, documentation and reconstruction and emphasised theorisations of dance across time and cultures – especially the relationship between dancing and writing as diverse sign systems embedded in social structures.

The anthology *Corporealities* (Foster 1996a) exemplifies this shift. All essays display a creative engagement with writing in relation to dance, while many of them also communicate in their form the content of their investigation. Evoking a complex choreography of power networks through movement and embodiment, the texts visualise the impact of different positions and voices. Such enlivening of language through the approach of choreography as a theory neither objectifies dancing nor does it substitute writing for dancing. Rather, the translation from dancing into writing is problematised without erasing structural differences between both forms.

Up to this point, the direct translation of dance into other sign systems had occurred only through various notation systems and the reverse move in music visualisation. With the focus on the translation of dancing bodies into writing, the essays in *Corporealities* shift their attention away from dance as an object to dancing as the choreographing of historical, social and aesthetic relationships. Such consideration of the structure of dance is no longer predominantly analytical but rethinks the form and its social context. This kind of writing still engages with archivisation and analysis, but with a different strategy for both. It situates them as choreographic activity and as part of the translation process rather than as a final product. Thus, the shift that occurred from *Reading Dancing* to *Corporealities* moved dance studies from an investigation of dance as a sign system to choreographing of relations. This transition was an important theoretical and political move and it allowed the discipline to establish a place in North American academia and to lastingly impact discourses in neighbouring disciplines.

The dance history and theory programme at Riverside started at a time of major shifts in university and social structures. As Readings (1996: 118) postulates, the cultural studies definition of 'culture' as no longer determined by national literary tradition or canon, shifts it into an umbrella term that has no specific referent anymore. As a result, Readings defines 'culture' – and I would add other terms, such as 'identity' and possibly 'choreography' – as a self-referential site and strategy, which loses its potential for intervention into hegemonic structures. The application and theorisation of these concepts performed valuable work in their initial utilisation. Their detachment from concrete social referentiality is not the cause of changes in academia and society, but a symptom. Readings aligns this 'dereferentialisation' with the shifts in the function of the university from a nationalising institution to a transnational corporation. Simultaneously with the end of the Cold War, the site of capital's self-reproduction also shifted from the nation-state to the global stage. If we align these developments, then a possible relationship between globalisation, corporatisation of higher education and post-structuralist strategies of intellectual inquiry come into view. Thus, for our discipline it might be valuable to investigate choreography as a seemingly unmarked site of inquiry to understand its potential complicity in the globalisation process and both its positive and negative effects.[12] Such reconsideration of choreography is especially constructive, because our discipline is still fairly young and the impact of changes in key concepts are felt acutely. I could envision a similar theorisation to the one that Münz attempted for theatricality. This would allow a comprehension of institutional interests in the construction of choreography, its disguises and its possible hegemonic moves.

Conclusion

National differences in the university and attendant social structures determined the models for dance studies in these three countries. *Tanzwissenschaft* at Leipzig originally served East Germany's nation-building demands on education with its attention to preservation of the final dance product through a focus on archivisation. The fading of East Germany's national structures enabled a questioning of archivisation. Surrey created a tangible object through a focus on analysis to establish distinct disciplinary methodologies and methods for dance studies. In the post-colonial national space of the UK, analysis – with its control over the object dance – emulated some of the hidden imperial dominance. The focus on analysis salved a conflict between increasing corporatisation of university structures and nationally regulated education because it provided the necessary disciplinary authority and cultural capital (Bourdieu 1988: 36). Riverside initially strove to create analytic systems for dance studies, yet shifted its focus toward choreography as a strategy for the theorisation of dancing. Choreography as a seemingly unmarked and neutral structure participates to a certain extent in the globalising hegemony of North American capital.

The three visions for dance studies and their materialisation into three programmes theorise dance with distinct, yet not wholly discrete, strategies. None of these approaches to the discipline are monolithic. Rather, they relate to each other and utilise aspects of each other's methodologies and those from neighbouring disciplines. In addition the three approaches had to engage with competing approaches in their national academic discourses, which complemented the three visions for the benefit of our discipline. I have stressed their distinctions to use them as models and to understand their politics in relation to the national and educational context in which they exist. I am aware that such international comparison and critique in itself is an authoritative and globalising strategy. I have been privileged in my ability to move between these national systems through my professional life. However, I want this privilege to further a discussion of relationships, accesses, dominances and erasures instituted through our disciplinary discourses and structures.

Notes

1 The concept of *Bildung* (the literal English translation as *education* does not encompass the extensiveness of the concept) originates in medieval theology. *Bildung* describes a process through which a subject strives to realise its own potential in order to get closer to the image of God. The concept of *Bildung* was eventually utilised in philosophical and pedagogical discourses by emphasising the unfolding of one's potential through education and also used as a political term for the creation of a national identity in Germany.

2 There are also conservatories in the USA, such as the Ailey School and the School of American Ballet. Such institutions play a defining role in canonical dance training in all three countries.

3 Although this was the first time a dance studies curriculum had been established in German higher education, other theorisations of dance had occurred in vocational and private institutions. In West Germany, Kurt Jooss' Folkwang School continued Laban's earlier investigation into the body's potentiality. Yet as with other pre-Second World War models, such investigation served a choreographic and technical educational mission rather than creating an independent, theoretical discipline.

4 Examples of everyday theatre are processions, festivals, executions, circus, religious acts, rituals and also the daily social conduct of people in society.

5 Janet Lansdale published under the names Adshead, Adshead-Lansdale and Lansdale. I refer to her as Lansdale, because this is the name she now uses.

6 Lansdale and Pauline Hodgens provide the theoretical foundation for the book, which is co-authored by them, Valerie A. Briginshaw and Michael Huxley.

7 Dance studies at the University of Surrey started as a PhD (MPhil) programme in 1982 and extended in 1983 to the MA and in 1984 into undergraduate education. A 1991 evaluation of the BA – then called Dance in Society – emphasised attention to non-Western forms and to the diverse cultural functions of dance in society throughout history (Adshead 1991: 7). The programme focused on periods or styles of dance across choreography, performance, appreciation and contextual studies. Except for choreography, these areas focused predominantly on the analysis and preservation of existing forms through technique classes, repertoire or notation. The current degree, called Dance and Culture, still adheres to this focus for the first two years of study, yet it broadens to include non-stage and media dances. Lansdale's initial vision still underwrites this degree, yet the degree became more inclusive over time by focusing on non-Western and social dance forms.

8 Marta Savigliano (1995: 224) points to lingering colonial powers in dominant academic discourses.

9 Such work is reflected in the University of Surrey's Dance Department's ongoing rethinking of its programmes.

10 The rethinking of epistemological power distinguishes Foster's vision for 'reading' from Lansdale's understanding of analysis.

11 The proposal for a PhD programme at the University of California, Los Angeles, submitted two months earlier, included these fields of study plus dance technique in its curriculum.

12 Choreography, as a seemingly unmarked structure, also has a colonising potential, especially when employed in transnational academic exchange.

30

SHIFTING PERSPECTIVES ON DANCE ETHNOGRAPHY

Theresa Jill Buckland

Since the 1990s, there has been a plethora of publications on dance that use ethnographic methodology. This literature and its associated research are often grouped under the rubric of 'dance ethnography', whether emanating from long-established disciplines such as anthropology, sociology, ethnology and folklore, or from the newer fields of dance studies, performance studies and cultural studies. According to the research aims of dance ethnography, all movement systems are viewed as socially produced by people in specific temporal–cultural circumstances; the people's conceptualisations, values and practices, which may, or more often may not, coincide with those of the researcher, form the principal focus of inquiry. Distinguished by intensive fieldwork, dance ethnography in the early twenty-first century admits no restriction on the kind of dancing to be investigated or on its participants, whether performers, observers or both.[1]

Key to the approach of dance ethnography is the quest to understand and communicate the emic, that is, the insider, perspective of the participants. Fundamental questions of who, what, where, when, how and why guide the fieldwork inquiry which variously deploys quantitative techniques such as questionnaires and structured formal interviews; but, more typically, ethnography is distinguished by the method of participant-observation, the qualitative mode of investigation initially developed in anthropology, though now widespread across many disciplines (Buckland 1999b; Krüger 2008). Techniques drawn from ethnography have grown in popularity in the study of dance, but the research aims and objectives of elucidating emic understanding among a community, however that is constituted, remain distinctive in the ethnographic project.

Ethnography within an anthropological framework normally does not presuppose final results in the sense of predetermining the focus of investigation. 'Let the fieldwork teach you' is a familiar refrain, a strategic approach which, although aiming to facilitate the discovery of fresh insights by privileging emic perspectives, does not preclude a thorough familiarity with existing accessible information and some consideration of what might be key concerns before stepping into the field. But the fieldworker must remain flexible, allowing experiences in the field to shape the principal lines of inquiry. Too rigid a focus upon examining gender, for example, among a group of dancers might ignore their concerns with respect to the authenticity of the repertoire and its transmission. On another occasion, an insistence on documenting movement patterns might fail to realise the importance of the spoken word in their conceptualisation of the dancing and its relation to other aspects of cultural life.

Until the closing decades of the twentieth century, ethnographic studies of dance were mostly restricted to dance practices that were positioned as Other to European and North American concert dance. Going into the field to produce dance ethnography was often a methodological necessity as the dancing to be investigated might well have lacked a significant critical and historical literature. Ethnography was a preferred and often necessary approach to dance study that espoused scholarly interest in genres that were variously labelled as primitive, folk, tribal, social, popular, vernacular, or simply not Euro-American. Normally the field of dance practice was far from the researcher's own social circle, cultural knowledge and geographical home. The researcher shifted across physical as well as conceptual terrains: in European folk studies, for example, fieldworkers journeyed from urban to rural environments for the purpose of collecting and studying dances from peasant culture; in anthropology, researchers frequently crossed whole continents, to observe and participate in the lives of peoples perceived to be remote from Eurocentric world views and technologies.

Scholarly discourse in the arts, humanities and social sciences underwent radical transformation in the later twentieth century, as postmodernism swept across former certainties of epistemological and political hierarchies in academia. Within the social sciences, postmodern anthropologists contested the construction of knowledge, the legitimacy of meaning and ethical implications of the researcher's position of power, leading a multi-stranded debate that was fuelled further by feminist discourse and the realities of post-colonialism (Barnard 2000: 139–77). Boundaries between disciplines blurred, new fields of study emerged and ultimate challenges to the paradigm of positivism resulted in a new emphasis upon the subjective, the partial and the individual. Through such dissent, fresh understanding with respect to both the media and morality of scholarly representation filtered into the study of dance, notably resulting in greater diversification in the genres of dancing to be studied. Further significant impact was a shift towards new locations of dance research in arenas such as performance studies and cultural studies (Desmond 1997a, 2000; Dils and Albright 2001). Within these fields of inquiry, ethnography gained fresh impetus as a means of investigation, although its migration into these new academic terrains usually decoupled the methodology from the research aims and theoretical objectives of the social sciences. If disciplinary ownership of methodologies has melted away since the mid-twentieth century, so too have the protective barriers around subjects of research claimed as proper to distinctive fields of academic inquiry. Dance has been no exception, even if, or possibly because, it is a comparative latecomer to academia. Widespread scholarly interest in 'the body', for example, has contributed to the appearance of research on dance undertaken by ethnographers for whom dance is not necessarily a principal professional concern (Doane 2006; Wainwright 2006), so that a healthy exchange of publication profiles now extends knowledge and understanding of the socio-cultural significance of dance. In this context of shifting disciplinary boundaries and the use of ethnography as a research tool in a variety of disciplines, a salient question concerns the distinctive contribution that dance ethnographers might make to scholarly knowledge and understanding. Specialist analysis, insight and representation of the dancing are central to the enterprise. Human movement as culturally patterned, learned, transmitted, conceptualised, experienced and evaluated remains vital to the dance ethnographic project.

Following the postmodern turn in the social sciences, the abstracted concept of culture, once the cornerstone of anthropological theory (even if forever debated), was discarded by postmodern anthropologists as an obsolete theoretical tool, blunted from overuse and now regarded in any case as rarely having been fit for purpose.[2] Consequently, by the 1980s, dance could no longer be viewed as a microcosm of culture, radical though that perspective had been when it first appeared only a decade earlier within the burgeoning dance scholarship of North America (Keali'inohomoku 1974). The holistic concept of culture had only just entered the arena of mainstream dance studies when its validity became insupportably fragile in the social sciences. According to postmodern discourse, culture as an entity did not exist, much less was it bounded, whole and homogeneous, its dance reflective of the culture's distinctive social structure and world view. With the demise of culture as a conceptual tool went its accompanying apparatus of text and structure; dances were replaced by dancing, the product by the process, and the abstract by the experiential (Browning 1995).[3]

Increasingly evident in publications on dance ethnography in the 1990s was the use of the cultural to replace culture as a central focus of analysis. Ethnographic perspectives began to emphasise the socio-cultural construction and movement of 'the body', shifting from the objectified study of dance in a cultural context to the experiential consideration of the emergent performance of cultural identities that are non-essential, fluid and relational. Key to this approach is the recognition and reflection upon personal experiences of the dynamic nature of cultural practices for both the researcher and the researched. Dance as cultural practice is no longer the study of an Other removed in time and space from the researcher, but an ongoing dialogue of conversants located within the same temporal and global frame. Such shifting perspectives have often been generated from the realisation of and need to address new situations in the field. The old models of geographically fixed communities of people who practised a culturally distinctive form of patterned movement are no longer tenable (Gore 1999; Amit 2000). Where now in the twenty-first century might the field(s) for dance ethnography be positioned in an increasingly geographically, socially and culturally mobile world?

In most twentieth-century dance ethnographies, the selected field sites were one sited, small scale and predominantly face to face in interaction. The people dancing within a community often shared ties of residential locality, kinship, occupation, religion and social status as well as being born, as it were, into a dance repertoire and way of moving.

Some research questions continue to demand long-term residence and immersion primarily in a single field site (Cowan 1990; Lowell Lewis 1992; Ness 1992; Mendoza 2000; Hughes-Freeland 2008). Such a pattern of fieldwork, even if classically anthropological in terms of the researcher's separation from their own home, does not, of course, replicate the theoretical perspectives of early-twentieth-century anthropology, but rightly engages with the people of such communities as contemporary players in the world.

Similarly, European dance ethnographers, when studying the dancing of migrant groups, as well as those of indigenous communities, situate the people and their lives in modern times (Ronström 1991; Dunin 2006) while investigating shifts in the danced articulation of ethnic identities. Since the late twentieth century, however, the focus of dance ethnographies has included more transient field sites that can be characterised as 'communities built around expressive culture' (Hast 1993: 21) rather than a specific locale or ethnicity, and where the members perform styles of dancing and moving as an act of choice, rather than accident of birth. Cynthia Novack's (1990) ethnographic history of contact improvisation, *Sharing the Dance* was one of the first published monographs to employ ethnographic methods and anthropological theory in a sustained study of a community built around a way of moving and that evinced specific American values of the period in which it gained ground. More recently, research into social dancing has gained from the ethnographic method (Penny 1999; Bosse 2008), often demythologising received opinion on the background and values of its participants.

The choice of field site(s) depends upon ethnographic purpose and method as well as conditioning the kind of documentation that might be undertaken. Even within the single site field, it is impossible for a sole fieldworker to be omnipresent, but multi-sited fieldwork may highlight the selection process that lies behind the fieldwork design, aiming to address conditions of contemporary fluidity of place and people. Dancing communities may be regional, national or worldwide in membership; they may sometimes be stable but are often shifting, thus posing new problems of representation for the researcher. Anthropologist Helena Wulff's (1998) *Ballet Across Borders* is an excellent example of a multi-locational ethnography, the fieldwork being undertaken with the British Royal Ballet, American Ballet Theatre and the Royal Swedish Ballet. The choice of ballet as a genre to be studied from this perspective underlines that the methodology and the anthropological framework are applicable to any dance practice, regardless of cultural status. Multi-sited ethnography is also the hallmark of Yvonne Daniel's (2005) *Dancing Wisdom* which investigates the centrality of movement in three African-sourced religious systems in which dancing is integral to the practice.

Emic perspectives may shift over time as well as vary from person to person and it is that partial rather than omniscient knowledge that contemporary dance ethnographers emphasise to their readers. Researchers no longer aim at a definitive representation of a whole, but rather disclose the terms upon which their fieldwork was undertaken, making explicit as far as they can, their own socio-cultural standing, knowledge and bias (Davies 2007). In so doing, the hidden third person author of traditional ethnography has been replaced by the explicit presence of the first person narrator.

First person accounts in ethnography communicate personal experiences in the field, making no claims to impossible generalisations, or inadequate or unethical interpretations of the beliefs and practices of Others. Such a strategy of representation lends itself well to the articulation of embodied experience in the field. By shifting away from the objectification of dance as structure to the sensations of dancing as process, many dance ethnographers now eschew linguistic analogies, developed in the 1960s and 1970s, in favour of first-hand narratives that employ his or her own body as a tool to document and investigate dance. Dance ethnologist and performance studies scholar Deidre Sklar's *Dancing with the Virgin* proceeds from the premise that movement 'combines felt bodily experience and the culturally based organization of that experience into cognitive patterns. Ways of moving are ways of thinking' (Sklar 2001: 4). Following fieldwork over a ten-year period, her somatic experiences led to a movement analysis and understanding of the cultural and spiritual dimensions embodied in the fiesta of Tortugas, New Mexico.

The researcher's body, however, is not, a *tabula rasa* upon which to inscribe new memory, nor, as anthropologist Brenda Farnell (1994) has warned, may assumptions about a universal conceptualisation of the body, movement and significance be made. Working from within the same discipline, Andrée Grau's (2005) comparative analysis of emic conceptualisations of the bodies of Tiwi dancers in Australia and of ballet dancers reveals how Eurocentric assumptions about 'the body' as singular and transcultural limit fuller understanding of dance as world view and impoverish our understanding of dance as cultural practice.

Among gifted writers, the evocation of dance through personalised sensate testimony may breathe fresh life and perception into the ethnographic monograph, enabling the reader who has not witnessed or participated in the dancing, to gain an empathetic kinetic experience, moving, as it were, with the researcher. A good example of such writing is anthropologist Julie Taylor's (1998) *Paper Tangos*, where in an endeavour to capture the dancing of tango, the author not only provides a highly personalised account of her experiences and impressions when dancing in Argentina, but includes a series of small photographs, located at the bottom of the pages, to be flicked quickly through to suggest sequential movement.

Anthropologist Sally Ann Ness's (2004) insightful examination of this development towards embodiment as a research strategy and mode of representation in dance ethnography underlines the often emergent and potential nature of the cultural in such writings. In these ethnographies, the participation end of the scale of the methodological spectrum of participant-observation dominates, arguably bestowing greater authentication on the scholarly claims of the researcher. The legitimating physical presence of the researcher in the field as eyewitness has now come to include the 'body witness' of the researcher, recalling and representing bodily sensation in an effort to overcome Cartesian dualities of analysis and communication. When cast as autoethnography, however, the more extreme representations of personal narrative may result in too limited a personal view, running the risk of becoming self-indulgent and unhinged from considerations of a cultural nature. Self-examination and self-disclosure in an ethnographic enterprise are ideally undertaken to reveal the cultural, whether that is collectivised as a company, school, class, region or country and so on. An ethnography of one person may fail to address what is held in common, however imprecise and labile that may be. The strength of ethnography, for all its flaws, is to throw light on and gain understanding of shared experiences that, at the same time, are rarely fully consensual but are conflictual, negotiated and emergent.

The expansion of dance studies in terms of genres to be examined, coupled with the shift towards the practice of anthropology at home, in the late twentieth century has brought into the frame numerous dance ethnographies in which the researcher undertakes fieldwork in a dance activity with which they are already familiar, and which they may describe from the position of an insider. In her ethnography of New York queer club culture, *Impossible Dance*, for example, Fiona Buckland (2002) explored a world with which she was already familiar as a social dancer, but which she investigated through ethnographic techniques of fieldnotes and interviews over a four-year period. Located in the field of performance studies, her investigation had the specific research aim, communicated to her consultants, of looking at the improvised social dancing inside the clubs as 'a valid cultural performance of identity and community' (ibid.: 186). Focused even more upon the researcher's body as a central locus in the fieldsite is Tomie Hahn's (2007) reflexive ethnography *Sensational Knowledge* which draws upon her thirty-year experiences with Japanese dance: beyond the dance studio and all that it embodied and signified, she realised, 'the dancers moving around me were in fact my field sites, and my own body a terrain to survey' (ibid.: xiv). Hahn's personalised history of dance learning and transmission further provides insight into issues of politics and ethics that resonate with the complexities and issues of biracial identity.

In classic anthropology undertaken from a Euro-American perspective, historical dimensions rarely figured, whereas in classic ethnology and folk-lore studies, the past was significant in legitimating issues of authenticity and ethnic identity. As anthropologist Susan Reed (1998) has identified in her review of the study of dance, a discernible trend since the 1980s has been analysis of dance's past histories, often from the political perspective of nationalist identity. In *Dancing from Past to Present* (Buckland 2006), dance researchers with long-term experience of fieldwork combine historical and ethnographic strategies to examine the significance of the past in con-temporary embodied cultural practice. Shifting time frames enable the eth-nographer to understand embodied collective memories held, negotiated and expressed through dancing, and their potency for different groups of people in specific socio-temporal circumstances.

The visual ethnography of dance has been comparatively slow to develop in spite of the comparative facility in carrying and using recording equipment today. Ethical concerns of representation as well as publishers' reluctance to invest costs in more than the printed text have continued to constrain access to visual representations of people dancing, both static and moving. Photographic stills as Farnell (1994) has argued are both inadequate representations of moving and insufficient for the analytical purposes of ethnography. Visual aids such as film, video and DVD do, however, assist in bringing the movement to life for the reader who may have no previous knowledge of the dancing. They are of particular value when constituted as standalone DVDs that explore and explicate emic understanding of musical and choreological relations (SOASIS/AHRC 2008). Some dance ethno-graphies have been published with video extracts that can be purchased separately from the publishers (Drewal 1992) or are published with DVD material (Mendoza 2000; Hahn 2007). A limited number of dance anthro-pologists have produced film as dance ethnography, notably Felicia Hughes-Freeland (1988, 1996) and Rena Loutzaki working with film director, Marianna Oikonomou (2006). The skills and costs needed, however, for such production, usually prevent the often sole dance ethnographer involved in an ethnographic project from pursuing this channel of repre-sentation. As yet, the potential of the Internet upon which to post ethnographic studies in dance, which might include text, stills and video and offer opportunity for feedback from consultants, is under-explored.[4]

The role of technology in the lives of dancing communities remains to be more fully investigated. In the twenty-first century, added to the potential of mobile phones and emails as means of eliciting and documenting material, websites, discussion forums, blogs and vlogs are a vital means of communication (Hine 2005) for dance aficionados whose community may be global. The phenomenon of *Numa Numa* and the *Evolution of Dance* on YouTube, for example, deserves ethnographic study, not least since dancing and its imitation ranks so high in terms of video posting and viewing. Though obviously not without problems of authentification and access to sociological information from those who post material, opportunities for dialogic ethnography, new modes of participant observation and insight into emic aesthetics and values abound on the Internet, suggesting alternative, frequently shifting modes of being and community. Alongside individualised representations of dancing by the researcher in the production of dance ethnographies, the disembodied world of the Internet may prove a new ethnographic space where multiple selves and others may both dance and speak with one another in a worldwide dialogue.

As a methodology, ethnography has long been disassociated from its parent discipline of anthropology and is employed across numerous disciplines outside the social sciences. In the process, researchers have added new inflections, shifting perspectives on the role of ethnography and its relation to theory (Atkinson *et al.* 2001). Ethnographic studies of dance have long histories stretching back into the nineteenth century, histories that can sometimes be overlooked in the new canon of dance studies, which tends towards a singular post-1980s history of publications from the United States. The realms of the past and of the comparative remain vital arteries in the body of dance ethnography, reliant for its vitality upon extensive and intensive fieldwork that has been meticulously researched and critically documented from a reflexive position. The challenges for dance ethnography, as a diverse field in the twenty-first century, are not only to employ ethnographic method to explore the individual and the familiar, genuinely illuminating though this is and can be, but also to point towards new lines of inquiry to reveal further how and why dancing may operate as discursive and affective social action of a peculiarly human order.

Notes

1 This brief essay, intended for students of dance studies, aims to introduce some of the main trends in dance ethnography since the 1980s and is based primarily upon monographs published in English. References are indicative rather than comprehensive. More fulsome accounts of the history and scope of dance ethnography may be found in Williams (2004), Frosch (1999) and Grau and Wierre-Gore (2006). Characterisations of late-twentieth-century trends may also be found in Reed (1998), Farnell (1999) and Sklar (2000).

2 This is not to say that the word 'culture' has been completely vetoed in dance ethnographies: rather, its limitations tend to be noted. For some anthropologists, notably Marshall Sahlins (1999), the potential of culture as a conceptual tool remains to be exploited rather than entirely jettisoned.
3 Structural approaches to dance analysis have not completely disappeared. See Kaeppler and Dunin (2007).
4 See Thomas (2002) for an example of dance ethnography on the Internet.

31

SLAMDANCING WITH THE BOUNDARIES OF THEORY AND PRACTICE

The legitimisation of popular dance

Sherril Dodds

I dunno, there was just mad crowd surges and stuff and, you know, you were just jumping up and down for all you were worth to the music ... I dunno, I was a young kid and I just was just like, 'wow', I was just totally overawed by it.

(Russ)

It's a fast aggressive style of music which requires a fast aggressive style of dancing ... I used to find it a great way of revealing frustrations. You've had a bad day, all pent up, it's one way to just release everything.

(John)

I mean people jump like against each other and stuff like that, but basically that's it. A lot of the gigs people are really jammed in, and like basically you are that crammed in you have no say in the matter.

(Tim)

The above quotations are taken from a series of interviews that I conducted in which punk fans spoke about their experiences of pogoing and slam-dancing at live music gigs.[1] Both dance styles are fast, furious and closely allied with punk music: pogoing requires a crowd of fans, tightly packed together, to jump frenetically on the spot with their arms held tightly by their sides; and slamdancing demands that participants bash into each other with chaotic bounding steps, while their arms punch and flail wildly in all directions. Indeed many of my own formative dance experiences were during my teen years at various concert halls and clubs in the North-East of England. I easily recall frenzied scenes of flying hair as we headbanged to Whitesnake, swaying in a sea of black clothes while I lost myself in the ethereal goth dancing that befitted Siouxsie and the Banshees, and slam-dancing on a beer-stained floor in the smoky haze of a Redskins gig. Yet when I went to university a few years later in the late 1980s, there was no opportunity for to me to reflect intellectually on these dance styles that were an important aspect of my adolescent experience. I was taught ballet and 'contemporary' dance technique, theoretical studies focused on late-nineteenth- and twentieth-century Western theatre dance and there was no existing work in the field of dance scholarship that examined slamdancing or popular social dance per se.

The notion of slamdancing provides a useful metaphor to consider how the popular idiom has disrupted the way that cultural practices are valued and conceived. In this chapter, I set out to examine how popular dance, as a neglected and marginalised area of somatic practice, has entered the academic terrain of dance scholarship. In much the same way that slamdancing intentionally barges into and knocks about fellow participants, the impact of popular dance on the intellectual field has demanded several radical shifts in the way in which scholars perceive and theorise this movement practice. In order to focus on how popular dance has shaped new directions in dance studies, first I seek to reflect upon the frameworks of value that produce and underpin scholarship in the arts and humanities. Secondly, I consider the problematics of defining popular dance as a discrete object of study. Finally I examine the emergence of popular dance as a legitimate subject of enquiry and consider how the movement practice insists upon theoretical and methodological approaches specific to itself. Fundamentally, this paper recognises a nascent validation of popular dance within the academy. Before arriving at this position, however, I begin with the notion of the Western art canon as this paradigm of cultural worth has been unequivocally influential in the neglect of the popular within dance studies.

Reading value from absolutism to relativism

The privileging of particular art works that are awarded high levels of artistic (and frequently economic) value has resulted in an elite aesthetic canon. Connor (1992) reflects that, until the mid-twentieth century, the humanities were informed by a Kantian logic in which objects possessed an inherent value that could be measured only in its own terms, therefore academic disciplines, such as literature and art history, simply sought to expose and reproduce those absolute values. It is this awarding of special value that produces the Western art canon and its criteria of worth. Within the discipline of dance studies, the hegemony of the canon is apparent from the way that the elite domain of theatre art dance has traditionally been the subject of intellectual enquiry, over and above popular forms of dance (Buckland 1999a; Desmond 2000; Malone 1996; Malnig 2001–2).

Herrnstein Smith (1983) identifies how the canon is a self-perpetuating phenomenon in that, once a work enters this framework of high-level value, it acquires a level of security. She describes how any contentious attributes, such as sexist or racist content, are overlooked in favour of its formal properties, hence its historicity is repressed. Herrnstein Smith further argues that the institutions that create and preserve the canon are organised by subjects who possess considerable cultural, and associated economic, social and political, power and who tend to reside in the dominant classes. Frith (1991) meanwhile suggests that it is the institutionalisation of the canon, in the form of galleries, museums, universities and so forth, that separates it from other cultural activities. Thus the dance that takes place in formal theatrical spaces before a paying audience is awarded higher levels of worth than that which occurs in dance halls, clubs, leisure centres and street sites.

The paradigm of an art canon reflects an absolutist model of value, which supposes that cultural artefacts contain pure, intrinsic value that is timeless and universal. Thus it privileges the 'object of value' rather than the process of evaluation (Connor 1993) and worth is measured through fixed standards and judgements (McGuigan 1992). The aesthetic canon relies heavily on the notion of inherent worth in order to ensure the stability and continuity of its hegemonic position. Indeed there are plentiful examples in the press and media that advocate the primacy of the canon through ridiculing or critiquing the latest popular trends and the inclusion of popular culture within the educational curriculum and academic arena.[2]

Yet irrespective of the social frameworks that seek to ensure its continuity, the stability of the canon has been called into question over the past few decades within the academy at least. Van den Braembussche (1996) contends the existence of inherent value as this is always informed by other systems of judgement rooted in the practical, sentimental, ornamental, historical, ideological and so on. Thus the value of art is always relative, sociohistorically constructed, biased and contingent. Frow (1995) argues that the elitism and authority of high art over a domain of culture denigrated as low, mass or popular is a dichotomy that is no longer justifiable. First, he identifies that high culture is also part of the free market economy and can be equally subject to mass production and marketing techniques. Secondly, in place of a singular dominant belief system that underpins the hegemony of high art, a range of hierarchies are at play as mass culture informs all kinds of cultural beliefs and values. Thirdly, the high/low cultural divide traditionally suggests a class correlation in which high culture is tied to the upper classes and popular culture appeals to the working classes. Frow (ibid.) insists that this class-based understanding of value is outmoded given that mass audiences are characterised by plurality, diversity and inclusion rather than singularity, uniformity and exclusivity. Finally, he suggests that within contemporary society, rather than a disdain for all things mass, there is an increasing play between high and popular forms.

This destabilisation of the high–low divide is equally apparent in dance practice whereby popular dance forms, such as hip hop and tango, are performed on the art dance stage, and producers of high art dance seek to popularise it through more accessible marketing campaigns and social inclusion projects. Similarly, in the academy, there has been a clear shift in research towards popular forms of dance expression (Buckland 1999a). There are now well-developed research clusters on African American vernacular dance,[3] period dances of the early twentieth century,[4] ballroom and Latin,[5] Lindyhop and swing,[6] and contemporary club dance[7] to name a few. Yet in spite of the fragility of the high–low paradigm, I will return to this later as it still informs how popular dance is delineated as a cultural practice.

The inclusion of dance practices outside the exclusive domain of high art reflects a relativist position which largely came about in response to the intractability of the absolutist stance. The past few decades of critical thinking denounce the essentialist belief in fixed and inherent values, thus exposing that which was considered 'natural' to be 'constructed' (Weeks 1993). Given that contemporary society is characterised by multiple and diverse beliefs (Hirst 1993), relativism accepts rather than passes judgement on this plurality, thus tolerating difference and diversity (Connor 1992). I want to note briefly, however, some of the critiques offered against relativism as I will return to this issue at the end of the chapter. As with the universalism of the canon, relativism is similarly accused of absolutism as it paradoxically privileges itself as a specified methodology (Hirst 1993); thus, if all 'truths' are relative, then so is the relativist hypothesis (Connor 1993). There is also the danger that liberal relativism exists as an apolitical intellectual strategy (Agger 1992). As Squires (1993) suggests, although postmodernism has brought an important critique to notions of hierarchy and truth, the privileging of relativism has led to a domain of sameness in which no sense of aesthetic judgement, ethical duty or epistemological objectivity can exist.

Yet in spite of the contradictions of relativism, its celebration of diversity and democratisation of cultural practices has led to a keen scholarly interest in popular forms of expression previously neglected or marginalised within the academy. Before examining the scholarly re-evaluation of dance that occurs in popular, social and vernacular contexts (Buckland 1999a) and how this has brought about shifts in approach, theories and methods, I want to reflect upon the term 'popular dance'.

What is popular dance?

Malnig (2001–02) comments that those dances described as popular, social or vernacular reveal a wide range of forms, skill levels, degrees of professionalism and performance contexts. Yet, although the label 'popular dance' is frequently employed to delineate dancing in quotidian life (ibid.), the term is riddled with ambiguity. One approach to defining the popular is to situate it in a paradigm of opposition. For instance in music, popular is set against 'classical' and 'folk' (Fiori 1983) and in cultural studies it is polarised with 'high culture' (Chambers 1986). Whereas 'high art' is profound, individual in its creation, non-participatory and independent of commercial pressures (Cutler 1983; Shepherd 1983), popular culture is entertaining, serialised, participatory and exists for commercial gain (Kassabian 1999; Storey 1997).

Birrer (1983) describes this as a 'negative definition' in that each classification is defined through what it is not. While some sense of the character of each classification begins to emerge, this structural model is fraught with contentions and exceptions as the boundary between art and popular culture proves to be temporary and fluid. For instance, although the origins of tap dance are located in a vernacular context, its transmission to a presentational stage context and the critical celebration of the technical and choreographic prowess of star performers places it within a set of discourses traditionally applied to high art. Similarly, the commercial world of music video and television advertising often call upon art dance choreographers, such as Michael Clark, Lea Anderson and Wayne McGregor, to brand mass-produced commodities as cutting edge and distinctive.

An alternative definition of popular dance conceives it in relation to a large proportion of the population (Buckland 1983). This quantitative approach views the 'popular' as an object or practice that is widely consumed (Shuker 1997; Storey 1997). Given that consumers determine what is popular with their economic capital (Burnett 1999), popular forms are then quantifiable through indicators such as sales figures, audience capacity, ratings, chart position and frequency of airtime (Shuker 1997). Yet this quantitative approach is contentious. For instance, there are no parameters to delimit the point at which a commodity becomes popular (Fiori 1983). By placing emphasis solely on those commodities that succeed in the market place, a vast quantity of cultural products that are 'potentially popular' but commercially unsuccessful is consequently neglected (Frith 1996). Another factor that skews a quantitative analysis is the manipulative character of the market in that it does not directly reflect consumer choice. Cutler (1983) argues that buying practices are complex and partial in that they are influenced by 'taste formation' and 'demand creation'. The reliance on market success to define popularity is even further problematised if the high–low dualism is brought into play. Whereas some high culture achieves vast sales figures, certain popular forms appeal only to niche audiences (Shuker 1998).

Clearly, the concept of popular dance is a slippery classification. While I would not wish to propose a rigid definition, it is possible to identify some common characteristics rooted in matters of historical context, economic structure, contexts of production and physical location. The explosion of popular dance styles, certainly in the United States and the United Kingdom, is closely tied to social changes in the late nineteenth and early twentieth centuries, such as assembly-line production, urbanisation and the development of mass communication systems, which brought about a clear divide between work and leisure time and, with this, prompted a boom in popular dance, music and cinema as recreational activities.[8] Thus, although popular dance is not necessarily subject to 'mass participation', it is often transmitted through, or closely allied to, the mass media. Unlike 'art dance', popular dance is rarely subsidised through 'public funds', therefore it is either created at low cost by individual agents/communities or else constructed for the purposes of commercial means by institutions such as the record industry, private dance schools, and film and television companies. Notably, these agents and institutions are often closely intertwined with popular dance. Although popular dance frequently develops within particular communities, it rarely stays at grass roots level as private corporations perpetually seek out new commercial enterprises.

Popular dance can occupy multiple sites that include stage, screen or 'street' locations, by which I mean common public spaces such as municipal halls, clubs, ballrooms, village greens, high streets and shopping centres, and can be performed by amateurs or professionals, depending on the 'performance context'. Although I would argue that it is generally positioned as distinct from 'art culture', in that it takes place in vernacular settings or commercial theatres, it can occupy 'art spaces' such as galleries, museums and subsidised performance venues. In spite of this contextual separation it is evident that popular dance can both influence and be influenced by art dance practices.

It is the pervasiveness of popular dance and its complex and multiple sites of production, performance and participation that have demanded new kinds of intellectual engagement with this rich yet malleable area of dance practice. In the final section of this chapter, I propose several strategies for the examination of popular dance practice that acknowledge its particularities and distinctiveness as a broad area of enquiry.

Some strategies for prioritising the popular

The need to examine the contexts through which popular dance is created and produced is clearly a primary concern. Since popular dance occurs in a variety of private and public locations that cross stage, 'street' and screen, the concept of site is key. I suggest that popular dance both shapes and is shaped by specific geographical, regional and architectural contexts, which raises important questions regarding the politics of space. For example, Fonarow (1997) offers a fascinating study of the physical organisation of an indie music gig that focuses on the function and status of participant dancing in relation to its spatial layout.

Although all dance is situated in an economic framework of production, as popular dance is frequently tied to a commercial remit through its location within the leisure and media industries, it is also necessary to consider these movement formations through a political economy lens. Cultural practices and representations are clearly informed by the socio-historical framework in which they evolve and this context impacts upon how cultural expression is circulated and subsequently consumed. Hence the context of production, modes of distribution and experiences of reception and consumption are fundamental to understanding the meanings and values that surround popular dance practice.

There are certainly some rich examples of how scholars engaged in the study of popular dance examine the context of production as a means to interrogate how the dance is shaped by and responds to particular materi-alities. For example, in Doolittle's (2001/2) paper on mass social dancing of the 1930s and 1940s in Alberta, Canada, the author addresses the changing historical conditions, the political and economic framework of this period, prescribed patterns of social behaviour regarding class, ethnicity and gender, legislative sanctioning and the shifting populations of urban and rural communities as a means to illuminate the dance practice. Hanna (2000) surveys the gender, religious and legal frameworks in which erotic dancing takes place and Sommer (2001–2) explores the historical, social and moral context in which underground house dancing occurs.

Not only are the conditions under which popular dance is produced sig-nificant, but also the means by which it is circulated and received. Popular dance is noted for its rapid transmission across different social groups through apparatus such as the global media or through face-to-face interac-tion. Buckland (1983: 326) identifies how the media and 'fashionable cen-tres' for dance play an instrumental role in the dissemination of popular dance and Desmond (1997a) recognises a complex process of appropriation, hybridisation and modification as social dance forms intersect with different audiences and participants. From this, questions of identity politics and the changing meanings that surround cultural practices come to the fore.

Several studies offer a considered account of how the dance form and its concomitant meanings are shaped by modes of distribution. For example, Daniel (1991) addresses the influence of the Ministry of Culture on the distribution of Cuban rumba; Desmond (1992) focuses on the marketing and commodification of hula through the tourist industry; Foley (2001–2) considers both local and global transmission of Irish step dance and Usner (2001–2) looks at the relationship between Internet discussion groups and neo-swing. Other scholars meanwhile focus specifically on consumption. The mass culture theorists of the early twentieth century denounced the popular as ideologically manipulative; it was conceived as a standardised and commercialised culture produced for mass consumption by an audi-ence delineated as passive and undiscriminating (Storey 1997). In the 1980s, however, a shift took place within cultural theory that challenged the notion of consumers as a homogeneous mass susceptible to the hegemonic force of mass culture; this perspective propounds that consumers, specta-tors and participants are actively involved in the creation of meaning through their ability to negotiate, interpret and appropriate popular formations to meet their own needs (Sedgwick and Edgar 1999).

This privileging of consumption is also evident within work in dance studies that seeks to address the popular. Young (1999) draws upon inter-view material, fanzines, databases and Internet discussion groups to give voice to the participants of goth club dancing and Stearns and Stearns (1994) employ considerable interview data to present an oral history of African American jazz dance. Since these authors integrate participant experience directly into the writing, the notion of consumption is rooted in embodied knowledge rather than abstract speculation. Other scholars raise issues of consumption to explore fundamental ideas about the dance prac-tice. For example, Cook (2000) investigates the 'private consumption' of ragtime dance in the domestic setting and the impact of this on cultural anxieties regarding class, race and gender; Stern (2000) examines the codifi-cation and standardisation of Latin dance to suit different consumer groups; and Osumare (2000) addresses the interface between the globalisation of hip hop and local interpretations in Hawaii. Clearly, questions concerning the contexts and apparatus through which popular dance is produced, the mechanisms by which it is circulated and close attention to how it is consumed and understood by its participants are central to grasping the complex workings of this embodied practice.

The question of methodological approaches to popular dance also requires a degree of reflection. Within early dance scholarship of the 1980s and 1990s, the influence of literary critical theory, in particular semiotics, structuralism and post-structuralism, clearly impacted on the discipline, prompting scholars to 'read' the dance as a 'text' (Adshead-Lansdale 1999a). Notably, a similar trajectory occurred in cultural studies in relation to the analysis of popular culture, but subsequently prompted a number of con-cerns. Billig (1997: 205) warns that as attention has turned to the media texts and commodities of mass culture in favour of lived practices and the ways in which people make use of these material and symbolic goods, cultural studies has become a 'depopulated discipline'. Agger (1992) similarly asserts that cultural studies is in danger of becoming a technical method that lacks any grounding in a social, historical or political context. While a detailed reading may facilitate intertextual flexibility and interpretive versatility, the material contexts and participant experiences of popular culture are sidelined (Ferguson and Golding 1997).

To some extent, the method of 'textual analysis' is a limited strategy for the study of popular dance. Whereas there is a repertoire in theatre art dance that can be treated as a relatively stable text, popular dance that exists as part of a dynamic social setting is subject to perpetual evolution and modification and personal interpretation of the dance is permitted and encouraged. It is therefore difficult to delimit a discrete text as such since the dancing often takes place over several hours and recurs across weeks, months and possibly years, but during this time there are multiple opportunities for stylistic changes and radical reinventions. Other popular dance forms constitute fleeting and short-lived crazes that are produced through niche markets and therefore go unnoticed by the wider population. Although textual analysis is a useful tool for the study of textual representations of popular dance, such as Malnig's (1998) examination of dance in women's journals or LaBoskey's (2001/2) reading of hip hop films, other kinds of research methods are required for the examination of the live embodied experience.

Clearly, historiography, in the form of archival research and oral histories, is one methodological approach that seeks to validate, locate and analyse those popular dance practices faded through time under the monolith of the Western art canon. Robinson's (2006) study of 1920s' African American jazz dance teachers relies heavily on archival materials to construct a picture of the social politics that infused their professional lives and Allen (1991) draws upon social commentaries and critical reviews from the popular press to raise questions of gender, class and race in late-nineteenth- and early-twentieth-century female burlesque performance. Qualitative field research within the disciplinary traditions of anthropology, sociology and cultural studies is also frequently called upon for the study of popular dance. Indeed several scholars insist upon the need to engage with the actual participants and consumers of popular culture as a way to understand the values and meanings that surround popular forms, rather than relying on the abstract position of an imaginary textually constructed reader (Frith 1991; Morley 1997). Jackson (2001/2), Usner (2001/2), Osumare (2000), Penny (1999), Sommer (2001/2) and Stern (2000) all employ empirical field data to respectively analyse African American vernacular dancing, neo-swing, hip hop, ballroom, housedancing and Latin American social dance.

As an end to this chapter, I want to return to the subject of value and the limitations of the relativist position. Given the expeditious transmission of popular dance forms through the global media, it is important to recognise its transnational character; yet it is equally necessary to interrogate formations of popular dance within its localised settings. Thus rather than simply viewing all values around popular dance through a relativist equivalence, it is useful to turn to the agents who create and participate in popular dance as a means to examine how they construct frameworks of value that inform and are informed by their dance activities. Significantly, participants may propagate values that are hierarchical and peculiar to their niche practice, therefore creating local value-systems that do not produce a relative 'sameness' but which exercise strong beliefs and inequities. It is here that qualitative field research is a key means to observe, analyse and discuss participant experience of popular dance. This is not to suggest that researchers are somehow able to access fixed and autonomous truth-values that reside in participant experience. In some of my own field research into pogoing and slamdancing, it was most apparent that, in addition to certain shared values articulated by the subcultural members, there was also opportunity for disagreement and contradictions. Indeed I would argue that the tensions that exist between the production, mediation and consumption of popular dance are central to understanding some of the distinctive characteristics of movement practices located within the popular domain. Much like the sweaty bodies that grapple with each other within the slamdancing scene, academics must also get to grips with the material realities of popular dance practice. Knowing the frameworks of significance and meaning through which audiences and participants appreciate popular dance allows for a reframing of its position within the academy from out of the margins and into a position of intellectual and embodied worth.

Notes

1 Between October 2004 and April 2006 I conducted a series of interviews with punk, heavy metal and ska fans in a research project that examined the frameworks of value that shape and respond to participant experience of subcultural dance.

2 In an online news article in the *Guardian* (Wednesday, 15 January 2003), Emma Brockes queries so-called 'Mickey Mouse degrees' that focus on culture and media subjects such as, for example, the singer Madonna, crossdressing and women's ice-skating <http://www.guardian.co.uk/politics/2003/jan/15/education.highereducation>, accessed 15 December 2008).

3 See Dixon Gottschild (1996, 2000); DeFrantz (2002); Jackson (2001/2); Malone (1996); Osumare (2000); Stearns and Stearns (1994); Valis Hill (1992 and 2001/2).

4 See Cook (2000); Doolittle (2001/2); Malnig (1998); Robinson (2006).

5 See McMains (2001/2, 2006); Penny (1999); Stern (2000).

6 See Usner (2001/2); Monaghan and Dodson (2000); Monaghan (2001/2).

7 See Gore (1997); Hall (2008); Pini (1997); Sommer (2001/2).

8 Although my intention here is not to explore cross-cultural notions of the popular, there is an underlying assumption that it exists as a Western phenomenon, which I would seek to challenge. In music and cultural studies, definitions of and research into the popular idiom reflect an imperialist position in their focus on forms located in Western Europe, North America and Australia (Aharonian 1983; Burnett 1999; Middleton 1997; Shuker 1998). Yet, in dance terms, there are practices that occur both in 'vernacular settings' and other 'popular fora' that would contend this ethnocentric reading: the Cuban rumba (Daniel 1995), the Brazilian samba (Browning 1995), the Argentinean tango (Savigliano 1995) and the screen dance performances of popular Bombay cinema (Shresthova 2004).

32

WHAT IS ART?

Betty Redfern

BOSWELL: Sir, what is poetry?
JOHNSON: Why, Sir, it is much easier to say what it is not. We all know
what light is; but it's not easy *to tell* what it is.

(James Boswell: Life of Johnson)

It is not unusual for those interested in the arts – though not, so they may
think, in philosophy – to ask nevertheless as a result of that interest questions which are of an indisputably philosophical kind. These are often of
the form, 'What is … ?'; for example, 'What is rhythm?', ' … form?',
' … dance?', and, not least, 'What is art?'

It may further be asked: 'Are ceremonial and ritual dances art? What
about folk dances, American square dancing, ballroom and tap dancing? Is
popular art a branch of art in general, or not art at all?' Or it might be said:
'Suppose someone creates a dance but never shows it to anyone – is that
art?' Perhaps even more interesting, philosophically speaking, is an undiscovered dance or music score. In other words, for something to count as
art must it be publicly accessible or can art be private?

Then what of talk of animals dancing, singing, painting, etc.? Can there be
animal art, or is art something created and presented only by human
beings? Must there be the intention to produce something to be seen as art?
What of objects found, say, on the beach (*objets trouvés*)? How is it that soup
tins, firebricks and so-called Readymades such as a bicycle wheel or a urinal
have been displayed – and apparently accepted – as art? Is it simply a matter
of someone declaring certain things to be art? Are 'happenings' in the
theatre to rank as art? What of accidents – stumbles, falls, collisions and
other chance occurrences on the part of dancers? Are extemporized dance
and music to rank as art, or must there always be some repeatable final
form? Is the term 'artwork' interchangeable with 'art', and does it imply
excellence, or can there be bad works of art?

I am not able, nor shall I even attempt, to deal fully with all these (and
similar) questions. Rather, I shall seek to identify the major philosophical
problems they raise in connection with the question, 'What is art?'

It may be noted first that this question is apt to be construed as a request for a definition of the term 'art' – a definition, moreover, of the sort that seeks to sum up the nature or essence of the thing in question in terms of a certain characteristic or set of characteristics that make it just what it is and not something else. Now if what is wanted here is a verbal definition that sets out both necessary and sufficient conditions for the correct application of the term, the request itself is of doubtful merit, for it suggests that something can be said in a brief space that is adequate for the thing that is up for definition. The very form of the question, 'What is ... ?', tends to place constraints on the kind of answer that is sought: it is expected to be all-embracing, but concise. Yet to attempt this in the case of a phenomenon as complex and varied as art would seem an impossible task.

Even within a limited period and within the same culture the manifestations of what is commonly regarded as art are extraordinarily diverse. Like 'beauty', 'aesthetic appreciation', 'form', and many other terms, 'art' would therefore seem to be precisely the kind that resists satisfactory definition in neat epigrammatic form, although examples of just such formulae abound: 'Art is expression of emotion', ' ... is significant form', ' ... is objectified subjectivity', and so on.

The problem is not, however, simply one of brevity. Rather, the question is whether 'art' is the kind of term that can be defined (in the strict sense) at all. It has certainly been the view of many philosophers since the second half of the twentieth century that it cannot; that the task is not merely as a matter of fact difficult, but logically impossible. The traditional quest for answers to 'What is art?', 'What is beauty?', and the like, has therefore been widely rejected as a proper subject for philosophical enquiry. To ask such questions, it has been insisted, is to misunderstand the kind of concept under review: no condition can be found necessary, let alone sufficient. Further, to prescribe a set of defining properties of art would restrict future development.

Traditional theories nevertheless often have the virtue of pinpointing aspects of art that are worthy of attention yet may have been neglected or distorted by previous accounts. Some definitions, often advanced with the express intention of revising an existing idea of art, might indeed be regarded as instances of 'persuasive definitions' – formulae that endow a word which has strongly emotive overtones with a particular meaning that the author tries to get others to accept as the 'real' or 'true' meaning.

What, however, were the purposes of traditional accounts of art? Many, if not most, would seem to have been principally concerned with the excellence of artworks, and with what makes for that excellence (the possibility of bad art was not usually considered – perhaps implicitly ruled out). Although, then, a strict definition might not be possible, it does not follow that nothing can be said about the character of whatever is under discussion. Some theories were attempting, for instance, to explain what sort of a phenomenon art is: for example, to make a case for the idea that it is a kind of play.

Thus what appear to be pithy definitions are often no more than short-hand summaries of substantial theses, which may provide important new insights into the subject. The extent to which traditional theories may still affect professional art criticism, as well as the responses of lay people, should not indeed be underestimated. Thus traces of doctrines derived from, for example, Wordsworth, Coleridge, Tolstoy, often remain deeply ingrained in people, even if their origins or wider implications are unknown.

What, however, have philosophers critical of traditional theorists them-selves had to say? Two major recommendations have been proposed. First, instead of asking 'What does "art" (or "work of art") mean?' we should consider how the word or phrase is commonly used and accepted in everyday language. Second, instead of trying to discover some property or properties common and peculiar to the various instances of (say) art, we should look for *family resemblances*. The model here is Wittgenstein's well-known advice in respect of a game:

> Don't say: 'There *must* be something common or they would not be called "games" ' – but *look and see* whether there is anything common to all.
>
> (Wittgenstein 1953: para. 312)

What we shall find, rather, is 'a complicated network of similarities over-lapping and crisscrossing'; somewhat like a rope held together by a vast number of fibres, even though no single fibre runs from one end to the other (Wittgenstein 1958: 87).

To take the first suggestion then: a highly abstract term such as 'art', unlike 'table' or 'tree', for instance, will be found to have a plurality of uses. This, of course, is evident from any dictionary. But listing 'skill', 'guile', 'craft', 'painting', etc. does not usually help when we ask, 'What is art?' Rather, we should examine how the word or phrase in question, along with its correlates and derivatives, is used in a range of familiar contexts, and compare and contrast those uses not only with one another but with those of other abstract terms that are relevantly similar.

We are then obliged to think more carefully about which sense we have in mind and to put forward reasons for or against a particular usage in a particular case. In striving to make clear what we mean, and thereby to achieve better understanding and communication with others, we shall probably soon find that we begin to draw parallels, to make distinctions, to notice interesting and significant differences and similarities. We are likely, too, in gaining a clearer idea of other people's conceptions of art, to become more precisely aware of what our own consists in, and to see what other perspectives we have (must have) in order to maintain this perspective consistently; we might even come to modify or change it altogether.

As regards the second suggestion, namely of family resemblances, a serious criticism often levelled at the model in general is that in the case of an actual family, one of whose members might resemble another in respect of the nose, another the lower lip, or the hair, gait, and so on, we already have the family determined for us. These traits are family likenesses because the individuals concerned belong together in the first place by virtue of genetic ties: if someone not related by blood happens to look like a Hapsburg or a Mitford, say, he or she could not be said to bear a *family* resemblance. But in the case of artworks, as well as many other things to which the model has been applied, how are we to identify the individuals between which likenesses are to be traced? What corresponds, that is, to the genetic tie? If we knew this, however, we might want to say, the puzzle as to what is to count as art would not have arisen in the first place.

One answer might be that we have to start with central cases which would seem indisputably to be art and then work outwards, so to speak. If, for example, *King Lear*, *Giselle*, *The Birth of Venus*, *The Magic Flute*, the *Eroica* symphony are not art, what is? We seek, that is, relevant similarities between such cases and other particular cases. But what is to count as relevant? For of course not any kind of similarity will do; it has to be of significance. For, given a little ingenuity, we could find likenesses between almost any two things. Yet if such a set of likenesses were to be worked out this would ultimately impose unacceptable limitations. It might be possible in principle – though in practice the task would be of overwhelming magnitude – to trace significant similarities among the vast body of items already acknowledged as artworks. But the exercise would be pointless; for even as we did so, some artist (especially a well-established artist) could come along with a new 'offering' which would cast doubt on any such scheme. This is not to say that no important similarity or similarities – as well as important dissimilarities – could be found between the new arrival and the rest; indeed, if it were otherwise, as I shall discuss further in a moment, there would be no reason to see it as art at all. But a particular set of resemblances laid down here and now, or at any other point in time, would be likely to exclude later candidates.

One aspect of the problem of resemblances which certainly requires elucidation has to do with the qualities or properties that are to be compared. For the terms 'qualities', 'properties', 'features' and such like are apt to give rise to a major problem, namely what is available to ordinary perception. For instance, several critics of traditional theories of art would seem to have supposed that what the authors of those theories had in mind when they spoke in 'essence' terms were qualities or properties of a directly observable kind – or what they thought was directly observable. Perhaps in some cases this was so, especially among those of a formalist persuasion, whose accounts do sometimes sound as if, for example, form, beauty, unity, harmony are actually *there* to be seen in the work. Yet such qualities have rarely been considered discernible in the way that features such as redness, hardness or circularity are thought of as discernible; moreover many traditional accounts of art focused not so much on artworks themselves as on, say, the (alleged) effect of art on the percipient; or on what was thought to be the creative artist's activity or mental state; or on the relationship between the artist and the public.

What might be more significant, therefore, are not directly manifested, but non-exhibited characteristics. Similarities and relationships between various objects, performances, etc., might, for example, be established in respect of origin, function, intention or purpose. We cannot, for instance, know that a dance is a work of art just by examining the movements involved; indeed we cannot even know that it is a dance. Rather, artworks are to be distinguished by their central role in a whole complex of social activities and practices that includes creating and producing, performing and presenting, criticizing and reviewing, marketing and financing, and so forth. The problem, of course, is how to provide a sufficiently precise characterization of such activities and practices so that they pertain specifically to art and not to other things as well. Nevertheless, the recognition of art as a social and historical phenomenon, quite unlike, say, sun, darkness, cold or stickiness, would seem vital for any satisfactory analysis of the concept. It is one of a vast host of concepts that require for their understanding a grasp of a whole culture.

To see something as a work of art then is not to recognize a brute fact, but depends on what can be known or taken for granted about the context of the object in question; and that context is of an *institutional* kind. As with, for instance, booking a ticket for a theatre – which may seem a very ordinary occurrence, yet in fact involves an intricate web of assumptions and beliefs that normally are not made explicit – so the knowledge needed to regard something as an artwork and to appreciate it *as* art requires acquaintance with the institutional framework in which such practices and activities are embedded.

Thus we are able, for example, to understand a set of bodily movements in terms of the art of dance and not (whatever outward similarities there may be) of, say, a magic ritual, a gymnastic display, or a set of therapeutic or physical fitness exercises, because we belong to a society in which, typically, one group – the audience – watches, and may pay money to watch, another group or an individual give a performance in a special space such as a theatre or *quasi*-theatre (e.g. a park, a school hall), where the proceedings are regulated by certain conventions. These conventions may, of course, be modified to a greater or lesser extent: audiences may be invited to participate themselves in some way; stages, lighting and special costumes may be dispensed with; a street may become, temporarily, 'the boards'. But no matter how experimental or revolutionary the presentation, either in terms of what is presented or how, there have to be sufficient likenesses between the old and the new frameworks for us to be able to accommodate any innovations within our existing concept of art. When we question whether something is a new form of art or not art at all, it is precisely when the institutional framework is strained to breaking point. But as long as a few conventions remain it is possible that our concept of art, or of a particular art form, is expanded and enriched, perhaps even drastically revised.

One of the most valuable points insisted on by writers who draw attention to the institutional character of art is that, just as there cannot be a private language, so is art essentially public. What is art cannot be determined according to personal whim or even the serious reflective judgment of a single individual. As with moral questions, nobody can set himself up as a solitary arbiter in respect either of his own 'works' or anyone else's – which is not, of course, to say that revolutionaries do not bring about change in the realms of both conduct and art, merely that no individual can ever be entirely independent of the standards of the culture to which he or she belongs. The most free-thinking radical is radical only in the light of what is generally accepted; revolutionaries and innovators have to be familiar with certain norms in order to revolt against them.

Recognition of the essentially public nature of art enables us to indicate answers to some of the questions raised at the beginning of this discussion. It will be evident, for example, that manuscripts and scores remaining unpublished, perhaps undiscovered, and choreographic inventions performed exclusively in private are not art, though it is merely fortuitous that they have not so far acquired this status. Neither are songs, poems, etc., as yet only 'in the composer's head', though this time for the very different reason that they *cannot* (logically cannot) be. For whereas in the first case it is only a contingent matter that what may be art is so far not known about, yet *could* be, in the second case there is nothing in sensuous form that is available for public scrutiny. Only when these two conditions (at least) are fulfilled can something be a candidate for art status, though success is not, of course, thereby automatically guaranteed.

This is sometimes apt to strike people as rather strange. Surely, it might be said, if something is an artwork it has always been an artwork, and always will be. How can the nature of something change simply as a result of its being regarded in a particular way? But, as should now be clear, a work of art is more than a physical phenomenon. The same physical object (which may be a set of movements, sounds, etc.) can therefore rank as art at one period of time, but not at another; in one place, but not elsewhere. Any sense of strangeness occasioned by this idea indicates a failure to grasp the significance of what has been discussed in the last few paragraphs, namely the social and historical character of art and the need, in any analysis of the concept, to take account of non-exhibited features of things, and of the customs and attitudes of a society in respect of certain objects and activities, the kind of *regard* in which they are held.

Once this is appreciated, however, we may begin to see how it is that such things as weapons, domestic utensils, masks or articles of clothing, whether from the everyday life of our own or another civilization, of our own day or of the past, may, appropriately treated, *become* art; how dances and songs, once an integral part of worship, say, or the celebration of some other occasion, can – again, appropriately treated – be, as it were, trans-formed, enter the domain of art. Removed from their normal context, such phenomena can take on a different character; they can acquire a new status, a new role in the life of the society that accords them this different treat-ment. And that society is thereby itself modified; for art not only derives its 'being' from the culture in which it emerges, but in turn contributes to, and indeed in some measure constitutes, that culture.

As with knowledge of any kind, we cannot start from scratch but have to begin from where we already are, with what we already know. Thus in the case of art our taking-off point has to be those instances which are meant to be seen as art, that is, which have been produced intentionally under the concept of art (even if an individual artist may not be explicitly aware of what that concept involves or be able to articulate it). Further candidates are considered in relation to acknowledged artworks against a background of established or, we might say, inherited standards and traditions – inher-ited inasmuch as we are brought up in a society in which human beings engage in art activities (in the wide sense referred to earlier).

A point made during the discussion of family resemblances perhaps needs to be stressed again here, however, namely, that to recognize some-thing as art is not a matter of searching for a *prescribed* set of similarities. The standards and traditions of art, far from being fixed or static, are con-stantly being enlarged and revised, as new dances, novels, films, operas and so on (as well as combinations of some of these) achieve the status of art, perhaps using new materials and new techniques and demanding new kinds of response and behaviour on the part of those who watch or listen or read.

Reference to what has gone on in the past as a necessary part of any satisfactory account of art does not, therefore, imply a rigid concept. Para-doxically perhaps, it is the continuity of certain cultural practices and norms that makes for its flexibility and elasticity; without them innovation would not be possible, for, as we saw earlier, traditions are necessary for there to be fresh developments. Modern dance, for example, originated as a direct consequence of classical ballet, and could be understood as a new kind of dance only against that background. Its exponents might have thought they were overthrowing everything, but they did not for some time attempt to dispense with, say, music or some other sort of sound accom-paniment, or with stages, audiences who sat in their seats to watch, and the like. And while some of these conventions, along with a number of others, have from time to time been abandoned by later choreographers, some connections with previous presentations remain, and have to remain (though it need not be the same connections that persist). Otherwise, as emphasized previously, these pieces could not be seen as art at all, maybe not even as dance.

Moreover artists are always limited not only by the nature of the medium (what can be 'said' in the dance cannot be said in literature, what is expressible in music is not expressible in sculpture, and so on); but also by the particular milieu in which that medium is used. For artistic techniques do not develop independently of the general cultural climate or of previous uses of paint, movement, words, etc.; the work of even the most highly creative artists grow out of the habits of thought and feeling integral to the society to which they belong and the language and art forms which both shape and enshrine that thought and feeling.

The fact that it is only in the light of what has already been accepted as art that new departures can be seen *as* new departures, means that newly admitted candidates – and most especially, perhaps, candidates presently seeking admission – are intelligible as art only to those with some knowledge of its history. This is not necessarily, or even usually, 'history of art' as a formal subject of study, however, but rather, first-hand acquaintance with individual artworks and art practices – in particular, of course, those belonging to the art form and the genre to which the newcomer most closely approximates. For they bring to their looking a store of experience that enables them to make significant comparisons such that a judgement is possible as regards the art (or non-art, or borderline art) status of whatever is in question. Indeed the knowledgeable spectator, listener, or reader – perhaps a critic, an art historian, a collector or a biographer – can often find a certain coherence between the items of an individual artist's total output, or that of a group, better than can the artist or group concerned.

Conversely, it is the man- and woman-in-the-street who are apt to be most resistant to change in the arts and to be puzzled by new developments. For they have literally lost their bearings; the fewer points of reference there are to existing artworks, the more restricted and the more readily upset are people's responses and expectations. What is required in such circumstances is someone who can latch on, as it were, to what is familiar: to repeat, we have to start with what *can* be seen as art. But all depends, as already indicated, on both parties being able to take for granted a whole range of shared concerns and values. The would-be appreciator will be able to grasp whatever similarities and comparisons a guide may point out only in so far as he or she is at home in the cultural milieu within which such similarities and comparisons make sense.

Once the point is established that the central cases of art are those intentionally produced under the concept of art, another of the questions posed at the beginning of this discussion may be taken up, namely the possibility of art among animals other than humans. For it now becomes evident that such a suggestion is hardly plausible. Certainly an observer or listener might find marks or movements or sounds made by birds, insects, etc., aesthetically interesting and might indeed display them in conditions normally reserved for art. But we cannot attribute *artistic* activity to non-human animals even in the case of, say, the singing of whales, or the movements and paint daubings of apes when these are intentionally produced and seem to be selected and arranged in some manner. For we are unable to say whether the intention and ordering in question involve the idea of making and presenting something which is primarily to be looked at or listened to, something which is typically altered, revised, improved upon or even scrapped altogether in order to make a better song, dance, painting or whatever.

The possibility of *dis*satisfaction on the part of an artist in respect of the look or sound of what he or she is doing is in fact as important as is that of satisfaction. In other words, critical appreciation goes hand in hand with making and performing: the artist pays attention to what he or she does not only (normally) in terms of taking care with movements, marks or sounds, but also in terms of what emerges, what makes for certain effects. He or she looks or listens reflectively, discriminatingly, and proceeds in the light of this assessment; he or she knows what he or she is doing and is able to imagine how others might respond. That is, he or she works against the background of certain criteria – though not a set of fixed criteria that can be laid down in advance, but criteria applied in relation to this particular effort.

Both the making and the looking or listening then take place not *in vacuo*, but in the light of other sounds, marks and movements that the artist has seen and heard, and has noticed other people, especially those known as *artists*, looking at and listening to, as well as talking about, displaying and presenting in particular ways: in short, against the background of what he or she has learned to conceive of as art. As a social activity of this kind, art is clearly outside the range of non-language users. An ape is no more *dancing* in the sense in which a human being dances than is a budgerigar *talking* when it imitates sounds of human speech. For that matter, neither are human beings dancing if they merely reproduce movements taken out of any context that makes those movements intelligible as dance.

To have a grasp of the concept of art, however, is not (as also with many other concepts) an all-or-nothing affair: there can be degrees of understanding ranging from the rudimentary to the more fully fledged; and it seems clear that this is a concept that goes on developing throughout childhood and, indeed, beyond. Even those individuals who go on to learn very little about art inevitably absorb a good deal about the forms and traditions of their own culture or sub-culture. For the idea of art is one that permeates our experience and plays an important part in shaping it. Indeed if it were to die out in a particular society, that society would not remain the same except for that single change: the whole fabric of its customs and practices, its habits of feeling and thinking, would be radically altered.

The way then in which debate about art tends to flow freely back and forth among specialists and non-specialists alike indicates that the answer to the question 'What is art?' is, in some sense, already known. The question presupposes that examples of art have already been identified. Moreover, as will have been evident throughout this discussion, we are also able to take for granted a great deal about art in general – for instance, that it is a complex phenomenon, that its manifestations are amazingly diverse and that it constantly undergoes change.

It has also become clear that the status of artworks is determined by history. Nevertheless, as Diffey (1969: 147) argues, there are occasions, especially in periods (such as our own) when the arts are subject to rapid change, when the question whether something is a work of art is not an idle one. For, while this has *normally* been settled, it does not follow that the decision can *never* be contested, though neither does the successful contesting of a particular case mean that nothing is settled. There is thus every reason why philosophers should continue to pursue their enquiries into the question 'What is art?'

The concept of art would certainly seem to be a classic case of the sort known as 'essentially complex and essentially contested' – a concept, that is, lacking full elaboration, yet nevertheless in general use. It is one that does not *as it happens* occasion endless disputes, but is *in the nature of the case* contestable; and will, as a rule, actually be contested. Although not resolvable by argument, such concepts are sustained by argument; they are essentially *appraisive* concepts, involving some kind of valued achievement which always admits of variation and modification. They therefore benefit, rather than suffer, from the constant scrutiny to which they are subjected.

BIBLIOGRAPHY

Ackroyd, P. (1995) *Blake*, London: Sinclair-Stevenson.

Adair, C. (1992) *Women and Dance: Sylphs and Sirens*, New York: New York University Press.

Adshead, J. (1981) *The Study of Dance*, London: Dance Books.

——(ed.) (1988) *Dance Analysis: Theory and Practice*, London: Dance Books.

——(1991) 'BA (Hons) dance in society', Course Document, Record of the Lever-hulme Trust Project 1982–88, University of Surrey, unpublished internal document.

Adshead-Lansdale, J. (1994) *Dance Analysis: Theory and Practice*, London: Dance Books.

——(1997) 'The "congealed residues" of dance history: a response to Richard Ralph's "Dance scholarship and academic fashion" – one path to a pre-determined enlightenment', *Dance Chronicle*, 20:1: 63–86.

——(ed.) (1999a) *Dancing Texts: Intertextuality in Interpretation*, London: Dance Books.

——(1999b) 'The concept of intertextuality and its application in dance research', in Society of Dance History Scholars, *Proceedings of the 22nd Annual Conference.*.

——(2006) 'Doctoral research in cultural change', in Burridge, S. (ed.), *Shifting Sands: Dance in Asia and the Pacific*, Braddon, ACT: Australian Dance Council.

Adshead-Lansdale, J. and Layson, J. (eds) (1983) *Dance History: An Introduction*, London: Routledge.

Agger, B. (1992) *Cultural Studies as Critical Theory*, London: Falmer.

Aggiss, L. and Cowie, B. (2006) *Anarchic Dance*, London: Routledge.

Aharonian, C.A. (1983) 'Latin-American approach in a pioneering essay', in Horn, D. (ed.), *Popular Music Perspectives 2*, Papers from the Second International Conference on Popular Music Studies, Reggio Emilia, IASPM: 52–65.

Ahmad, A. (1992) *In Theory: Classes, Nation, Literature*, New York: Verso.

Albright, A.C. (1997) *Choreographing Difference: The Body and Identity in Contemporary Dance*, Middletown, CT: Wesleyan University Press.

——(2007) *Traces of Light: Absence and Presence in the Work of Loie Fuller*, Middletown, CT: Wesleyan University Press.

Albright, A.C. and Gere, D. (eds) (2003) *Taken By Surprise: A Dance Improvisation Reader*, Middletown, CT: Wesleyan University Press.

Allen, G. (2000) *Intertextuality*, London: Routledge.

Allen, M.H. (1997) 'Rewriting the script for South Indian dance', *The Drama Review* 41: 63–100.

Allen, R. (1991) *Horrible Prettiness: Burlesque and American Culture*, Chapel Hill, NC: University of North Carolina Press.

Amit, V. (ed.) (2000) *Constructing the Field: Ethnographic Fieldwork in the Contemporary World*, London: Routledge.

Anderson, B. (1983) *Imagined Communities: Reflections on the Origin and Spread of Nationalism*, London: Verso.

Anon. (1910) 'Courrier des Theatres' *Figaro* 19, 23 and 25 June.

——(1932) 'Announcing "Great Day" ', programme announcement', James Weldon Johnson Collection, Beinecke Rare Book and Manuscript Library, Yale University.

Appadurai, A. (1996) *Modernity at Large: Cultural Dimensions of Globalization*, Minneapolis, MN: University of Minnesota.

Aronowitz, S. (2000) *The Knowledge Factory: Dismantling the Corporate University and Creating True Higher Learning*, Boston: Beacon Press.

Aronson, A. (2008) 'The power of space in a virtual world', in Hannah, D. and Harsløf, O. (eds), *Performance Design*, University of Copenagen: Museum Tusculanum Press, pp. 23–37.

Aschengreen, E. (1974) 'The beautiful danger: facets of Romantic ballet', trans. Patricia N. McAndrew, *Dance Perspectives* No. 58.

Atkinson, P., Coffey, A., Delamont, S., Lofland, J. and Lofland, L.H. (2001) *Handbook Of Ethnography*, London: Sage.

Auster, P. (1998) 'White spaces', in *Selected Poems*, London: Faber & Faber.

Ayrey, C. and Everist, M. (eds) (1996) *Analytical Strategies and Musical Interpretation: Essays on Nineteenth and Twentieth Century Music*, Cambridge: Cambridge University Press.

Bachelard, G. (1994) *The Poetics of Space*, Boston, MA: Beacon Press.

Bagchi, J. (1990) 'Representing nationalism: ideology of motherhood in colonial Bengal', *Economic and Political Weekly* 25: WS65–71.

Bales, M. and Nettl-Fio, R. (2008) *The Body Eclectic: Evolving Practice in Dance Training*, Champaign, IL: University of Illinois Press.

Banes, S. (1986) 'Pointe of departure', *Boston Review* I, 5: 12–13.

——(1998) *Dancing Women: Female Bodies on Stage*, London: Routledge.

Bannerjee, A. (2007) 'Paratopias of performance: the choreographic practice of Chandralekha', unpublished paper presented at the Annual Conference of the Congress on Research in Dance, Barnard College, New York.

Barnard, A. (2000) *History and Theory in Anthropology*, Cambridge: Cambridge University Press.

Bartenieff, I., Hackney, P., Jones, B.T., Van Zile, J. and Wolz, C. (1984) 'The potential of movement as a research tool: a preliminary analysis', *Dance Research Journal* 16, 1: 3–26.

Barthel, G. and Artus, H. (2007) *Vom Tanz zur Choreographie: Gestaltungsprozesse in der Tanzpädagogik*, Oberhausen: Athena Verlag.

Barthes, R. (1972) *Mythologies*, trans. Annette Lavers, New York: Hill & Wang.

——(1977) *Roland Barthes by Roland Barthes*, New York: Hill & Wang.

Battersby, C. (1989) *Gender and Genius*, London: The Women's Press.

Bauer, U. (2006) 'Melting away', *Performance Research*, 11, 2: 145–7.

Baxmann, I. and Cramer, F.A. (eds) (2005) *Deutungsräume: Bewegungswissen als kulturelles Archiv*, München: K. Kieser Verlag.

Beaumont, C. (1938) *The Complete Book of Ballets*, New York: G.P. Putnam's Sons.

Beisser, A.R. (1970) 'The paradoxical theory of change', in Fagan J. and Shepherd, I. L. (eds), *Gestalt Therapy Now*, New York: Harper.

Benjamin, A. (1993) 'In search of integrity', *Dance Theatre Journal* 10, 4 (Autumn): 42–6.

——(1995) 'Unfound movement', Presented at the CDET conference 1995, published in abridged version in *Dance Theatre Journal*, 12, 1, Summer.

——(2001) *Making an Entrance*, London: Routledge.

Benjamin, W. (1969) trans. H. Zohn, 'On some motifs in Baudelaire', trans. H. Zohn, in Arendt, H. (ed.), *Illuminations*, New York: Schocken Books.

——(1999) *The Arcades Project*, Cambridge, MA: The Belnap Press of Harvard University Press.

Benois, A. (1936) 'The decor and costume', in Brahms, C. (ed.), *Footnotes to the Ballet*, London: Lovat Dickinson.

——(1941) *Reminiscences of the Russian Ballet*, London: Putnam.

Berland, J. (1993) 'Sound, image and social space: music video and media reconstruction', in Frith, S., Goodwin, A. and Grossberg, L. (eds), *Sound & Vision: The Music Video Reader*, London: Routledge.

Berliner, P. (1994) *Thinking in Jazz: The Infinite Art of Improvisation*, Chicago, IL: University of Chicago Press.

Berry, J. (2005) *Reclaiming the Ivory Tower: Organizing Adjuncts to Change Higher Education*, New York: Monthly Review Press.

Best, D. (1974) *Expression in Movement and the Arts*, London: Lepus.

——(1992) *The Rationality of Feeling*, Brighton: Falmer.

Bhabha, H.K. (1994) *The Location of Culture*, London: Routledge.

Bharucha, R. (1990) *Theatre and the World: Essays on Performance and Politics of Culture*, Columbia, MO: South Asia Publications.

Billig, M. (1997) 'From codes to utterances: cultural studies, discourse and psychology', in Ferguson, M. and Golding, P. (eds), *Cultural Studies in Question*, London: Sage.

Birrer, F. (1983) 'Definitions and research orientation: do we need a definition of popular music?' in Horn, D. (ed.), *Popular Music Perspectives 2: Papers from the Second International Conference on Popular Music Studies*: 99–105.

Blanco Borelli, M. (2006) 'A case of hip(g)nosis: an epistemology of the mulata body and her revolutionary hips'. PhD dissertation, University of California, Riverside.

Bosse, J. (2008) 'Salsa dance and the transformation of style: an ethnographic study of movement and meaning in a cross-cultural context', *Dance Research Journal* 40, 1: 45–64.

Bourdieu, P. (1988) *Homo Academicus*, Stanford, CA: Stanford University Press.

Bousquet, M. (2008) *How the University Works: Higher Education and the Low-Wage Nation*, New York: New York University Press.

Boyd, V. (2003) *Wrapped in Rainbows: The Life of Zora Neale Hurston*, New York: Scribner.

Brandstetter, G. and Klein, G. (eds) (2007) *Methoden der Tanzwissenschaft*, Bielefeld: Transcript.

Brown, J.M. (ed.) (1979) *The Vision of Modern Dance*, Princeton, NJ: Princeton Book Company Publishers.

Brown, T. and Rainer, Y. (1979) 'A conversation about *Glacial Decoy*', *October* 10 (Autumn): 29–37.

Browning, B. (1995) *Samba: Resistance in Motion*, Bloomington, IN: Indiana University Press.

Buber, M. (1937) *Buber I and Thou*, London: Continuum.

——(1965) *The Knowledge of Man: A Philosophy of the Inter-human*, trans. M.S. Friedman and R.G. Smith, New York: Harper & Row.

Buckland, F. (2002) *Impossible Dance: Club Culture and Queer World-Making*, Middletown, CT: Wesleyan University Press.

Buckland, T. (1983) 'Definitions of folk dance: some explorations', *Folk Music Journal* 4, 4: 315–32.

——(1999a) 'All dances are ethnic, but some are more ethnic than others: some observations on dance studies and anthropology', *Dance Research* XVII, 1: 3–21.

——(ed.) (1999b) *Dance in the Field: Theory, Methods and Issues in Dance Ethnography*, Basingstoke: Macmillan.

——(ed.) (2006) *Dancing from Past to Present: Nation, Culture, Identities*, Madison, WI: University of Wisconsin Press.

Buckle, R. (1975) *Nijinsky*, Harmondsworth: Penguin.

Burnett, R. (1999) *The Global Jukebox: The International Music Industry*, London: Routledge.

Burt, R. (1995) *The Male Dancer: Bodies, Spectacle, Sexualities*, London: Routledge.

——(1998) *Alien Bodies: Representations of Modernity, 'Race' and Nation in Early Modern Dance*, London: Routledge.

——(2005) 'Raimund Hoghe: *Sacre, Rite of Spring*' <http://ballet-dance.com/200503/articles/Hoghe20050223.html> [accessed 20 April 2007].

Buscher, J. (2009) 'The Choreography of the Click Wheel', unpublished paper presented at Dance Under Construction XI, University of California, Los Angeles, May 1.

Butler, J. (1989) 'Sexual ideology and phenomenological description: a feminist critique of Merleau-Ponty's phenomenology of perception', in Allen, J. and Young, I.M. (eds), *The Thinking Muse, Feminism and Modern French Philosophy*, Bloomington: Indiana University Press.

Butterworth, J. and Wildschat, L. (2009) *Contemporary Choreography: A Critical Reader*, London: Routledge.

Carby, H. (1994) 'The politics of fiction, anthropology, and the folk: Zora Neale Hurston', in Fabre, G. and O'Meally, R. (eds), *History and Memory in African-American Culture*, New York: Oxford University Press.

Carroll, L. (1984 [1871]) *Through the Looking Glass: And What Alice Found There*, Puffin: Harmondsworth 1984.

Carter, A. (ed.) (1998) *The Routledge Dance Studies Reader*, London: Routledge.

——(ed) (2004) *Rethinking Dance History: A Reader*, London: Routledge.

——(2005) *Dance and Dancers in the Victorian and Edwardian Music Hall Ballet*, Aldershot: Ashgate.

Cassell, E. (1985) *Talking with Patients*, vol. 2, Cambridge, MA: MIT Press.

Castaldi, F. (2006) *Choreographies of African Identities: Négritude, Dance, and the National Ballet of Senegal*, Champaign, IL: University of Illinois Press.

Chaki-Sirkar, M. (1993) 'New directions in Indian dance', in J. Irani (ed.), *The Statesman: Festival*, Calcutta.

——(1994) 'The emergence of dance culture in Bengal', in Roy, S. and Ghosal, S. (eds), *Images and Perspectives*, Calcutta: Nariseva Sangha and Engage Publishers.

——(1997) *Chandralekha*, New Delhi: HarperCollins.

Chakravorty, P. (1998) 'Dance hegemony and nation: the construction of classical Indian dance', *South Asia* 21: 107–20.

——(2000) 'Choreographing modernity: Kathak dance, public culture, and women's identity in India', PhD dissertation, Temple University.

——(2008) *Bells of Change: Kathak Dance, Women and Modernity in India*, Kolkata: Seagull Books.

Chambers, I. (1986) *Popular Culture: The Metropolitan Experience*, London: Methuen.

Chao, Y. (2000) 'Dance culture, and nationalism: the socio-cultural significance of Cloud Gate Dance Theatre in Taiwanese society', PhD dissertation, Laban Centre, UK.

——(1997) *The Nation and its Fragments*, Calcutta: Oxford University Press.

Chapman, J. (1978) 'An unromantic view of nineteenth-century Romanticism', *York Dance Review* 7: 28–40.

Charles, Prince (2008) 'My interest is in celebrating the culture of food', *The National Trust Magazine*, Vol. 115, 21–3.

Chatterjea, A. (2004) *Butting Out: Reading Resistive Choreographies through Works by Jawole Willa Jo Zollar and Chandralekha*, Middletown, CT: Wesleyan University Press.

Chatterjee, P. (1986) *Nationalist Thought and the Colonial World: A Derivative Discourse*, The United Nations University, London: Zed Books Ltd.

——(1989) 'Colonialism, nationalism and colonized woman: the context in India', *American Ethnologist*, 16: 622–33.

Chen, Y. (2005) 'The Eastern invasion: Cloud Gate Dance Theatre's *Smoke*', unpublished paper, presented at the Asia Pacific International Dance Conference, organized by the World Dance Alliance and University of Malaya, Kuala Lumpur, July 6–10.

Chidiac M. and Denham-Vaughan, S. (2007) 'The process of presence: energetic availability and fluid responsiveness', in *British Gestalt Journal* 16, 1: 9–19.

Ching, L.T.S. (2001) *Becoming 'Japanese': Colonial Taiwan and the Politics of Identity Formation*, Berkeley, CA: University of California Press.

Chowdhury, I. (1998) *The Frail Hero and Virile History*, Calcutta: Oxford University Press.

Cixous, H. (1995) 'The place of crime, the place of pardon', in Drain, R. (ed.), *Twentieth Century Theatre*, London: Routledge.

Cixous, H. and Calle-Gruber, M. (1997) *Rootprints: Memory and Life Writing*, London: Routledge.

Claid, E. (2002) 'Standing still ... looking at you', *Research in Dance Education* 3, 1: 7–19.

——(2006) *Yes? No! Maybe ... Seductive Ambiguity in Dance*, London: Routledge.

Clark, V. (1994) 'Performing the memory of difference in Afro-Caribbean dance: Katherine Dunham's choreography, 1938–87', in Fabre, G. and O'Meally, R. (eds), *History and Memory in African-American Culture*, New York: Oxford University Press.

Clifford, J. (1988) *The Predicament of Culture: Twentieth-Century Ethnography, Literature, and Art*, Cambridge, MA: Harvard University Press.

CGDT (1993) *Cloud Gate Dance Theatre: Twentieth Anniversary Photo Album*, Taipei: Cloud Gate Dance Theatre Foundation.

Cohen, S.J. (1972) *Doris Humphrey: An Artist First*, Middletown, CT: Wesleyan University Press.

——(ed.) (1974) *Dance as a Theatre Art: Source Readings in Dance History from 1581 to the Present*, New York: Dodd Mead.

——(1976) 'The English critic and the Romantic ballet', *Theatre Survey* XVII, 1: 82–91.

Cohn, N. (1969) *Rock from the Beginning*, New York: Hill & Wang.

Coles, A. (ed.) (2000) *Site Specificity: The Ethnographic Turn*, London: Black Dog Publishing.

Connor, S. (1992) *Theory and Cultural Value*, Oxford: Blackwell.

——(1993) 'The necessity of value', in Squires, J. (ed.), *Principled Positions: Postmodernism and the Rediscovery of Value*, London: Lawrence and Wishart.

Cook, N. and Everist, M. (eds) (1999) *Rethinking Music*, Oxford: Oxford University Press.

Cook, S. (2000) 'Talking machines and moving bodies: marketing dance music before World War I', in CORD, DCA, NDA and SDHS, 'Dancing in the Millennium' Conference Proceedings, Washington.

Coomaraswamy, A. K. (1957) *The Dance of Shiva*, rev. edn, New York: The Noonday Press.

Coombe, R.J. (2000) *The Cultural Life of Intellectual Property: Authorship, Appropriation and the Law*, Durham, NC: Duke University Press.

Cooper, E. (1986) *The Sexual Perspective: Homosexuality and Art in the Last Hundred Years in the West*, London: Routledge & Kegan Paul.

Coorlawala, U.A. (1992) 'Ruth St. Denis and India's dance renaissance', *Dance Chronicle* 15: 123–48.

——(1994) 'Classical and contemporary Indian dance: overview, criteria and choreographic analysis', PhD dissertation, New York University.

——(1996) 'The birth of Bharatanatyam and the Sanskritized body', *CORD Conference Proceedings*.

Copeland, R. (1990) 'In defence of formalism', *Dance Theatre Journal* 7, 4:4–7, 37–9.

Copeland, R. and Cohen, M. (1983) *What is Dance? Readings in Theory and Criticism*, Oxford: Oxford University Press.

Copper, J.F. (1996) *Taiwan: Nation-State or Province?* 2nd edn, Boulder, CO: Westview Press.

CORD (2009) 'Dance, the disciplines, and interdisciplinarity', *Dance Research Journal*, Congress on Research in Dance, special issue: 41:1 (Summer).

CORD/CEPA (2009) 'Proceedings: Global perspectives on dance pedagogy – research and practice', Congress on Research in Dance/Centre of Excellence for Teaching and Learning in Performing Arts, Special Conference, de Montfort University, Leicester.

Cowan, J.K. (1990) *Dance and the Body Politic in Northern Greece*, Princeton, NJ: Princeton University Press.

Croce, A. (1979) *Afterimages*, New York: Vintage Books.

Csordas, T. (1993) 'Somatic modes of attention', *Cultural Anthropology* 8: 135–56.

——(1994) *The Sacred Self: A Cultural Phenomenology of Charismatic Healing*, Berkeley, CA: University of California Press.

——(1999) 'Embodiment and cultural phenomenology', in Weiss, G. and Haber H. F. (eds), *Perspectives on Embodiment: The Intersections of Nature and Culture*, New York: Routledge.

Cutler, C. (1983) 'What is popular music?' in Horn, D. (ed.), *Popular Music Perspectives 2*, Papers from the Second International Conference on Popular Music Studies, Reggio Emilia, IASPM: 3–12.

Daly, A. (1987) 'The Balanchine woman: of hummingbirds and channel swimmers', *The Drama Review* (TDR) 31, 1: 9–19.

——(1995) *Done into Dance: Isadora Duncan in America*, Bloomington, IN: Indiana University Press.

Daniel, Y. (1991) 'Changing values in Cuban rumba: a lower class black dance appropriated by the Cuban revolution', *Dance Research Journal* 23, 2: 1–10.

——(1995) *Rumba: Dance and Social Change in Contemporary Cuba*, Bloomington, IN: Indiana University Press.

——(2002) 'Cuban dance: an orchard of Caribbean creativity', in S. Sloat (ed.), *Caribbean Dance from Abakuá to Zouk: How Movement Shapes Identity*, Gainesville, FL: University of Florida Press.

——(2005) *Dancing Wisdom: Embodied Knowledge in Haitian Vodou, Cuban Yoruba, and Bahian Condomblé*, Champaign, IL: University of Illinois Press.

Davies, C.A. (2007 [1999]) *Reflexive Ethnography: A Guide to Researching Selves and Others*, London: Routledge.

Davies, S. (1989) 'The artist's view', *Dance Theatre Journal* 7, 2 (Autumn): 8–9, 27.

——(2002) *Woman's Hour* interview with Jenny Murray, 24 September, <http://www.bbc.co.uk/radio4/womanshour/2002_39_tue_04.shtml > (accessed 1 September 2008).

DeFrantz, T. (2002) *Dancing Many Drums: Excavations in African American Dance*, Madison, WI: University of Wisconsin Press.

——(2004a) *Dancing Revelations: Alvin Ailey's Embodiment of African American Culture*, New York: Oxford University Press.

——(2004b) 'The black beat made visible: hip hop dance and body power', in Lepecki, A. (ed.), *Of the Presence of the Body: Essays on Dance and Performance Theory*, Middletown, CT: Wesleyan University Press.

——(2005) 'African American dance: philosophy, aesthetics, and "beauty" ', *Topoi: An International Review of Philosophy* 24, 1: 93–102.

Deleuze, G. (1988) *Foucault*, trans. Séan Hand, Minneapolis, MN: University of Minnesota.

——(1991) *Coldness and Cruelty*, New York: Zone Books.

——(1996) *Crítica y Clínica*, trans. T. Kauf, Barcelona: Anagrama.

Deleuze, G. and Foucault, M. (1977) 'Intellectuals and power', in Bouchard, D. (ed.), *Language, Counter-Memory, Practice: Selected Essays and Interviews by Michel Foucault*, New York: Cornell University Press.

Dempster, E. (1988) 'Women writing the body: let's watch a little how she dances', in Sheridan, S. (ed.), *Grafts: Feminist Cultural Criticism*, London: Verso.

——(1999) 'Ballet and its Other: modern dance in Australia', in Brannigan, E. (ed.), *Movement and Performance (MAP) Symposium*, 25 and 26 July 1998, Melbourne: Ausdance.

Denby, E. (1986) *Dance Writings*, London: Dance Books.

Derrida, J. (1981) [1972] *Dissemination*, trans. B. Johnson, Chicago, IL: University of Chicago Press.

——(1995) 'The rhetoric of drugs', trans. P. Kamuf *et al.*, in Weber, E. (ed.) *Points*, Stanford, CA: Stanford University Press.

Desai, J. (2004) *Beyond Bollywood: The Cultural Politics of South Asian Diasporic Film*, New York: Routledge.

Desjarlais, R. (1992) *Body and Emotion: The Aesthetics of Illness and Healing in the Nepal Himalayas*, Philadelphia, PA: University of Pennsylvania Press.

Desmond, J. (1991) 'Dancing out the difference: cultural imperialism and Ruth St. Denis's "Radha" of 1906', *Signs: Journal of Women in Culture and Society* 17, 1: 28–49.

——(1992) 'Hula hips and smiling lips: Americans abroad at home' in Society of Dance History Scholars, *American Dance Abroad: Influence of the United States Experience*, Proceedings of the SDHS 15th Annual Conference: 37–45.

——(ed.) (1997a) *Meaning in Motion: New Cultural Studies of Dance*, Durham, NC: Duke University Press.

——(1997b) 'Introduction', in Desmond, J. (ed.), *Meaning in Motion: New Cultural Studies of Dance*, Durham, NC: Duke University Press.

——(2000) 'Terra incognita: mapping new territory in dance and "cultural studies" ', *Dance Research Journal* 32, 1: 43–53.

——(2001) *Dancing Desires: Choreographing Sexualities On and Off the Stage*, Madison, WI: University of Wisconsin Press.

Diffey, T.J. (1969) 'The republic of art', *British Journal of Aesthetics* 9: 145–56.

Dils, A. and Albright, A.C. (eds) (2001) *Moving History/Dancing Cultures: A Dance History Reader*, Middletown, CT: Wesleyan University Press.

Doane, R. (2006) 'The habitus of dancing: notes on the swing dance revival in New York City', *Journal of Contemporary Ethnography* 35: 84–116.

Dodds, S. (2001) *Dance on Screen: Genres and Media from Hollywood to Experimental Art*, Basingstoke: Palgrave.

Dolin, A. (1985) *Last Words*, London: Century.

Doniger, W. (1998) *The Implied Spider*, New York: Columbia University Press.

Doolittle, L. (2001/02) 'The trianon and on: reading mass social dancing in the 1930s and 1940s in Alberta, Canada', *Dance Research Journal* 33, 2: 11–28.

Drewal, M.T. (1992) *Yoruba Ritual: Performers, Play, Agency*, Bloomington, IN: Indiana University Press.

Dubey, M. (1995) 'Gayl Jones and the matrilineal metaphor of tradition', *Signs* 20, 2: 245–67.

duCille, A. (1993) *The Coupling Convention: Sex, Text, and Tradition in Black Women's Fiction*, New York: Oxford University Press.

Dumas, R. (1998) 'On film: an interview by Deborah Jowitt', *Writings on Dance* 17: 1–14.

Dunagan, C. (2005) 'Dance, knowledge, power', *Topoi: An International Review of Philosophy* 24, 1: 29–41.

Duncan, I. (1927) *My Life*, New York: Liveright.

Dunin, E.I. (2006) 'Romani dance event in Skopje, Macedonia: research strategies, cultural identities, and technologies', in Buckland, T.J. (ed.) *Dancing from Past to Present: Nation, Culture, Identities*, Madison, WI: University of Wisconsin Press.

Dyer, R. (1990) *Now You See It*, London: Routledge.

——(1993) 'I seem to find the happiness I seek', in Thomas, H. (ed.), *Dance, Gender and Culture*, London: Macmillan.

Eco, U. (1984 [1979]) *The Role of the Reader: Explorations in the Semiotics of Texts*, Bloomington, IN: Indiana University Press.

Eichenbaum, R. (2008) *The Dancer Within: Intimate Conversations with Great Dancers*, Middletown, CT: Wesleyan University Press.

Eksteins, M. (1989) *The Rites of Spring: The Great War and the Birth of the Modern Age*, Boston, MA: A Mariner/Peter Davison Book, Houghton Mifflin Company.

Essed, P. and Goldberg, D.T. (2002) 'The social injustices of sameness', *Ethnic and Racial Studies* 25, 6, November: 1066–82.

Erdman, J. (1996) 'Dance discourses: rethinking the history of the "Oriental dance" ', in Morris, G. (ed.), *Moving Words: Re-writing Dance*, New York: Routledge.

Farjeon, A. (1994) 'Choreographers: dancing for de Valois and Ashton', *Dance Chronicle* 17, 2: 195–206.

Farnell, B. (1994) 'Ethno-graphics and the moving body', *Man* (now *Journal of the Royal Anthropological Institute*), 29, 4: 929–37.

——(1999) 'Moving bodies, moving selves', *Annual Review of Anthropology* 28: 341–73.

Favel, F. (2005) 'Waskawewin', *Topoi: An International Review of Philosophy* 24, 1: 113–15.

Featherstone, M. (2001) 'The body in consumer culture', in Johnston, J.R. (ed.), *The American Body in Context*, Wilmington, DE: Scholarly Resources, Inc.

Ferguson, M. and Golding, P. (eds) (1997) *Cultural Studies in Question*, London: Sage.

Fiori, U. (1983) 'Popular music: theory, practice, value', in Horn, D. (ed.), *Popular Music Perspectives 2*, Papers from the Second International Conference on Popular Music Studies, Reggio Emilia, IASPM: 13–23.

Flitch, J.E.C. (1913) *Modern Dancing and Dancers*, London: Grant Richards Ltd.

Fokine, M. (1961) *Memoirs of a Ballet Master*, London: Constable.

Foley, C. (2001/2) 'Perceptions of Irish step dance: national, global and local', *Dance Research Journal* 33, 1: 34–45.

Fonarow, W. (1997) 'The spatial organization of the Indie music gig', in Gelder, K. and Thornton, S. (eds), *The Subcultures Reader*, London: Routledge.

Foster, S. (1986) *Reading Dancing: Bodies and Subjects in Contemporary American Dance*, Berkeley, CA: University of California Press.

——(1991) 'Proposal for a Ph.D. in dance history and theory at UCR', University of California unpublished internal document.

——(1995) *Choreographing History*, Bloomington, IN: Indiana University Press.

——(ed.) (1996a) *Corporealities*, London: Routledge.

——(1996b) 'The ballerina's phallic pointe', in Foster, S. (ed.), *Corporealities: Dancing, Knowledge, Culture, and Power*, London: Routledge.

——(1996c) *Choreography and Narrative: Ballet's Staging of Story and Desire*, Bloomington, IN: Indiana University Press.

——(2002) *Dances That Describe Themselves: The Improvised Choreography of Richard Bull*, Middletown, CT: Wesleyan University Press.

——(2003) 'Taken by surprise: improvisation in dance and mind', in Albright, A.C. and Gere, D. (eds) *Taken By Surprise: A Dance Improvisation Reader*, Middletown, CT: Wesleyan University Press.

——(ed.) (2009) *Worlding Dance*, New York: Palgrave MacMillan.

Foster, S., Rothfield, P. and Dunagan, C. (2005) 'Introduction', *Topoi: An International Review of Philosophy* 24, 1: 3–14.

Foucault, M. (1972) *The Archaeology of Knowledge*, New York: Pantheon.

——(1977a) *Discipline and Punish: The Birth of the Prison*, New York: Vintage Books.

——(1977b) 'What is an author?', in Bouchard, D. (ed.), *Language, Counter-Memory, Practice: Selected essays and Interviews by Michel Foucault*, Ithaca, NY: Cornell University Press.

——(1984) 'Nietzsche, genealogy, history', in Rabinow, P. (ed.), *The Foucault Reader*, New York: Pantheon Books.

——(1984) *The Foucault Reader*, Paul Rabinow (ed.), New York: Pantheon Books.

——(as Maurice Florence) (1994) 'Foucault, Michel, 1926–', trans. C. Porter, in *The Cambridge Companion to Foucault*, Cambridge: Cambridge University Press.

——(1997) 'Of other spaces: utopias and heterotopias' in Neil Leach (ed.), *Rethinking Architecture*, London: Routledge.

Foulkes, J. (2002) *Modern Bodies: Dance and American Modernism from Martha Graham to Alvin Ailey*, Chapel Hill, NC: University of North Carolina Press.

Franko, M. (1989) 'Repeatability: reconstruction and beyond', *Theatre Journal* 41, 1: 56–74.

——(1995) *Dancing Modernism/Performing Politics*, Bloomington, IN: Indiana University Press.

——(1996) 'History/theory, criticism/practice', in Foster, S. (ed.), *Corporealities: Dancing, Knowledge, Culture, and Power*, London: Routledge.

——(2002) *The Work of Dance: Labor, Movement, and Identity in the 1930s*, Middletown, CT: Wesleyan University Press.

Franko, M. and Richards, A. (2000) *Acting on the Past*, Middletown, CT: Wesleyan University Press.

Freud, S. (1962) *Three Essays on the Theory of Sexuality*, trans. and ed. J. Strachey, New York: Basic Books.

Frith, S. (1991) 'The good, the bad, and the indifferent: defending popular culture from the populists', *Diacritics* 21, 4: 101–15.

——(1996) *Performing Rites: On the Value of Popular Music*, Oxford: Oxford University Press.

Frosch, J. (1999) 'Dance ethnography: tracing the weave of dance in the fabric of culture', in Fraleigh, S. H. and Hanstein, P. (eds), *Researching Dance: Evolving Modes of Inquiry*, London: Dance Books.

Frow, J. (1995) *Cultural Studies and Cultural Value*, Oxford: Oxford University Press.

——(2006) *Genre*, London and New York: Routledge.

Gaerlan, B. (1999) 'In the court of the sultan: orientalism, nationalism, and modernity in Philippine and Filipino American dance', *Journal of Asian American Studies* 2, 3: 251–87.

Garafola, L. (1989) *Diaghilev's Ballets Russes*, Oxford: Oxford University Press.

Gautier, T. (1973) *The Romantic Ballet as seen by Théophile Gautier: being his notices of all the principal performances of ballet given at Paris during the years 1837–1848*, trans. Cyril Beaumont, New York: Dance Horizons.

Gautier, T., Chasles, P. and Janin, J. (1845) *Les Beautés de l'Opéra*, Paris: Soulié.

Geertz, C. (1973) *The Interpretation of Cultures*, New York: Basic Books, Inc.

George, D.E.R. (1999) *Buddhism as/in Performance: Analysis of Meditation in Theatrical Practice*, New Delhi: D.K. Printworld.

Gere, D. (2004) *How to Make Dances in an Epidemic: Tracking Choreography in the Age of AIDS*, Madison, WI: University of Wisconsin Press.

Gerschick, T. (2000) 'Toward a theory of disability and gender', *Signs: Journal of Women in Culture and Society*, 25, 4: 1263–8.

Giannachi, G. and Stewart, N. (eds) (2005) *Performing Nature: Explorations in Ecology and the Arts*, Bern: Peter Lang.

Giersdorf, J. R. (2008) 'Dancing, Marching, Fighting: Folk, the Dance Ensemble of the East German Armed Forces, and Other Choreographies of Nationhood', *Discourses in Dance*, 4.2 39–58

Gilroy, P. (2004) *Between Camps: Nations, Cultures and the Allure of Race*, London: Routledge.

Gitelman, C. (2003) *Liebe Hanya: Mary Wigman's Letters to Hanya Holm*, Madison, WI: University of Wisconsin Press.

Gitelman, C. and Martin, R. (eds) (2007) *The Returns of Alwin Nikolais: Bodies, Boundaries and the Dance Canon*, Middletown, CT: Wesleyan University Press.

Giurchesu, A. (1990) 'The use of traditional symbols for recasting the present: a case study of tourism in Rumania', *Dance Studies* 14: 47–64.

Giurchesu, A. and Torp, L. (1991) 'Theory and method in dance research: a European approach to the holistic study of dance', *Year Book for Traditional Music* 23: 1–10.

Gluck, C. (1985) *Japan's Modern Myth: Ideology in the Late Meiji Period*, Princeton, NJ: Princeton University Press.

González, R. (2002) *Cine Cubano: Ese ojo que nos ve*, San Juan: Editorial Plaza Mayor.

Gore, G. (1997) 'The beat goes on: trance, dance and tribalism in rave culture', in Thomas, H. (ed.), *Dance in the City*, London: Macmillan.

——(1999) 'Textual fields: representation in dance ethnography', in Buckland, T. J. (ed.), *Dance in the Field: Theory, Methods and Issues in Dance Ethnography*, Basingstoke: Macmillan.

Gottschild, B.D. (1996) *Digging the Africanist Presence in American Performance: Dance and Other Contexts*, Westport, CT: Praeger & Greenwood Press.

——(2000) *Waltzing in the Dark: African American Vaudeville and Race Politics in the Swing Era*, New York: St. Martin's.

——(2005) *The Black Dancing Body: A Geography from Coon to Cool*, Basingstoke: Palgrave Macmillan.

Goulish, M. (2000) *39 Microlectures: In Proximity of Performance*, London: Routledge.

Graff, E. (1997) *Stepping Left: Dance and Politics in New York City, 1928–1942*, Durham, NC: Duke University Press.

Graham, M. (1950) 'Martha Graham is interviewed by Pierre Tugal', *Dancing Times* October: 21–2.

——(1991) *Blood Memory: An Autobiography*, New York: Doubleday.

Grau, A. (1992) 'Intercultural research in the performing arts', *Dance Research* 10: 3–27.

——(2005) 'When the landscape becomes flesh: an investigation into body boundaries with special reference to Tiwi dance and Western classical ballet', *Body and Society* 11, 4: 141–63.

Grau, A. and Jordan, S. (2000) *Europe Dancing: Perspectives on Theatre, Dance and Cultural Identity*, London: Routledge.

Grau, A. and Wierre-Gore, G. (eds) (2006) *Anthropologie de la danse: genése et construction d'une discipline*, Paris: Centre National de la Danse.

Grosz, E. (1989) *Sexual Subversions*, Sydney: Allen and Unwin.

——(1990) 'Sexual relations', in *Jacques Lacan: A Feminist Introduction*, London: Routledge.

——(1995) *Space, Time and Perversion: Essays on the Politics of Bodies*, London: Routledge.

——(2001) *Architecture from the Outside*, Cambridge, MA: MIT.

Guest, I. (1972 [1954]) *The Romantic Ballet in England: its Development, Fulfilment, and Decline*, London: Dance Books.

——(1980 [1960]) *The Romantic Ballet in Paris*, London: Dance Books.

——(1969) 'Dandies and dancers', *Dance Perspectives* 37.

——(1984) *Jules Perrot: Master of the Romantic Ballet*, London: Dance Books.

Gunaratnam, Y. (1997) 'Culture is not enough: a critique of multi-culturalism in palliative care', in Field, D., Hockey, J. and Small, N. (eds), *Death, Gender and Ethnicity*, London: Routledge.

Habermas, J. (2001) 'Modernity: an unfinished project', in Malpas, S. (ed.), *Postmodern Debates*, New York: Palgrave.

Hagood, T.K. (2000) *A History of Dance in American Higher Education*, Lewiston, NY: Edwin Mellen Press.

Hahn, T. (2007) *Sensational Knowledge: Embodying Culture through Japanese Dance*, Middletown, CT: Wesleyan University Press.

Hall, J.L. (2008) 'Mapping the multifarious: the genrification of dance music club cultures', in Lansdale, J. (ed.), *Decentring Dancing Texts*, Basingstoke: Palgrave.

Hall, S. (1992) 'The question of cultural identity', in Hall, S., Held D. and McGrew, T. (eds), *Modernity and its Future*, Cambridge: Polity Press.

Halprin, A. (1995) *Moving Towards Life*, Middletown, CT: Wesleyan University Press.

Hammergren, L. (1995) 'Different personas: a history of one's own', in Foster, S. (ed.), *Choreographing History*, Bloomington, IN: Indiana University Press.

——(2004) 'Many Sources, Many Voices', in Carter, A. (ed.), *Rethinking Dance History: A Reader*, London: Routledge.

Hanna, J.L. (2000) 'Ballet to exotic dance: under the censorship watch', in CORD, DCA, NDA and SDHS, *Dancing in the Millennium Conference Proceedings*, Washington, DC, pp. 230–4.

Hannah, D. (2007) 'Containment + contamination: a performance landscape for the senses at PQ03', in Banes, S. and Lepecki, A. (eds), *The Senses in Performance*, London: Routledge.

——(2008) '*Her Topia*: a dance-architecture event', in Hannah, D. and Harsløf, O. (eds), *Performance Design*, University of Copenagen: Museum Tusculanum Press.

Haraway, D. (1988) 'Situated knowledges: the science question in feminism and the privilege of partial perspective', *Feminist Studies* 14, 3: 575–99.

Hartman, S. (1997) *Scenes of Subjection: Terror, Slavery, and Self-Making in Nineteenth-Century America*, New York: Oxford University Press.

Harvey, D. (1989) *The Condition of Postmodernity: An Enquiry into the Origins of Social Change*, Oxford: Basil Blackwell.

Hast, D.E. (1993) 'Performance, Transformation, and Community: Contra Dance in New England', *Dance Research Journal* 25, 1: 21–32.

Hay, D. (2000) *My Body, the Buddhist*, Middletown, CT: Wesleyan University Press.

Heath, C. (1977) *The Beauties of the Opera and Ballet*, New York: Da Capo Press.

Heath, S. (1991) 'The turn of the subject', in Burnett, R. (ed.), *Explorations in Film Theory: Selected Essays from Ciné-Tracts*, Bloomington, IN: Indiana University Press.

Hemenway, R. (1977) *Zora Neale Hurston: A Literary Biography*, Champaign, IL: University of Illinois Press.

Herrnstein Smith, B. (1983) 'Contingencies of Value', *Critical Inquiry* 10, 1: 1–35.

Hill, L. and Paris, H. (eds) (2006) *Performance and Place*, Basingstoke: Palgrave MacMillan.

Hine, C. (2005) *Virtual Methods*, Oxford: Berg.

Hirst, P. (1993) 'An answer to relativism', in Squires, J. (ed.), *Principled Positions: Postmodernism and the Rediscovery of Value*, London: Lawrence & Wishart.

Hodson, M. (1985) 'Ritual design in the new dance: Nijinsky's *Le Sacre du Printemps*', *Dance Research* 3, 2: 35–45.

Holt, H. (1933) Letter to R. Wunsch, 28 January, Department of College Archives and Special Collections, Rollins College.

Honour, H. (1979) *Romanticism*, New York: Harper & Row (Icon Editions).

Hoy, D. (1999) 'Critical resistance: Foucault and Bourdieu', in Weiss, G. and Haber H.F. (eds), *Perspectives on Embodiment: The Intersections of Nature and Culture*, New York: Routledge.

Hughes-Freeland, F. (2008) *Embodied Communities: Dance Traditions and Change in Java*, New York: Berghahn Books.

Hurston, Z.N. (1925) Letter to A.N. Meyer, 10 November, Hurston-Annie Nathan Meyer Correspondence, American Jewish Archives.

——(1931) Letter to C.O. Mason, 15 October, Alain Locke Papers, Manuscript Division, Moorland Spingarn Research Center, Howard University.

——(1933) Letter to E. Grover, 1 February, Department of Special Collections, George A. Smathers Libraries, University of Florida.

——(1939) Works Progress Administration interview by Herbert Halpert, sound recording, June, Jacksonville, FL, Archive of Folk Culture, Library of Congress.

——(1996) *Dust Tracks on a Road*, New York: Harper Perennial.

——(1999) 'The Fire Dance', in Bordelon, P. (ed.), *Go Gator and Muddy the Water: Writings by Zora Neale Hurston from the Federal Writers' Project*, New York: W.W. Norton & Company.

Husserl, E. (1931) *Cartesian Meditations*, The Hague: Nijhoff.

Huxley, M. (1999) 'Some historical origins of the choreographed body as a modernist statement', unpublished paper given at the annual meeting for the Congress on Research in Dance, Pomona College, Claremont, California.

Huyssen, A. (1986) *After the Great Divide*, London: Macmillan.

Hycner, R. and Jacobs, L. (1995) *The Healing Relationship in Gestalt Therapy*, Gouldsboro, ME: The Gestalt Journal Press.

Irigaray, L. (1985) *This Sex Which is Not One*, trans. C. Porter, New York: Cornell University Press.

Iwabuchi, K. (1994) 'Complicit exoticism: Japan and its Other', from *Continuum: The Australian Journal of Media and Culture*, special issue on Critical Multiculturalism, O'Regan, T. (ed.), 8, 2 <http://www.mcc.murdoch.edu.au/readingroom/8.2/Iwabuchi.html>.

Iyer, A. (1997) 'South Asian dance: the traditional/classical idioms', in Iyer, A. (ed.), *Choreography and Dance: South Asian Dance*, Amsterdam: Harwood Academic Publishing.

Jackson, J. (2001/2) 'Improvisation in African-American vernacular dancing', *Dance Research Journal* 33, 2: 40–53.

Jackson, S. (2004) *Professing Performance*, Cambridge: Cambridge University Press.

Jakobson, R. (1960) 'Closing statements: linguistics and poetics', in Sebeok, T. (ed.), *Style in Language*, Cambridge, MA: MIT Press.

——(1972) 'Linguistics and poetics', in De George, R. and De George, E. (eds), *The Structuralists: From Marx to Lévi-Strauss*, New York: Anchor Books.

Jeyasingh, S. (1995) 'Imaginary homelands: creating a new dance language', *Border Tensions: Dance Discourse*, Proceedings of the Fifth Study of Dance Conference, Guildford: University of Surrey.

——(1997) 'Text context dance', in Iyer, A. (ed.), *Choreography and Dance: South Asian Dance*, Amsterdam: Harwood Academic Publishing.

Johnson, D. (2005) 'The poised disturbances of Raimund Hoghe', *Dance Theatre Journal*, 2: 36–40.

Jordan, S. (1992) *Striding Out: Aspects of Contemporary and New Dance in Britain*, London: Dance Books.

——(2000) *Moving Music: Dialogues with Music in Twentieth Century Ballet*, London: Dance Books.

Jordan, S. and Thomas, H. (1994) 'Dance and gender: formalism and semiotics reconsidered', *Dance Research* XII, 2: 3–14.

Jowitt, D. (1977) *Dance Beat: Selected Views and Reviews, 1967–1976*, New York: Marcel Dekker.

——(1988) *Time and the Dancing Image*, Berkeley, CA: University of California Press.

Kaeppler, A.L. (1985) 'Structured movement systems in Tonga', in Spencer, P. (ed.), *Society and the Dance*, New York: Cambridge University Press.

Kaeppler, A.L. and Dunin, E.I. (eds) (2007) *Dance Structures: Perspectives on the Analysis of Human Movement*, Budapest: Akadémiai Kiadó.

Kamuf, P. (1988) *Signature Pieces: On the Institution of Authorship*, Ithaca, NY: Cornell University Press.

Kant, I. (2005) [1797] *Der Streit der Fakultäten*, Hamburg: Felix Meiner Verlag.

Karina, L., Kant, M. and Steinberg, J. (2004) *Hitler's Dancers: German Modern Dance and the Third Reich*, New York: Berghahn.

Kassabian, A. (1999) 'Popular', in Horner, B. and Swiss, T. (eds), *Key Terms in Popular Music and Culture*, Oxford: Blackwell.

Kaviraj, S. (1994) 'On construction of colonial power: structure, discourse, hegemony', in Engles, D. and Marks, S. (eds), *Contesting Colonial Hegemony*, London: British Academic Press.

Keali'inohomoku, J. (1969/70) 'An anthropologist looks at ballet as a form of ethnic dance', *Impulse*, San Francisco: Impulse Publications, pp. 24–33.

——(1974) 'Dance culture as a microcosm of holistic culture', in Comstock, T. (ed.), *New Dimensions in Dance Research: Anthropology and Dance: The American Indian*, CORD Research Annual 6: 99–106.

Kellner, D. (ed.) (1994) *Baudrillard: A Critical Reader*, Oxford: Blackwell.

Kersenboom-Story, S. (1987) *Nityasumangali: Devadasi Tradition in South India*, New Delhi: Motilal Banarasidass.

Keynes, G. (ed.) (1966) *Blake Complete Writings*, London: Oxford University Press.

Khokar, M. (1997a) 'Devadasis in tights and ballet slippers, what?', *Sruti*, 154 (July): 21–6.

——(1997b) 'Male dance in America: the original catalyst', *Sruti*, 150 (March): 19–25.

King, K. (2005) 'The dancing philosopher: for Susan Leigh Foster', *Topoi: An International Review of Philosophy* 24, 1: 103–11.

Kirstein, L. (1935) *Dance: a Short History of Classical Theatrical Dancing*, New York: G.P. Putnam's Sons.

——(1969) *Dance: A Short History of Classical Dancing*, New York: Continuum.

Kleist, H.V. (1984) *Der Zweikampf, Die heilige Cäcilie, Sämtliche Anekdoten, Über das Marionettentheater*, Stuttgart: Reclam.

Kraut, A. (2008) *Choreographing the Folk: The Dance Stagings of Zora Neale Hurston*, Minneapolis, MN: University of Minnesota Press.

——(2009) 'Race-ing choreographic copyright', in Foster, S. (ed.), *Worlding Dance*, Basingstoke: Palgrave MacMillan.

Krüger, S. (2008) *Ethnography in the Performing Arts: A Student Guide*, The Higher Education Academy: Palatine.

Laban, R. (1966) *Choreutics*, London: Macdonald and Evans.

LaBelle, Brandon (2008) *Street Noise on the contours and politics of public sound*, Hannah, Dorita and Harslof, Olav, *Performance Design*, Copenhagen: Museum Tusculanum pp. 159–177.

LaBoskey, S. (2001/2) 'Getting off: portrayals of masculinity in hip hop dance in film', *Dance Research Journal* 33, 2: 112–20.

Lacan, J. (1985) 'God and the *jouissance* of the woman,' trans. J. Rose, in Mitchell, J. and Rose, J. (eds), *Feminine Sexuality: Jacques Lacan and the Ecole Freudienne*, New York: W.W. Norton.

Lakhia, K. (1995) *Nritya Parva*, Ahmedabad: Abhigam.

Lane, J. M. (2005) *Blackface Cuba, 1840–1895*, Philadelphia, PA: University of Pennsylvania Press.

Langer, S. (1953) *Feeling and Form*, New York: Charles Scribner's Sons.

Lansdale, J. (2006) 'A response to Susan Manning', *SDHS Newsletter* XXVI, 1: 2–4.

——(2007) *The Struggle with the Angel: A Poetics of Lloyd Newson's Strange Fish*, Alton: Dance Books.

——(ed.) (2008) *Decentring Dancing Texts: The Challenge of Interpreting Dances*, Basingstoke: Palgrave Macmillan.

Larasati, D. (2006) 'Dancing on the mass grave: cultural reconstruction post Indonesian massacres', unpublished PhD dissertation, University of California, Riverside.

Lauretis, T. de (1984) *Alice Doesn't: Feminism, Semiotics, Cinema*, London: Macmillan.

Lepczyk, B.F. (1981) 'A contrastive study of movement style in dance through the Laban perspective', EdD dissertation, Teacher's College, Columbia University.

Lepecki, A. (2006) *Exhausting Dance: Performance and the Politics of Movement*, New York: Routledge.

Lesschaeve, J. (1985) *The Dancer and the Dance: Merce Cunningham in Conversation with Jacqueline Lesschaeve*, New York: Marion Boyars.

Levin D. (1985) *The Body's Recollection of Being: Phenomenological Psychology and the Deconstruction of Nihilism*, London: Routledge & Kegan Paul.

Lieven, Prince P. (1980) 'Vaslav Nijinsky', in Steinberg, C. (ed.), *The Dance Anthology*, New York: New American Library.

Limon, J. (2001) *Jose Limon: An Unfinished Memoir*, Middletown, CT: Wesleyan University Press.

Lin H. (1989) *Shuo wu* (On Dance), Taipei: Yuan-liu Publishers.

——(1993) 'Legacy in China', *China Times*, 13 November.

——(2002) *Cicada*, Taipei: Ink Publishing Company.

Lin, H. *et al.* (1976) *Cloud Gate Dance Talk*, Taipei: Yuan Liu Publishers.

Lin, Y. (2004) 'Choreographing a flexible Taiwan: Cloud Gate Dance Theatre and Taiwan's changing identity, 1973–2003', Doctoral dissertation, University of California, Riverside.

Lowell Lewis, J. (1992) *Ring of Liberation: Deceptive Discourse in Brazilian Capoeira*, Chicago, IL: University of Chicago Press.

Lu, S.H. (2007) *Chinese Modernity and Global Biopolitics: Studies in Literature and Visual Culture*, Honolulu: University of Hawaii Press.

Lung Y., *et al.* (2003) *Cloud Gate at Thirty [Yunmen Sanshi]*, Taipei: Cloud Gate Dance Theatre.

Lyotard, J.F. (1984 [1979]) *The Postmodern Condition: A Report on Knowledge*, trans. G. Bennington and B. Massumi, Manchester: Manchester University Press.

McCance, D. (2004) *Medusa's Ear: University Foundings from Kant to Chora L*, New York: State University of New York Press.

McDonagh, D. (1976) *The Complete Guide to Modern Dance*, Garden City, NY: Doubleday.

McFee, G. (1992) *Understanding Dance*, London: Routledge.

——(1999) *Dance Education and Philosophy*, Aachen: Meyer & Meyer Sports.

McGuigan, J. (1992) *Cultural Populism*, London: Routledge.

McKenzie, J. (2001) *Perform or Else: From Discipline to Performance*, London: Routledge.

Mackrell J. and Craine, D. (eds) (2004 [2000]) *Oxford Dictionary of Dance*, Oxford: Oxford University Press.

McLeod, L. (1993) 'The self in gestalt therapy theory', in *British Gestalt Journal* 2, 1: 25–40.

McMains, J. (2001/2) 'Brownface: representations of Latin-ness in dancesport', *Dance Research Journal*, 33, 2: 54–71.

——(2006) *Glamour Addiction: Inside the American Ballroom Dance Industry*, Middletown, CT: Wesleyan University Press.

——(2008) 'Dancing Latin/Latin dancing: salsa and DanceSport', in Malnig, J. (ed.), *Ballroom, Boogie, Shimmy Sham, Shake: A Social and Popular Dance Reader*, Champaign, IL: University of Illinois Press.

Main, L. (2005) 'The dances of Doris Humphrey: creating a contemporary perspective through directorial interpretation', *Dance Research: The Journal of the Society for Dance Research* 23, 2: 106.

Malnig, J. (1998) 'Athena meets Venus: visions of women in social dance in the teens and early 1920s', *Dance Research Journal* 30, 2: 34–62.

——(2001) 'Two-stepping to glory: social dance and the rhetoric of social mobility', in Dils, A. and Albright, A.C. (eds), *Moving History/Dancing Cultures*, Middletown, CT: Wesleyan University Press.

——(2001/2) 'Introduction', *Dance Research Journal* 33, 2: 7–10.

——(2008) *Ballroom, Boogie, Shimmy Sham, Shake: A Social and Popular Dance Reader*, Champaign, IL: University of Illinois Press.

Malone, J. (1996) *Steppin' on the Blues: The Visible Rhythms of African American Dance*, Urbana, IL: University of Illinois Press.

Manning, S. (1993) *Ecstasy and the Demon: Feminism and Nationalism in the Dances of Mary Wigman*, Berkeley, CA: University of California Press.

——(2004) *Modern Dance/Negro Dance: Race in Motion*, Minneapolis, MN: University of Minnesota Press.

——(2006) 'Letter from the President', *SDHS Newsletter* XXVI, 2: 1–2.

Marcuse, H. (1977) *The Aesthetic Dimension*, London: Macmillan.

Marglin, F.A. (1985) *Wives of the God-King*, New York: Oxford University Press.

Marinis, M. de (1993) *The Semiotics of Performance*, Bloomington, IN: Indiana University Press.

Marranca, B., Robinson, M. and Chaudhuri, U. (1991) 'Criticism, culture, and performance: an interview with Edward Said', in Marranca, B. and Dasgupta, G. (eds), *Interculturalism and Performance*, New York: Oxford University Press.

Martin, E. (1994) 'Chapter seven: flexible systems', in *Flexible Bodies: The Role of Immunity in American Culture from the Days of Polio to the Age of AIDS*, Boston, MA: Beacon Press.

Martin, J. (1965[1939]) *Introduction to the Dance*, New York: Norton and Dance Horizons.

Martin, R. (1996) 'Overreading the promised land: towards a narrative of content in dance', in Foster, S. (ed.), *Corporealities: Dancing, Knowledge, Culture, and Power*, London: Routledge.

——(1998) *Critical Moves: Dance Studies in Theory and Politics*, Durham, NC: Duke University Press.

Massey, D, (2005) *For Space*, London: Sage.

Mauss, M. (1973) 'Techniques of the body', *Economy and Society* II, 1: 70–88.

Maxwell, R. (ed.) (2001) *Culture Works: The Political Economy of Culture*, Minneapolis, MN: University of Minnesota Press.

Meduri, A. (1996) 'Nation, woman, representation: the sutured history of the devadasi and her dance', PhD dissertation, New York University.

——(1988) 'Bharata Natyam: What are you?', *Asian Theatre Journal*, 5, 1 (Spring): 1–22.

Meinhof, U.H. and Smith, J. (eds) (2000) *Intertextuality and the Media*, Manchester: Manchester University Press.

Mendoza, Z.S. (2000) *Shaping Society through Dance: Mestizo Ritual Performance in the Peruvian Andes*, Chicago, IL: University of Chicago Press.

Merleau-Ponty, M. (1962) *Phenomenology of Perception*, trans. C. Smith, London: Routledge and Kegan Paul.

Middleton, R. (1997) *Studying Popular Music*, Milton Keynes: Open University Press.

Miller, N. (1995) *French Dressing*, New York: Routledge.

Monaghan, T. (2001/2) 'Why study the lindy hop?', *Dance Research Journal* 33, 2: 124–7.

Monaghan, T. and Dodson, M. (2000) 'Has Swing dance been revived?' in CORD, DCA, NDA and SDHS, 'Dancing in the Millennium' Conference Proceedings, Washington: 317–20.

Moore, C.-L. (1999) 'The choreutic theory of Rudolf Laban: form and transformation', PhD thesis, University of Surrey.

Moore, R. (1997) *Nationalizing Blackness: Afrocubanismo and Artistic Revolution in Havana, 1920–1940*, Pittsburgh, PA: University of Pittsburgh Press.

Morley, D. (1997) 'Theoretical orthodoxies: textualism, constructivism and the "New Ethnography" in Cultural Studies', in Ferguson, M. and Golding, P. (eds), *Cultural Studies in Question*, London: Sage.

Morris, G. (1996) 'Introduction', in Morris, G. (ed.), *Moving Words: Re-writing Dance*, London: Routledge.

Mueller, J. (1986) *Astaire Dancing: The Musical Films*, London: Hamish Hamilton.

Münz, R. (1989) 'Theatralität und Theater. Konzeptionelle Erwägungen zum For-schungsprojekt "Theatergeschichte"' *Wissenschaftliche Beiträge der Thea-terhochschule 'Hans Otto'* 1: 5–20.

Nancy, J.-L. (1994) 'Corpus', in MacConnell, J.F. and Sakarin, L. (eds), *Thinking Bodies*, Stanford, CA: Stanford University Press.

Neale, S. (1983) 'Masculinity as spectacle', *Screen* 24, 6: 2–19 Limelight Editions.

Ness, S. (1992) *Body, Movement and Culture: Kinesthetic and Visual Symbolism in a Philippine Community*, Philadelphia, PA: University of Pennsylvania Press.

——(1997) 'Originality in the postcolony: choreographing the neoethnic body of Philippine dance', *Cultural Anthropology* 12, 1: 64–108.

——(2001) 'Dancing in the field: notes from memory', in Dils, A. and Albright, A.C. (eds), *Moving History/Dancing Cultures: A Dance History Reader*, Middletown, CT: Wesleyan University Press.

——(2004) 'Being a body in a cultural way: understanding the cultural in the embo-diment of dance' in Thomas H. and Ahmed, J. (eds), *Cultural Bodies: Ethnography and Theory*, Oxford: Blackwell.

Nijinska, B. (1981) *Early Memoirs*, London: Faber & Faber.

——(1986) 'On movement and the school of movement', in Baer, N. (ed.), *Bronislava Nijinska: A Dancer's Legacy*, San Francisco: The Fine Arts Museums of San Francisco.

Novack, C.J. (1986) 'Sharing the dance: an ethnography of contact improvisation', PhD dissertation, Columbia University.

——(1990) *Sharing the Dance: Contact Improvisation and American Culture*, Madison, WI: University of Wisconsin Press.

O'Flaherty, W.D. (1980) *Women, Androgynes and Other Mythical Beasts*, Chicago, IL: University of Chicago Press.

Ohno, K. and Ohno, Y. (2004) *Kazuo Ohno's World from Without and Within*, trans. John Barrett, Middletown, CT: Wesleyan University Press.

O'Neill, J. (1985) *Five Bodies: The Human Shape of Modern Society*, Ithaca, NY: Cor-nell University Press.

Ong, A. (1999) *Flexible Citizenship: The Cultural Logics of Transnationality*, Durham, NC: Duke University Press.

Orbell, Margaret (1995) *The Illustrated Encyclopedia of Maori Myth and Legend*, Christchurch: Canterbury University.

O'Shea, J. (1998) 'Traditional Indian dance and the making of interpretive commu-nities', *Asian Theatre Journal*, 15, 1 (Spring): 45–63.

——(2006) 'Dancing through history and ethnography: Indian classical dance and the performance of the past', in Buckland, T. (ed.), *Dancing from Past to Present: Nation, Culture, Identities*, Madison, WI: University of Wisconsin Press.

——(2007) *At Home in the World: Bharata Natyam on the Global Stage*, Middletown, CT: Wesleyan University Press.

Osumare, H. (2000) 'Performance and performativity in global hip hop: Hawai'i as case study', in CORD, DCA, NDA and SDHS, 'Dancing in the Millennium' Conference Proceedings, Washington: 334–8.

Ovid (2004) *Metamorphosis*. Translated by David Raeburn. London: Penguin.

Parmenter, M. (2008) 'Hand to hand: intentionality in phenomenology and con-temporary dance', MA thesis, University of Auckland.

Paxton, S. (1986) 'Small dance', in *Contact Quarterly* 11, 1: 48–50.

PCD (1839) *Petit Courrier des Dames*, (1839–[41]) Paris: Imprimerie de Dondy, Dupré.

Penny, P. (1999) 'Dancing at the interface of the social and the theatrical: focus on the participatory patterns of contemporary competition ballroom dancers in Britain', *Dance Research*, 17, 1: 47–74.

Perls, F. (1969) *Gestalt Therapy Verbatim*, Moab, UT: Real People Press.

Perls, F., Hefferline, R. and Goodman P. (1951) *Gestalt Therapy Excitement and Growth in the Human Personality*, London: Souvenir Press Ltd.

Petermann, K. (1980) 'Aufgaben und Möglichkeiten der Tanzwissenschaft in der DDR', *Material zum Theater* 125: 49–65.

Pettus, A. (2007) 'End of the melting pot? The new wave of immigrants presents new challenges', *Harvard Magazine*, May–June: 44–53.

Phelan, P. (1993) *Unmarked: The Politics of Performance*, New York: Routledge.

——(1996) 'Dance and the history of hysteria', in Foster, S. (ed.), *Corporealities: Dancing Knowledge, Culture and Power*, London: Routledge.

Phillips, K. (2005) 'Absurdism, anarchy and mime', *Dance Theatre Journal*, 20, 1: 21–5.

Piedra, J. (1997) 'Hip poetics', in Delgado, C.F. and Muñoz, J.E. (eds), *Everynight Life: Culture and Dance in Latino America*, Durham, NC: Duke University Press.

Pini, M. (1997) 'Cyborgs, nomads and the raving feminine', in Thomas, H. (ed.), *Dance in the City*, London: Macmillan.

Pooler, J.A. (2002) *Demographic Targeting: The Essential Role of Population Groups in Retail Marketing*, Aldershot: Ashgate.

Porter Abbott, H. (2002) *The Cambridge Introduction to Narrative*, Cambridge: Cambridge University Press.

Praz, M. (1967) *The Romantic Agony*, London: Thames & Hudson.

Preston-Dunlop, V. (1999) *An Extraordinary Life*, London: Dance Books.

Programme (1932) *The Great Day* programme, 10 January, John Golden Theatre, Prentiss Taylor Papers, Archives of American Art, Smithsonian Institution.

——(1939) *The Fire Dance* programme, 25 January, New Auditorium, Orlando, Florida, Department of Special Collections, George A. Smathers Libraries, University of Florida.

Rainer, Y. (1974) *Work 1961–1973*, New York: New York University Press.

Ralph, R. (1995) 'On the light fantastic toe: dance scholarship and academic fashion', *Dance Chronicle* 18, 2: 249–60.

Ramsey, K. (1997) 'Vodou, nationalism, and performance: the staging of folklore in mid-twentieth-century Haiti', in Desmond, J. (ed.), *Meaning in Motion: New Cultural Studies of Dance*, Durham, NC: Duke University Press.

Ransom, J. (1938) *A Short History of the Theosophical Society*, Madras, India: Theosophical Publishing House.

Readings, B. (1996) *University in Ruins*, Cambridge, MA: Harvard University Press.

Redfern, B. (1983) *Dance, Art and Aesthetics*, London: Dance Books.

Reed, S.A. (1998) 'The poetics and politics of dance', *Annual Review of Anthropology* 27: 503–32.

Reiwoldt, O. (ed.) (2002) *Brandscaping: Worlds of Experience in Retail Design*, Basel: Birkhäuser Verlag.

Ritsema, J. (2004) 'Lecture on improvisation', unedited lecture presented at Dance Unlimited, postdoctoral dance education, in Arnhem, Holland, 6 October.

Rivière, J. (1983) *'Le Sacre du Printemps'*, in Copeland, R. and Cohen, M. (eds), *What is Dance?* Oxford: Oxford University Press.

Roberts, D. (1996) 'Reconstructing the patient: starting with women of color', in Wolf, S. (ed.), *Feminism and Bioethics: Beyond Reproduction*, New York: Oxford University Press.

Robins, K. (1991) 'Tradition and translation: national culture in its global context', in Corner, J. and Harvey, S. (eds), *Enterprise and Heritage: Crosscurrents of National Culture*, London: Routledge.

Robinson, D. (2006) '"Oh, you Black Bottom!" Appropriation, authenticity and opportunity in the jazz dance teaching of 1920s New York', *Dance Research Journal* 38, 1 and 2: 19–42.

Ronström, O. (1991) 'Folklore: staged folk music and folk dance performances of Yugoslavs in Stockholm', *Yearbook for Traditional Music* 23: 69–77.

Rosen, C. and Zerner, H. (1984) *Romanticism and Realism: The Mythology of Nineteenth Century Art*, New York: W.W. Norton and Co.

Ross, J. (2000) *Moving Lessons: Margaret H'Doubler and the Beginning of Dance in American Education*, Madison, WI: University of Wisconsin Press.

Rouhiainen, L. (2003) 'Living transformative lives: Finnish freelance dance artists brought into dialogue with Merleau-Ponty's phenomenology', PhD dissertation, Theatre Academy, Helsinki.

Roy, S. (2007) 'Sacre: The Rite of Spring', the *Guardian*, 10 April, <http://www.guardian.co.uk/stage/2007/apr/10/dance> (accessed 20 April 2007).

Ruhl, A. (1932) '"Second nights" review of The Great Day', 17 January, *New York Herald Tribune*.

Sachs, C. (1937) *World History of the Dance*, trans. Bessie Schönberg, New York: W.W. Norton.

Sahlins, M. (1999) 'Two or three things that I know about culture', *Journal of the Royal Anthropological Institute* 5, 3: 399–421.

Said, E. (1987) *Orientalism*, New York: Vintage Books.

Sarup, M. (1988) *Post-Structuralism and Postmodernism*, Hemel Hempstead: Harvester.

Savigliano, M. (1995) *Tango and the Political Economy of Passion*, Boulder, CO: Westview Press.

——(1996) 'Fragments for a story of tango bodies (on Choreocritics and the memory of power)', in Foster, S. (ed.), *Corporealities: Dancing, Knowledge, Culture, and Power*, London: Routledge.

——(2003) *Angora Matta: Fatal Acts of North–South Translation*, Middletown, CT: Wesleyan University Press.

Schiller, F. (2000) *Über die ästhetische Erziehung des Menschen in einer Reihe von Briefen*, Ditzingen: Reclam.

Scott, A.B. (2001) 'Dance', in Maxwell, R. (ed.), *Culture Works: The Political Economy of Culture*, Minneapolis, MN: University of Minnesota Press.

——(2002) 'Articulations of blackness in Salvador Bahia, Brasil', paper presented at the meeting Blackness in Global Contexts: Reflections on Experiences of Blackness from a Transnational Perspective, University of California, Davis.

SDHS (2007) *Proceedings: Thirtieth Annual Conference: Re-thinking Practice and Theory/ Repenser pratique et théorie*, Centre National de la Danse, Paris, France, Society of Dance History Scholars joint conference with CORD.

——(2008) *Proceedings: Thirty-first Annual Conference: Looking Back/Moving Forward*, International Symposium on Dance Research, Skidmore College, Saratoga Springs, New York.

Second, A. (1844) *Les Petits Mystères de l'Opéra*, Paris: G. Kugelmann/Bernard-Latte.

Sedgwick, P. and Edgar, A. (eds) (1999) *Key Concepts in Cultural Theory*, London: Routledge.

Seremetakis, N. (ed) (1994) *The Senses Still: Perception and Memory as Material Culture in Modernity*, Chicago, IL: University of Chicago Press.

Servos, N. (1984) *Pina Bausch: Wuppertal Dance Theatre, or the Art of Training a Goldfish: Excursions into Dance*, trans. P. Stadie, Cologne: Ballett-Buhnen-Verlag.

Shakespeare, W. (1914) *Romeo and Juliet* Act 1 Sc. 5 lines 11–21, in Craig, W.J. (ed.), *The Complete Works of William Shakespeare*, London: Oxford University Press.

Shea Murphy, J. (1995) 'Unrest and Uncle Tom: Bill T. Jones/Arnie Zane Dance Company's last supper at Uncle Tom's cabin/the promised land', in Shea Murphy, J. and Goellner, E. (eds), *Bodies of the Text: Dance as Theory, Literature as Dance*, New Brunswick, NJ: Rutgers University Press.

——(2009) 'Mobilizing (in) the archive: Santee Smith's Kaha:wi', in Foster, S. (ed.), *Worlding Dance*, New York: Palgrave MacMillan.

Sheets-Johnstone, M. (1966) *The Phenomenology of Dance*, London: Dance Books.

——(1984) 'Phenomenology as a way of illuminating dance', in Sheets-Johnstone, M. (ed.), *Illuminating Dance: Philosophical Explorations*, London: Associated University Press.

Shepherd, J. (1983) 'Definition as mystification: a consideration of labels as a hindrance to understanding significance in music', in Horn, D. (ed.), *Popular Music Perspectives 2*, papers from the Second International Conference on Popular Music Studies, Reggio Emilia, IASPM: 84–98.

Shih, S. (2003) 'Introduction', in *Postcolonial Studies: Culture, Politics, Economy*, special issue based on the 'Remapping Taiwan' Conference at UCLA (2000), 6, 2: 143–53.

——(2007) *Visuality and Identity: Sinophone Articulations Across the Pacific*, Berkeley, CA: University of California Press.

Shildrick, M. and Price, J. (1996) 'Breaking the boundaries of the broken body', *Body and Society*, 2, 4: 93–113.

Shimakawa, K. (2004) 'Loaded images: seeing and being in "Fan Variations" ', in Mitoma, J., Trimillos, R.D. and Jorjorian, A. (eds), *Narrative/Performance: Cross-Cultural Encounters at APPEX*, Los Angeles, CA: Center for Intercultural Performance <http://www.wac.ucla.edu/cip/appexbook/loadedimages.html>.

Shresthova, S. (2004) 'Swaying to an Indian beat ... *Dola* goes my diasporic heart: exploring Hindi film dance', *Dance Research Journal* 36, 2: 91–101.

Shuker, R. (1997) *Understanding Popular Music*, London: Routledge.

——(1998) *Key Concepts in Popular Music*, London: Routledge.

Siegel, M. (1995) 'On multiculturality and authenticity: a critical call to arms', in Gere, D. (ed.), *Looking Out: Perspectives on Dance and Criticism in a Multicultural World*, New York: Schirmer Books.

Siegmund, G. (2006) 'Raimund Hoghe', <http://kulturserver-nrw.de/home/rhoghe/> accessed 27 July 2006.

Singer, M. (1958) 'The great tradition in a metropolitan center: Madras', *Journal of American Folklore* 71, 281: 349–88.

Sirkar, R. (1997) 'Contemporary Indian dance', in Mukherjee, B. and Kothari, S. (eds), *Rasa*, Calcutta: Anamika Kalasangam.

Sklar, D. (2000) 'Reprise: on dance ethnography', *Dance Research Journal*, 32, 1: 70–81.

——(2001) *Dancing with the Virgin: Body and Faith in the Fiesta of Tortugas, New Mexico*, Berkeley, CA: University of California Press.

Sloterdijk, P. (2000) *La Mobilisation Infinie*, Paris: Christian Bourgeois Editeurs.

Smith, P. (2008) email correspondence with Emilyn Claid, 20 September.

Sobchack, V. (2005) '"Choreography for one, two, and three legs" (a phenomenological meditation in movements)', *Topoi: An International Review of Philosophy* 24, 1: 55–66.

Sokolova, L. (1960) *Dancing for Diaghilev*, London: John Murray.

Sommer, S. (2001/2) 'C'mon to my house: underground-house dancing', *Dance Research Journal* 33, 2: 72–86.

Sparshott, F. (1984) 'The dancing body: divisions on Sartrian ground' in Sheets-Johnstone, M. (ed.), *Illuminating Dance: Philosophical Explorations*, London: Associated University Press.

Spencer, P. (ed.) (1985) *Society and the Dance*, New York: Cambridge University Press.

Spinelli, E. (2007) *Practising Existential Psychotherapy*, Los Angeles, CA: Sage Publications.

Spivak, G. (1985) 'Can the subaltern speak? Speculations on widow-sacrifice', *Wedge* 7/8 (Winter/Spring): 120–30.

——(1994) 'Can the subaltern speak?', in Taylor, D. and Villegas, J. (eds), *Negotiating Performance: Gender, Sexuality, and Theatricality in Latino America*, Durham, NC: Duke University Press.

Squires, J. (1993) 'Introduction', in Squires, J. (ed.), *Principled Positions: Postmodernism and the Rediscovery of Value*, London: Lawrence & Wishart.

Srinivasan, A. (1984) 'Temple prostitution and reform: an examination of the ethnographic, historical and textual content of the devadasis of Tamilnadu, South India', PhD dissertation, Wolfson College.

——(1985) 'Reform and revival: The devadasi and her dance', *Economic and Political Weekly* 20, 44 (November): 1869–76.

Srinivasan, P. (2007) 'The bodies beneath the smoke or what's behind the cigarette poster: unearthing kinesthetic connections in American dance history', *Discourses in Dance* 4, 1: 7–47.

Staemmler, F. (2006) 'The willingness to be uncertain – preliminary thoughts about interpretation and understanding in gestalt therapy', in *International Gestalt Journal* 29, 2: 11–42.

Stearns, M. and Stearns J. (1968) *Jazz Dance: The Story of American Vernacular Dance*, New York: Schirmer Books.

——(1994) *Jazz Dance: The Story of American Vernacular Dance*, 2nd rev. edn, New York: Da Capo.

Stern, C. (2000) 'The implications of ballroom dancing for studies of "Whiteness"', CORD, DCA, NDA and SDHS, 'Dancing in the Millennium' Conference Proceedings, Washington, DC: 394–9.

Stoneley, P. (2006) *A Queer History of the Ballet*, London: Routledge.

Storey, J. (1997) *An Introduction to Cultural Theory and Popular Culture*, 2nd edn, Hemel Hempstead: Prentice Hall/Harvester Wheatsheaf.

Taylor, J. M. (1998) *Paper Tangos*, Durham, NC: Duke University Press.

Tharu, S. and Lalita, K (eds) (1991) *Women Writing In India, 600 BC to the Present*, New York: The Feminist Press at the City University of New York.

Thomas, H. (1993) *Dance, Gender and Culture*, London: Macmillan.

——(ed.) (1997) *Dance in the City*, New York: St. Martin's Press.

——(2002) *Dancing into the Third Age: Social Dance as Cultural Text*, <http://www.dance.gold.ac.uk>.

——(2003) *The Body, Dance and Cultural Theory*, Basingstoke: Palgrave Macmillan.

——(2004) 'Reconstruction and dance as embodied textual practice', in Carter, A. (ed.), *Rethinking Dance History: A Reader*, London: Routledge.

Thompson, R.F. (1966) 'Dance and culture, an aesthetic of the cool: West African dance', *African Forum* 2, 2: 85–102.

——(1983) *Flash of the Spirit: African and Afro-American Art and Philosophy*, New York: Vintage Books.

Todd, M.E. (1937) *The Thinking Body*, Hightstown, NJ: Dance Horizons/Princeton Book Company.

Tomko, L.J. (1999) *Dancing Class: Gender, Ethnicity, and Social Divides in American Dance, 1890–1920*, Bloomington, IN: Indiana University Press.

——(2004) 'Considering causation and conditions of possibility: practitioners and patrons of new dance in progressive-era America', in Carter, A. (ed.), *Rethinking Dance History: A Reader*, London: Routledge.

Toombs, K. (1992) *The Meaning of Illness: A Phenomenological Account of the Different Perspectives of Physician and Patient*, Dordrecht: Kluwer Academic Publishers.

Trubridge, S. (2007) 'Beyond the Veil', *Theatre Forum*, 30 (Winter/Spring): 3–10.

Tschumi, B. (1995) *Questions of Space: Lectures on Architecture*, London: Architectural Association.

——(1996) *Architecture and Disjunction*, Cambridge, MA: MIT Press.

Tuan, Y. (1977) *Space and Place: the Perspective of Experience*, London: Edward Arnold.

Turner, J. (1995) 'Control of the passes, describing the fictions of Bali', *Border Tensions: Dance Discourse*, Proceedings of the Fifth Study of Dance Conference, Guildford: University of Surrey.

Usner, E. (2001/2) 'Dancing in the past, living in the present: nostalgia and race in southern California neo-swing dance culture', *Dance Research Journal* 33, 2: 87–101.

Valis Hill, C. (1992) 'Buddy Bradley: the "invisible" man of Broadway brings jazz tap to London', *American Dance Abroad: Influence of the United States Experience* Proceedings of the SDHS 15th Annual Conference, California: 77–84.

——(2000) *Brotherhood in Rhythm: The Jazz Tap Dancing of the Nicholas Brothers*, New York: Oxford University Press.

——(2001/2) 'From Bharata Natyam to bop: Jack Cole's "modern" jazz dance', *Dance Research Journal* 33, 2: 29–39.

Van den Braembussche, A. (1996) 'The value of art: a philosophical perspective', in Klamer, A. (ed.), *The Value of Culture: On the Relationship Between Economics and Arts*, Amsterdam: Amsterdam University Press.

Vatsyayan, K. (1982) *Dance in Indian Painting*, New Delhi: Abhinav Publications.

——(1989) 'Dance scholarship: the complex Indian situation', in Au, S. and Peter, F. (eds), *Beyond Performance: Dance Scholarship Today*, Berlin: Centre of the International Theatre Institute.

——(1995) 'The future of dance scholarship in India', *Dance Chronicle* 18: 485–90.

——(1997) *The Square and the Circle of the Indian Arts*, New Delhi: Abhinav Publications.

Venkataraman, L. (1990) 'Lets get physical', *The Telegraph* (Calcutta), August.

Victora, C. (1997) 'Inside the mother's body, pregnancy and the "emic" organ "the body's mother"', *Curare* 12: 169–75.

Wainwright, S.P. (2006) 'Varieties of habitus and the embodiment of ballet', *Qualitative Research* 6, 4: 535–58.

Warner, Marina (2002) *'Stone Girl' Murderers I have Known and Other Stories*, London: Chatto and Windus, pp. 105–118.

Weeks, J. (1993) 'Rediscovering values', in Squires, J. (ed.), *Principled Positions: Postmodernism and the Rediscovery of Value*, London: Lawrence & Wishart.

Werner, Katja (2003) 'Tanzgeschichten', *Dance Europe*, December, <http://kultur-servernrw.de/home/rhoghe/en/en_tanzgeschichten.html > accessed 27 July 2006.

White, H. (1980) 'The value of narrativity in the representation of reality', *Critical Inquiry* (Autumn): 5–27.

Williams, D. (2004 [1991]) *Anthropology and the Dance: Ten Lectures*, Champaign, IL: University of Illinois Press.

——(2008) *a little by little, suddenly* <www.sky.writings.blogspot.com/2008_07_01_archive.html> accessed 10 September 2008.

Williams, J.F. (2003) 'Who are the Taiwanese? Taiwan in the Chinese Diaspora', in Ma, L.J.C. and Cartier, C. (eds), *The Chinese Diaspora: Space, Place, Mobility and Identity*, Lanham, MD: Rowman & Littlefield Publishers, Inc.

Willis, J. (1999) 'Dying in country: implications of culture in the delivery of palliative care in indigenous Australian communities', *Anthropology and Medicine* 6, 3: 423–35.

Wilson, R. (1997) *Bringing them Home: Report of the National Inquiry into the Separation of Aboriginal and Torres Strait Islander Children and their Families*, Canberra: Human Rights and Equal Opportunity Commission.

Winkler, E. and Jarchow, P. (1996) *Neuer Künstlerischer Tanz*, Dresden: Tanzwissenschaft e.V. and Palucca Schule Dresden.

Winter, M.H. (1974) *The Pre-Romantic Ballet*, London: Sir Isaac Pitman and Sons.

Wittgenstein, L. (1953) *Philosophical Investigations*, trans. G.E.M. Anscombe, Oxford: Blackwell.

——(1958) *The Blue and the Brown Books*, Oxford: Blackwell.

Wollen, P. (1987) 'Fashion/orientalism/the body', *New Formations* 1: 5–33.

Wong, Y. (2002) 'Towards a new Asian American dance theory: locating the dancing Asian American body', *Discourses in Dance* 1, 1: 69–90.

——(2009) 'Michio Ito and the trope of the international', in Foster, S. (ed.), *Worlding Dance*, New York: Palgrave MacMillan.

Worton, M. and Still, J. (eds) (1990) *Intertextuality: Theories and Practices*, Manchester: Manchester University Press.

Wu, C. (1995) *Orphan of Asia*, Taipei: Vista Publishing Co.

Wu, J. (1993) 'Using movement to create stories: Lin Hwai-min's rapid improvements', in *Cloud Gate Dance Commentaries*, Taipei: Cloud Gate Dance Foundation.

Wu, M. (ed.) (2000) *The Concise Dictionary and Chronology of Taiwan's History*, Taipei: Yuan-liu.

Wu, P. (1969) 'The white snake: the evolution of a myth in China', PhD dissertation, Columbia University.

Wulff, H. (1998) Ballet Across Borders: Career and Culture in the World of Dancers, Oxford: Berg.

Yang, C. (1991) 'Er-hua de Lishi Shiyi Zheng: Xiangtu chungfang (Historical Amnesia Gone Awry: Revisiting Hsiangtu)', in Liu-li Guan-dian (Diasporic Perspectives), Taipei: Zhili Evening News Publications,.

Yang, M. (1998) Cloud Nine: Lin Hwai-min and Cloud Gate Dance Theatre, Taipei: Commonwealth Publishing Co.

——(2003) The Young Hwai-min, Taipei: Commonwealth Global View Publishers.

Yontef, G. (1993) Awareness, Dialogue and Process, Gouldsboro ME: The Gestalt Journal Press.

Young, T. (1999) 'Dancing on Bela Lugosi's grave: the politics and aesthetics of gothic club dancing', Dance Research XVII, 1 (Summer): 75–97.

Youngerman, S. (1974) 'Curt Sachs and his heritage: a critical review of world history of the dance, with a survey of recent studies that perpetuate his ideas', CORD News 6, 2: 6–19.

Yu, T. (1993) 'Regarding Cloud Gate's new dance drama Xu Xian', in Yu, K. et al. (eds), Cloud Gate Dance Commentaries, 3rd edn, Taipei: Cloud Gate Dance Foundation.

Zhang, Y. (2000) 'Cinematic remapping of Taipei: cultural hybridization, heterotopias, and postmodernity', unpublished paper presented at the 'Remapping Taiwan: Histories and Cultures in the Context of Globalization' conference, UCLA.

Zhou, Z. (2001) Cursive: The Birth of a Dance, Taipei: Ecus Publishing House.

Zimmer, E. (2000) 'Fusing Shakespeare, hip-hop dance', The Philadelphia Inquirer: Weekend cover story, 16 June.

Internet sources

http://www.cloudgate.org.tw.
http://www.destinationhollywood.com/movies/westsidestory/mediagallery_content.shtml.
http://etext.lib.virginia.edu/Shakespeare/works.
http://www.puremovement.net.
http://www.romeoandjuliet.com/party/palace.html.
http://www.westsidestory.com/site/level2/archives/productions/movie.html.

Visual and aural sources

Bausch, P. (1975) Le Sacre du printemps (The Rite of Spring), performed by the Tanztheater Wuppertal.

Chang C. (1987) 'Cloud Gate episode', from Stage Meditations, Public Television Service (Taipei).

——(2003) Cloud Gate Dance Theatre at Thirty, Public Television Service (Taipei).

Forsythe, W. (1999) William Forsythe Improvisation Technologies: A Tool for the Analytical Dance Eye (CD-ROM and booklet), Cologne, ZKM Karlsruhe.

Graham, M. (1961) *Night Journey*, directed by Alexander Hammid, Knoll Productions.
——(1976) *Cave of the Heart*, Public Broadcasting Service.
Harris, R. (2000) *Rome & Jewels*, Richard and Karen Carpenter Performing Arts Center, California State University, Long Beach, 4 November.
Hughes-Freeland, F. (1988) *The Dancer and the Dance*, London: Royal Anthropological Institute, 16mm/VHS format.
——(1996) *Tayuban: Dancing the Spirit in Java*, London Royal Anthropological Institute, VHS format.
Jordan, S. (1987) *Rushes (Davies): Analysis of Three Duets*, University of Surrey: National Resource Centre for Dance.
Lin, H. (1987) *Legacy*, Taipei: Cloud Gate Dance Theatre Foundation.
——(1996) *Tale of the White Serpent*, Taipei: Cloud Gate Dance Theatre.
——(1998) *Rite of Spring, 1984*, Taipei: Cloud Gate Dance Theatre.
——(2000) *Moon Water*, Directed by Ross MacGibbon, RM Associates/LGM/MEZZO.
——(2002) *Cursive*, directed by Chang Chao-tang, Jingo.
——(2006) *Cursive II*, BBC Opus Arte.
Luhrman, B. (1997) *William Shakespeare's Romeo & Juliet*, 20th Century Fox Home Entertainment.
Martínez Solares, G. dir. (1954) *Mulata*, Tekila Films, DVD 2005.
Newson, L. and Hinton, D. (1993) *Strange Fish*, BBC/RMArts video. Also available on DVD (2007) Arthaus Musik.
Nijinsky, V. (1987) *Le Sacre du printemps (the Rite of Spring)*, reconstructed by Millicent Hodson for the Joffrey Ballet.
Oikonomou, M. (dir.) (2006) *My Place in the Dance*, VHS, 52 mins, Greece: Hellenic Broadcasting Corp. ERT, Mega Channel, Cynergon.
Ross, D. (2000) *Rome & Jewels* soundtrack.
SOASIS/AHRC (2008) *Bàtádádé Technique*, SOASIS DVD Series, London: SOAS (School of Oriental and African Studies), Research Centre for Cross-Cultural Music and Dance Performance, University of London.
Tale of the White Snake: Peking Opera from China (2000) Three-volume VCD published by Yangtze Chiang, distributed in Taiwan by Rontm company.
Viva Tonal [Tiaowu Shidai or, The Dance Age] (2003) Public Television Service (Taipei).
West Side Story, Columbia Records CK 32603, CD reprint.
William Shakespeare's Romeo & Juliet: Music from the Motion Picture (1996) Capitol Records CDP 7243 8 37150 9.
Wise, R. and Robbins, J. (1961) *West Side Story*, Metro-Goldwyn-Mayer [MGM Home Entertainment 1998].

INDEX